Karyn Bosnak was born and raised in the suburbs of Chicago. She is a daytime television producer turned Internet guru who likes (but can't afford) the finer things in life. She now resides in Brooklyn, New York. She can be reached at www.savekaryn.com

SAVE KARYN

One Shopaholic's Journey to Debt and Back

Karyn Bosnak

CORGI BOOKS

SAVE KARYN
A CORGI BOOK : 0 552 15165 3

First publication in Great Britain

PRINTING HISTORY
Corgi edition published 2004

1 3 5 7 9 10 8 6 4 2

Set in Garamond by
Kestrel Data, Exeter, Devon.

Corgi Books are published by Transworld Publishers,
61–63 Uxbridge Road, London W5 5SA,
a division of The Random House Group Ltd,
in Australia by Random House Australia (Pty) Ltd,
20 Alfred Street, Milsons Point, Sydney, NSW 2061, Australia,
in New Zealand by Random House New Zealand Ltd,
18 Poland Road, Glenfield, Auckland 10, New Zealand
and in South Africa by Random House (Pty) Ltd,
Endulini, 5a Jubilee Road, Parktown 2193, South Africa.

Printed and bound in Great Britain by
Cox & Wyman Ltd, Reading, Berkshire.

Papers used by Transworld Publishers are natural, recyclable products made from wood grown in sustainable forests. The manufacturing processes conform to the environmental regulations of the country of origin.

This book is dedicated to my big sister, Lisa,
and her crazy curly hair.
Long live Lou Lou Bell and Squeaky!

AUTHOR'S NOTE

While this book is a work of nonfiction, I have made a few changes along the way to protect the privacy of those mentioned. For obvious reasons, I have changed the names of numerous people in the book, as well as altered their descriptions.

In addition to those changes, I have taken certain storytelling liberties to help move the events along, but it has been my intent to stay true to the story as it happened. Enjoy!

THE SUMMER I STARED AT THE CEILING

Have you ever made such a mess of things that you were sure there was no way out? That's basically the story of my life. In June 2002, I was in that position: dead broke and $20,000 in the hole. How did I end up that way? Well, I guess you could say it all started three years earlier, during what I now refer to as 'the summer I stared at the ceiling.'

It was May 1999, and I was twenty-six years old. I was living and working in Chicago. I wasn't unhappy. I was just unfulfilled. I realized that there must be more to life than what I had experienced so far. I was born in Illinois, raised in Illinois, went to school in Illinois, and was working in Illinois. That summer all I did was stare at the ceiling and think. I didn't know who I was. I was the person that my parents raised, but I never felt like my *own* person. I felt like an extension of them, and an extension of my job. I felt defined by my friends. All I did was stare and think.

At the end of the summer, the conclusion that I came to was this: I had to get the hell out of Illinois. I needed to pack my bags, leave the Windy City, and move to a faraway land. I needed to be alone to figure out exactly who Karyn Bosnak was. And the faraway land that I chose to be alone in was . . . New York! I had been there once – for a day. But I liked it, and I had seen tons of episodes of *Friends* and *Seinfeld*, and decided that it was going to be my new home.

The next year all I did was work and save money. Well, I tried to save money, let's just say that, but I've never been really good in that department. But I saved enough to pay for a one-way plane ticket and an apartment. I had enough for everything, except the movers. I had to charge the movers . . .

THE RISE

May 2000

ONE

American Express

Karyn Bosnak
400 E. 57th St.
New York, NY 10010

Date	Payee	Amount
May 20, 2000	Mini-Moves Chicago, IL, to New York, NY	$ 2,050.00
May 20, 2000	United Airlines Chgo O'Hare to NY LaGuardia	$ 235.00
May 22, 2000	Barnes & Noble	$ 75.00
Jun 1, 2000	Otto Tootsie Plohound	$ 173.00
Jun 2, 2000	Duane Reade	$ 32.00
Jun 2, 2000	Trattoria Pesce & Pasta	$ 30.00
Jun 3, 2000	The Wiz – Cell Phone	$ 108.00
Jun 3, 2000	Bed Bath & Beyond	$ 313.00
Jun 3, 2000	ABC Carpet & Home	$ 217.00
Jun 5, 2000	Kate's Gifts	$ 42.00
Jun 10, 2000	Intermix	$ 159.00
	Total	**$ 3,434.00**

Grand Debt Tally $3,434.00

THE MOVE

I awoke that morning to a buzzing in my ear. My head was throbbing. The night before we had a big party to wrap up the ninth season of *The Jenny Jones Show*, where I had worked for four years. (No, I wasn't there for the murder, so don't ask.) As desperately as I wanted to leave Chicago, I was sad to say good-bye to all of my coworkers, some of whom I had become very close with throughout the years.

The buzzing stopped and then started up again. I finally realized that it wasn't my alarm clock, but my doorman buzzing my apartment. I got out of bed and went to answer the intercom.

'Karyn, it's Robert the doorman. Your mom's here,' a voice said.

Ever since I've lived alone, I've had an apartment with a doorman. It's always made me feel safe. Sure, doorman apartment buildings are more expensive, but how can you put a price on safety? This particular apartment was on Oak Street – the Madison Avenue of Chicago. If you walked straight out the front door of my apartment building, you'd hit Barneys. That was good for me, a girl who grew up shopping.

'Oh, right. Let her up.' I was moving to New York the next morning. My mom was there to help me pack and was planning to stay overnight so she could take me to the airport. It was my last day in Chicago.

I love my mom. But she was part of the reason that I decided to move. She'd do *anything* for me, and I knew that and always took advantage of it. I was hoping New York would make me feel more independent, so I wouldn't call my mother every minute to ask for her help. 'Help' to me usually ment 'help with some cash,' which meant 'I spent too much at Marshall Field's and I need help paying the bill.' And Mom was always there in that department.

After packing all day, we slept for a few hours before we had to get up and leave for my 6.00 A.M. flight. I was going to bring some of my clothes with me, and movers were coming to my apartment the following day to pick up the rest of my stuff. The reason for the early flight was that I had a job as a producer for a new court show called *Curtis Court* and had to be at work at noon the day I arrived.

That morning my mom and I woke up, loaded the car, and drove to the airport in silence. I've always had this horrible separation anxiety when it comes to my mother. When I was little, I would cry at school because I wanted my mom. My sister, Lisa, who is two years older than me, would have to leave her class and come to help my teacher quiet me down. I also was unable to sleep over at any of my friends' houses until I was in fourth grade because again, I would cry at bedtime because I missed my mom. I would fake being sick and have my friend wake her parents up and tell them that I needed to go home. Every time I'd attempt a sleep-over, my mom always knew the midnight phone call would come, and would get in her car to come pick me up.

After the twenty-minute ride to O'Hare, we pulled up to the United Airlines departure terminal. I got out of the car and my mom popped the trunk. The bell cap came over and took my bags out of the back. I had five of them.

'You are only allowed to check two bags,' he said.

'What? Why didn't they tell me that on the phone? I need all of these bags,' I said.

Now, I admit that I've never been a light packer, but I *had* to have all these bags. My apartment wouldn't be ready for me to move into until two weeks after I got to New York, so I had to bring some of my clothes, purses and shoes with me. And two weeks of clothes meant five suitcases.

'Sorry, miss. I can't change the rules.'

So, I had to carry on three bags. Three *big* bags. These were not overnighter-size bags either. They were suitcases.

I turned around and looked at my mother, who was

wearing her sunglasses so I wouldn't see her tears, but I knew they were there.

'Mom, don't cry!' I said. 'Please don't cry or you'll make me cry.'

'I'm sorry, I can't help it. Why won't you let me come in with you?' she asked.

'Because if you come in with me, you'll make me cry, that's why.'

I looked at my mom and hugged her. I closed my eyes. I've always thought that if I closed my eyes when I cried the tears would stay in.

'Okay,' she said and continued to hug me. Hard. I couldn't breathe.

I didn't want to say the word 'good-bye,' because I knew that would have pushed me over the edge. So I just said 'I love you,' and pulled away quickly. Without looking at my mom, I turned around and pushed the heavy cart with my three suitcases through the automatic door.

After checking in and looking around for a while, I finally found a seat at the gate that accommodated me and my three suitcases. After I sat down, I looked to the left and saw someone familiar dart behind a pole. I couldn't see the person's face, but I could see the outline of a black Kate Spade purse. It was my mom! She was watching me!

'Mom,' I said, getting her attention, 'you're not supposed to be here!'

'I know but I couldn't help it! I just wanted to make sure you got on the plane,' she said as she wiped the stream of tears coming down her face.

'I can't believe you did this!' I said, now bawling. 'I didn't want to cry!'

She straightened my blouse and counted all three of my bags to make sure they were there.

'Now boarding Flight 668 to New York LaGuardia,' a man said over the loudspeaker.

'I have to go.'

'Okay. I love you,' she said.

'I love you too,' I said and gave my mom one last big hug. She wouldn't let go. I finally broke away from my mom's arms and walked toward the boarding area, gave the man my ticket and turned one last time. My mom blew me a kiss, and I caught it, smacked it on my lips, and blew one back.

After hitting all the passengers with my bags on the way to my seat and sitting next to a chatty German dude, the flight from Chicago to New York took off, and landed an hour and a half later. I was now home.

THE ARRIVAL

Since my apartment wasn't ready yet, I had made arrangements to stay with a girl I used to work with named Ann Marie, and her husband, Bill.

After a short cab ride from the airport, I arrived at their apartment with all five of my suitcases in tow. They lived in a swanky pad on the Upper West Side. It was a doorman building with a beautiful view of the city.

This arrangement came about because I was going to be working with Ann Marie at my new job. *Curtis Court* was a new *Judge Judy*-type of daytime court show that was set to premiere in September. I was one of six producers. Ann Marie was also a producer. The staff started two weeks before me, and I was the last person to arrive, so it was important that I use this weekend to catch up.

So my boss arranged for Ann Marie to take me to the office that first day to show me around.

After unpacking some of my stuff, Ann Marie and I walked a few blocks to where our offices were. Once we arrived, I followed her upstairs to the third floor, where our desks were.

'Here's your cube,' she said, pointing to a short cube, no more than six feet by six feet.

'A cube?' I asked.

'Yeah, I know it sucks, but we all have them. These facilities are just too small to fit everyone, and there aren't enough offices to go around.'

I was so excited for my first producing job and I got stuck with a cube. How could that be? I was a New York City television producer for a syndicated daytime television show from King World Productions, the same people that distributed *Oprah*, and I got a cube. A short cube. The walls didn't even go above my shoulders.

Anywho, I settled into my short cube and Ann Marie explained how producing a court show worked. She told me that there were these employees called 'stringers' who go to small claims courts around the country and make copies of the small claims cases that people file. Once someone files a small claims case it becomes public record, so anyone can go and do this. They make the copies, and then the copies are handed out to the producing teams, which consist of one producer and an associate producer. The producer or the AP then cold call the plaintiff or defendant and try to convince them to come on the show. If they do, then they plead their case to James Curtis, the host/judge.

It sounded easy enough. So I got my claims and started calling. And calling. And calling. And everyone hung up on me. How could someone not want to come on a television court show? After about an hour, I decided to give up and decorate my desk instead.

An aesthetically appealing work environment is a very important thing. After asking Ann Marie to point me in the direction of the supply closet, I made my way there and started thinking about what color scheme I'd choose. Okay, I couldn't get *really* elaborate because I had a short cube, but I could make it somewhat cozy. When I got to the supply room, I was saddened to see a few three-ring binders, some legal pads, yellow Post-its, and a few Bic pens. That was it. I moved some boxes thinking I'd find some bulletin boards and colored paper behind them, and perhaps some fluorescent pink highlighters too, but I found nothing. There wasn't a desk pad to be found. No colored paper clips in the house. Nada. Zilch. Just some plain paper and pens. I expected being a New York television producer would be a bit more glam than it was. I guessed wrong.

Disappointed, I made my way back to my cube and pretended to work for another hour. Finally, Ann Marie and I decided to leave and go back to her apartment.

THE APARTMENT

Despite a slow first day, the next two weeks at work flew by. I eventually got the hang of cold calling and managed to book a few cases for my first week of shows. Before I knew it, it was time to move into my apartment. On June 1st, after going back to Ann Marie and Bill's apartment and packing up my stuff, I hopped into a cab and told the driver my destination.

'Four hundred East Fifty-seventh Street, please,' I said.

'No problem,' he replied.

While in the backseat, I stared out the window and watched as the driver made a few turns until he finally turned left on 57th Street. Looking out my window I stared in utter amazement. What a beautiful street I lived on! As the driver headed east, I started flailing all over the backseat, switching between the right and left windows as fast as I could just so I could see all that my new street had to offer.

Oooh, lookie! There's Carnegie Hall! It was so big and pretty! I wasn't much into classical music, but I bet all fancy New Yorkers went to Carnegie Hall! There's the Russian Tea Room. What was I coming up to on the left? Bergdorf Goodman? Wow! Now *that* looks historic. I had never been to that department store before. And what beautiful window displays they had! Window displays really say a lot about a store, and their displays said 'expensive and cool.' I'd have to make a note to go there.

Just then the cab came to a screeching halt at a red light at Fifth Avenue. As we sat there waiting for the light to turn green, I looked south down Fifth Avenue and noticed that it never ended. There was just one store after another. This was my neighborhood. I felt so, what's the word . . . rich?

As the light turned green, we continued our journey across 57th Street and one after another the stores kept coming. We passed Louis Vuitton, Burberry, Prada, and the Four Seasons. I know that the Four Seasons isn't a store, but it is still fancy nonetheless. In the distance I saw big poles shooting out of a building with Gucci flags hanging down from them. Wow. The Gucci in Chicago was in a mall. This one had flags. The cab passed a cute shoe store called . . . Otto Tootsie Plohound? What a cute name!

Before I knew it we were passing Second Avenue and were just one block from my new home. On my right we passed a place called Mr Chow. I had heard of Mr Chow before. It was a very fancy Chinese restaurant where all the famous people went to eat.

A few seconds later I saw my building. It was a large white monstrosity on the corner on 57th Street and First Avenue. The awning said 400 East. That was it. That was home. Wow, it was big. As we pulled up, a doorman in a suit and a hat came to the cab and opened my door.

'Hello!' I said to him as I stepped out of the cab, 'I am moving in today!'

'Oh, welcome,' he replied in some sort of accent. 'My name is Sam.'

'Well, hello, Sam. I'm Karyn.'

'Welcome, Miss Karyn,' he said as he made his way to the back of the car to get my bags out of the trunk. 'What apartment are you moving into today?'

'4E.'

'Okay, well, come this way.'

I paid the driver and followed Sam into the building. Right inside the lobby was a beautiful desk with another doorman standing behind it who was so short he could barely see over the counter.

'Hi, I'm Edson,' he said, introducing himself.

'This is Miss Karyn,' Sam said, 'she's here to move into apartment Four-E.'

'Oh, great,' Edson said. 'The superintendent left your key for you.'

'Great, thanks,' I said, taking the key.

Sam and I walked toward the elevator and I assumed he would take me to my apartment, but when the elevator door opened, there was yet a third doorman inside.

'Hi! I'm Osei,' he said.

'Osei, this is Miss Karyn,' Sam explained. 'She is here to move into apartment 4E.'

'Hi, Jose!' I said.

'No, Osei. O-S-E-I,' he said, correcting me.

'Oh, I'm sorry. I totally know how you feel,' I said, apologizing. 'My name is Karyn with a y. It's spelled K-A-R-Y-N, not K-A-R-E-N. And I get really annoyed when people get it wrong.'

I guess I like the spelling of my name now, but I didn't always. I hated it when I was little. I could never have pencils, key chains, or pads of paper with my name on them because it was always misspelled. It sucked. So I felt for Osei.

'Osei will take you to your apartment, Miss Karyn,' Sam said.

'Great!' I answered as me and my five suitcases boarded the elevator and rode up to the fourth floor.

'There are a lot of doormen here,' I said.

'Yes. There are always at least three of us on duty. One to greet you, one at the desk, and one in the elevator.'

'Wow,' I said, 'fancy.'

The doors opened, and Osei pushed my suitcases to the left and three doors down to 4E. I pushed my key into the lock and the door opened. It was the cutest apartment! Osei unloaded my suitcases and put them just inside the door.

I didn't know if I should tip him or not. I mean, he'd just unloaded all of my suitcases. I've lived in other buildings with doormen before, but there was only one and they never helped me up to my apartment. But this was New York, after all, and I bet these guys got tipped. George Jefferson tipped Bentley all the time and Bentley expected him to. And if Osei is used to getting tips and I don't tip him, then he's not going to like me and he's going to tell all the other doormen not to like me either. And the last thing I wanted was to be known as the new cheap girl who just moved into apartment 4E. So I decided to tip Osei. I reached into my wallet and gave him a $20 bill. That assured that I'd be in good with the doormen and they would believe that I belonged in a swanky place like this.

'Thank you,' he said.

'You are welcome,' I replied.

Osei left and I turned around and looked at my apartment. It was the first time I had seen it. Even after plopping down $4,000 for it. It's not the easiest thing to get an apartment in New York, especially when you're living in Chicago. But I knew this guy who used to live in this building and he gave me the phone number to the management office. So I called them up and found out that a studio apartment just happened to be available when I needed one. The rent was $1,800 a month, which was more than I wanted to spend. But in order to find something cheaper, I'd probably have had to use an apartment broker (that's what you have to do here) and that would have cost me about $2,200 more (10 percent of the annual rent), so I decided to take it. So I mailed off my $4,000 for the security deposit and first month's rent, and crossed my fingers that it would be okay. And okay it was! All 475 square feet of it!

It had hardwood floors and three big windows that looked out onto the corner of First Avenue and 57th Street. I also had two big closets, and a small kitchen with a short fridge. The bathroom was a bit old, but it would do just fine. As I looked around the apartment, my eyes stopped at the front door. I realized there was a big hole in it.

I found a funny-looking phone right next to the door and picked it up. It immediately rang the lobby. Cool. Edson picked up.

'Hi, Edson, it's me, Karyn, in Four-E,' I said.

'Hello, Miss Karyn,' he replied.

I liked that they called me Miss Karyn. It made me feel special.

'Hello. Edson, there's a big hole in my front door, maybe where a lock is supposed to be? Did my apartment not come with a lock?'

'Oh, no, just the knob lock. It doesn't come with a dead bolt, you have to buy your own.'

'Really. Huh. Where do I get one of those?'

'There's a hardware store down the street. They have them.'

'Okay, thanks, Edson,' I said, and realized I was a bit hot. 'Oh, one more thing. Edson, how do I control the air?'

'Oh, Miss Karyn, there's no air conditioner in there. You have to buy one of those too.'

'Oh, okay,' I said and hung up.

No lock and no air. Maybe I should have asked about those things before I moved in. All the apartments I ever lived at in Chicago came with air. I wonder why they didn't in New York. And a lock. What kind of place doesn't come with a lock?

Oh well. I decided to hide my suitcases in the closets and venture out to the hardware store. But when I got outside, I remembered that cute little shoe store called Otto Tootsie something . . . You know, I can always get a lock, and it really wouldn't be that hot for another few months. So I decided to check out the shoe store instead . . .

A NICE PAIR OF WALKING SHOES

Otto Tootsie Plohound was a short fifteen-minute walk away, straight down 57th Street. I couldn't wait to see the shoes that I'd seen from far away in the cab up close. As I approached the store, my heart started racing. I walked in and was surrounded by hundreds of shoes. The walls were lined from top to bottom with shelf after shelf of shoes and more shoes and more shoes. These shoes weren't like anything that Nine West sells or even Bloomingdale's for that matter. These puppies were the coolest things I had ever seen!

I walked around and slowly looked at the shoes. I looked at the brand names and had never heard of any of them. Oh, wait, there's Miu Miu. I've heard of that. Miu Miu is the cheaper line from the Prada people. I picked up a pair and looked at the bottom: $250. Ouch! That's not very cheap to me. I quickly put those shoes down and continued to make my way toward the back of the store. In the distance I saw a great pair of sandals. They were kind of clunky, but in a city chic kind of way. I turned them over to reveal the price: $280. Oh c'mon! I started to pick up all the pairs sitting around them and they were all that much. These shoes were expensive! Just then I looked down at my Steve Maddens. There was a tear at the corner of the leather strap. Yuck. They were cruddy. They were teeny-bopper. I decided to continue my search for a pair of shoes that I could afford. Surely they couldn't *all* be that expensive.

Finally, after picking up almost every shoe in the place, I found a great pair for $160. They were the cheapest pair there. But they were cute. They were tan and red and looked great with my jeans all cuffed up. And I really wanted a pair of shoes from Otto Tootsie Plohound.

Now, I didn't have any money because I had been in New York for all of two weeks and I hadn't gotten paid yet. But what I did have was an American Express card. You see, I had to pay for my first month's rent when I signed the lease for my new apartment, so I technically didn't have to pay rent until July, which was a whole month away. So I decided that it was okay if I charged a few things on my Amex card. I made a vow to use it only for emergencies, and this was an emergency! Well, not really, so I struck a deal with myself to justify the purchase: I would charge the shoes, and then walk to and from work every day for a month. Since the bus was $1.50 either way, I'd save myself $60 in a month. It was June. It wasn't too hot outside, work wasn't that far, and I could use the exercise anyway. Doing this would be the same as taking the bus every day and spending $100 on a new pair of sandals, which is pretty reasonable. I needed them anyway. The ones I had on right now would probably break any day now. So I pulled out my Amex card and swipe, sign, they were mine!

By the time I was done, it was too late to go to the hardware store, so I headed back toward my apartment. All three of my doormen greeted me.

'Hello, Miss Karyn,' they all said in unison with big smiles on their faces.

They were so nice. They were going to become my new friends.

'Hello, everyone!' I replied.

Sam asked me if I had luck finding a lock. I explained to him and the other doormen that I got sidetracked. I asked them again why I didn't have a lock, and suggested that maybe there was some sort of a mistake. They told me again that none of the apartments came with locks and I had to get my own. But they suggested that I ask the superintendent if he had one that I could buy from him. Sure, I thought. I bet he has the same lock that he took off my door before I moved in and now he's going to sell it back to me. Oh well, I guess it's just the way things worked in New York.

Osei was at the elevator and pushed the button for me. Phew! Good thing he was there! I don't think I would have been able to find the 4 button alone, let alone push it. I got out at my floor and unlocked my knob lock with my key and entered my apartment. It was so small, but it was just perfect. I loved it.

I unpacked my five suitcases and then realized that I had nothing to sleep on because my furniture hadn't arrived yet. So in my little 'bed nook' area, I piled up some of my clothes and made a bed. I laid down, covered myself up with some more of my clothes, and tried to get comfortable. I was so excited to be there that I didn't care how hard the floor was beneath me. I closed my eyes and fell fast asleep.

The next morning I was awoken at the crack of dawn by the immense sunlight that was pouring in through my three big windows. Wow, it was bright. My back hurt. I put my hands over my head and stretched myself as much as I could. And I screamed. I love to stretch and scream.

Manhattan is set up like a grid. The streets run east and west, and the avenues run north and south. From the very east of Manhattan to the very west of Manhattan, the city is about two and a half miles wide. My new apartment was at the very east of Manhattan on East 57th Street and First Avenue. My new job was on the west side of Manhattan on West 57th Street and Tenth Avenue.

I got ready for work, put on my new walking sandals, locked my knob lock and headed out the door. I was so excited for my first day's walk to work! My new sandals were so fine! I pushed the elevator door button and was greeted by Sam's smiling face.

'Ah, good morning, Miss Karyn,' he said.

'Top of the mornin' to ya, Sam!' I replied.

When I got downstairs, I bid farewell to Sam and the other doormen and started on my commute.

It was such a beautiful day! As I walked down the street, I

looked into all the fancy buildings. Some of the lobbies were really nice. All of them had doormen. There were people everywhere. It was a busy morning.

After a few minutes, I started to get a bit winded and looked up at a street sign. Third Avenue. Only seven more to go. I continued on and tried to walk more slowly, but I realized that if I didn't hurry it up I was going to be late for work. These blocks were long!

Almost forty minutes later, I finally arrived at Tenth Avenue. Work was farther away than I thought. My feet ached. They hurt. I pulled one of the leather straps away from the top of my foot and saw a huge blister. Damn! There was a blister in the same place on the other foot too. Maybe my feet just needed to get used to these sandals and build up some calluses.

When I got upstairs, I immediately went to the bathroom to remedy the situation. I looked in the mirror and was horrified at my appearance! What had happened to me? I was pretty when I left my apartment! I had a sweaty face, flat hair and smudgy mascara. And my feet were all grubbed up with street grime. I was a mess! It wasn't even that hot outside. I had to figure something out. I couldn't walk to work every day if it meant looking like a wet dog when I arrived. I found some Band-Aids in the first-aid kit on the wall and put them on my blisters. I'd survive.

As I walked to my desk and sat down, Gwen, a producer who sat next to me, noticed that I was limping.

'Are you limping?' she asked.

'Oh, no. I'm fine. I just have a small blister. New sandals,' I said, kind of embarrassed. 'I walked to work.'

'You walked to work? Where do you live?'

'On Fifty-seventh and First. It's not that far.'

'Not that far? That's all the way across town! I'd never walk to work. Why don't you just take a cab?' she asked.

'I really like to walk to work. It's a really easy walk, just down Fifty-seventh.' I didn't want to tell her that I bought shoes that I couldn't afford, and in order to make it up to my checkbook I had to walk to work for a month.

'Yeah, I can tell by your blisters. Not far at all,' she said and laughed as she turned away.

Why did it matter to her if I walked to work? I noticed that people in New York tell you what's on their mind. I grew up in the Midwest. If someone told me they had blisters, I would have asked them if they needed anything. Gwen wasn't being rude. She was just being direct. Five minutes later she probably would have forgotten about our conversation. Whereas I remembered it and felt stupid for walking almost three miles to work just so I could buy a nice pair of shoes. Maybe she was right.

Later that day, I decided to get some personal stuff done and called the phone company to have the phone set up at my new apartment. They told me that I would have to wait for two weeks. I then decided to call the moving company to find out when my furniture would be arriving. They'd picked it up two weeks ago exactly, so I expected it any day now. I found the number on my receipt.

'Mini-Moves,' a woman answered.

'Hello, I'd like to check on the status of my furniture,' I said. 'I just moved from Chicago to New York.'

'Do you have your job number?' she asked.

I read the job number on my receipt to the woman on the phone. She put me on hold. I held and held. Ten minutes later I was still holding. Just then the woman came back.

'I'm sorry, miss, but we can't find your furniture.'

'What do you mean you can't find my furniture?' I asked. 'You've had it for two weeks. And the guy I talked to on the phone told me it would be here early next week.'

'Miss, settle down,' she said, 'I just can't find it in the system. Let me look into this and I'll call you back later.'

'Okay,' I replied. What kind of moving company loses your furniture?

Later that afternoon, the woman called me back and told

me they *think* they *might* have found my furniture in a warehouse in Illinois, but wouldn't be sure it was mine until Monday. They *think*. They *might*. Damn.

Upset, I packed up my stuff and decided to go home early. My first case was on Monday, so I took some work home to make sure I was prepared, as well as some cases to call on because I was still getting caught up. I made my way outside and hopped into a cab. I was cranky, I was tired, my back hurt from the wood floor the night before, and there was no way I was going to walk all the way home with my blisters. I'd give it another try on Monday, but today, I was taking a cab.

OH, MY ACHIN' BACK!

On my way home, I stopped by a drugstore to get some stuff, and as I was paying, I picked up a New York City *Zagat* guide that was sitting by the counter. If you are from a small town, then you may not know what a *Zagat* guide is. It is a book that surveys all of the best restaurants in the city. Most major cities have a *Zagat* guide. I vowed to myself that I was going to visit every restaurant in that guide because I love to eat out!

That night I went home and sat on the floor. I pulled out my cases from work and realized I couldn't call on them because I didn't have a phone. So I decided to eat dinner and go to bed early. I couldn't cook because I didn't have any of my pots or pans because the moving company lost my furniture, even though they *think* they *might* have found it. So I decided to order in from this cute little Italian place that I saw across the street.

When I was done, I found the page in the *Zagat* guide that listed Trattoria Pesce & Pasta and circled it. Next to it I wrote, 'By myself on wooden floor with plastic silverware and a hole in the door.' I vowed to hit more restaurants and planned on doing this for every restaurant I would go to. I made up a new rule. I'd only eat at places in my guide, and never eat at the same place more than once. There were just too many to choose from, and it would be a fun little game anyhow.

The next morning I was again woken up at the crack of dawn by the sun coming up. I'd have to get some curtains soon. I turned on to my side and could barely move. My clothes weren't the best mattress I had ever slept on. And I have slept on tons of mattresses, let me tell you. Kidding. Not really. Anywho, my back was busted and I needed to fix this situation.

I decided to take a trip to Bed Bath & Beyond – a place that wasn't in my *Zagat* guide but was in my *Moving to New York* guide. In the two weeks that I had been here, I had now acquired six guidebooks. They all had different information in them and I wanted to make sure I knew as much about this city as possible. I had become a guidebook whore.

I got dressed and headed in search of the subway. It was a beautiful day. I pulled out my special laminated subway map (guaranteed by the saleslady to last me a lifetime) and found the closest stop to my apartment building. This would be the third time on the subway for me, and the first time on my own. I figured out where I needed to go, bought a subway card and waited for the train.

Chicago had a train – the El – but it was an elevated train, not a subway. The El actually did have a line that went underground – the red line – but I rarely took it. I wasn't scared on the New York subway. I was just grossed out.

If you have never been in the New York subway in the summertime, then that's a *good* thing. Just like Martha says. It smelled like something I had never smelled before in my whole life. It was ripe.

I tried to breathe in through my nose and out through my mouth, so the stink wouldn't pass through my mouth. I didn't want that stink on *my* tongue. Because we all know what stink is: it's little floating particles of whatever it is that's causing the stink. And my guess was that this stink was being caused by either mold (and I have allergies), or rotting rodents (and I have a general distaste for those as well). I briefly thought about investing in one of those paper facemasks that doctors use to keep their spit and stuff out of the patients they operate on, but thought that people might look at me funny if I wore one of those.

Soon enough the train came and I was saved. After a short ride, I arrived at my destination. The Bed Bath & Beyond was only a short walk away. I poked around the store for what seemed like hours.

After checking out an inflatable bed for a while, I decided to buy a queen-size feather bed instead. I'd sleep on that until my furniture was found, at which point I'd put it on top of my mattress where it belonged. I've always wanted a feather bed anyway, so I guess there was never a better time to buy it.

After checking out all the brands they had to offer, I picked the most expensive one they had. Why buy the cheap one, when for only a few dollars more you can get the best? I adopted this philosophy in college when I wanted a new blender. My mom wanted to buy me a cheap one, and I said, 'Why buy the cheap one, when the best one is only eighty dollars more?' She looked at me, shrugged her shoulders and said, 'I guess you're right.' And I got the nice blender. But in this case, the cheap one was $80, and the nicest one they had was $230. But I needed to look at it like it was an investment.

I took the feather bed, along with a nice chenille blanket, up to the register to pay. Afterward, I asked them if I could leave it there and pick it up later when I was done shopping. There was this rug place I had heard about, and it was only a few blocks away. I really wanted to check it out. They said yes, and with that I was off.

The name of the store was ABC Carpet & Home, and everybody at work kept telling me that I'd have to go there. A few blocks away, I found the store. There were two stores actually – one with just rugs, and one across the street with just furnishings. I decided to go into the one with just rugs first.

The place was enormous and was filled with rugs. Some were hanging up, others were lying down. There were two floors too. I poked around and saw some of the prices, and most of them were really expensive. I made my way to the back and realized that I had just stumbled upon the rugs that were on sale.

My eyes stopped on a stack of eight-feet-by-ten-feet floral wool woven rugs that were in a pile on the floor. They were so pretty! I looked at the price and noticed that they were $800. That's a steal for a wool woven rug! I flipped through the stack and found one that I really liked. I thought about it and thought about it, but I couldn't bring myself to summon a salesman and tell him that I wanted it. It might have been a steal at $800, but I didn't have $800. If I wanted this rug, I was going to have to charge it. And I said that I would only use my American Express card for emergencies. The feather bed could be considered an emergency, but the rug couldn't.

I looked down at the rug again and noticed that the one I wanted didn't have a price on it. Come to think of it, it did look a bit smaller than the others in the pile, so maybe it didn't belong here, and maybe it wasn't $800. A salesman was standing nearby, so I decided to ask him.

'Excuse me, how much is this rug?' I asked. 'I think it's a bit smaller than the others here, and they are eight hundred dollars.'

'Um,' he said, hesitating, 'I think it's two hundred dollars.'

Two hundred dollars! No way! No how! I told him that I'd take it, and he wrote up a tag and pinned it to the rug. As I bent down to help him roll it up, I realized that it *was* the same size as all the others. Oops. Now, if you were in my situation, would *you* tell the guy that you'd made a mistake and the rug probably was $800 like the others? Or would you grab it, run to the register to pay, and then get the hell out of the store?

I chose to do the latter. Think what you may. But I bet the extra $600 to a big fancy store like this is just a drop in the bucket. I was just one little girl in a big city on a budget. It was a big drop in the bucket to me. The rug was on sale anyway, and they were probably happy to get rid of it so they could move some new merchandise in. My mother would not be proud. She once made my sister and me go back to the grocery store because the cashier forgot to ring up a six-pack of soda. But she wasn't here and wouldn't have to know the story behind this rug.

I walked with the guy and waited while he wrote up my sale. He wasn't moving fast enough. I thought for sure that any moment he was going to realize what he did and change the price. I tried to not look him in the eye and talk to him about the weather. Yep, that's it. I'd keep him occupied so he forgot about the rug. When it was time to pay, I pulled out my Amex card and gave it to him. Swipe, entering amount, dialing, going through . . . gosh, this was taking a long time! Every other time when I charge things it seems to take just a second. But this time seemed to be taking forever. Finally, the machine spit the receipt out and I signed on the dotted line. It was mine!

I practically ran out the front door with my rug. It wasn't that heavy because it was woven and didn't have a backing. But it was bulky. But that didn't stop me from hightailing it outta there as fast as I could. I hopped into the first cab I saw and headed back toward Bed Bath & Beyond to pick up my feather bed.

One hour and two cab rides later, I arrived home. I unfolded the rug and laid it out on the wood floor. It was gorgeous! I then put my feather bed on top of that and laid down. Ahhhh! Nice. I heard a noise come from the hallway and looked up at the door to find an eye staring at me through the hole in my door. I still hadn't gotten a lock. I screamed.

'Oh, I'm sorry,' said a voice from the hallway, 'I'm Spiro, the super. I heard you needed a lock.'

I wanted to yell at him for scaring me, but it's just not in me. 'Oh, don't worry. I was just resting,' I said, rising.

I walked to the door, opened it, and let him in. Spiro was about five feet six, bald with glasses. He seemed nice enough and pretty harmless.

'I have a lock that I can sell you for $75,' he said. 'They usually sell for around $300 down the block.'

'Oh, really? They're that expensive? Wow. Um, I guess . . . sure, I'll take it,' I said reluctantly. Now obviously the last thing that I wanted to be spending $300 on was a lock for my door, so I should have jumped at the chance to buy the lock for $75 from Spiro. But I didn't have any cash. If I went to the store to buy a lock, I could have charged it. But if I bought it from him, I would have to pay him cash. So I didn't really want to buy it from him, and was unsure why I said I would. Payday was one week away.

'Great. I'll bring it up and put it on the door and everything,' Spiro said, heading toward the door.

'Okay,' I replied, having no clue how I was going to pay him. 'Sounds good. I'll see you later.'

'Oh, I'll be right back,' he said.

As soon as Spiro left, I pulled out my cell phone and called American Express to see how I could get a cash advance so I could pay Spiro. I had bought a cell phone on the way to Bed Bath & Beyond that morning. I needed it to do work because my phone wouldn't be hooked up for at least two more weeks. It was an emergency. It was a cute Motorola with a flippy thing on the bottom that covered up all the numbers. Anywho, I called American Express and they told me that I couldn't get a cash advance from them, because American Express is a *charge* card, not a *credit* card. Oh, yeah, right. That's why I got one in the first place.

I'm not really great with money. I never have been. So

when I opted to move to New York, I decided to cancel all of my credit cards and get only an American Express card. I did this because American Express is a *charge* card, not a *credit* card – meaning that I have to pay off the balance in full every month. They don't let you carry over balances to the next month. By only having an American Express card, I decided that I would be less likely to charge up frivolous items. But a lock for my front door wasn't a frivolous item. A lock was a necessity.

'But all I need is a hundred dollars,' I begged to the woman on the phone.

'I'm sorry, but you can't get that with this card,' she said. 'And just so you know, your balance is $3,434 and $2,581 of that is due in one week.'

'Um, great, thanks. Bye,' I said and hung up.

Crap. I had been here for two weeks exactly and hadn't gotten paid yet. And that American Express lady just told me that I owed more than what I expected my next paycheck would be. But I could figure that out later. Back to Spiro and the lock. How was I going to pay him $75?

A few seconds later, he came to my front door.

'Oh, hi,' I said. 'Spiro, before you put that on, I just realized that I left my checkbook at work, and I don't have an ATM card yet, so I probably won't be able to pay you until sometime next week.'

'Oh, don't worry about it. I'll put it on anyway. You shouldn't be sleeping here with a big hole in the door,' he said. 'Just leave it in an envelope with the doormen when you are able to get it.'

How nice was that?

'Thank you so much,' I said.

'When I was downstairs, I noticed I have an air conditioner too that I can sell to you if you want. I'll give you that and the lock for $200.'

He was so nice to let me pay him next week that I felt like I *had* to buy the air conditioner. So what if it was something he was trying to unload? I'd have to get one eventually anyway.

'That would be great. I'll leave the money in an envelope for you next week.'

Spiro finished installing the lock and left. I laid down on my feather bed again on my nice, new oriental rug, in the middle of my empty apartment, with no more hole in the door and fell asleep. I'd had an exhausting day.

IS IT THE BLACK?

Before I knew it, it was Monday, and time for my first case. I was nervous, to say the least. Working in television was never something that I set out to do. I just sort of ended up there. I've always been a 'go-with-the-flow' type of girl. I never make the plans, I just 'go-with.' I end up places. And I just ended up in television.

After having a gazillion majors in college, I finally graduated with a bachelor's degree in marketing. After graduation, I worked at Hyatt Hotel's corporate office in the marketing development office for six months. The Hyatt job was boring, to say the least. And the only reason I wanted to work there was for the free hotel rooms. But after I started, I found out that I had to work there for a whole year before I got those. So one day while trying to get my first year under my belt, my college roommate and good friend Tracy called me up and told me that *The Jenny Jones Show* was looking to hire a new audience producer.

Tracy and I met and bonded in college when we joined the same sorority – and we both hated it. We thought that dressing up in matching outfits, holding candles, and singing songs to girls telling them that they were our best friends was a bit strange. How could they be our best friends when we'd just met them? And weren't we just a bit too old to be dressing up? I thought so. Tracy felt the same way.

'All you have to do is jump around and clap your hands all day. Basically, you are a glorified cheerleader,' she said, describing the job at *Jenny Jones*. It sounded good to me. So I quit my Hyatt job, interviewed and got hired at *The Jenny Jones Show*, and stayed for four years. And that's how I ended up working in television. It was never something I set out to do. I just ended up there.

As audience producer at *Jenny*, my job was to make sure the audience was very enthusiastic and involved in every show. I was therefore in the studio for every single show taping for four years. At two hundred shows a season, that's eight hundred shows.

During that time I learned a lot. So when I knew that I was going to move to New York, I interviewed for a producer position at the new court show. The jump from audience producer to producer would be a big one, but I felt that I was ready for the challenge.

I got ready and went to work early, because I wanted to be extra prepared for my first big show day. My guests were from Texas, and arrived on Sunday afternoon. The case involved a thirty-five-year-old woman who was suing a man for hanging her wallpaper upside down in her kitchen. The man said that the woman told him to hang it that way, and added that it was so ugly that he couldn't tell which way it was supposed to go. He was counter-suing for emotional distress because he said after the wallpaper was hung the plaintiff started harassing him, and called his wife a 'fat pig.'

On the way to work, I called my mom from my cell phone for that extra boost of confidence.

'Hi, Mona!' she said. My mom has called me Mona since high school because she thinks that I 'whine, moan and complain' too much. It's her nickname for me.

'Hi, Mom,' I said. 'My first show is today and I'm really nervous. Will you say a prayer to grandma for me and ask her to make sure it's a good one?' Not like I couldn't say a prayer by myself, but I thought God would be more apt to listen to my mom because she went to church every Sunday. I'm Catholic, so I had a bit of the Catholic guilt for not going to church on a regular basis.

'Yes, I will,' she said.

'Do it right now while I am on the phone,' I said.

'Okay. Hold on,' she said. We sat there for a few seconds silence until my mom said she was done.

'Thank you, Mama. Okay, I have to go now,' I said. 'I love you.'

'I love you too,' she said and hung up. I missed my mom. It's times like these when I'm nervous that I just want to crawl up and sit on her lap. It's always safe there.

Around 9:00 A.M., my guests arrived for their case, which was scheduled to start taping at 10:30 A.M. I greeted them in their green rooms and after talking with them a bit, was confident it was going to be a good one. The blond Texan was really high energy. I mean *really* high energy. Her twin sister came with her, and asked me if she could testify on her behalf to tell Judge Curtis that she was an honest person. They were dressed alike. They told me how they were both former Bud girls. They actually told everybody how they were both former Bud girls. But they didn't look like Bud girls. I wondered if they ever looked like Bud girls.

Shortly before the case was scheduled to begin, I walked into the studio and took my place on the side of the stage where the producer and the executive producer, who is my boss, stand during the taping. My boss, the woman who hired me, was Mary, a woman who is famous in the world of daytime television. She is an Emmy-winning producer who had been in the business for years. And I wanted so much to impress her.

Soon enough, the show began and the plaintiff told the judge all about how the defendant hung her wallpaper upside down.

'It has tulips on it, Your Honor. Everyone knows that tulips grow upward. What kind of tulips grow downward?

None. That's what kind,' she said. The judge asked the defendant what his side of the story was.

'Well, she told me to hang it that way,' he said. 'And I had to ask her because it's ugly and I couldn't tell which way was up all by myself. It looked the same any way you hung it.'

'Excuse me, Your Honor,' the plaintiff interrupted. 'I just want to tell you that he tried to come on to me when he was hanging my wallpaper. He was taking his time hanging it, not paying attention to what he was doing because he wanted me. I mean, I was a former Bud girl, Your Honor. It was many, many years ago, but I was.' Of course she was.

'That is untrue,' the defendant argued back. 'After I hung the wallpaper up, she started calling *my* house and harassing my wife because she wanted *me*. That's why I'm countersuing her for harassment. She called my wife a fat pig.'

The judge asked the plaintiff if this was true.

'Well, Your Honor,' she said, pointing at the defendant's wife, 'she *is* a pig. Just look at her. She's a pig.' I felt bad for the defendant's wife, but I had to laugh because the plaintiff was in her mid-thirties and was acting like a teenager.

At the end of the case, while the judge was delivering his verdict, the plaintiff kept interrupting him. He banged his gavel and looked at her. He was a very large African American man with a powerful voice, and she was just a small Texan with big blond hair and a sister to match.

'Why aren't you listening to me? Is it the black?' he asked while tugging at his black judge robe.

'Oh, no, Your Honor. We don't hate blacks,' she replied, pointing to herself and her sister. With that, the judge burst into laughter and just shook his head. I had to bite my lip to stop from laughing.

'That's not really what I asked you, but I'm glad to know that you don't hate black people,' he said.

A few moments later, after the judge composed himself, he made his ruling. The plaintiff was not rewarded any money and the defendant was found not guilty for hanging her wallpaper upside down, because, well, it was ugly and looked the same any way you hung it. He then banged his gavel and went back to his chambers. Okay, he didn't really have chambers – it was more like a dressing room, but it always sounded more courtlike to say chambers. Afterward, I looked at my boss to see what her reaction was. She smiled at me and patted me on the back.

'That was good,' she said, hurrying off to get ready for the next case. 'You rock, sister!'

I did it! I produced my first case! And it was good! And I rocked!

I walked backstage and said good-bye to the litigants, and went back to my desk to get ready for my case the next day. It was a couple suing a dog groomer over a bad haircut on their Maltese.

So far this court show thing was kind of fun. Nothing was too serious. There weren't parents wanting to send their out-of-control teens to boot camp, or girls trying to find out if their boyfriends were indeed the fathers of their babies. It was just good old-fashioned small claims cases. Sure you had your 'ex suing an ex' case every now and then, or a family member suing another family member. But more often than not it was pretty lighthearted. And that was good because I liked lighthearted, fun things.

After about an hour, I decided to take a walk to an office supply store to jazz up my short cube. A few blocks down I found a gift store/office supply place that had a lot of cute frames and stuff. This stuff would do just fine. $42 later, I walked out of the store, got something to eat, and headed back to the office.

POTENTIALLY GAY BRAD

Later that afternoon, my best friend from home, Naomi, called to tell me that she was going to set me up on my first blind date in New York with a guy named Brad, who worked in the New York office of her company. The big date was set for Saturday night. Naomi told me she likes to call Brad 'Potentially Gay Brad' because he was just that: potentially gay.

'Naomi, why would you set me up with someone who is potentially gay?' I asked.

'Because he's cute,' she said.

'Okay,' I said. That was a good enough reason for me.

The next day, Potentially Gay Brad called me on the phone and asked me to go to dinner that Saturday night. I already had plans with a couple that both Naomi and I knew from Chicago, who also now lived in New York, otherwise known as the Swingers. Naomi and I call the Swingers 'the Swingers' because they have been known to pick up a third every now and then. But they were nice, and attractive – right out of a J. Crew catalog. I never swung with them, but I couldn't help but think about swinging every time I was around them. Not that I wanted to, but I couldn't keep my mind from wandering that way. I wondered how they asked someone to swing with them. Did they just come right out and say it? Or did they just casually began rubbing someone's forearm at a bar? I wondered how things like that happen. What if they asked me to swing with them this Saturday night? What would I say?

'Um, excuse me, Karyn, we think you're great and all, and were wondering if you would be interested in having sex with us?'

What would I say if they asked me that?

'Um, ooh . . . yeah. I'm sorry. You know, I think you're *really* nice people, and you sure are swell, but I'm not really into gettin' it on with a married couple.' No, that might offend them . . .

I'd say, 'Gosh, I think swinging is *really* great, but I just swung last night with a different couple, so I'm not much up for makin' sweet, sweet love with you right now. But maybe later.' Yes, that's it! That's what I'd say! Just to be safe and make sure this didn't happen, I asked Brad if he would like to join us, and he accepted my invitation.

Saturday came before I knew it, and Mrs Swinger and I decided to go shopping so I could get a little something new for my date. Since moving to New York, I kept having the feeling that most of my clothes were 'Midwestern.' I'm not a hillbilly or anything, but I just didn't look as chic as most of the women did in this city. I was 'cute.' But now that I lived in New York, I wanted to be snazzy.

Since Mrs Swinger lived on the Upper West Side, she took me to Columbus Avenue to go shopping. There were all sorts of cute little stores. We went to Betsey Johnson (I just *love* her frilly dresses) and a place called Olive & Bette's. They had the hippest T-shirts I ever saw for only like $70! We walked and shopped for hours, and eventually stumbled upon a store called Intermix. Now, I had never heard of Intermix before, but with one look in the window, I knew that we were destined to meet.

We walked in and my jaw dropped. They *did not* have stores like this in Chicago! All of the clothes were hanging on long racks that ran along the walls on both sides of the store. In the middle, they had *more* long racks, and a few tables with clothes folded on top of them. It was very well lit too, which in my opinion helped me to see the inner beauty of the clothes.

I walked up to the racks and began looking through the cutest clothes I had ever seen in my whole life. They had Earl Jean and Marc Jacobs – all the same clothes that I saw in my fashion magazines. I felt like a jailbird on the loose! I couldn't flip through the racks quickly enough. Surely my blind date would fall in love with me if I wore an outfit from here! Then we'd live happily ever after! While perusing the store, I stopped dead in my tracks when I saw the prettiest sheer coral top hanging from one of the racks across the store. (Coral was very hot that summer, remember? Charlize Theron wore that coral dress to the Academy Awards and BAM! Coral bloomed. The rest is fashion history.)

I ran and pulled it from the rack. It was exquisite! I picked up the tag to see the size, and was happy to see that it was a medium. Just my size! I then looked at the price – $148. That wasn't too bad. It was good quality, you know? I tried it on and it fit perfectly. And damn did it make me look skinny! I *had* to have this top. Brad might be the one, you know? You just can't take chances with blind dates. *Every* one might be the one. So I took that coral top up to the register, pulled out my Amex card, and swipe, sign, it was mine.

Later that night, I put on my new top and paired it with a pair of great Shelli Segal black pants that I already had. The plan was to meet at the Swingers' for a drink before going to dinner.

I was happy that I decided to take my chances with Potentially Gay Brad. Now nothing is wrong with being gay, some of my best friends are gay. But being potentially gay and being set up with *me* is a recipe for disaster. I don't know what it is, but several of my former boyfriends have *turned* gay after going out with me. So it just seems that the guys that I do go out with that are 'potentially' gay usually *are* gay. For example, Doug, my first high school boyfriend and first love of my life, is now a gay social worker. Luke, my serious college boyfriend who I wanted to *marry*, now works in a flower shop. Voluntarily. The list goes on. So if you are at all unsure about your sexuality, one date with me should clear up which side of the fence you're on.

Anywho, I arrived at the Swingers' apartment before Brad, and sat on the couch in my new coral top and waited for his arrival. Mr Swinger came and sat next to me. A chill went up my spine. Is this how it happens? I thought. Is Mr Swinger going to make his big move? He reached across me and I thought, 'Get your hands off me!' until I saw him grab the remote.

'Sorry to reach. Are you okay?' he said, noticing the frightened look on my face.

'Oh, I'm fine,' I said, embarrassed for a moment. 'I'm just nervous about my date.'

A few moments later the buzzer rang, which meant Brad was in the lobby and on his way up to the Swingers' apartment.

Although Naomi assured me Brad was cute, you just never know with these things. There was a knock on the door, and I walked over in my smart coral top and opened it to find Brad standing there. He was cute! He was really, really cute! And he was exactly my type, which meant that he was probably gay.

Brad sort of looked like a cross between Jude Law and Prince William. He was devastatingly beautiful! He had light brown wavy hair that looked so soft. I just wanted to touch it. Oh, and those eyes! They were piercing blue. And he was *my* date! I was so happy that I'd splurged on the Intermix top . . .

'Hi, Karyn? Brad,' he said.

'Hi,' I replied and kinda just stared . . . for a while . . .

'Can I come in?' he asked, snapping me back to reality.

'Oh, yeah, sorry,' I said, blushing. 'Come in.'

'Great. Cute shirt, by the way!'

Yup. Just as I suspected: Gay. How many straight men comment on your shirt before they really know you? None. That's how many.

Nonetheless, Potentially Gay Brad, the Swingers and I had a drink, and then set out to find a place to eat. We ended up going to a little Italian cafe called Pomodoro and ate outside.

As I sat in my chair and watched all the people walk by, I couldn't help but notice how fashionable they all were. I looked down at my top and felt like one of them. I felt like I fit in.

During dinner, the Swingers got drunk and became really touchy-feely. Brad and I looked at each other and just smirked. It was really quite funny and I was glad that we both noticed, and *noticed* that we both noticed. It sort of became our little joke throughout the evening. Every time Mr Swinger would glance over at his wife and stare at her chest, Brad and I would kick each other under the table. We were bonding.

After two bottles of wine and a great dinner, the check came. The Swingers got into some sort of drunken squabble and decided they wanted to go home. Brad and Mr Swinger took care of the bill.

As all four of us walked outside, I couldn't help but feel nervous. Was Brad going to say he wanted to go home too, or was he going to ask me to go out for another drink? I was a bit buzzed from the wine at dinner and *did* feel some sort of chemistry, but I didn't know if it was mutual.

'Do you want to go out for another drink?' Brad asked.

I was so excited! He liked me! Maybe. Or maybe he was just being nice. But I didn't really care.

'Yeah, definitely,' I said, trying to contain my excitement and sound casual.

We bid our farewell to the Swingers, who proceeded not to look at each other and sway in their drunken standing positions.

'Bye,' they said in unison, and then seemed angry that they had said it in unison.

'Bye,' Brad and I said as we watched them stumble into a cab.

Tense and buzzed, I looked over at Brad. He looked at me. We both burst into laughter.

'They were wasted!' Brad said, laughing.

'No kidding! You know, I don't know them very well,' I said, trying to make the statement sound like some sort of disclaimer.

'Yeah, right,' he said jokingly. We decided to walk to a cheesy Greek bar on the corner and get another drink there.

'Yeah, I know,' he continued, 'Naomi told me they were a bit odd.'

'She did?' I asked, surprised.

'Yeah. She told me they like to hook up with other people.'

'Really? She told you that! That's so funny, I heard that too, and I'm always so nervous every time I'm alone with them,' I said.

'Yeah, about as nervous as I was when you invited me there for drinks. I was thinking you may be into that sort of thing too and invited me over there to make the moves on me.'

'Liar!' I said, laughing and hitting him. He grabbed my hand.

'I swear!'

'Brad,' I said, looking him straight in the eye, 'I, Karyn, am *not* a swinger.'

'Good,' he replied, looking me square back in the eye, 'I, Brad, am not either.'

After a night of endless flirting, I decided that Potentially Gay Brad might not be gay after all. Sure, he had all the mannerisms of a gay man, and was well groomed, but he was so flirty! And we had such chemistry . . . After two more drinks, Brad walked me all the way home. It was such a beautiful night. He told me all about the neighborhood that my new apartment was in. It was a neighborhood called Sutton Place and he said it was very ritzy – old-money ritzy. Like the Vanderbilts used to live in the neighborhood and stuff.

When we arrived at the entrance to my building, Brad politely kissed me on the cheek and said good-bye. The cheek? Okay, Brad just turned back into Potentially Gay Brad. What kind of man in his twenties kisses a hot girl in a sexy coral Intermix top on the cheek to say good night? My loins were burning and his weren't? Oh, well. I smiled and thanked him for the lovely night. Despite the kiss, or lack thereof, I still had a crush. And I think he did too . . .

I turned and walked through the front door, and when I was almost at the elevator, I looked back over my shoulder at Brad, who was still standing there watching me with a big smile on his face. Yeah, he had a crush too . . .

TWO

AMERICAN EXPRESS

American Express

Karyn Bosnak
400 E. 57th St.
New York, NY 10010

Date	Payee	Amount
	PREVIOUS BALANCE	$ 3,434,00
Jun 11, 2000	Gracious Home	$ 432.00
Jun 12, 2000	American Express Gift Cheques	$ 325.00
Jun 13, 2000	Petland	$ 75.00
Jun 17, 2000	Diesel Backpack	$ 108.00
Jun 17, 2000	Barnes & Noble	$ 16.00
Jun 17, 2000	Jim's Health & Fitness	$ 96.00
Jun 17, 2000	D'Agostino Grocery	$ 213.00
Jun 23, 2000	Manhattan Transit Authority	$ 34.00
Jun 26, 2000	Intermix	$ 138.00
Jun 29, 2000	American Express Gift Cheques	$ 325.00
	PAYMENTS	– $ 3,000.00
	Total	**$ 2,196.00**

JENNIFER CONVERTIBLES

Karyn Bosnak
400 E. 57th St.
New York, NY 10010

Date	Payee	Amount
Jun 12, 2000	Couch	$ 1,774.00
	Total	**$ 1,774.00**

Grand Debt Tally $3,970.00

NO USE CRYIN' OVER LOST UNDERWEAR

That Monday my alarm clock woke me up at 7.00 A.M. The new curtains that I bought on Sunday kept the sun out nicely. They were an emergency. They were an emergency because I am not a morning person, and my day gets off to a bad start when I'm not able to sleep in. The windows were so big that I had to buy six panels to cover them completely. I bought six sheer panels at a store called Gracious Home I found on the Upper East Side. Gracious Home is a home store that carries everything from doorknobs and curtains to French linens for your table. And just like ABC, it was split into two stores right across the street from each other. I wondered if a lot of stores did this in New York. Anyway, I bought the panels and a nice long rod, and some pretty tiebacks for when I felt like letting the sunlight in.

But as much as the curtains were an improvement, the feather bed wasn't much better than sleeping on a pile of clothes. I could still feel the hardwood floor beneath me and my back still hurt.

I got ready for work and decided that I would try to walk to work again in my new sandals. Maybe my feet just needed to get used to them. I put on some fresh Band-Aids and off I went.

All I can say is that I tried. But a few blocks later, I looked down at my feet and again they were a big aching Band-Aid mess. As I stopped to try to readjust the straps, I looked around at all the other women walking to work. They had on heels and sandals and their feet seemed just fine. Maybe mine were extra sensitive. The logical thing for me to do would be to walk to work in a different, more comfortable pair of shoes, and then change into my sandals when I got there. But I didn't really want to do that. My sandals looked really nice, and I wanted people to see me in my new sandals. Besides, I think it's tacky when women walk to work in fancy business suits and sneakers. Women in Chicago did this all the time, but I noticed that women in New York did not. Or at least they didn't while walking down 57th Street.

Out of nowhere, a big bus pulled up and stopped right in front of me. I looked up and realized that I was at a bus stop. I decided to jump on because my feet just couldn't take it. Luckily I had $1.50 in change in my purse, because I didn't have a subway card and the bus didn't make change. After paying, I made my way to the back and found a seat. The bus was a lot cleaner than the subway. The people were better looking too. As I sat in my seat and peered out the window, I came to terms with the fact that I had to give up on trying to walk to work. It was just too much of a hassle. I looked a mess when I got there, and honestly, my feet just couldn't take it.

The traffic was horrible, but the bus dropped me off right in front of my building. I looked down at my watch and realized I was twenty minutes late. My boss was a stickler for promptness, and so far I had been on time. So I decided to get a coffee and a muffin.

You see, the best thing to do when you are late is get a coffee and a muffin. Then you drop your bag/purse/briefcase/coat just outside of where your boss happens to be and walk in with just your coffee, as if to say, 'I've already been here (and was probably here before you, actually) and just left to get some coffee. But now I'm back and am heading to my desk to get back to what I was working on.' Once you've made sure your boss sees you, it's safe to go back and get your bag/purse/briefcase/coat.

This morning I did just that. And it worked. Like always. As I sat down, I logged on to the Internet and went to American Express's website. I just wanted to check my balance again to make sure the lady on the phone had it right. She sure did. It was $3,000. As freaked out as I was about the balance, I also started to think about how I was going to pay

Spiro. I then noticed something on the left-hand side of the screen: American Express Gift Cheques.

American Express Gift Cheques. Hmmm. I clicked on the link and was taken to the page. 'Better than a gift certificate – the American Express Gift Cheque,' it said. 'Overnight delivery available.'

I started to read further.

'Available in denominations up to $100,' it said. From what I gathered, people could order these checks, charge them to their American Express card, and give them to someone as a gift. That person could buy whatever they wanted, and pay for it with a Gift Cheque. They were kind of just like traveler's checks, but had a different name.

I started to think. I remembered that the last time I used traveler's checks on a vacation, I had some extra left over when I got home. So I called up the traveler's check company and asked what I should do with them, and they told me that I could just cash them or deposit them into my checking account. Just then a light went off in my head!

I decided that I'd get these American Express Gift Cheques and give them to *myself* as a gift! Then I'd deposit them into my checking account. That's it! I knew there must be a way to get some cash out of my American Express card.

Sure, there were fees. But I needed the money now, kind of like how Wimpy on *Popeye* needed his burgers. He was on to something when he said, 'I'll gladly pay you Tuesday for a hamburger today.' Well, I'd rather pay them $20 at the end of the month for $300 today.

After figuring out what I needed, I decided to get $300 worth. That would cover the amount I had to give to Spiro and give me a bit extra to last me until Thursday, which was payday. After clicking on the 'Order Now' button and choosing the overnight delivery option, I was all set. Federal Express would deliver my Gift Cheques tomorrow before noon, at which point I'd take them to my bank and deposit them right into my checking account. They'd go in just like cash!

As I leaned back and smiled, my phone rang. It was my friend Mark in Chicago, who was taking care of my cat until this week, when he was going to fly with him to New York to drop him off.

'Honey, hi!' Mark said.

'Hi! How's my baby?' I said.

'I'm fine!' he answered, knowing full well I was talking about my cat.

I have always been a bit obsessed with my cat. His name is Elvis. Well, his full name is Elvis the Bush Cat. My mom found him in a bush about five years ago while visiting a friend in a shady town north of Chicago called North Chicago. It's kind of like 'the hood' there, and Elvis was just living in a bush outside her friend's house for a few weeks. One day while my mom was there, he came out of the bush to say hello and he was all beat up. He had a big hole in his leg where he must have been attacked or something, his tail was broken, and so was his front tooth.

So my mom is like a big 'save the animals' fanatic and took him to the vet, who gave him stitches and fixed him all up. But she is allergic to cats, and asked me if I would take him. I didn't have a pet at the time and wanted one, so I said yes.

I had a cat once, but I had to get rid of him. His name was Kitty, and I got him while in college. A few years after that, I moved into a new apartment with a friend in Chicago. The apartment wasn't very big, and I don't think Kitty was very happy there because he weighed eighteen pounds. He was big.

One day my roommate came home and told me that she was allergic to him and asked me to get rid of him. The thought seemed ludicrous to me, until I looked at big fat Kitty, who seemed unhappy anyway. I ended up giving him to a good family friend who had met Kitty before and was very fond of him. She had a house with a yard and Kitty ended up being really happy there. But I cried and cried when I had to give him away. It was horrible.

A few months later that same roommate went to the Humane Society and came home with a cat. Seriously. She made me get rid of *my* cat and then got *herself* one. She said she was only allergic to my cat. That's a bunch of crap.

But you know, everything happens for a reason. And if I'd still had Kitty when my mom called about finding Elvis, I might have decided not to take him. And Elvis and I were destined to be together.

I named him Elvis because I like the name, not just because I'm a huge fan of the King. Although when I was a little girl, I used to *love* Elvis. My mom had the *Elvis – Aloha from Hawaii* eight-track tape, and I would play it on our stereo in the basement. And I would think that a miniature Elvis was really singing to me from inside the speakers. I would just lie there all day and listen to him.

So Elvis it was. It wasn't until a few months later that he landed his full and proper name of Elvis the Bush Cat. It was the holiday season and I put up a Christmas tree and he started attacking it and scaling the side of it. I decided that he must be having flashbacks to his wild days living in the bush and must have thought there were animals inside. He still acts the same crazy way every Christmas when the tree comes out. So Mark was watching Elvis until I moved into my new apartment.

'Not you, dumbass,' I said. 'How is my baby Elvis?'

'He is good. And I am happy to get rid of him,' Mark said.

Mark is a high-maintenance gay man. I like to call him Mo, which is short for Homo, which is short for High-Maintenance Homosexual. He has jet-black hair and ice-blue eyes and is so good-looking that it's sometimes painful to be friends with him. He doesn't act gay, so women everywhere, including me at one point, always fall madly in love with him. When we first met, I was *positive* that I could change him, but

I was wrong. He's as gay as they come. And he's now one of my greatest friends in the whole world.

Mark gave me the details of his flight, and told me to expect him that Wednesday. He was arriving in the middle of the day, and I would have to go to my apartment to meet him.

When I hung up the phone, I decided I'd call the moving company to see if they'd found my furniture yet. I really needed it to arrive by that Wednesday because I had company coming. I called and was of course transferred around a million times before I finally got a man on the phone who knew the whereabouts of my furniture: in a warehouse outside of Chicago.

'You've had it for two weeks and it hasn't even left Illinois?' I asked.

'Sorry, miss, we don't know what happened. You should have it in a couple of weeks.'

'A couple of weeks just won't do,' I said, starting to cry. 'You have all of my stuff. You have my clothes, my underwear. I really want my underwear.'

'Miss, there's no use crying over lost underwear. We'll try to get it to you as quickly as we can.'

'Listen, dude, this isn't spilled milk here. It's my underwear. And it's not just my underwear, for that matter. It's everything I own. I feel so displaced. I want my stuff. I want my underwear,' I said.

I can't really explain why I got so emotional over my underwear, but I did. I wanted my stuff and was sick of living out of five suitcases. And the feather bed *seemed* like it would make a fine mattress, but the truth was that it sucked. The wood floors were very hard to sleep on. I was tired. I was cranky. I wanted my bed. I wanted my underwear.

I hung up the phone and decided to take a walk and get some fresh air and something to eat. It was a bit early for lunch, but I was depressed and hungry. While I was walking down the street, I saw a Jennifer Convertibles in the distance. I always see their flyers in the Sunday papers. They have couches in there for like $400 and stuff. I decided to check it out. On my way into the store, I noticed the American Express card logo on the door. I mean, if this wasn't an emergency, then I don't know what was. I browsed around for a while and looked at what they had to offer. The flyer was right. Some of the couches were dirt cheap, but they were also butt ugly. I then started to thinking about the blender in college, and the feather bed that I'd just bought, and asked myself, 'Self, why buy the cheap one when the nice one is only a thousand dollars more?' I mean a couch is an investment. There's no use spending $400 on a cheap one. If I was going to buy one, then I might as well *buy* one. And I was being responsible about this. I was in Jennifer Convertibles, for crying out loud. I wasn't in the Bloomingdale's furniture department, or at some other fancy Italian furniture place. I was at Jennifer Convertibles: the home of cheap couches.

In the corner I saw a nice gorgeous brown velvet sofa that would go perfectly with my new rug. I asked the salesman if I could buy the floor sample. He said no.

'Why not?' I asked.

'Because it's not for sale. You have to order one,' he replied.

'But I really need a couch now, like today. I have company coming in two days.'

'Listen, I can try to put a rush on one if you want to order it, but it is our policy not to sell the floor samples.'

I sat down on the sofa and cried.

'How about a chair? Can I buy that chair over there and take it home today?' I asked, pointing to the most hideous blue-and-white-striped club chair.

'No, sorry. It's the same thing as the couch. You have to order it.'

'Okay,' I said, giving in, 'I'd like to order this couch, please.'

The salesman started to write up the paperwork. I sat on the floor sample and sulked.

'Do you want to put a price hold on the matching chair, ottoman, and love seat?' he asked.

'Sure, I guess,' I said, not knowing what a price hold was. The salesman could tell by the confused look on my face that I had no idea what I just agreed to.

'That means if the price goes up at all, you can buy it for the same price that it is today. That's $50 extra per item. It's a good deal.'

'Oh, okay,' I said.

'Okay, miss, the grand total is $1,774.00. Would you like to open up a Jennifer Convertibles credit card?' he asked. 'There is no payment due and no finance charges for four months.'

I looked down at my American Express card. I was holding it in my hands. Putting almost $1,800 on a *charge* card that I *have* to pay off every month didn't seem that wise. And even though I didn't want another credit card, the idea of no payment due and no interest charged for four whole months seemed like a much better option. I would easily be able to save this money in four months, at which time I would pay it off in full.

'Sure, I'd love to open up a store credit card, sir. Thank you.' In less than ten minutes, I was applied, approved, charged and out the door. I got back to my office and saw Ann Marie on my way in.

'How was lunch, Karyn?' she asked.

'Great, thanks,' I said, one couch heavier and $1,800 lighter with one more credit card in my wallet.

ELVIS THE BUSH CAT

The next morning, I left a check for Spiro at the front desk on my way to work The American Express Gift Cheques were delivered to me at work right on time. I deposited them into my checking account at lunch. I decided that if I could just get past these moving costs I'd be fine.

Brad called me later that afternoon and asked me to go to dinner Wednesday night. I told him that Mark was coming into town, and he invited him to come along as well.

Before I knew it, it was Wednesday. I'd already broken the news to Mark that he had to stay in a hotel or sleep with me on the floor, and he opted for the hotel. But he was going to call me when he arrived, and meet me at my apartment to drop off Elvis before checking in.

Around noon, Mark called me to tell me that he and Elvis were leaving LaGuardia and on their way to my apartment. I snuck out the back door at work, 'on my way to lunch,' and jumped in a cab so I could get home fast to meet them. I was so excited!

'Four hundred East Fifty-seventh Street, please,' I said to the cab driver.

'Oh, lady . . .' the cab driver whined in a thick accent.

'Oh, lady what?' I asked.

'Oh, lady, that's all the way across town.'

'Yeah, so what? I know it's not that far, but I need to get there quickly,' I said, thinking he was mad because it wasn't that far.

'That's not it, lady. The traffic is bad this time of day, and it will take a long time to get across town. You should walk.'

Oh, not this. I still couldn't walk because I had blisters all over my feet.

'I have heels on,' I said, lying. 'You have to take me.'

'Fine by me,' he said shortly.

The car slowly started to move and then stopped abruptly. Then it started again and stopped abruptly again. It couldn't possibly be this bad.

'Was there an accident?' I asked.

'No, lady, I told you already,' he answered. 'This is what it's like trying to go crosstown in the middle of the day. Welcome to New York. Sheesh.'

I looked down at my watch. I had been in the car for all of ten minutes and had moved ten yards. I hadn't even gone one block yet. The car slowly started up again, and then stopped. This continued for almost an hour.

I looked up and realized that I was only two blocks from home, so I decided to pay the guy and walk the rest of the way. I knew Mark would already be waiting for me.

'Oh, gee, thanks, lady,' he said. 'Make me get stuck in this crap for an hour and give me a dollar.'

'You know, it's not my fault, sir, and sometimes people have to go crosstown.' I quickly figured out that New York is one of the only places I know where I can walk somewhere in thirty minutes or drive there in an hour.

When I got to my apartment, Mark was already there waiting. So was Elvis in his pet taxi.

'I can't believe you didn't buy me the Kate Spade pet carrier like I asked you to,' Mark said. 'I was embarrassed to walk through the airport with this one.'

Mark has this way of joking, but pretending he's serious. I get the sense of humor and knew he didn't really expect me to buy him the Kate Spade pet carrier. But if a stranger just overheard our conversation, they would think he was serious.

'Mark, he goes in his pet carrier once a year on his way to the vet. That's it. He's agoraphobic. You know that. He doesn't want a Kate Spade pet carrier.'

I like to give human qualities, and even human neuroses, to my pets.

'How do you know he doesn't want one? Have you asked him?'

'As a matter of fact I did,' I said, 'I called him last week when you weren't home, and he said he was fine with this black one,' I said.

'Huh. Well, still, this is an ugly pet carrier,' he said.

We took the elevator up to four and arrived at my empty apartment. I put the cat carrier on the ground and opened it up. Elvis the Bush Cat peered out. He looked scared. I picked him up and he hugged me. He does this. He wraps his kitty arms around your neck and hugs. I call it 'putting out.' He's not picky. He'll put out for anyone.

I looked down at him and noticed that he had a bad case of the flakes. Kitty dandruff.

'Mark,' I said, complaining, 'didn't you ever brush him? He's got dandruff.'

'Ew. No,' he said, 'he wouldn't come out from under my bed for the past three weeks. Why can't he brush himself?'

'He tries, but he can't hold the brush. No thumbs,' I said.

Elvis may be cute, but suave he is not. He frequently gets the flakes, which are really noticeable because he's black and white, but mostly black on his back, where the flakes are. He also barfs everywhere on a daily basis. I think that he may be bulimic because he does it right after he eats.

He's grubby. What else can I say? He came from a bush. And he just flew first class to live on 57th Street in New York. That's a long way from the 'hood.

'Oh, baby, did you miss your mommy?' I asked. He didn't answer me, and I could only assume that meant yes. He just kept hugging me and was hanging on for dear life. He was terrified.

'He was actually really good on the flight,' Mark said. 'He didn't make a peep the whole way here.'

'Yeah, well, I think he had a big going-away party last night with all his kitty friends, so maybe he was hungover.'

After a few minutes of mommy-kitty lovin', I showed Elvis his new pink litter box and his new food bowl and martini glass that I'd bought the night before. Elvis always drinks his water from a martini glass. A few minutes later, we locked up and left the building. Mark and I, that is. Not Elvis.

After my horrible commute home I decided to walk back to work, and Mark walked with me.

'What are you doing tonight?' he asked.

'I went on this date about a week ago with a guy named Brad that Naomi set me up with. And I'm supposed to go out with him tonight again. I told him that I had a friend coming in town and he told me to bring you. Do you want to come?'

'Yeah, that sounds good,' Mark said.

Halfway to work, Mark and I went our separate ways. He took a left down Madison Avenue because, well, he's gay and likes to shop. I kept going straight toward work.

'I'll call you later,' he said.

'Okay, bye, beautiful boyfriend!' I yelled toward him down the street. He looked at me embarrassed because I'm not his girlfriend. He's a big Mo.

KARYN'S GOT A BIG OLE BUTT

That night Mark and I met Brad out at a restaurant called Rosa Mexicana. It was right across the street from my apartment, and it was in my *Zagat* guide. It was known as one of the best Mexican restaurants in the city. It was Brad's choice.

I told Mark all about Potentially Gay Brad being potentially gay. So he was all prepared to let me know what his professional opinion was.

Mark came over as I was getting dressed. I was rummaging through the same clothes that I had been rummaging through for the past five weeks. I finally pulled out a pair of black pants and a yellow tunic button down and began to put it on.

'Honey, no,' he said, 'you are not wearing that.'

'Why not?' I asked. 'What's wrong with it?'

'Because you look like a cow in it,' he answered. 'It's too big and baggy. You know what I noticed today?'

What, dear Mark God, who just called me a cow? Enlighten me.

'Women in New York wear everything tight. It doesn't matter if they are big, small, fat or skinny. They all wear tight clothes. And it looks good. Nothing's wrong with having a big booty, honey. And you should try showing it, rather than hiding it.'

Just like my Mo to bring me down, then bring me back up again.'

'Really, you think?' I asked.

'Yes. Leave the pants on, but change the shirt,' he said. 'Let me see what you have.'

Mark started flipping through my clothes and found a tight yellow T-shirt.

'Here, wear this,' he said, handing it to me.

'Okay,' I said, I put the T-shirt on and looked at myself in the mirror. I felt so fat! I'm not what you would call fat, but I'm not stick-skinny either. I have curves, but only on the bottom. I'm flat as a board on top.

'Mark, now I look like a cow,' I said. 'My hips are so wide.'

'Honey, shut up. It's womanly. Thank Jennifer Lopez. She made girls like you with big asses acceptable in society again.' He continued laughing. 'Without her you'd be nothing.'

Sometimes I wonder why I'm friends with Mark, but I love him too much to question it. He's so vain, would he want to go out with a woman who looked like a lard-ass? The answer is no, so I decided to trust his judgment and wear the tight T-shirt with the tight black pants.

'You need bigger boobs,' Mark added.

'No duh,' I said, pulling out my jelly silicone breast enhancers. They are called Curves and are a small-breasted woman's best friend. I started to put them into my water bra to balance myself out. I was going for a double whammy tonight!

'Much better,' Mark said.

We left and headed toward the restaurant. We arrived five minutes late. Not bad for me. Brad was already waiting at the bar. He was cuter than I remembered.

'Hi,' I said, looking down, incredibly self-conscious about what I was wearing.

'Hi,' Brad replied and gave me a kiss on the cheek. I started to blush. I get nervous and awkward during times like these.

I can't help it. I can come across so self-assured at times, and so self-conscious and nervous at others.

I introduced Mark to Brad, and the three of us mingled by the bar for a few minutes until the hostess came to show us to our table.

Rosa Mexicana was the best damn Mexican food I had ever eaten in my whole life! They had these pomegranate margaritas that were mouthwateringly good. And they made guacamole from avocados right in front of your face. It was dreamy good! Hot diggity damn it was tasty!

Now, the last thing I wanted was to feel full and fat while dressed in my skintight New York style-clothing, so I only ate half of my meal. Sadly. The waiter came to ask me if I was full and I said, 'Oh, yes, stuffed.' What a lie. What a waste.

We all had too many margaritas during dinner, and Brad excused himself to go to the bathroom.

'So what do you think?' I asked Mark as soon as Brad was out of sight.

'I like him,' he said, 'I don't think he's gay.'

'Really?!' I asked, drunk and excited.

'Really,' answered Mark, 'he's cute too.'

'I know!' I said with my voice shrilling in excitement. Several people turned around to look.

'Honey, you need to fix that voice.'

Fixing my voice was something that Mark and I had been working on for a good year now. We saw on *Oprah* once where this lady had a 'voice makeover' and learned how to speak lower and more slowly. L-o-w-e-r and more s-l-o-w-l-y. She said it made people take her more seriously.

I needed a voice makeover. And a vocabulary makeover too. When I was a younger girl I saw the movie *Valley Girl* and started talking really singsongy and saying the words 'like' and 'for sure' all the time. I'm older now, but I still can't seem to get rid of the shrill and shake the words from my vocabulary. In fact, 'grody' is still one of my favorite words ever. So is 'dude.' And since I'm from the Midwest, most of my favorite adjectives are 'nice,' 'pretty' and 'cool.'

So about a year ago, Mark and I decided that it was time for me to change my voice. I bought a 'vocabulary builder' book from the bookstore and learned one new word a day. And I'd practice and practice at lowering the pitch in my voice. Mark would call me on the phone for my test, and I'd answer in my new voice.

'H-e-l-l-o-w-w . . .' I'd say, l-o-w-e-r and more s-l-o-w-l-y while trying to think of a sentence to use my new word in.

'Honey, good!' Mark would say. But that was usually the end of my serious voice because I'd burst into laughter. It's very hard for me to keep a straight face when I talk in my l-o-w-e-r and more s-l-o-w-l-y voice, because it's just not me.

Anywho, I promised him that I would work on it.

'Honey, your boobs look big,' Mark said to give me that extra boost of confidence right before Brad walked up.

'Thanks,' I whispered.

The two of them split the bill. That was nice. My two boyfriends bought me dinner. We left the restaurant and walked toward my apartment. Mark bid us farewell and hopped in a cab to his hotel, and Brad decided to come up to see my apartment.

As we walked toward the elevator, I got that nervous feeling again. I could feel the chemistry between us, the same chemistry I felt the first night we went out. Or maybe it was just the margarita. Whatever caused it, it was there.

We arrived at my door and I unlocked the lock and showed him in. It still didn't have any furniture, except curtains, a rug, a feather bed, and now a cat.

'It's nice,' Brad said as he walked toward the windows and pulled back the curtains, 'it's great.'

'Do you like it?' I asked.

'Yeah,' he said, walking back toward me.

'I don't really have anywhere for us to sit,' I said, leaning against a wall.

'That's okay,' he said.

With that said, Brad walked up to me and kissed me. Standing up. Slowly and softly. It was a real kiss this time. Not one of those cheek ones. He had nice soft lips. We stood there and kissed for a while, and it was kind of awkward, but what was I to do? Tell him he'd have to go because it was awkward to kiss while standing up? I don't think so. He was hot! And I had too many margaritas in me to care. I was quite happy just standing up and kissing. And happier that he just slid his hands down to my round Jennifer Lopez-sized booty. Ooh . . . what was he trying to do down there?

Brad had one hand on my booty, and the other on the bottom of my thigh, and I think he was trying to . . . lift me up? Maybe? Was he going to try to carry me or something? I was embarrassed that I was too heavy for him to lift, so I pressed my shoulders against the wall behind me and tried to push up to help him out. But nothing! This poor guy was trying to get it on with me and my big fat booty just wouldn't lift into the air. Damn! I had to go on a diet! But what kind of diet should I do? Should I do the Zone? The Atkins Diet? Ooh, no. I tried that one before and I got all light-headed. No, what kind should I do? Damn! I was being felt up by Brad and all I could think about was what kind of diet I was going to go on. Focus, Karyn, focus . . . hands are on your booty. Okay, there we go. Back to Brad, and his lips, and his hands on my booty that will not budge. I'll just pretend that I don't want to be lifted up. Because that's what you always do when you think that you are too fat to be lifted. You just pretend that you don't want to. Resist it. Then he won't think he wasn't able to lift me because I was too fat, he'll just think that I didn't want to be lifted.

After a few more minutes of kissing, I told Brad that I had to work early and it was best if we said good-bye. I could have stayed there for a good long while just doing what we were doing, but I wanted another date, so I decided that I needed to call it quits at this. Can't give it all away on the second date. And besides, any minute now his hands would have wandered upward and he would have felt the double whammy going on in my bra.

With that I walked Brad to the door and he kissed me again good-bye. He really was a good kisser. I sort of giggled a nervous little giggle and said good-bye.

'Bye,' he said, 'I love you.' No, I'm just kidding. He didn't say that last part.

I closed the door and locked it behind him. I then walked to the window and peered out the corner onto the street. A few seconds later I saw Brad cross the street and hop into a cab. He was so cute. And he just felt my butt. I'd have to do something about my butt. And my v-o-i-c-e.

I walked back and laid on my feather bed. I looked in the closet and saw Elvis peering out at me.

'Elvis, come here, baby,' I said. He crawled out and into my arms. 'You're still the number-one man in my life.' With Elvis perched on my shoulder, I pulled out my *Zagat* guide. I found Rosa Mexicana, circled it and wrote, 'My two boyfriends, some Curves and my booty.'

PAYDAY

The next day I woke up with a smile on my face. I got dressed for work and hopped on the bus. I was getting used to this commute. It wasn't so bad.

I didn't have any cases today, so I got off a block early and went to Starbucks. But this time I passed up the latte and opted for an Iced Grande Café Americano. That's three shots of espresso and some water over ice. Nice. Refreshing. Nonfat. I eyed all the muffins and passed on them too. I was going to get skinny!

I got to work and started calling on prospective cases. This job wasn't too bad so far. I was getting the hang of it. And it paid better than my last job. Oh, come to think of it, today was payday! I'd finally be receiving my first paycheck for my first two weeks of work. I needed it so badly!

My salary was about $1,500 a week, which is kind of low for a court show producer. Normal court show producers made about $1,700 a week or higher. But I wasn't 'normal,' considering that I'd never produced a day of television in my life. When they were staffing the show, the company was looking to hire six producers, but they also needed to adhere to a tight budget. By the time I was interviewed, they had already hired five of them, and were looking for just one more to hire for cheap. So I agreed to take a smaller salary just for the opportunity. No one else would have hired me as a producer, but my boss saw something in me that she liked. And she was friends with my former bosses, who were confident that I could do the job. So it worked out for both of us.

So, $1,500 x 2 weeks = $3,000. So after taxes I expected my first paycheck to be about $2,100 or so. I looked at the clock. It was 10:00 A.M. Time to get to work. Someone told me that the paycheck lady came around at lunchtime, so I set an alarm on my computer at noon to remind me to keep my eye out for her.

I worked for the next two hours, and right at the same time that my alarm went off, I saw her. The paycheck lady! She was going desk to desk and dropping off people's paychecks. She was moving really slowly. People never move fast enough when you need them to and you're staring at them, you know?

A few moments later, my time had come. She arrived at my desk and gave me my first paycheck.

'Thank you,' I said cheerfully. I opened my check and looked at the amount: $1766.66? That can't be right. Did I get paid for all the days that I worked? I looked more closely at my check and realized that it was correct. State tax and city tax were so high! All in all, the government took 41 percent of my paycheck. That's a crock.

I left for lunch and went to the bank to deposit my check. I figured that I could send my next two checks to American Express to be caught up, and then use the one after that to pay my rent. So that was my plan. But I'd have to have some spending money, so I kept $266, and decided to just send them $1,500.

Later that afternoon, as I was calling on court cases, the little envelope at the bottom of my computer started flashing. I went to my inbox and saw an e-mail from Brad.

To: Karyn
From: Brad
Re: Last night

Hey there smiley girl, how are you feeling today? I am exhausted. I had a great time though. I am leaving tomorrow to go to the Hamptons. I have a share in a summer house there. What are you doing?

Let's make a plan for next week when I get back. Are you free?

Brad

Hmm. Mark was leaving tonight, and wouldn't be here for the weekend, Ann Marie and her husband were going out of town, and Brad and the Swingers were really the only people I knew in the city. And I was afraid to be alone with the Swingers. So, I didn't have any plans for the weekend. But I wasn't going to tell *him* that. I decided to just be vague. When all else fails, be vague.

To: Brad
From: Karyn
Re: Re: Last night

Hi! Yes, last night was very fun. Thank you very much for dinner. I actually have a very busy weekend ahead of me . . . :)

E-mail me when you get back next week. I'd love to get together, but probably can't until at least Wednesday.

Have fun this weekend!

Karyn

There. That was good. I hit the Send button and my e-mail was off. I was kind of disappointed that I wouldn't see him this weekend, but I'd get over it.

That weekend all I did was walk around the city. And that kept me busy, so see? My feet were actually getting a bit used to my new sandals, so I wore those. The city was so big – everything about it! The streets were wide. The sidewalks were wide. The buildings were tall. The blocks were long. Manhattan isn't that big, or at least it didn't look like it on a map, but every inch of it was jam-packed with stuff.

I discovered a street fair and saw a couple of people wearing cute backpacks that had a strap that went across their chests diagonally. I liked the way they looked. I tried a cheap one on at the street fair, but instead opted to get a Diesel one I found at a store nearby. It was cooler. Hipper. I noticed that Mark was correct in his assessment that all New Yorkers wore tight clothes. I saw *plenty* of this at the street fair.

It was kind of fun to roam around the street fair by myself. You know how on *Cheers* they say 'Sometimes you want to go where everybody knows your name'? Well, sometimes you don't. Sometimes you want to go where no one knows you. At least I did. What I really hated about living in Chicago was that every time I went anywhere, I always would run into someone I knew. I was sick of going to the store and seeing someone from college, or going to the park and seeing someone from high school. Some people find comfort in things like this. But I found it annoying. I wanted to be alone and anonymous. That is why I came to New York. To figure out who I was.

On my way home I bought a fitness book that told me that

in order to lose fat, I needed to exercise and keep my heart rate between 134 and 154. Any lower and I wouldn't burn fat, and any higher I would stop burning the fat. So I bought a heart monitor at a fitness store to help me keep track. This was an investment in my health, and something that would last a long, long time. I planned to go running when I got home.

I have always liked to go running at night because it's when everyone has their lights on and you can look inside the windows and see what people's homes look like. I used to do this in Chicago all the time. I'm not a pervert or anything. I'm just fascinated with how people live.

So that night, I put on my heart rate monitor, got out my Walkman, and headed toward the Upper East Side. I was going to burn all the excess fat away on my butt and get skinny! Soon, Brad would be able to lift me into the air and throw me on my bed, once it arrived.

I ran all the way up Park Avenue and passed doorman after doorman and looked into lobbies that were utterly amazing. Since most apartments were higher up, I couldn't see a lot and decided to turn down a side street to check out some brownstones. There were so many beautiful brownstones in New York, and I couldn't wait to look inside.

For the next few blocks, I stared at fancy paintings and chandeliers. I saw a family eating at a long dining room table, with candles burning and everything. I thought people only ate like that in the movies. I stopped and watched them for a while. I wished I lived like that. I think a lot of people wish they lived like that. It looked comfortable. It looked like they had no worries.

I continued on my way and saw brownstone after brownstone. There were hundreds, maybe thousands in this neighborhood. How could that many people be that wealthy? I was going to be that wealthy someday.

A few blocks up I cut over to Fifth Avenue and ran past the Metropolitan Museum of Art, past the Guggenheim, and past where I heard that Jackie O had lived. The Upper East Side had a crisp clean feeling to it. I decided right then and there that I was going to concentrate on my job more so that one day I could buy myself one of these houses. There was a lot of money to be made in television. And I was going to make it.

That Sunday, I went into the office to get ahead with some work. I decided that I was going to be a very successful television producer. I was going to focus more on my work and move up quickly. This was the career that I chose, and I was going to be good at it.

THREE

AMERICAN EXPRESS

® **American Express**

Karyn Bosnak
400 E. 57th St.
New York, NY 10010

Date	Payee	Amount
	PREVIOUS BALANCE	$ 2,196,00
Jul 4, 2000	Crunch	$ 80.00
Jul 5, 2000	American Express Gift Cheques	$ 325.00
Jul 5, 2000	New York Magazine Subscripton	$ 30.00
Jul 6, 2000	Manhattan News	$ 25.00
Jul 6, 2000	Manhattan Transit Authority	$ 60.00
Jul 6, 2000	D'Agostino Grocery	$ 337.00
Jul 10, 2000	Virgin Records	$ 25.00
Jul 29, 2000	Red Salon	$ 318.00
Jul 29, 2000	Lucy Barnes Clothing	$ 140.00
Aug 5, 2000	Bloomingdale's – Gucci Sunglasses	$ 260.00
Aug 5, 2000	Bloomingdale's – Rebecca Taylor	$ 151.00
Aug 5, 2000	Barneys – Fresh Cosmetics	$ 30.00
Aug 5, 2000	China Grill	$ 140.00
	PAYMENTS	– $ 1,500.00
	Total	**$ 2,617.00**

JENNIFER CONVERTIBLES

Karyn Bosnak
400 E. 57th St.
New York, NY 10010

Date	Payee	Amount
	PREVIOUS BALANCE	$ 1,774.00
	Total	**$ 1,774.00**

Grand Debt Tally $4,391.00

The next week at work was great. I booked some great cases and made my boss proud. I've always gotten along very well with my bosses. It's very important to me not to let them down. I have a very good work ethic and always have since I was younger. I started working when I was fifteen years old at a local family-owned drugstore/gift shop. My mom would never let me call in sick or show up late. And those habits stuck with me as I got older and moved on to more jobs. In my four years at *Jenny Jones*, I never called in sick once.

Brad called and we went to a movie. He then went away for the weekend again, and then called me again the next Monday. It was very difficult to form a relationship with someone who kept jetting off to the Hamptons every weekend. But I suppose I only did just meet him and there was no sense in rushing it.

My furniture also finally arrived. And of course, the only day they could deliver it was a day that I had two cases taping in the studio. So I couldn't be home to meet the movers, or more importantly, to tip them so they would be gentle with my furniture. I planned on sending the tip in an envelope though the next day, as soon as I got home and made sure my furniture was all okay. It wasn't their fault that their moving company sucked.

However, since the movers didn't know that I planned on sending the tip, they decided to stack all my furniture sideways in my apartment. It was a huge disheveled mess when I got home. And I stayed up half the night trying to arrange it just so I could sleep. I didn't send the tip.

At the end of the week, my next paycheck arrived and I went to the bank to deposit it. Just like I had planned, I sent the whole thing to American Express again. While this made me catch up and kept me current, I didn't have any spending money left over for things like transportation to work, phone bills, cell phone bills and food. So I charged everything until my next paycheck. I charged my Metrocard for the bus. I charged my groceries. I charged the cute top that I got to go to the movie with Brad. And I got some more Amex Gift Cheques and cashed them for those places that didn't accept American Express.

I kept running every night and felt good. I lost five pounds. Basically my life was working, working out, and occasionally going out with Brad. On a weekday, when he wasn't in the Hamptons, of course. Before I knew it, it was July.

Brad of course went to the Hamptons for the Fourth. So did the Swingers. I hadn't really met anyone else yet in the city, so I didn't have big plans for the holiday, which happened to fall on a Tuesday. We had the day off work, but had to be back at work on the fifth.

I hate when holidays fall in the middle of the week. And I hate it more when employers give you the holiday off, but not the day after, especially a holiday like the Fourth of July, because everything happens at night on the Fourth of July. So I'd rather work on the fourth in the daytime and have the fifth off to recuperate.

So on the Fourth, I set out for my daily jog, having decided to go when it was light out instead. I headed in my usual direction, toward the Upper East Side. Two blocks away, I noticed a gym, Crunch. I didn't have any intentions of joining, but I went inside to check it out. I walked in the door and headed down a long spiral staircase to where the gym was. I walked up to the front desk and asked the very fit chick behind the counter if I could have a tour. She picked up the phone and called someone. A few seconds later, a short buff guy came over to me.

'You Karyn?' he asked.

'Yes, I am,' I replied.

'Hi, I'm Robert. I'll give you a tour.'

Robert and I walked all over the gym and he showed me

all it had to offer. Holy shikeys, this gym was huge! They had a big climbing wall that looked like a mountain. They had a boxing ring. Not that I'd use either of those things, but they were cool.

They also had all sorts of cool aerobic classes. One of them was called Ab, Thighs & Gossip, where your teacher was a drag queen who read all the latest Hollywood gossip to you from the weekly tabloids. Another was called Broadway Dance Series, where people from actual Broadway plays would teach an aerobics class based on the dance moves in the play.

I'm not an athletic person. I never have been. I'm not one of those people who gets off on going to the gym. I'm extremely uncoordinated. But this sounded so cool! For sure if I belonged here I'd go to these classes! I'd be so fit.

'How much is it?' I asked.

'Well, today is your lucky day. Since it's a holiday, we waive the membership initiation fee of $250, so it's free to join. Then there is a monthly membership charge of $80.'

Free! It's my lucky day! I wasn't really financially in the position to join, but if I didn't join today, I'd have to pay $250 when I did. That's like four months of membership dues. So, I looked at it this way: I could join today for free and start paying $80 a month. Or (in order to break even on the same deal) I could wait until November to join, and then pay the $250 and $80 a month. Either way I'd come out the same.

November was a long way away, and October can be cold. And if it was, was I still going to want to run outside? Probably not. And if I am in a serious workout mode by then, do I want to jeopardize it, when in the end I'm going to come out the same financially anyway? Heavens no!

So I opted to join Crunch today! I sat down with Robert, gave him my Amex for my first month's dues, and told him to charge it monthly for the dues thereafter. While he filled out all the paperwork, I looked up at the wall and read the Crunch Philosophy that was painted there.

We at CRUNCH warmly welcome people from all walks of life regardless of shape, size, sex or ability.

People *don't have to feel flawless* to feel at home at CRUNCH. We don't care if you're 18 or 80 . . . fat or thin . . . short or tall . . . muscular or mushy . . . blond or bald . . . or anywhere in between.

CRUNCH is *not competitive*, it is *non-judgmental*, it is not elitist, it *does not represent a kind of person.*

CRUNCH is a *gym; a movement which is growing* as we continue to perfect our ability to create an environment where our members don't feel self-conscious, and *don't worry about what others think.*

At the heart of the CRUNCH core, stands a tremendously *experienced and energetic staff* dedicated to creating an environment where *everyone feels accepted* . . .

A truly unique place.

That was nice. That's the kind of gym that I wanted to belong to. I briefly wondered if I *would* be working out with eighty-year-olds. Probably not. But if so, I wondered what machines they used the most. Probably the treadmills. Anywho, I was now a member of Crunch gym – A truly unique place.

UNAVAILABLE FUNDS VS INSUFFICIENT FUNDS

The next day I got paid and mailed my rent check for July. It was a few days late, but I didn't think it would be that big of a deal. And because I was super cash-poor, I had to get some more American Express Gift Cheques to have some spending money, as well as charge my bus card and groceries again. Everyone took American Express. Even Starbucks, which was good because I don't like making my coffee at home.

I lived right across the street from a grocery store called D'Agostino. It was really nice and carried organic produce. My favorite thing to eat was the lettuce in a bag with organic chicken breasts. Monica on *Friends* had a canvas D'Agostino bag that she used to carry her groceries home in, and I bought myself one too. It is important to conserve.

During the next two weeks, things got more serious at work. The show went into production full swing, and one producer quit, which put a bit more pressure on the rest of us to pick up the slack. Brad called twice to go out, but I had to cancel because of work. He hadn't called or e-mailed since, and I couldn't help but feel neglected.

Before I knew it, it was payday again. Once more I had to send the whole thing to American Express, so I went to my bank's ATM to make a deposit. At the end of the transaction, I looked to see what my balance was. The screen said $3,600. Huh? How could that be? Did my rent check not clear yet? I mailed it over two weeks ago, so I wasn't sure how it couldn't have. I decided to look into it further.

I pushed the button at the bottom of the screen that said 'Account History.' A few seconds later, a list of recent transactions appeared. I looked through the list and saw that the check to the phone company had cleared, as had the one to American Express. But there was no sign of my rent check. I then noticed a charge for $30 for something called a Non-Available Funds fee. I had no idea what that was.

I pushed the button at the bottom of the screen that said 'More History' and was taken to another screen with more transactions. It was then that I saw it – check 115 for $1,800 returned! Oh my gosh! That was my rent check! They returned my rent check! How could this be though? I *had* money in my account! I pushed the Exit button as fast as I could, took my receipt and made my way up to the teller. I had to find out how this happened.

I waited in line for what seemed like forever until it was my turn to talk to a teller. When I was up, I headed toward the very last teller window, where the small light was blinking, signaling she was available.

'Hi,' said the young woman behind the desk. She was the enemy.

'Hello,' I said, trying to remain calm while handing her my deposit receipt. 'I was just depositing my paycheck into my checking account and noticed that you *wrongly* sent my rent check back last week. I had money in my account, which I deposited the week before. I want to know what happened.' I was near tears. I couldn't believe they sent my rent check back.

'Let me take a look,' she said while typing a bunch of numbers into her computer. 'Hmmm . . . It looks like it was sent back because you had non-available funds.'

'What do you mean non-available funds? I had the money in there!'

'Yes, you had it in there, but it wasn't available yet.'

'What does that mean?' I asked.

'Well, I'm assuming the check you deposited was an out-of-state check since it looks like it took so long to clear. When you deposit out-of-state checks, it takes five days for them to clear. They don't clear automatically. It's during that time that your funds are non-available. So any checks that come through against those funds, bounce.'

'Five days? That's crazy. It's a paycheck. Of course it's going to clear. In Chicago, all the funds from my paychecks were available the next day.'

'This isn't Chicago,' she said, 'and all this was probably explained to you when you opened your account.'

'I don't think it was,' I snapped back, trying to remember if it was. No, I don't think that it was.

'Well, now you know. You can take out $100 one day after, and $300 two days after you deposit an out-of-state check,' she said.

'Thanks. That was my rent check you sent back. What am I supposed to do now?' I asked.

'I don't know, call your landlord?' she said rudely.

'Gee, thanks,' I said, walking away.

I couldn't believe it. I couldn't believe that I bounced my first rent check. I know I was mad at the bank, but it was ultimately my fault, I guess. It was an honest mistake though. I'm sure my landlord would understand. Ugh. I'd have to call them to tell them what I did.

Later that afternoon I made the dreaded phone call to my landlord. I was so embarrassed. I explained the whole story to the accounts payable woman. She told me not to worry, but said that I needed to send a cashier's check for the $1,825 – my rent plus a $25 fee – to be current. So, on my way home from work that night, I went back to the bank, but this time to a different teller, to get my cashier's check.

BUDGET CUTTING

The next week I was sitting at my desk working. Gwen, who was sitting next to me, was going through a nasty divorce and had just hung up on her soon-to-be ex-husband. I tried not to listen but with short cubes, you couldn't keep many things private. I had e-mailed Brad earlier in the day and was waiting to see if he e-mailed me back.

A few hours later, a return e-mail still hadn't come. Disappointed, I went to the bathroom and looked at myself in the mirror. In my best Stuart Smalley impression I said, 'I'm good enough. I'm smart enough. And doggone it, people like me.' Naw, I didn't say that. But I did look in the mirror and catch a glimpse of my roots.

Now, I'm a blonde, but I'm not a *real* blonde. I'm also not one of those 'I bought a bottle of blonde at the drugstore and now I'm a kind of orange-blonde.' I'm a 'I've had my hair colored and highlighted for so long that I don't know what the real color is anymore' blonde. It looks great. It looks natural. I've actually had it highlighted since I was in grade school. As a matter of fact, I was the first girl in my grade school with highlights. And Guess jeans for that matter. They were the two-toned kind.

But back to my roots. They were horrible. I needed to get them done immediately. But finding a good colorist in a new city is not as easy as it sounds. You just can't waltz into a place and ask for highlights. You have to seek out the good people. Back in Chicago, Naomi and I were experts at this. We had been to every salon in the city. We'd find someone who we liked and go to them for a while. Then they'd get really comfortable with us, and would start making little screwups, like not making it look as natural or something. And the next month we'd be off to find someone else. We were hair whores.

I had just read an article all about the best colorists in New York, but I couldn't remember what magazine it was in. Was it *Glamour*? Was it *Allure*? I just couldn't recall. It could be any one of a hundred. I'm sort of addicted to beauty magazines. I read all of them every month. They're good for me. I am really on top of my game the first few days after I read them. I eat better, I pay more attention to penciling in my eyebrows, I deep condition my hair – they make me want to be a better person.

There is nothing that I love more than going into a bookstore or a magazine shop and seeing the brand-new cover of a magazine that I haven't yet read. I get so excited! I grab it off the shelf, and buy it up as quickly as I can. It's one of my favorite pastimes. Some people play soccer. Some people play chess. Me? I read beauty magazines.

My new apartment had a twenty-four-hour magazine shop right across the street, and they had *every* magazine there –

even the foreign ones with the big, thick glossy covers. So if I was ever bored, or couldn't sleep or something, I would go to the magazine shop and buy a bunch of magazines. They accepted American Express.

After visiting all the magazine websites that I had bookmarked on my computer, I finally remembered that it was *Allure*. Yes! That was it! *Allure*. They actually had a guide to the best colorists in the city right on their website. Let's see . . . they listed Oscar Blandi, Garren New York, Pierre Michel, and Louis Licari. Yes, these all sounded familiar. They were the same people mentioned in the article. I started at the top of the list and started calling to see if I could get an appointment for that Saturday. It was an emergency!

'Louis Licari,' a woman said.

'Hi! I'd like to make an appointment for a single process, a full head of highlights and a haircut for this Saturday,' I said. Since my hair is brown (I think), colorists have to single process the roots to bump it up a notch to a lighter brown so it's not so dark. Then they give me blond highlights on top of that. Doing this makes it look less 'skunky.'

'Yes, no problem. Do you have anyone particular that you'd like the color or cut with?' she asked.

'No, not really. I'm new to the city,' I said.

'Okay, I have Michelle open at 10.00 A.M. for the color, and David open at noon for the cut. Does that sound good?' she asked.

'Yes, that sounds great,' I said. 'Thank you so much. Oh, by the way, what do your prices start at?'

I don't know what possessed me to ask this question. But this was New York, so I thought I'd better ask.

'Your single process will begin at $100, the highlights will begin at $200, and your cut will begin around $125.'

Huh? I always got my hair done at the nicest salons in Chicago and it never cost me $400. After tip it would be like $480! That's almost $500! I usually paid about $200 tops. I didn't know what to do. I didn't want to cancel right then for fear of sounding cheap.

'Uh . . . okay. See you Saturday,' I said, hanging up.

I quickly started to call the other salons to see what their prices started at. One after another they all told me the same prices. How could that be? There are millions of fake blondes in New York, and they can't all pay $400 a month to get their hair colored. What was I going to do?

I looked down and noticed a *New York* magazine sitting next to me. If you live in New York, then a subscription to *New York* magazine is a must. It's a weekly guide to what's going on in the city. It highlights the best *Zagat*-rated restaurants, the hottest clubs, has pictures of various socialites and celebs at the latest charity events and parties. I started flipping through it. Surely they must have a beauty guide. All of a sudden a headline grabbed my attention.

Sales & Bargains: Style Setters
This week's highlights: A fab haircut doesn't require a second mortgage or months on a waiting list: These stylists are pros at budget cutting.

Holy smokes! What timing! This is exactly what I needed! The article started out . . .

Manhattan is so taken by the cult of the hairdresser that it sometimes seems there's nobody between Garren or Fekkai (at $350 a trim) and your local barber . . .

It was like God was speaking to me. He knew I had to get my hair done and didn't know where to go! It was a sign. I kept reading the article as it went on to list five places that offered bargain haircuts. One by one I called them all, and one by one they told me they were booked. I had one left to call. It was a place called Red Salon.

Tired of minimalism? Red Salon is done up nineteenth-century-boudoir-style, with deep-red curtains and chandeliers. The atmosphere is low-key in a downtown way, drawing everyone from Lou Reed and the Cardigans to Vogue *and* Allure *editors. You'll pay $70 to $100, depending on the cut, not the stylist (so it's great for a trim). Highlights are $135 to $175.*

Only in New York would $70 for a haircut be considered a bargain. But I didn't have time to look any further. Red Salon was my last chance. I picked up the phone and asked if they had any openings for Saturday. And they did! I was in! My appointment was at 11.00 A.M. with a guy named Vlad.

Phew! That was a close call! With a smile on my face, I picked up the phone to cancel my appointment with Louis Licari.

'Louis Licari,' a voice answered.

Crap! It was the same woman who took my appointment. I was hoping I'd get someone different.

'Yes, I need to cancel an appointment for Saturday. It looks like I have to go out of town last minute,' I said, lying.

'Okay, miss. What's your name?' she asked.

'Karyn Bosnak, I just made the appointment. I just found out that I have to go out of town for work and won't be able to make it.'

'Oh, okay. Did you want to reschedule?' she asked.

'Oh, no. I'll call you when I get back.'

'Okay. You are all canceled then,' she said.

'Thank you,' I said hanging up the phone.

I figured the new place would be at least $100 cheaper. And that was good enough for me.

SHAMPORGASM

Before I knew it, Saturday came and I headed for the subway to go to my hair appointment. Brad hadn't returned my e-mail from earlier in the week, but I wasn't going to let it get me down. I looked on my map and saw that Red Salon was located on West 11th Street in the West Village. I had been to the West Village once before I moved here. It was so pretty and felt very European. It was the reason I wanted to move here. So I found the closest subway and headed downtown.

I wasn't a big fan of the subway, and had only been on it a few times. I usually used the bus or cabs to get around town. The subway was just so hot and stinky! And my hair was always flat and my makeup was always runny after I took it. Yuck! But today it didn't matter so much because I was going to get my hair done. So off to the subway I went.

I found the correct train and sat down in my seat. As the train started moving, I noticed a little boy sitting to the left of me. I smiled at him and he blushed. I laughed and looked away. I then looked back at him and crossed my eyes. He blushed again and gave me a big smile this time. A few seconds later I stuck out my tongue at him and made little devil ears with my fingers. I was going for a laugh here. But instead his smile disappeared and he started screaming. Oops! It wasn't *that* scary. His scream quickly turned into tears and I looked away and pretended that I had nothing to do with it. Out of the corner of my eye, I saw his mother shoot a nasty look in my direction, but I pretended not to notice. I decided that it was best not to mess with people on the train. The *'clientele'* down there was a bit more rough than it was on the crosstown 57th Street bus.

With that I started to zone out like I always do when I travel. Whether traveling by cab, bus or train, I space out. I don't know how long I was zoned out, but all of a sudden over the loudspeaker I heard something like, 'Mex Top Brookland.'

Huh? Then I heard it again, a bit more clearly, 'Next stop Brooklyn.'

Oh my gosh! I stood up really quickly and jumped out the closing door. I looked at the signs in the station. They said

Brooklyn Bridge. I didn't know if that meant I was on the Manhattan side of the Brooklyn Bridge, in the middle of the Brooklyn Bridge, or all the way in Brooklyn itself. I headed toward a map on the wall.

I didn't know anything about Brooklyn, except that it's on the other side of the river and it's a whole other world over there. I saw it in the movies, and it was always kind of scary. And I worked with a guy who lived in Brooklyn and he was scary too.

After figuring out where I was on the map, I was relieved to see that I was not in Brooklyn, but one more stop and I would have been. I totally missed my stop. I looked down at my watch and realized that I had two minutes to get to my appointment before I was late. Crap. With that I went upstairs and flagged down a cab. I hopped in and gave the driver the address of the salon.

A few minutes later, the cab pulled up to the salon, and I paid him and jumped out. The salon was on the bottom floor of a brownstone on a beautiful tree-lined residential street. It wasn't big at all. It was very quaint. I walked in the front door and gave my name to the guy at the front desk. He told me to have a seat.

While he summoned my hairstylist, I looked around and felt very comfortable. It was a very peaceful place. The walls were painted red, and it was dark and cozy.

A few minutes later, my stylist came out and introduced himself. He was of medium build and had brown hair and brown eyes. He was good-looking. And I think he may have been straight.

'Hi, Karyn. My name is Vlad,' he said.

'Hi,' I said, 'sorry I'm late.'

'No problem,' he said.

I followed Vlad to the back of the salon to his chair. He looked at my hair and convinced me to skip the single process and just get highlights and lowlights instead. It would make it look more natural and would go 'better with my skin tone,' he said. I trusted him, and went along with the plan.

For the next hour, Vlad put foils in my hair. He really took his time and I kind of liked it. It was relaxing. Red Salon wasn't one of those big salons with bright lights and a million people. Everyone's station was kind of hidden, and very private. Vlad and I had a very nice conversation. He told me all about his girlfriend (I was right!), and I told him all about Chicago, and why I moved to New York and he understood it. Usually when I told people that I moved to New York to be alone, they were always like, 'Huh?' But Vlad understood what I meant. I love hairdressers. They are always so nice.

When he was done foiling, he sent me to sit under a dryer in the back. I fell asleep. I'm not sure how long I was under there, all I know is that I was awoken by another guy who was really, really cute. He led me to the shampoo chair in a back room. The lights were dark and there were candles burning on the wall. It was very soothing. Now what I'm about to tell you might have never happened. I might have still been sleeping under the dryer and dreamt the whole thing. But something's telling me I wasn't.

It started out very innocently. I sat down in the chair and leaned my head back against the bowl. The shampoo guy – I didn't get his name – started to remove the foils, and rinse out the color. He then put some shampoo in his hand and started rubbing. And rubbing . . . He was massaging my head, and soon moved to my temples. And then moved to my neck. And ooh . . . I was in pure ecstasy. My spine started tingling, and soon my whole body was too. This is why they charge so much at these New York salons! I was so turned on from this shampoo guy! Did he like me? Or did he do this to all the shampoo-ees. I didn't even remember what he looked like, but I was ready to give him my flower. Oh wait, I gave my flower away a long time ago. Let me rephrase that – I was ready to give him my virtuous body. Yes, my virtuous body!

If anyone had so much as touched the tops of my thighs,

I would have been sent over the edge. One wrong slip of a knee would have sent me into orgasm heaven. Boy, did I enjoy that shampoo! Almost fifteen minutes later, he tapped me on my shoulder to signal that he was done. I didn't even realize that he had rinsed and conditioned my hair. I opened my eyes and stared at him in a daze from my spot in the shampoo chair. I didn't want to get up. I wanted a cigarette and I don't smoke. That shampoo was one of the best things that has ever happened to me in my whole life. It was by far much better than some sex I've had.

Reluctantly I got up and walked back to Vlad's chair in a daze. My eyes were half open. I had that come-hither look going on.

'Are you okay?' he asked.

'Fine,' I said, smiling, 'just fine.'

With that, Vlad started cutting my hair. He cut the back with a razor, to make it look all jagged and funky. It was so cool! It was very Meg Ryan. It was cooler than any cut I had ever had. And the color was even better. He really was right, it did go better with my skintone.

When it was all said and done, I went to the front to pay. The total was $295 before tax and tip. I figured I needed to tip Vlad at least 20 percent, and I *had* to give that shampoo guy at least $10 – but he was worth so much more. I bet he gets a lot of dates doing what he does. I was tempted to ask him out, except that I'm too shy, and he probably wasn't on my team anyway. So the total ended up being $387. I was only allowed to charge the total and tax though, not the tip. I had a feeling this was the case, and was prepared. So I gave them my Amex card and forked over $70 cash for the rest. It was a lot, but it was so worth it. Getting your hair done in New York is just expensive, I guess.

I left the salon and wandered around the West Village for a while with my new haircut. I had my new sandals on too. And I still had that come-hither look in my eye. As I walked down the street, I noticed that a few people stared at me. Yep, my haircut's hot! I know it. I strutted down the street like I owned it. Until I tripped on a rock. Then I slowed down.

After buying a cute red silk top in a store off Bleecker, I noticed a bunch of people gathering around a store, or was it? A bakery? Yes, it was a bakery. The sign outside said Magnolia Bakery, and the line was out the door. It smelled so amazing! I think I read about that place in my *New York* magazine. Maybe I hadn't and just used that as an excuse to get a treat. But I hadn't eaten since before I got my hair done, and that was hours ago. And I worked up quite an appetite after that shampoo. I was hungry and decided to wait in line and buy myself a treat.

I waited in line for almost fifteen minutes. I noticed that everyone was buying a cupcake, so that must be the thing to get. It was self-serve and I got to pick out my own. I opted for a yellow cupcake with pink frosting and white sprinkles. I like pink.

I walked outside and sat down on a bench and bit into my cupcake. Holy smokes! It was dreamy. This cupcake was not like your normal bakery cupcake. This cupcake tasted better than even your grandma's cupcakes. It was dee-lish!

I sat outside with my new cool hair color, and my new cool haircut, while wearing my new cool sandals and ate the best cupcake of my life. The breeze was perfect. I smiled. Today was heaven.

THE FIVE B'S: BLOOMINGDALE'S, BERGDORF, BENDEL, BARNEYS & ME

By the time Monday came, I went to work and felt great with my new haircut and color. Everyone commented on how great it looked and I felt like the $387 was so worth it. As I sat down at my desk to get started on my day, the phone rang.

'*Curtis Court?*' I answered.

'Is Karyn there?' said a cute-sounding guy's voice.

'This is Karyn,' I said.

'Karyn, my name is Sam. I am a personal trainer at Crunch and I see that you just joined.'

'I *did* just join, Sam!' I said, flirting back.

'Well, did you know that you get one free personal training session when you join Crunch?' he asked.

'No, I didn't know that,' I said.

'What's your fitness goal, Karyn?' Sam asked.

'To burn fat,' I said.

'And what are you doing to burn fat? Don't tell me running on the treadmill.'

'I *am* running on the treadmill.' I hope Sam didn't look at my chart and see that I hadn't been there in over a week.

'You need to build muscle to burn fat more efficiently, Karyn,' he said. 'I can show you how to do that.'

'Really?' I asked.

'Yes, do you want to come in for your complimentary training session?' Sam asked.

'Yes,' I replied, 'when do you want to do it with me?' I asked. I then blushed because I just asked him when he wanted to do it with me. 'I mean – well, you know what I mean,' I continued. Sam laughed.

'How about next Wednesday around 8.00 P.M. sometime,' he said.

'8.00 P.M. on Wednesday sounds great,' I said. 'Should I ask for you?'

'Yep, just check in like always, go to the locker room, then check in at the personal training desk and ask for me.'

A personal trainer! I was so excited! And he sounded so cute! All of my workout clothes were such a mess. I would need something nice to wear. I had to look cute. And besides, new workout clothes would motivate me to get back on the fitness wagon.

That Saturday I decided to venture out in search of workout gear. I walked outside and took a left on 57th Street. My plan was to go to Niketown. I passed it frequently on the way to work, and holy Jordans it was *huge*!

A few blocks later, as I approached Lexington Avenue, I looked to the right and noticed an enormous building a few blocks down. It took up the whole block and had to be at least eight stories high. At the front of the building, a bunch of national flags were billowing in the breeze. I wondered what it was. Was it an embassy? I knew I lived by the UN, but I thought that it was in the opposite direction of this.

I decided to check it out because I wasn't in that much of a hurry to get to Niketown. As I approached the building, I started to read the large letters above the entry doors that spelled out the name of the building. What was it spelling? B-L-O . . . I was over a block away and couldn't tell. As I got closer I started to make out some more letters. B-L-O-O-M . . . Could it be what I thought it was? My heart started to flutter. B-L-O-O-M-I-N-G . . . Yes, yes it was! That big building with the flags wasn't an embassy at all! That big building was Bloomingdale's!

Holy sweet Jesus I found home! I had never seen such a large department store in all of my twenty-seven years on this earth! We had a Bloomingdale's in Chicago, but it wasn't *that* big. This one took up the whole block! And with all the flags it looked so regal! I picked up my pace to get there more quickly. I couldn't wait to get inside. As I approached the corner and the entry, I was startled by a car horn.

A disgruntled cab driver gave me the finger and yelled at me as he almost ran me over. I looked up and realized that I didn't have a Walk sign and was almost in the middle of the street.

'Ooh, sorry,' I said, pointing at the store, smiling, 'Bloomingdale's.' The cab driver just looked at me and shook his head.

I love shopping and have since I was a little girl. When my sister and I were little, we were two little homely kids. I was kind of greasy, and she had crazy curly hair that stuck up everywhere. We didn't have many friends. But when I was eight years old, my mom bought me a yellow satin roller-skating jacket that said 'Hot Rollers' on it, and all of a sudden all of the kids in school liked me. It was a hot jacket – let me tell you. You could say I learned the power of clothes at an early age.

Things only got worse as I got older.

When my mom married my stepdad, we started spending the weekends on his boat on Lake Michigan. (He was a big boater.) My sister and I were still a bit grubby, and now all of a sudden we had to start hanging around the rich kids – the kids of my parents' boating friends. And I'll be honest – my Hot Rollers jacket didn't fly too well with those kids at the lake. They all had on Polo and stuff, and didn't want to be our friends and that hurt our feelings. We would cry sometimes. So my mom, doing what any mom would do, bought us Polo, too, so we'd fit in with the other kids. And it worked. As soon as we showed up with the little horsies on our shirts, they liked us.

The 'power of a Hot Rollers jacket' turned into the 'Power of a Polo.' And as I got older, that Polo shirt turned into Guess jeans, Vuarnet sunglasses, and eventually: the Gucci purse.

My love of purses began in high school. I went to a private all-girls Catholic high school, and we had to wear a uniform, which consisted of your typical plaid skirt and polyester blazer. With that, we had to wear solid color socks and a solid color top with a collar. Not very creative. So the way the girls expressed themselves was with their purses. Your purse became like an ID tag. It became your shield. It became who you were. And I didn't want to be the girl with the Liz Claiborne clutch. Because at my high school, the Liz Claiborne clutch didn't cut it. It was private, and a lot of the girls that went there came from wealthy families. At my high school, you needed to have a Gucci, a Louis Vuitton, or a Fendi. By the time I hit high school, the 'Power of a Polo' turned into the 'Power of a Purse.' As I got older, I never let go of my love of designer goods.

Anywho, back to Bloomingdale's. I backed up and got back on the curb and waited for the little walking man to turn from orange to white, signaling it was okay for me to cross the street. I waited and waited for what seemed like an eternity. Just one little street stood between the largest Bloomingdale's I had ever seen in my life and me. I watched all the people go in and out of the store while I waited on the curb. And waited. A few minutes later, the green light turned yellow, and then red. The cars stopped. And finally, the little walking man turned white, as if to say, 'Come, my child. Come follow me into the promised land.' That little white walking man held the keys to heaven, I mean Bloomingdale's. And *he* decided when you were allowed to come in. He was the gatekeeper. I looked up at him and bowed. He knew how important it was to work this corner.

I put one foot in front of the other and stepped off the curb. I walked across the street in what seemed like slow motion. A few moments later, I had arrived. I looked at the series of doors. They were big and heavy. I picked one and pulled it open. I was inside. I looked around at all the people and took a deep breath. I was in the purse section. How perfect!

I started to walk around. My mind was moving so fast that I barely comprehended what I was looking at. They had Louis Vuitton and Fendi, and Versace and D&G. The purses were endless!

I made my way to the other side of the store and came across the sunglasses counter. I love sunglasses! Purses and sunglasses! How perfect. I tried on a pair of killer Gucci shades. They were burgundy and too big for my face. But that was the way they were supposed to look. Paired together with my new hair, they looked amazing. *I* looked amazing. I *had* to have these sunglasses. As I handed over my Amex card, I justified the purchase to myself. I hadn't bought a new pair of sunglasses in quite some time. In fact, almost two seasons. So one pair of sunglasses at $240 was just like getting two pairs at $120 each season. And that wasn't too bad.

Sunglasses in hand, I made my way to the next floor. I looked out onto row after row of brightly lit counters and mirrors. This must be the makeup floor. How perfect! I love makeup! I love purses and sunglasses and makeup! They had every brand name you could think of. Prescriptives, MAC, Bobby Brown, Trish McEvoy – you name it. I was like a kid in a candy store! The counters were endless. I think they went on forever! In the distance I saw an escalator heading up and decided to see where it went. I was on a mission. I wasn't leaving this store until I had examined every square inch of it.

The second floor was the home of women's clothing. It was so big and there were so many clothes. Now I'm no sports expert, but I'm guessing that it was the size of several football fields. I immediately pulled out my cell phone and called my friend Naomi in Chicago.

'Hello?' she answered.

'You are never going to believe where I am and it's the most *amazing* place I've ever been to,' I said.

'Where?' she asked anxiously.

'Bloomingdale's. I have just discovered Bloomingdale's in New York. And it's the biggest place I have ever been in my whole life. You have *no idea* how big it is. I wish I had a camera so I could take a picture and send it to you. It's that big.'

'Really, tell me more!' she said, excited.

'Okay, I am approaching a section called Elements. They have the cutest clothes in the whole world in this section. It's very girly stuff and very nice. And ooh, it's expensive,' I said, picking up a price tag. 'Have you ever heard of Rebecca Taylor?'

'No,' Naomi answered, 'who is she?'

'I have no idea, but she designs some cute clothes! Here's a lovely pink silk sleeveless top that's $140. And this section is only one section out of like a hundred! And I'm only on the second floor. I haven't even been to the others. I've never seen anything like this ever. The Chicago Bloomingdale's has nothing on this place.'

'No way. Oh, I have to come!' she said. 'I think at the beginning of next month some people are going to New York for business. I bet you that I can tell my boss that I have some really important business to do there too and that they'd let me go.'

'Oh my gosh, you have to come! You'd never believe it.'

'Tell me more,' she said.

With the Rebecca Taylor top in hand, I proceeded to walk Naomi through most of the floor before hanging up. Yes, this is what excited girls do when they find cute clothes. At least that's what my friends and I do anyway. Whether we are in the smallest boutique or the biggest department store, we call each other when we find great stuff. I discovered that the whole back half of the second floor was the shoe section. They had lots of shoes.

Three hours later, after buying that top, and exploring more women's clothing on the third and fourth floors, and furniture on the fifth floor, and housewares on the sixth floor, and bath and bedding on the seventh floor, and children's clothing on the eighth floor, I took the elevator all the way back down to one. I was exhausted. I was speechless. As much as I didn't need the Rebecca Taylor top, I decided to look at it like it was part of an investment in a new wardrobe. Yep. Slowly, I was going to phase out all of my baggy, cute Midwestern clothes, and replace them with chicer, tighter, New Yorkey things.

As I left Bloomingdale's, I turned to get one last look. Wow! It was so big! And it was just three blocks from where I lived. I decided to skip Niketown for the day and headed down 60th Street toward Central Park to see what I could find to eat. I was light-headed and realized that it was probably because I hadn't eaten anything. The sun was shining and it was a beautiful day! I pulled out my new sunglasses and put them on. When I got to Madison Avenue, I noticed that Barneys was to the right. Oh no! Not another one! This city is like one big shopping mall. Everywhere I turned there were stores. I bought a hot dog from a street vendor and sat on the sidewalk and ate it. It was good. When I was finished, I decided to just browse through Barneys to see what they had.

Now, I may be a Bloomingdale's girl when it comes to clothing, but I have always been a Barneys girl when it comes to makeup and perfume. Bloomingdale's has a bigger clothing selection and it's a bit more affordable than Barneys. They also have some good necklaces and stuff for under $100. It's more 'user-friendly,' as I like to say. But I hate the perfume that they carry. All department store perfumes are too 'perfumey' for me. They all smell too much alike and smell too much like alcohol. And most department stores don't carry any really cool new makeup lines, just the standard Prescriptives and MAC and stuff.

But places like Barneys carry the *best* perfumes and makeup. So does Henri Bendel. Chicago used to have a Henri Bendel, and Naomi and I would go every weekend and spend hours in the makeup department. We'd try on lip gloss and sparkles, and have our eyes done. It was so fun! But then one Christmas it closed down. We were *so* sad. It was truly the end of an era. That's when we discovered the Chicago Barneys. And I ended up moving right across the street from it, and lived there until I moved to New York.

Anywho, I crossed the street and went inside. It was just as I suspected! Bigger and better than its Chicago counterpart! The whole first floor was filled with makeup and purses. Near the back I found some nice body lotion called Lychee from a company called Fresh. It smelled so glorious! And it was in a glass bottle. How classy! It was $28, but so worth it! I wouldn't have to wear perfume with it. And what man wouldn't want me while wearing this lotion? I smelled like candy! I wanted to eat my arm off!

About an hour later, I emerged from Barneys with only my lotion in hand. I was so proud of myself for not buying anything else. I was so exhausted that I decided to head home. I went down Fifth Avenue toward 57th Street so I could walk along the park. A few blocks down I passed the Plaza Hotel. It had big flags billowing from it as well, just like Bloomingdale's. New York was so fancy! And I was too in my new sunglasses.

I passed Bergdorf Goodman, but did not go in. I'd have to save that one for a special day. I was just too tired. While waiting on the corner, I noticed that Henri Bendel was just one block down Fifth Avenue as well. Bloomingdale's, Barneys, Bergdorf, Bendel – the four Bs of New York. And I couldn't help but think I belonged here, seeing that my last name was Bosnak. I was the fifth B.

That night I went home and met Ann Marie and another coworker named Jodi out for dinner at a place called China Grill. Jodi was the senior producer at *Curtis Court* and she was so nice! I wore my new Rebecca Taylor top. This is what life is like in New York, I thought. Good people, good clothes, good food, and good times. I needed some money, so I charged the whole dinner and both Ann Marie and Jodi paid me cash.

That night when I got home, I pulled out my *Zagat* guide, circled China Grill, and wrote, 'Some coworkers, Rebecca Taylor, and me – the Fifth B.'

FOUR

AMERICAN EXPRESS

American Express

Karyn Bosnak
400 E. 57th St.
New York, NY 10010

Date	Payee	Amount
	PREVIOUS BALANCE	$ 2,617,00
Aug 6, 2000	Bloomingdale's – Active Wear	$ 324.00
Aug 7, 2000	Niketown	$ 378.00
Aug 8, 2000	Bloomingdale's – Active Wear	– $ 324.00
Aug 9, 2000	Crunch	$ 900.00
Aug 10, 2000	Manhattan Transit Authority	$ 60.00
Aug 12, 2000	D'Agostino Grocery	$ 300.00
Aug 12, 2000	Virgin Records	$ 58.00
Aug 12, 2000	Banana Republic	$ 205.00
Aug 12, 2000	Flying A	$ 65.00
Aug 13, 2000	Bloomingdale's – Burberry Coats	$ 702.00
Aug 13, 2000	Bloomingdale's – BCBG	$ 151.00
Aug 13, 2000	Bloomingdale's – Burberry Coats	– $ 702.00
Aug 13, 2000	Bloomingdale's – BCBG	– $ 75.00
Aug 13, 2000	Sushiya	$ 25.00
	PAYMENTS	– $ 1,451.00
	Total	**$ 3,233.00**

JENNIFER
CONVERTIBLES

Karyn Bosnak
400 E. 57th St.
New York, NY 10010

Date	Payee	Amount
	PREVIOUS BALANCE	$ 1,774.00
	Total	**$ 1,774.00**

Grand Debt Tally $5,007.00

THE WORKOUT CLOTHES

'So let me get this straight,' I said to the male litigant on the phone. 'Your ex-girlfriend is suing you because she thinks you caused a tumor that's on her head?'

'That's right. She says it happened when I dropped her on her head while dancing a few years ago. You could say she do-sied when she should have doed,' he said with a thick Minnesota accent. He was in his fifties.

'Well, like I said, we'd love to hear your case at *Curtis Court*. And your ex-girlfriend, the plaintiff, already agreed to come here, so it's up to you. Once again, if you lose we will pay her the monetary settlement that she's awarded, and if you win – well, you win. Also, she will sign papers saying that she won't appeal the verdict, so she can never take you back to court again for this matter.'

'Well, then I'm game too. That woman's a nut, I tell ya! Falls don't cause tumors. I was even really nice after it happened, and put a steak on her head and everything,' he said.

'A steak? Huh. Well, you can explain all of that to the judge when you get here,' I said.

'I will,' he said. 'I have to go to work now, so why don't you call me later and we can go over the details. I should be home around five.'

'Sounds good,' I said. 'I'll call you then. Bye.'

'Bye,' he said as he hung up the phone.

A steak on the head. I wondered if he really did that. I only thought people did that in cartoons. And in *Rocky*. I think someone did it in *Rocky* too.

As I leaned back in my chair and thought about steaks on heads, I caught a glimpse of my new Nike gym bag underneath my desk. I had my first big training session with Sam after work and was pumped up! Especially after all I went through buying workout gear.

That past Sunday I realized that I still hadn't bought the workout clothes that I set out to buy on Saturday, so I went back out in search of some goods. And I ended up right back at Bloomingdale's, but this time in the active wear department. I bought some shirts, pants and a sports bra, which came to about $300. It was more than I wanted to spend, but it was an investment in my health! Well, that and I wanted to fit in with the other girls at Crunch.

But on my way home from Bloomingdale's, I decided to check out Niketown just in case they had cooler stuff. And you know what? They did! I mean, sure I'd fit in just fine at Crunch with my Bloomingdale's clothes. But with my Nike clothes, the other girls would want to fit in with *me*. So I decided to buy my workout clothes there (and even got a pair of shoes to match) and took the other ones back to Bloomingdale's on my way home.

After daydreaming about myself walking through Crunch in my new clothes and my new shoes, I didn't feel like going back to work. So I decided to get some personal stuff done and make a few phone calls. The first thing I did was call the bank to find out if my rent check had cleared yet. I had deposited my paycheck the previous Thursday, but waited until Monday to mail my rent check off in order to give it time to clear. I didn't want a repeat of last month. After pushing a few buttons and finally getting a live person on the phone, I was relieved to find out that my rent check hadn't gone through yet, but the funds from my paycheck were fully available. So I was in the clear!

My thoughts then shifted to my American Express bill. I knew a payment was due any day, but I didn't know exactly when or how much it was. So I called the phone number on the back of my card and again pushed a few buttons until I got a live person on the phone. I just hate those automated services.

'American Express,' a woman said.

'Hi,' I said, 'I'd like to know when the payment is due on

my account, please, and how much it is that I should be paying you.'

'Can I have your account number?' she asked.

'Sure,' I said, reading it to her from my card. The woman looked up my account and then asked me my mother's maiden name and my social security number and all the other things they ask you for 'your protection.' And after a few seconds she spoke.

'Payment is not due until next Thursday and it looks like you owe $2,552 – no, wait . . . You had a credit come through, so you only owe $2,228,' she said.

'What do you mean a credit?' I asked with excitement. Was someone else paying my bill for me? How cool would that be?

'You had a credit issued from Bloomingdale's for $324,' she answered.

'Oh,' I said with disappointment. No one was paying my bill for me. 'I bought something Saturday and returned it on Sunday,' I said. 'Why is the credit on this bill though? I thought it would be on the next bill since I already got this month's statement in the mail.'

'No, American Express always applies credits to the current amount due. The $324 charge from when you *bought* the clothes will appear on your next statement though,' she said.

'Oh, okay,' I said.

'Anything else I can help you with?' she asked.

'Um, no,' I answered. I then started thinking. 'Wait, yes. So if I bought something for $100 tomorrow and then returned it the next day, the credit would be applied immediately and I'd only owe $2,128 on Thursday, and the $100 charge would be applied to next month's statement?'

'Yes,' she said with a laugh, aware of the fact that I just figured out a way to lower my current payment due, 'that's exactly what would happen.'

'Oh, okay. I'm not saying that I'll do that or anything, I was just wondering,' I said, trying to sound casual. 'Thanks for all your help.'

'You are welcome,' she said.

No freaking way! I wondered if that would really work? I owed $2,200 to American Express and there was no way that I could pay it all by next Thursday. I could actually only afford to send them about $1,400 or so, which would leave me owing $800. But according to this lady on the phone, if I bought and returned $800 worth of stuff by next Thursday, in addition to making my $1,400 payment, then I'd be all caught up! The $800 credit would be applied to the current bill, and the charge would be applied to next month's bill. The buying and returning wouldn't affect my overall balance at all. It would just buy me more time to pay up to American Express! Kick butt!

I had to try this to see if it would work. But I'd have to pick a place that would give me a refund if I returned something. Not one of those 'store credit only' kind of stores. Department stores always gave refunds. So did places like the Gap. But I'd get more bang for my buck at a place like Bloomingdale's. I could buy fewer more expensive items there than at a place like the Gap. So Bloomingdale's it was! I decided to go over the weekend.

I went back to work and before I knew it, it was the end of the day. It was time for my trainer! I turned off my computer and got ready to go. I grabbed my gym bag and headed out the door. Gwen was lurking nearby.

'Where are you going?' she asked, looking at my gym bag.

'To see my personal trainer,' I said proudly. Ha. I had a personal trainer. I felt so cool saying it.

'You have a personal trainer?' she asked with skepticism.

'Yes. Well, I mean it's my first time going tonight, but I do,' I replied.

'Isn't that expensive?' she asked.

'No more expensive than taking a cab to work every day,' I answered.

'Oh,' she said with a puzzled look on her face. She had no clue what my last comment meant. I was right, she did forget about our conversation about my blisters.

'Well, I gotta run,' I said. 'Bye.'

'Bye,' she said. 'Have fun.'

THE PERSONAL TRAINER

After a short bus ride and a fast walk, I arrived at Crunch. I walked down the long spiral staircase, checked in at the front desk, and went to the locker room to change. Five minutes later I emerged looking fabulous in my white Nike T-shirt with green and blue trim on the sleeves, and tight blue Nike workout pants that flared at the ankle. My silver-and-blue gym shoes topped off the outfit and were so new and pretty! I walked over to the personal training desk and checked in.

'Hi, I'm here to see Sam,' I said to the woman standing behind the counter.

'What's your name?' she asked.

'Karyn,' I answered.

'Sam,' she said over the loudspeaker, 'Karyn is here.' She then motioned for me to have a seat on a nearby bench. I sat down and waited. I hoped this Sam was as cute as he sounded on the phone. A few minutes later, a short guy with light brown hair approached me with a smile on his face.

'Karyn?' he asked.

'Yeah,' I said, standing up, 'hi.'

'I'm Sam,' he said, extending his hand, 'nice to meet you.'

'It's nice to meet you too,' I said, shaking it.

Sam was cute! Not really my type, but cute! He was a bit too short and beefy for me, and had some facial hair, which I'm not a fan of, but all in all, I'd say he was cute. I decided that I'd put him in the running too to be my New York boyfriend. I had to stop being so picky and had to start giving every eligible man a chance. You just never know with these things.

I followed Sam downstairs to another level of the gym, where I had not yet gone. Most of the free weights and 'boy machines' were on this floor. When I usually go to the gym, I run on the treadmill, do the elliptical machine, or ride the stationary bike. I rarely use the machines. But when I do use the machines, I use the 'girl machines.' The girl machines are the pretty ones that are easy to use with the pin that you stick in the weight. The boy machines are the ones that don't have the pins, the ones that you have to actually put the weights on yourself. Those were too difficult for me to figure out, so I always stayed away. But Sam was all about the boy machines.

Before we started working out, he asked me what my fitness goal was.

'Well, my main concern is my butt,' I said, 'it's just too big and not toned. I'd like to fix it up.'

'Fix it up?' he asked, laughing. 'What is it, a car?'

'Yes,' I said. 'Well, no, it's not a car, but yes, I want to fix it up. You know, make it look good, lift it in the air.'

'I'm just kidding. I know what you mean. And today is your lucky day, my lady, because I'm a butt man,' he said, laughing. 'I always have been. So every time I get a female client, I work on their butt the most. I might do it for selfish reasons, but I haven't had any complaints yet.'

'Cool,' I said. 'So then let's get to it.'

'Yes, let's get to it,' he replied.

For the next hour, Sam gave me the workout of my life. Like I said earlier, I'm not really a 'gymsy' kind of girl either. He put heavy weights on a bar and made me lift it up and down. He made me hold weights in my hands and do lunges across the room. I even did some boy machines. And he kept calling me 'my lady.'

'Come with me this way, my lady,' he'd say. And I kind of liked it. It made me feel special.

Toward the end of the workout, Sam started telling

me what to expect if I hired him as my trainer. He started talking about building muscle and burning fat, and increasing metabolism and all sorts of things that were just plain boring. I zoned him out when I caught a glimpse of my new outfit in the mirror. Damn, I was stylin'! I looked good! I wondered if Sam liked my outfit. Come to think of it, he hadn't even commented on it.

'So, like I was saying,' he said, 'I could completely transform your butt in ten weeks.'

'Huh,' I said, tuning him back in. Now he was speaking my language. 'Ten weeks? Really?'

'Yes. But you'd have to come see me twice a week,' he answered.

'Twice a week?' I asked. 'How much is it?'

'It's $90 a pop,' he said.

Wow! That's expensive! I started doing the math. If I saw him twice a week for ten weeks, that would be $1,800. I didn't have that kind of money. But I knew that I'd never be able to do all the exercises by myself that he made me do that day. And I did just discover my new buy-and-return trick. And he was a butt man, after all. What better person to have me work on my butt than a butt man? I looked at Sam and then at my butt.

'Okay, I'll do it,' I said impulsively. 'Do I have to pay for it all at once?' I asked.

'No. You can split it up and pay for ten sessions now, and ten sessions later,' he said.

'Cool,' I said.

My workout soon wrapped up and Sam and I walked over to the personal training desk. The woman behind the counter wrote up a sales slip for my ten personal training sessions. The total was $900. I handed over my American Express card to pay.

Sam and I agreed that he'd see me every Monday and Wednesday night at 8 P.M. I bid him farewell and headed back to the locker room. I was too tired to shower or change, so I just grabbed my bag and headed home. I felt really nauseous, which Sam said was normal and would go away.

As I wobbled down the street toward my apartment building, I passed the Mr Chow restaurant. Every time I walked by Mr Chow, fancy cars and limousines were always parked outside. I would always wonder what famous person was inside eating dinner. And then the next day in the *New York Post* I would read it was Puff Daddy or some other big star. It was kind of exciting.

But tonight I wouldn't have to guess, because at the same time that I was passing the front entrance, the back door of a black limousine opened. One man got out, and then turned around to help another man out. When I looked to see who it was, my eyes lit up. It was Stevie Wonder! I just wanted to belt out my very own Stevie Wonder musical medley and start dancing right on the street. I could do all the hits – 'Superstitious!' (snap! snap! snap!) 'Isn't she luuuvly' (clap!) 'My Cherie Amour' (clap! clap!) . . . But I didn't.

I looked down at my sweaty gym clothes and was embarrassed because I looked a mess! I sure was glad Stevie was blind! I stopped to let him walk in front of me and then not thinking, I waved at him. My excitement took over! The guy who was helping him just looked at me and laughed, but I didn't care. Because I just saw Stevie Wonder, but he didn't see me!

When I got home, I looked through my CDs for some Stevie Wonder and was disappointed to realize that I didn't have any. I'd have to make a note to buy some next time I was out. I took off my workout clothes and headed toward the shower. On my way there, I stopped to look at my naked body in the mirror. 'Ten weeks to a new you!' I said to my bare butt. It didn't respond.

THE PET STORE GUY

The next morning I woke up and couldn't move. I was so sore from my workout that I could barely get out of bed. I sat up slowly and leaned forward and tried to stretch my head to my knees. Ouch! My legs ached!

After a few minutes of slight stretching, I slowly rose and got ready for work. It took me twice as long as it usually did. When I finally left, it was just my luck that the elevator wasn't working that morning and I had to take the stairs. And going down stairs when you are sore is horrible. It's actually worse than going up.

I started my descent and every step down was more painful than the one before. Other people taking the stairs just whizzed right by me. I almost lost my balance a few times from the breeze. I finally arrived on the first floor and said hello to the doormen, who assured me that the elevator would be working by the time I got home. I may have lived only four floors up, but those four floors seemed like forty.

That day at work, it hurt just to sit at my desk. Every time I moved in either direction, I would wince in pain. The thought of going out to lunch seemed crazy, so I had the local deli deliver me a tuna melt. And fries. I was hungry. Working out worked up quite an appetite in me. Just as I started eating my sandwich, my phone rang.

'*Curtis Court*,' I answered with a mouth full of tuna.

'Karyn,' said a familiar male whiny voice, 'hey, it's Paul. How you doing?'

Paul? Who's Paul? Oh, wait. It was a guy that a friend of mine had set me up on a date with. I'd gone out with him one night for dinner after work the week before, and it was just horrible. He told me that he waxed his back within the first five minutes of me meeting him. He owned a bunch of pet stores or something. Eww! Why was this joker calling me again?

'Oh, hi,' I said, lacking excitement. 'How are you?'

'Good, thanks. So I got the tickets for the show Saturday night and wanted to let you know the plans,' he said.

Saturday night? What plans? Huh? Just then I realized that I'd forgotten to cancel on him. He had asked me to do something this weekend and I said yes, thinking I would cancel but I forgot. Oh crap! Not another night with this guy! I had to think of an excuse quickly.

'Oh, my, is that this Saturday night?' I asked, still racking my brain for an excuse. 'I forgot all about it.'

'Yes, it is this Saturday and I already bought the tickets. So you aren't bailing on me, young lady,' he said, trying to sound charming.

'Oh, um . . .' I said, still at a loss for words. I just couldn't think of anything to say. 'Um, okay. What are the plans?' I asked, realizing that I was trapped.

'Well, I thought that you could come here to my apartment for a drink, then we could go to dinner at this great sushi place around the corner, and then on to the concert after that,' he said.

'Okay,' I said reluctantly. I did not want to go out with this loser again, but I'd forgotten to cancel and he'd already bought the tickets and well, it was just too late to do anything. So I had to do the right thing and just go. He was a friend of a friend, after all.

'Alrighty then. I'll see you at eight.' Paul gave me his address and I kicked myself for forgetting to cancel. How could I have been so forgetful? But the damage was done, so I would just have to suck it up and go. This date definitely wasn't worth a new outfit. But then again, maybe I'd buy myself something just to make the night more fun. A bad date in a new outfit would be more fun than a bad date in an old outfit. Right? Right.

* * *

Saturday night came and I got ready at my apartment. As I listened to my new Stevie Wonder CDs (I bought the box set and put it on shuffle – cuz how can you choose just one Stevie Wonder CD?), I put on my new Banana Republic shirt and skirt that I bought to make the night more enjoyable. I also got one of those sparkly rhinestone belts that clips to itself and hangs down. And I got a necklace to match it. I bought those at this cute little store in SoHo called Flying A.

As I hopped in a cab to go to Paul's apartment, I realized that my body was still sore from the workout and decided to use it as an excuse to call it an early night. Paul's apartment building was a fancy high-rise. Way fancier than mine. He lived on the twenty-third floor. When I knocked on his door, I heard a dog bark from inside. A few seconds later, Paul opened the door.

'Hi, Karyn,' he said. He was wearing a blazer with a T-shirt underneath and a pair of jeans. He'd worn the same thing last time. He was a real Mr Miami Vice. 'Sorry about the barking,' he said, referring to a big golden retriever in the corner. 'She gets excited when we have company.'

'Oh, no problem. I love dogs,' I said, entering his apartment and walking toward the dog. 'What's her name?'

'Goldie,' he said. 'She's great. She's getting old though.'

'Hewwo, Gowdie,' I said in my 'animal voice.' Like any normal person, I save my 'animal voice' for when I'm alone or with friends. I don't use it in front of men I'm attracted to, and I try not to use it in public too much either. But I wasn't trying to impress, so I pulled it out here too. The dog looked up at me and panted. She was so cute! I felt sorry that she was stuck living with this loser.

I wasn't being overly mean. He really was a loser. After our first date, he pushed his drunk self all over me in a cab and told me that he wanted to please me 'down there.' Seriously. I had known him for four hours – and we didn't hit it off. He had been rude to our waiters all night and was just horrible. So you would have felt sorry for his dog too. But maybe she was happy. He did own some pet stores, after all. If my parents owned a few department stores, I'd be happy as a clam!

While Paul made us drinks in the kitchen, I checked out his apartment. Just like when I go running at night, I like to see how people live. It had one bedroom, a nice-size bathroom, and a balcony that overlooked Central Park. Not too shabby. I walked out onto the balcony and Goldie followed.

A few minutes later, Paul sat down next to me and Goldie crashed in between us. (Tank you, Gowdie!) We chatted for a while, and for a moment I thought that maybe the night would be tolerable. He told me how Goldie understood the words 'walk' and 'outside' and how he has to spell them out in front of her, because she freaks when she hears them. I told him all about Elvis the Bush Cat, and Sam, my new trainer. And to get him prepared for my early departure, I told him that I was still in pain from the workout.

'I seriously can't move,' I said. 'My body just aches.'

'I could fix that for you,' he said.

'Huh?' I asked naively.

'Your body,' he said, looking at me 'down there' again. 'I know just the thing that will take all your pains away.' He was so gross. I couldn't believe he just said that to me. I looked at him and then looked down at Goldie.

'Gowdie, bay-by. Do you want go *outside*? Huh? Do you want to go for a *walk*?' I asked teasingly. With that, Goldie jumped up and started to run around in circles. She then looked at Paul and started barking. Paul looked up at me and gave me a dirty look.

'Now why did you have to go and do that?' he asked, obviously irritated.

'I just wanted to see if you were telling the truth,' I said with a smirk on my face.

'Well, now you know I was,' he said. He stood up and headed toward the kitchen. 'I have to take her for a walk now,' he yelled back at me. 'Do you want to come with me?'

'Oh, no, thanks. I'll wait up here,' I said proudly. Paul put Goldie's leash on her and told me he'd be back in about ten minutes. Ahh . . . ten minutes all to myself. I sat on the couch and enjoyed it.

When Paul returned a short while later, I asked him when we were going to eat. He looked down at his watch, which was a Rolex, and made sure I could see it.

'Well, the concert starts kind of late, so maybe we should wait a while,' he said.

'Late? How late?' I asked. 'I'm kind of tired and I don't want to stay out that late.'

'Well, not that late,' he said, avoiding the question. 'Yeah, you know you're right. Let's go eat now.'

'Okay,' I said. I said good-bye to Goldie, and Paul and I headed out the front door.

We walked to the sushi restaurant, which was only a couple blocks away. It was bright and empty, and not exactly the kind of place where you'd take a Saturday-night date. But who was I to complain?

My friends and I always debate if a sushi restaurant is a good place to take a date. Basically you are shoving large pieces of raw fish into your mouth, which isn't very attractive. And sometimes the pieces are just too big to fit, and half of it ends up on your face, which is even less attractive. But I wasn't there to impress Paul, so I guess it didn't matter.

Seeing as how there was no big backup in the kitchen, the service was pretty speedy. I made a note of the restaurant name, but doubted that it was in my *Zagat* guide. *Zagat*-rated restaurants usually have a sign in the window and this one didn't have one. But the food actually looked pretty good. Well, at least mine did anyway. When I looked over at Paul's, I noticed something that looked like a raw egg on top of each piece of sushi.

'What's that?' I asked, pointing to it.

'They're quail eggs,' he said. 'They're so good.'

'They don't look very good,' I said.

‘Oh, but they are,’ Paul said while lifting a piece of sushi up, balancing it so that the slimy quail egg wouldn’t fall off. With one big swoop, he shoved the whole thing in his mouth. The quail egg burst instantly, and yellow goo oozed all over the inside of his mouth. I normally wouldn’t stare at this type of thing, but since he chewed with his mouth open, I kind of didn’t have a choice. It was the most grotesque thing I’ve ever seen. Some pieces of rice were hanging out on his lip too. They either fell out, or never made it in to begin with. I thought I was going to vomit. I suddenly agreed with my friends: a sushi restaurant is a very bad place for a date.

I looked down at my plate and tried not to look at Paul for the rest of the meal. I had to concentrate on my own raw fish. Every so often, I heard eating noises like ‘mmmm’ and ‘ooooh’ coming from his side of the table. He’d made these same noises last time we went out. Didn’t this boy’s mama ever teach him table manners?

When we were done, the waiter cleared the table and left the check. Paul picked it up and paid for it.

‘Thank you,’ I said.

‘No problem. I’ll take you to every good restaurant in the city if you want,’ he said.

‘Thanks,’ I said, trying to smile. I wanted to say ‘No, thanks,’ but I decided to be polite.

We left the restaurant and jumped in a cab to head toward the club. I tried to talk the whole way there because I didn’t want him to make any sudden moves on me again like last time. When we arrived, there was a line to get in, so we waited. I looked up at the sky and yawned.

‘Are you tired?’ he asked.

‘Yes, I actually am. I had a really long week,’ I said. As much as this was my plan to escape early, it was true. I really was exhausted. When we finally arrived at the front of the line, Paul handed the guy our tickets. I looked at my watch. It was 10:30 P.M.

We entered the club and walked upstairs to the second level, where the band was supposed to play. Every time I asked Paul what time they were going to start, he avoided answering me.

'I'll go get us some drinks,' he said. Fine by me.

A few minutes later he returned with our drinks and quickly slammed his. He then went back to the bar to get another. And another. I quickly realized that he was completely wasted.

When I wasn't looking, he snuck up behind me and wrapped his arms around my stomach and pressed himself against me. And boy was he excited! And boy was I irritated! I quickly pulled away.

'I really wish you wouldn't do that,' I said.

'Why not? What's wrong?' he asked in a drunken haze, trying to stroke my hair.

'Um . . .' I said searching for an excuse.

'Um . . . what?' he asked.

'Um . . . I'm a lesbian, that's what's wrong,' I finally said proudly. Yes, that was it! That was a good excuse. 'I'm gay!' I yelled.

Just then about five people turned around to stare. I felt like Ellen DeGeneres on that coming-out episode. I don't know why I just couldn't say 'I don't like you,' but I couldn't. I was a chicken. So I just told him that I was a lesbian. It was easier.

Paul just looked at me and then a perverted smile crept across his face. 'Cool,' he said, shaking his head up and down. Oh no! I just turned him on more! I'm positive that as he was looking at me he was thinking about the last lesbian porn movie he'd rented.

I turned my head and looked away. Just then I looked up and saw a big clock on the wall. It was midnight. I had been there for an hour and a half already and the band hadn't started yet. I looked at Paul. He was still looking at me, smirking.

'Paul, seriously, what time does the band start? We've been here for an hour and a half,' I said shortly. I felt like I was talking to a child. He started laughing.

'What's so funny?' I asked.

'They don't go on until 1.00 A.M. I didn't want to tell you because I knew you were tired,' he said.

'Did you think I wouldn't notice?' I asked, irritated.

'No, I knew you would eventually,' he answered. 'But I was hoping you'd be drunk by the time they started and would forget that you were tired.'

'Well, I didn't forget. And I'm even more tired than when I got here. I really want to go home,' I said.

'Okay, in a bit,' he said.

Well, a bit came and a bit left. A warm-up band finally started and they were horrible. Every time I asked Paul if we could go, he said 'in a bit.'

When I couldn't take it anymore, I decided to go downstairs to escape the noise.

'I'm going to go to the bathroom,' I said to Paul.

'Okay,' he said, swaying back and forth. He was spilling his drink everywhere.

As I walked down the stairs to where the bathrooms were, I let out a big exhale. It was much quieter. As I waited in line, I looked to the left and noticed that the front doors were propped wide open. I saw a taxi drive by, and then another one. I looked up at the stairs leading back to the second floor, and then back through the open doors at the taxis. And before I knew it, I walked right out those doors and hopped into one of those taxis.

'Four hundred East Fifty-seventh Street, please,' I said to the driver. As the cab pulled away, I turned and looked at the club. Paul was inside. He had no clue that I'd just left. For a split second I felt guilty, but just for a split second. Otherwise, I felt great!

When I got home, I told my doormen all about my horrible date and they just laughed. I asked them if they thought I should call him and tell him that I went home and they said no.

'It may sound mean, Miss Karyn, but hopefully it will teach him to listen to a woman next time she asks him to go home,' Sam said.

'I guess you are right, Sam,' I said. I bid the doormen good night and went upstairs to go to sleep.

The next morning I awoke to a message on my voice mail from Paul, asking me why I'd left the bar. I didn't even hear the phone ring. He said something like 'you must have gotten sick.' How dense could a guy be? On my way out to get the paper, the doormen told me that Paul came to the building drunk at 4.00 A.M. looking for me.

'I told him that you were safely upstairs asleep,' Osei said. 'He wanted me to call up to your apartment, but I refused because it was too late. He then got disorderly and started yelling, and we had to kick him out of the building.'

'Oh, I'm so sorry,' I said.

'That's okay, Miss Karyn,' Osei said. 'He was a loser.'

'I know,' I said.

When I got back to my apartment, I called Paul back out of courtesy to tell him that I was alive. I got his voice mail.

'Hi, Paul, it's Karyn,' I said. 'I'm so sorry that I left you at the bar last night, but I really just wanted to go home. I hope you understand. Anyway, I hope the band finally started and it was good. Take care.' I hung up the phone and sighed a sigh of relief. I then hopped in the shower and got ready for my day. I had some buying and returning to do!

THE BUY

Bloomingdale's looked just as lovely this Sunday as it did last Sunday. The flags were billowing, the clothes were fluffy, and the sunglasses were shiny. As I roamed around the store, I pondered what to buy. I decided that the best thing to do was to buy one big item, and then a smaller one to make up the difference.

The thing is, when I don't have any money and shouldn't be buying things, I want them really, really badly. So I charge them and feel satisfied, and then briefly guilty, then satisfied again. But today I *had* to buy something. I didn't necessarily want something in particular. I wasn't looking for a new outfit for a date, or looking for a new pair of shoes or something. Today I *had* to buy something because I *had* to return something. I was under pressure. And because I was under pressure, I became very indecisive. Even though I was going to return whatever it was I was going to buy.

Anyway, after roaming around the store for almost an hour, I finally found the item. It was a beautiful $650 Burberry trench coat. I found my size on the rack and tried it on. I don't really know why I did this, because I was just going to return it anyway. But if I was going to splurge on a $650 coat, then I wanted to at least pretend like I was going to keep it.

I walked over to the three-way mirror and looked at the coat. Damn I looked good! The coat was khaki and had the signature Burberry plaid on the inside. It really blew my Banana Republic one out of the water! It was just gorgeous! Now I know why Burberry is so expensive. This coat fit so nicely! It really was much better quality. After making sure the other women in the section saw how fabulous I looked in my new Burberry coat, I took it off and walked up to the counter to pay for it. The woman rang it up.

'The total is $702,' she said. 'How will you be paying for that?'

'American Express. I don't leave home without it,' I said, giggling. I was so excited to buy the coat that I was downright slaphappy!

She ran my card through and I was approved. I was kind of nervous because I didn't know if I had a limit. I forgot to ask the woman that on the phone. I signed on the dotted line and it was official: I was now the proud owner of a Burberry coat!

'Shall I hang it for you?' the saleslady asked.

'Oh, yes, please, I don't want it to wrinkle,' I said. 'I have to wear it to a big occasion tomorrow,' I added to make it sound believable. The saleslady didn't really care about my big occasion, so I shut up. What kind of big occasion would I have on a Monday that required a Burberry coat anyway?

'A business lunch,' I said out loud. Yes, that's what kind! The saleslady just looked at me. She didn't really care. When she was done hanging the coat, she passed it to me over the counter, and I thanked her.

'Thank you,' I said. Phew! Got the big one out of the way! I was nervous. I felt like a criminal. Now all I had to do was buy something around $100 and I was done. For that I decided to go to the BCBG section.

A short trip on the down escalator took me right to the BCBG section. A table in the front had some super cute T-shirts on it. They were black and white with some pretty designs on them. I looked at a price tag and saw that they were $70 each. With that, I grabbed two in my size – one black and one white – and brought them up to the counter. The total ended up to be $151. Perfect! I was done!

I decided to take my stuff home and wait a few hours and then go back to return it. I was hoping by the time I got back there that the women I bought the items from wouldn't be there anymore. If they were, I wasn't sure what I would say to them – especially the coat lady. Should I tell her that my business lunch was canceled? No, that's not good. Ah! I know. I'd tell her that I found another coat that I like better. At Saks . . . yes, Saks. That's it. I went to Saks and found another coat that I like better so I wanted to return this one.

To pass the time, I straightened up my apartment a bit. And I pet Elvis. He was in desperate need of some lovin'. He's always in desperate need of some lovin'. When I got home, I noticed that he had been humping a sweater of mine that was on the floor. He does this all the time, and has since I got him. The first time I caught him 'making muffins' I sort of freaked out and picked him up to stop him. And I was horrified when I saw that his 'pink thing' was sticking out. He's neutered and I didn't think that was supposed to happen to neutered cats. So I freaked out and called the vet, telling them that they didn't get it all when they did the job.

'That "pink thing," Karyn, is his penis,' the vet said to me. 'When we neuter cats, we only remove their testicles, not their penises. If we cut his penis off then he wouldn't be able to pee, now would he?'

'I guess not,' I said. 'So he's totally normal?'

'Totally,' the vet answered.

Anywho, Elvis humps anything that's soft and fluffy. I once caught him on top of a stuffed animal and was tempted to take a picture and send it to my friends as 'kitty porn.' But I opted to let the little bugger hump in peace, in the privacy of his own home.

I picked up the phone to make a call and realized that I had voice mail. I had three, in fact. I was popular! I pushed the button to listen to the first.

'Uh, hi, Karyn. This is Paul,' said a grumbly voice. 'Uh, I'm glad to hear you are okay. I was worried when I couldn't find you and just assumed that you probably got sick.' Yeah, sick of you, I thought. 'So let's try to get together again sometime next weekend if you're free. Okay, bye.'

Are you kidding me? How dense can a guy be? I left him in a bar. In the middle of a date, mind you. I went to the bathroom and just never came back. And he wants to know if I want to go out again. Oy vay! I deleted the message and went on to the next call.

'Hi, Karyn, it's your mother. Listen, my friend Pandy has a son who lives in New York and we want to set you up with each other. He's supposed to be really good-looking and has a really great job. You remember Pandy, right? She brought me that nice gift basket last time you were home. Anyway, call me.'

As great as this sounded, I was a bit worried. My mom isn't always the greatest at picking out suitable men for me. I let her set me up on a date once before. Once. It was horrible.

You see, my mom used to work at the local orthodontist's office. One day while I was living in Chicago, she called me and told me that she gave my phone number out to some guy who happened to be a patient there.

'I know I didn't ask you,' she said, 'but he's a pilot for Northwest. A *real* pilot. He's thirty-five years old and just adorable.'

'Wait, go back. Why is he a patient there?' I asked. 'Does he have braces, Mom!?'

'Oh, no, not anymore. He just got them taken off. He came in to be fit for his retainer,' she said.

'A retainer? Mom, that's worse!' I yelled. 'He doesn't have a head gear, does he?'

'No, he doesn't have a head gear! And quit being mean! You better be nice to him when he calls you! I told him that you were nice!'

'I am nice,' I said, 'to men who don't wear retainers, that is.'

'Karyn!'

'Oh, I'm just kidding, Mom. I'll be nice. I promise.'

A few days later, my mom's pilot called for a date. And true to my word, for my *Mom's* sake, I was nice to him.

I was nice when he asked me to take a train to the suburbs to go out to dinner because he didn't want to drive into the big bad city. I refused, but I was nice. I was also nice when the date had to start at 5:30 P.M. so he could beat the traffic into the big bad city. And I was nice again when I watched him pick the corn out of his teeth during dinner.

But my favorite part of the evening, when I was the *nicest*, came when we were having a drink after dinner. We were sitting across from each other at a table talking when he stopped and reached in his pocket.

'Do you mind if I put my retainer in?' he asked me.

'Um . . .' I said, startled, 'um, no. Go right ahead.' With that said, he pulled out his retainer and showed it up in the roof of his mouth with his two thumbs. Then after a few seconds of adjusting and biting up and down, he was set. Don't worry about going to the bathroom to do that or anything. Just pull it right out here in front of your date. No problem.

'Thanks,' he said. 'Now, where were we?'

Um, I honestly forgot. Before the night was over he told me how he and his 'buddy' just got season passes to the local theme park, Six Flags. He asked me if I had ever been there.

'When I was twelve,' I said. He was thirty-five.

Yep, I was nice all night. And because of that, I'm always a bit cautious when my mom wants to set me up with someone. I deleted my mom's message and went on to the third.

'Hi, Karyn,' said a familiar voice, 'it's Brad.' Brad! It was Brad! The message continued. 'I just want to apologize for not calling you back. I've been crazy at work and I know it's not an excuse, but I'd love to get together sometime this week if you are free. Give me a call. Oh, yeah, and in case you threw it away, my number is 555-1234. Bye.'

I couldn't believe he called! I felt like maybe I should be angry, but I couldn't really be because I was excited. I pushed Repeat and listened to the message again. Aaah . . . Brad. I then saved it and hung up.

THE RETURN

I decided to wait to call Brad back and got ready to go back to Bloomingdale's to do my return. I got my purse, made sure my Amex was in it, found my keys and then looked at the phone. I decided that I wasn't going to play games, and called

Brad right then. I picked up the phone and dialed his number. Before I knew it, it was ringing. And ringing. I hoped he was home. A few seconds later he answered.

'Hello?' he said. Oh, he sounded so cute!

'Brad? Hi, it's Karyn,' I said.

'Karyn! Hi! I was hoping you'd call back! I'm so sorry that it's taken me so long to get back to you. I've just been crazy at work and have actually been doing a lot of traveling,' he said.

'Oh, no problem. I know the feeling very well,' I said.

'So what's up? How is work? When does your show premiere?' he asked.

'Monday, September 11th, but we have a really crappy time slot in New York, so it's going to be on at like three in the morning or something. You'll have to tape it.'

'I will definitely. Just let me know when.'

'I will,' I said. I was excited to talk to him. And I really didn't have any reason to be angry. We weren't seriously dating or anything. And I didn't want to come across as some possessive freak. So I was cool. Cool as a cucumber.

'So, we have to get together soon. What are your plans this week?' he asked.

'This week? Well, I have a trainer now and I see him Monday and Wednesday,' I said, trying to impress him. 'So I guess that leaves Tuesday or Thursday.'

'A trainer? Wow. Little miss workout,' he said, teasing.

'Yes, a trainer. It's actually kind of funny and a very big deal for me because I'm very uncoordinated and have no idea what I'm doing in a gym.'

'Well, I'm impressed,' he said. Ahh! It worked! 'Tuesday is really good for me, so let's go out then. I'll take you to dinner to celebrate your trainer.'

'Sounds good,' I said.

'Okay. I'll give you a call tomorrow with details,' he said.

'Until then,' I said. 'Bye.'

'Bye,' he said.

I hung up the phone and threw my body back on my bed and smiled. Dinner with Brad on Tuesday. I was so excited! What was I going to wear? I got up and started going through my closet. I passed up the coral shirt because I'd already worn it with him. And I didn't want to wear the one I got to go out with the Pet Store Guy, well, because I decided it was bad luck. My Rebecca Taylor shirt was at the cleaners and wouldn't be ready until Wednesday. What to wear, what to wear . . .

I then looked over at the Bloomingdale's bag sitting on the floor by the front door. One of those BCBG shirts inside would be perfect. I know I was supposed to return them, but I decided to try one on just to see how it looked.

I went in the bag and pulled out the white one first. It had the outline of an orchid or some kind of flower in black on it. But the outline was really big, so you couldn't really tell what it was. It looked kind of 'rocker,' but rocker in a good way, not rocker in a Lita Ford way.

I slipped the T-shirt over my head and stood in front of the mirror. Oh, it was nice . . . And my boobs looked so big in it. I wouldn't even have to wear my water bra or my Curves with it. Just a plain old padded bra would look just fine.

I then decided to try on the black one as well just to see how it compared. Looking more closely I noticed that they were the same T-shirt, the colors were just reversed. I slipped this one over my head and looked in the mirror. Oh! Oh, we had a winner! The black one was so much better – hands down! I had to keep this one. I could just return the other one and the Burberry coat and probably still create enough 'credit' to offset my payment for the month.

With that, I hung the black T-shirt up in my closet and put the white one back in the bag, and headed back to Bloomingdale's. The closer I got to the store, the more nervous I became. Once I arrived, I went to the coat section and started to stake out the place looking for the same saleslady. After checking out the counter, I didn't see her and realized that I must be safe. She was gone. I felt relieved. I walked up and put my coat on the counter.

'Hi,' I said to the saleslady behind the counter. 'I just bought this coat and wanted to return it. I didn't wear it. I didn't even take it out of the bag, to be honest. I just found one that I liked better at a different store. I'm sorry.'

'Oh, that's no problem, miss,' the saleslady said. She was so nice. I don't know why I was so nervous. She took my coat out of the bag and found the tag and started the return. I held my head down and waited.

'It's a beautiful coat,' she said.

'Oh, yeah, it is. It's great. I just found the cutest one at Saks though. I'm so sorry,' I said.

'Oh, don't worry about it,' she said, 'I understand. I always buy and return things because I can never tell if I truly like something until I get it home.'

'I know exactly how you feel! I always do that too!' This was true. I did know how she felt. I am a big believer in the 'skinny mirror' conspiracy theory – because I look like a supermodel when I'm in some fitting rooms. I've even thought about sending my photos into Elite when I'm in some fitting rooms. Could you imagine if I did?

'Um, miss, were you high when you sent us these pictures?' they'd ask me.

'No, seriously, if you'll just come with me to Bloomingdale's fitting rooms, you'll see how hot I am,' I'd say.

Anywho, when she finished ringing the return, I signed my American Express credit slip and thanked her. I turned around and walked toward the down escalator. That was so easy that this next one should be a breeze. When I got to the BCBG section, I again scoped out the area and saw that the same girl was working the register. Oh, who really cares? It was one shirt. I walked up and took it out of the bag.

'Hi. I want to return this,' I said. The saleslady looked up at the shirt and then looked at me.

'Didn't you just buy this?' she asked rudely.

'Yeah, I bought two actually, and I just don't like this one,' I said. She sighed.

'Can I have your credit card, please?' she asked, irritated. I just wanted to yell, 'Chill out, lady. It's only seventy bucks. I just returned a $650 coat upstairs and they didn't hassle me.' But I didn't. I just smiled and handed over my card. She pushed a few buttons, swiped my card, and before I knew it, I was out the door.

I walked out of Bloomingdale's and let out a sigh of relief. I did it. I succeeded in doing the buy and return. Now I just hoped it worked. I should be able to find out by tomorrow.

On my way home, I picked up dinner at a nearby sushi restaurant that was in my *Zagat* guide. That night as I ate by myself, I looked out the window into an apartment building across the street. It was getting dark outside, and I could just start to make out the inside of some of the apartments. One in particular caught my attention, and I briefly stopped eating and stared. Inside, the light from a hanging chandelier glowed and fire from a few random candles flickered as a couple danced together with wineglasses in their hands. It was sweet.

After a few moments, I looked back down at my plate and continued to eat alone. When I was finished, I pulled out my *Zagat* guide, circled the sushi restaurant and wrote, 'Me, all alone after a buy-and-return, with the chandelier people across the street.'

FIVE

AMERICAN EXPRESS

American Express

Karyn Bosnak
400 E. 57th St.
New York, NY 10010

Date	Payee	Amount
	PREVIOUS BALANCE	$ 3,233,00
Aug 20, 2000	Bloomingdale's – Nick & Nora	$ 147.00
Aug 22, 2000	Bloomingdale's – Cacharel	$ 270.00
Aug 26, 2000	Red Salon – Hair	$ 318.00
Aug 26, 2000	Saks Fifth Avenue – Nars	$ 198.00
Aug 26, 2000	Saks Fifth Avenue – Clarins	$ 54.00
Aug 26, 2000	Saks Fifth Avenue – Kiehl's	$ 67.00
Aug 26, 2000	Saks Fifth Avenue – Lingerie Dept.	$ 778.00
Sep 11, 2000	Manhattan Transit Authority	$ 60.00
Sep 11, 2000	Elena's Salon – Wax	$ 102.00
Sep 11, 2000	Crunch	$ 900.00
Sep 23, 2000	Red Salon – Hair	$ 318.00
	PAYMENT	– $ 1,451.00
	Total	**$ 4,994.00**

JENNIFER CONVERTIBLES

Karyn Bosnak
400 E. 57th St.
New York, NY 10010

Date	Payee	Amount
	PREVIOUS BALANCE	$ 1,774.00
Sep 12, 2000	Late Charge	$ 25.00
Sep 12, 2000	Finance Charge	$ 36.00
	Total	**$ 1,835.00**

Grand Debt Tally $6,829.00

On Monday, I called American Express and was delighted to find out that the buy and return was successful! I mailed off my check for $1,451 and was set for the month. With that under my belt, I was able to concentrate on my Tuesday-night date with Brad, which turned out to be a success as well. My shirt was a success, my Red Salon haircut and color was still a success, and damnit – I was a success. He took me to a great Mexican restaurant downtown called Mi Cocina, which was deeelish. And afterward, I invited him back to my apartment and he was deeelish!

I'm not one to kiss and tell, but let's just say as quickly as I showed him my cherry wood sleigh bed, we were thrashing around on it like wild animals. And during the thrashing, something awfully peculiar happened. I reached for Brad's zipper but was stopped in mid-zip. No, the zipper wasn't stuck. Brad actually stopped me himself. What kind of man stops a woman from undoing his zipper? A potentially gay man, that's what kind.

Brad ended up sleeping over, but nothing too exciting happened. The next day, when I got to work, I called my friend Naomi in Chicago to tell her all about it.

'He slept over,' I said, 'but nothing major happened or anything. It was like he didn't want me to go there or something.'

'What do you mean he didn't want you to go there?' she asked.

'I mean we were fooling around, and I went for it, you know, and he stopped me.'

'Oh, I have to work with him, I don't want to hear this,' she said.

'Well, you were my friend before you started working with

him, so you have to. And you are the one who set me up with him, so you have to have to,' I said.

'Well, maybe he has a little penis,' she said. 'But then again, he is Potentially Gay Brad.'

'He's not gay!' I said.

'If you say so. I mean you're the one who can't get in his pants, not me,' she said. 'But I have very good news.'

'What?'

'I'm coming to New York next week! On Monday! I convinced my bosses that I had some serious work to do there and they are letting me go!' she said.

'Cool! I'm so excited!' I said. 'You can see my apartment. More importantly, you can see Bloomingdale's!' I said. I hadn't seen Naomi in three months.

'So listen to this,' she said, 'I'm staying Monday and Tuesday night. And I was thinking that we could go to dinner Monday with my expense account and then you can shack up with me at my hotel. We can have a slumber party.'

'Where are you staying?' I asked.

'Prepare yourself,' she said.

'I'm prepared,' I said, anxiously awaiting.

'The Plaza!' she said, screaming. I screamed back.

'The Plaza! Eloise lives there!' I said, referring to the little fictional girl who lives in the hotel.

'Is that that little bitch in the book?' Naomi asked.

'Yes,' I said. 'And please don't refer to her like that. Okay, I am going to move my training appointment to the morning.'

'Good,' she said. 'Then Tuesday night I have to go to dinner with Brad and some other people from work. You should come to that too actually. I don't think anyone would care.'

'I'll see if he invites me. I don't want to throw myself into a mix with all his coworkers if he doesn't want me there.'

'I agree,' she said. 'Okay, well then, I'll call you when I get in on Monday.' Who is she kidding? She'd call me tonight, and then I'd call her tomorrow. Naomi and I talk on the phone every day, twice a day. It was like I hadn't moved.

'Okay,' I said. With that, I hung up the phone.

Brad and I went out again that Saturday night, and he again came over afterward and stayed the night. And again he was weird with his zipper. But he did ask me to join him and Naomi for dinner on Tuesday night with their coworkers, so I was happy about that. I was anxious to see how he would act toward me in front of other people.

On Monday morning I woke up at 6:30 A.M. so I could get to Crunch by 7.00 A.M. to meet Sam. As planned, I moved my training appointment up so I could go to dinner with Naomi that night.

I left work around 8.00 P.M. to meet Naomi at a new restaurant called Guastavino. Guastavino just opened and was located underneath the 59th Street Bridge. The ceiling of the restaurant was the actual restored base of the bridge. I was the first to arrive and waited at the bar. And waited at the bar. Naomi finally arrived twenty minutes late.

'Hi!' she shrieked while hugging me.

'Hi!' I shrieked back. It was so nice to see her again! 'How are you?'

'Oh, I'm drunk,' she said.

'You're drunk?'

'Yeah. We had this meeting this afternoon, and then afterward everyone left and went to this bar by the office, and now I'm just wasted. Oh, and Brad was there,' she said, like she had some scoop.

'He was?' I asked. 'Did he say anything?'

'No, but this guy he works with asked me what was up with Brad and my friend – which is you. That means that Brad must have told him about you.'

'That's kind of good. Right?' I asked.

'I think so because he probably wouldn't have said

anything if he didn't like you,' she added. 'But I'm drunk, what do I know.'

'We'll see how he acts tomorrow night,' I said.

The hostess led Naomi and me to our table, where we proceeded to order whatever we wanted because she had an expense account! The food was good, but the people watching was better. Guastavino was filled with older rich men and the women looking to meet them. It was a Monday night, a normal weeknight, and women were decked out in Diane von Furstenberg dresses, high heels, and costume jewelry. They were dressed to kill.

After dinner, Naomi and I walked the three short blocks to where I lived so I could show her my apartment and grab my overnight bag.

'It's so small,' she said.

'I know but it's cute, isn't it?' I said.

'Yeah, it's really cute,' she said. 'Is that where the alleged zipper debacle took place?' she asked, pointing at my bed.

'Yes, it is,' I answered. We both stared at the bed silently and just shook our heads for a while.

'Anyway,' I said, turning to Naomi, 'I have a surprise for you.'

'I love surprises! What is it?' she asked.

'I bought us matching pajamas for our slumber party!' I said, pulling out two sets of Nick & Nora flannel pajama sets from my closet.

'Oh my gosh, I love Nick and Nora!'

'I know, aren't they cute?' I said. She agreed. We decided to both change into our pajamas right then before we went to the Plaza. It was more fun that way. On the way out, I introduced Naomi to my doormen and we asked them if they would take a picture of us. We were excited for our slumber party and were going to capture the event on film. They took our picture, and then hailed us a taxi. A few minutes later, we arrived at the hotel. As the taxi pulled into the circular drive, a bell cap walked over and opened the door. We asked him if he would also take a picture with us, and he obliged.

'We are so trashy,' I said, turning to Naomi.

'Oh, I know it. But it's so fun!'

We looked up at the hotel, which was all lit up and just seemed to glow. We then followed the bell cap inside and just stood there and stared. It was so elegant! There were crystal chandeliers, oriental rugs, oil paintings, and flowers everywhere. It was so opulent! We did not belong in a place like the Plaza. Especially in our pajamas. The bell cap pointed out the front desk. Naomi and I just looked at each other and burst into laughter. A few seconds later we composed ourselves and approached the man behind the counter.

'Hi,' Naomi said to the man behind the desk, 'we're here to check in.'

'Can I have your name, please?' he asked.

'Sure, my name is Naomi and this is my friend Karyn,' she said. 'The room is under my name though.' The man seemed charmed by our delightful demeanor, as I am sure he deals with a lot of stiff people here every day.

'We're having a slumber party,' Naomi whispered to him as he typed her name into the computer. 'We're not lesbians or anything.' The man looked up.

'A slumber party?' he asked, noticing our matching pajamas. 'Well, I hope you two have a nice time.' While we waited for the man to finish checking us in, another bell cap came over and took our bags. We guessed he was going to take them to our room.

'Okay, Miss Naomi and Miss Karyn, I've just checked and because we have some more availability, I have upgraded you two delightful young ladies to a suite. More room to enjoy your slumber party.'

'A suite? Really?' Naomi turned to me and we both started to jump up and down.

'Cool!' I said. 'We get to stay in a suite at the Plaza!'

'Thank you so much!' we said in unison.

'Is Eloise gonna be on our floor?' I asked the man.

'No, miss, I'm sorry, she lives on a different floor,' he said.

'How about Kevin McCallister?' I asked. 'Is he still here?'

'Who?' he asked.

'Kevin McCallister – Macaulay Culkin. *Home Alone*,' I clarified.

'Oh, no, miss, he checked out a while ago.'

'Okay,' I said.

'Here is your key card. Enjoy. And thank you for coming to the Plaza,' he said.

On our way to the elevator, Naomi and I saw the picture of Eloise that hangs in the lobby and proceeded to take pictures by it. We rode the elevator up to our room, which was on the eighth floor, and again took photos in the elevator. We found our room, and Naomi put the key in the lock.

'Are you ready?' she asked.

'I'm ready,' I said.

Naomi proceeded to open the door and we walked in.

'Oh. My. Gosh!' we said in unison.

The room was so beautiful! And big! It was bigger than my apartment. Two crystal chandeliers were hanging from the high ceiling. The walls had silk wallpaper that was set off by beautiful molding. On one side of the room, there was a huge mahogany television cabinet, and next to that a door to a walk-in closet, which was about as big as my apartment. On the other side of the room, there was a couch and two club chairs, along with a door to the bathroom. And a huge king-size bed was smack dab in the middle.

'Could you imagine living in a place like this?' I said to Naomi, wherever she was.

'It's amazing!' she yelled from the bathroom. 'They have two robes with "The Plaza" written on them in here.'

'Oh I want one!' I said, running to take a look.

'I bet we have to pay for them if we take one,' she said. She then lit up, 'But that's what expense accounts are for!'

'Cool!' I said, trying a robe on. She put one on too.

A few moments later there was a knock on the door.

Naomi and I jumped.

'Are we expecting visitors?' I asked.

'No,' she said. 'Did you order a stripper?'

'No,' I replied.

'Oh, I bet it's our bags,' she said. 'Crap! Do you have any money? We have to tip him.'

'I don't have anything,' I said. 'I'm dead broke.'

'But you look good,' she said, 'and that's important.'

'Thank you,' I said.

Naomi found her purse and scrounged together $5 from the bottom in change. It was better than nothing, I guess. We then opened the door.

'Hello there,' we said in unison while wearing our matching pajamas and matching Plaza robes.

'Well, hello, ladies,' said the bell cap. 'Looks like you are having a nice time. Here are your bags. Shall I bring them in?'

'Oh, please do,' we said.

'Would you like me to turn down your bed?' he asked.

'Oh, no, sir, we can do that on our own,' Naomi said while handing him our tip.

'Very well then,' he said as he turned to leave.

That night we climbed in bed. After talking for what seemed like hours, we finally started to drift off to sleep.

'Naomi,' I said on the brink of sleeping.

'Yes?' she answered.

'You're kinda like my sugar mama,' I said.

'I am, aren't I?' she said.

'Thanks,' I said.

'You are welcome,' she said. 'Just no funny business under the covers.'

'I promise,' I said. Girlfriends are the best.

ONE DIVINE NIGHT

The next day I met Naomi at Bloomingdale's after work. She may have technically been in New York on business, but we both knew that Bloomingdale's was the real reason she came. She was just as taken aback by the size of the store as I was, and we each bought a great outfit for our dinner out with Brad that night. I bought a cotton Cacharel button-up shirt-dress, which would be perfect for the tapas restaurant and wine bar called Divine Bar, where we were going to meet Brad later that evening.

Naomi and I arrived at the restaurant about twenty minutes late and saw Brad waiting with a couple of friends at the bar. He greeted us each with a kiss, and then introduced us to a guy he worked with named Lou and another business associate who was visiting from another country named Ali. Ali was from Yemen, and Lou . . . well, Lou was from Long Island.

During dinner the wine flowed freely, and all of us had a very good time. Ali was single and looking for a girlfriend, and told Naomi and me that his ideal woman would act as his servant. Apparently in Yemen this was a normal thing. But Ali was now in America, and Naomi and I quickly had to remind him of it.

Brad sat next to me and frequently put his arm around me and grabbed my hand all throughout dinner. He was very touchy-feely, which I didn't mind at all. Every time he showed affection, Naomi kicked me under the table. When dinner was through, Naomi and I went to the bathroom.

'Okay, I take it back,' Naomi said to me once the bathroom door closed.

'Take what back?' I asked.

'He's not gay,' she said. 'He's totally into you.'

'I know!' I said. 'Then why can't I get him to go for it in the sack?'

'It's gotta be small,' she said, laughing. 'It really is the only logical explanation.'

'Maybe he's religious or something,' I said, hopeful.

'Oh, he's not religious!' she said, laughing. 'Perhaps he's just a prude and isn't used to slutty girls like you.'

'I'm not a slut,' I said, grabbing for my lipstick.

'Oh, I'm kidding,' she said. 'Maybe he just needs motivation. Do you have any sexy lingerie or something? Maybe he just needs to be turned on a bit more.'

'Not really. All I have is a pair of silk geisha pajamas that I bought in Thailand, and my Nick and Nora flannel pajamas from last night.'

'Slip the flannels, those won't turn anyone on. But the geisha ones might work. If they don't, then he's a lost cause.'

'Okay,' I said.

We went back to the table and finished our drinks. Afterward, we all went dancing at a nearby club. After about an hour, we said our good-byes. Ali and Naomi went back to their hotels, Lou went back to Long Island, and Brad came over to my apartment.

As Brad and I were kissing on the couch, I started thinking about my geisha pajamas. I didn't know exactly when to pull them out. Finally, a few minutes later Brad got up to move to the bed, and I decided that it was a perfect opportunity to change.

'Can you hold on a second?' I asked.

'Sure,' he said.

I ran over to my dresser, grabbed my red pajamas and went into the bathroom. As I unfolded them, I noticed they were a bit wrinkly, but I doubted he'd notice. I quickly changed, and looked in the mirror. I looked cute, but cute wasn't exactly what I was going for. I was missing something . . . What was I missing? Makeup! Yes, makeup! Fun, slutty makeup would do the trick!

I reached in my makeup bag under the sink and pulled out my black eyeliner. On my upper lid right at the edge of my lashes, I drew a super-thick line that made me look very geisha-like. When I was done, I stood back to reexamine myself. Yes! That did the trick! I looked like every man's geisha dream! If I were Brad, I'd want to pull down my zipper. With that, I walked out of the bathroom, dimmed the lights and walked over to where Brad was sitting on the bed.

'Herro, Brad. Mee Kareeen. Me hewe to make you—'

Brad started laughing and cut me off. 'Okay, stop talking, please, because you look hot, and your fake Asian accent is about to ruin it.' With that, Brad grabbed me and pulled me onto the bed. I started laughing. He jumped on top of me and we started kissing. Wow! These PJs sure did throw a spark into things.

A little while later, as things were heating up, I decided to go for the zipper once more. Very slowly, I reached my hand down there and started to pull. One notch . . . and then another notch . . . and then another notch. He didn't try to stop me. I waited a bit more, and then decided to go for the gusto. With one big swoop, I pulled the zipper the rest of the way down. It worked! Long live the geisha!

Soon enough Brad completely wiggled out of his pants, and after that my geisha pajamas fell off too. It was just me and Brad – body to body. I know what you are wondering. Was it small? Well, a real woman never tells. But I've never been a real woman, so I'll tell you it was just perfect!

That night Brad slept over again, but when I woke up the next morning he was gone. I looked over and saw a note sitting on the edge of my bed and grabbed it.

Karyn,
Good morning, beautiful geisha girl! Thanks for the glorious night. I had an early morning meeting and didn't want to wake you. I'll give you a call later.
Brad
PS – Loved the pajamas. Do you have more where those came from?

Beautiful geisha girl! Wowie! With a smile on my face, I got ready and went to work. Later that afternoon, I called Naomi. She was at the airport waiting for her flight.

'Hello?' she said.

'He's not gay and it's not little,' I said.

'What's not little? Oh wait! No way!' she screamed.

'Way!' I said. 'The pajama thing worked. And I gotta get more! My sex life depends on it.'

'Get more what?' she asked confusedly.

'More pajamas!' I said. 'I need more! I'm going to go to Saks this weekend. I hear they have a stellar lingerie department.'

'Oh I love Saks,' she said.

'Me too! I love sex too!' I said.

'*Saks*. I love *Saks*. Well, sex too, but also Saks,' she said.

'Okay, so I'll keep you posted on my progress,' I said. 'And thanks again for letting me shack up with you at the Plaza.'

'You are welcome,' she said, 'just don't go fallin' in love and forget all about your sugar mama.'

'I won't,' I said.

SEXY SAKSY SLEEPWEAR

The remainder of the week was crazy at work. The show was set to premiere in just two weeks, so the pressure was on all of the producing teams to pump out the best cases that we could. I worked long hours on Thursday and Friday, and had plans to see Brad again Saturday night. So that meant that Saturday was my day to lingerie shop.

I got my hair done at Red Salon again in the morning, and headed out to Saks Fifth Avenue afterward to get started. I was a big fan of the Saks in Chicago, and was sure that the New York original wouldn't let me down. And after another one of those shamporgasms, I was really in the mood!

Just as I suspected, the Saks in New York was amazing.

The first floor was filled with makeup and purses, and the second floor and up was all clothing! Before I headed upstairs to get started, I stopped by my favorite makeup counter, Nars, to get some blush.

I hadn't been to the Nars counter in ages and was delighted to find out that they had many new products. I try to seek out products that say they are one thing but can also be something else. You really get more bang for your buck with those types of things. Which is why I bought an eye shadow/eyeliner called Night Clubbing. It was jet black with a hint of sparkle and even though I doubt I'd wear it to a lot of clubs, it looked cool. I also bought a red stain called Pussycat that could be used on both your lips and your cheeks. However, it worked better on your cheeks when mixed with a bronzing stick called Palm Beach, so I bought one of those too. And since I could also use the bronzing stick on my eyes, it was okay. And to make the stain more versatile for my lips, I bought two lip glosses that changed the color a bit. I got a pink goopy one to tone it down called Baby Doll, and an orange-coral one that brightened it up called Sunset Strip.

I also got something called a Push Eyeliner Brush that helped apply the black eye shadow/eyeliner by pushing it right into my lashes. And I also got some eye makeup remover to help take it off. So with all of that in addition to the basics that I went there to buy, which was really just blush in my favorite color, Desire, the total came to almost $200! It was pricey, but all the stuff would last me a long time.

Not far from the Nars counter was the Clarins counter. And they were giving away a free gift with any purchase over $50. I had been eyeing their Body Lift cream for a while now, ever since I read an article in a magazine that said it really worked. They said that in addition to getting rid of cellulite, it actually took inches off your thighs! And with all the lingerie that I was planning on wearing, I figured now was a perfect time to buy some. And since one bottle was $50, I would be able to get the free gift!

After leaving the Clarins counter, I headed toward the escalator, but I stopped dead in my tracks when I saw the Kiehl's counter. I was running low on two of my favorite hair necessities, the Leave-In Hair Conditioner and Crème with Silk Groom, as well as my favorite lip balm, Lip Balm #1. They ran me about $67, but would last a long time.

After all the distractions, I finally made it up to the floor where the lingerie department was. I started looking around and saw some bras and panties by the designer La Perla. I frequently saw La Perla ads in magazines, so I decided to check them out. After finding a bra that I liked, I was horrified to see that the price was almost $200! I looked at a couple more and discovered that they all were that much! Who in their right mind would spend $200 on a bra? Not me.

I quickly moved on and soon found the nightgown section, because that was what I was there to buy. They had long ones and short ones, cotton ones and silky ones. I liked the way the long ones looked, so I decided to grab a couple of those. As my hands were getting full, a saleslady came up to me and asked me if I needed a fitting room.

'Oh, yes, please,' I said while handing her all my nighties. She led me to a fitting room that she said no one knew about.

'It's huge, and it's hidden away from the others, so it's always empty. You'll love it,' she said.

Once we arrived, I was delighted to see that she was indeed correct. It was enormous, and almost as big as my apartment. Yes, it's a sad day when a fitting room at a department store is as big as your apartment, but I tried not to let it get me down.

As I undressed and started to put on the nightgowns, I imagined myself sashaying around in my fabulous but small New York apartment, looking like Krystle Grant Jennings Carrington or Alexis Morrell Carrington Colby Dexter Rowan. I used to watch a lot of *Dynasty* when I was younger, and always dreamed of looking like those women. Maybe someday someone would even name a perfume after me. I bet all fancy New York women had fancy silk nightgowns like these.

As thoughts of a perfect life filled my head, I slipped an Oscar de la Renta silk nightgown off the hanger and over my head. I adjusted the straps and turned around to look in the mirror and . . . ugh! It looked just horrible! I did not look like Alexis or Krystle. I was too short and my breasts were too small to pull a long nightgown off.

With little hope, I tried the other long nightgowns on as well, and each one brought me the same reaction. Not good. Back to the drawing board.

I gave the long nightgowns back to the saleslady, and she suggested I try younger more hip styles from designers like Only Hearts and Eberjey. With her help, I picked out a cute tie-dyed sheer camisole and brief set, and an orange-and-yellow short nightgown. I also selected some short D&G spaghetti-strap nightgowns.

After a short while, I went back to my favorite hidden fitting room and tried them on. And bingo! She was right. The shorter nightgowns and camisole sets looked so much better on me! After trying them all on, I gave the saleslady two Only Hearts camisole sets and one Eberjey nightgown to hold, and went back out to see what else I could find. I never knew lingerie could be so fun!

After three more trips to the fitting room, I ended up also giving the saleslady a D&G nightgown, two more short nightgowns and a great camisole/pant set by Josie Natori, and a great bra and panty set from a designer called Princess Tam-Tam. I wasn't there to get bras and panties, but once I saw this set, I just couldn't pass it up! It was periwinkle and had the most beautiful lace stitching I ever saw! And every girl should have at least one nice bra and panty set.

On my way up to the counter to pay, I grabbed a few more black lace boy-cut undies that I knew would look so flattering on my big booty. As the saleslady rang it all up, I tried to add it all up in my head. It couldn't be that much. A few seconds later she was done.

'Okay, the total is $778,' she said.

'How much?' I asked, shocked that it was so expensive.

'$778,' she repeated. 'You had two Only Hearts camisole sets for $72 each, one Eberjey nightgown for $80, one D&G nightgown for $123, one Natori camisole/pant set that was $100, two Natori nightgowns for $50 each, one Princess Tam-Tam bra for $72, one pair of Princess Tam-Tam panties for $42, and three pairs of Wacoal black lace panties for $20 each. That comes to $721. And with tax the total is $778.'

I stood there in awe not knowing what to do. It was expensive, but I had to be honest with myself. I was twenty-seven years old and wasn't going to be a spring chicken much longer. So I needed these nighties to look as sexy as I could because I needed to land a man. So they were kind of like an investment. An investment in my sex life and an investment in my future. Just like my favorite makeup products, they served two purposes. And if they didn't work with Brad, then hopefully they'd work with the next guy.

And how 'out of style' can lingerie really go? Sexy is sexy. Lace panties have been in style forever and weren't going anywhere. These weren't like a trendy top or something. They were pajamas. Lingerie. I'd be able to wear them for seasons. So I needed to chill out and not fret over my $778 lingerie purchase. It was going to be okay. With that, I gladly handed over my Amex card, and a few moments later I was out the door.

On my way home, I passed St Patrick's Cathedral and tried not to look because I didn't want God to know I had sexy lingerie in my Saks bag. It was bad enough that I hadn't been to church much lately. I didn't want him to know I was also having premarital sex. All that 'no going to heaven if you sin' stuff that was drilled into my head during Catholic school really stuck with me.

When I got home, I opened my pajama drawer. There

comes a time in your life when you have to say good-bye to old T-shirts and college sweatshirts that have been masquerading as pajamas for years and make room for more adult stuff. And for me, now was that time. As I cleaned out my drawer, I put the old stuff in a bag and decided to give it to Catholic Charities with hopes that it might help me get back in good with God again. Surely he'd forgive me after I gave my old clothes to people who needed them.

Later that night Brad and I went to dinner, and when he came over afterward I put on the cute tie-dyed Only Hearts camisole set. And it worked. I again got in his pants, and again woke up with a smile on my face.

Over the next two weeks, Brad slept over almost every night. Things were going pretty well between us. And my financial life seemed to be picking up as well. American Express upgraded me to a Gold card. And if they were confident that I could pay it off every month, then so was I! Life was good!

THE BIKINI WAX

The second weekend in September, my dad came to visit me. He arrived on Friday afternoon, and I left work early so we could get an early start on our weekend of sightseeing. Well, that and we had to eat 'supper' by 5.00 P.M. because he has a bad case of indigestion. My dad is relatively conservative. He is big on having a savings account. So just to appease him, I got myself one. There wasn't any money in it, but I had one.

Despite not knowing the city all that well, I think I did a fine job being tour guide that weekend. In addition to taking him to all the basic New York landmarks, I took him to a few of my favorites as well! Like SoHo for some great shopping, and Madison Avenue for some more great shopping! And it was there that we experienced what would become my second New York celebrity sighting: Ted Danson walking into Barneys. Sam Malone himself!

On Sunday, we visited the famous St Patrick's Cathedral, and actually attended mass there. I was kind of afraid to enter for fear of being struck down by God, but then I remembered that he forgives people's sins.

All in all, my dad seemed to enjoy his visit, but he had a couple of concerns about New Yorkers. For one, he wondered why no one talked to each other in public places, like on the train for example. When you are from the Midwest, you talk to everyone, I guess. I know I do. But in New York people didn't do that so much.

'Everyone just sits there and puts their Walkmans on, and no one says anything to each other,' he said. I told him that I thought it was a safety thing.

Another thing that bothered him was the phrase 'on line.' In the Midwest, when people go to the store, for example, they wait 'in line' to pay. But for some reason, everywhere you go in New York people always say 'on line.' 'Please wait on line for your tickets.' Or, 'You have to stand on line to pay for those.' This is incorrect and I shared this concern with my dad.

On Monday morning, I bid him farewell and he left to go back home. As I got ready for work I tried to look extra special because it was a special day for me both professionally and personally. It was the premiere of *Curtis Court* and the staff was having a party in the studio. And I also decided that today was the day that I was going to explore a new area of personal hygiene: the bikini wax.

The bikini wax was something I had read a lot about lately, and I had never gotten one before. It seemed to be something that all New York women did. And every salon from hair salons to nail salons offered them. After asking my friend Tracy in Los Angeles and Naomi in Chicago about them, I still was unsure about what to expect. So I decided to just go for the gusto and made an appointment at a salon uptown.

As I sat in the studio during our party and listened to boss after boss make speeches, all I could think about was my appointment. Like a hair salon, I didn't really know where to go. I read about a place called J. Sisters but couldn't get an appointment there quickly enough. So I went to a place that I found in the phone book. I would never do this for my hair, but unlike a bad haircut or color, a bad bikini wax could be hidden.

Later that afternoon, I went to a small salon on the Upper East Side owned by a Russian woman. I walked in and told them my name at the front desk, and waited patiently on a bench to be called into the back for my wax. The salon was rather barren (excuse the pun), and there was no big waiting room or anything. While sitting on the bench waiting to be called, I could see into the back of the salon. It looked like each 'waxing station' was separated by those fake wall partitions, kind of like office cubicles. In fact, I bet the company that makes these cubicle walls could market them specifically to waxing salons as 'pubicle cubicles.' My guess is that it's an untapped market and they'd make a fortune.

Anyway, the waxing seemed to be taking place in these pubicle cubicles, just like my cube at work. Except the walls were high. Could you imagine if they weren't?

'Hey there,' I'd say to the woman next to me, 'looks like you are overdue for your wax. What are you getting done today? A Brazilian?'

'Yeah,' she'd say. 'Gosh, I just love what they did to yours. What is that, a French wax? Say, bikini wax technician, could you make mine look like hers? Do you think that style would look right on me? I just love the way it looks on her.'

But the walls of the pubicle cubicles were high, so we didn't have to worry about any unnecessary conversation. A few moments later, a woman appeared holding a piece of paper.

'Karreen?' she said, rolling the *r*. I stood up.

'Right dees way,' she said.

I followed the woman to my assigned pubicle cubicle, and

a few seconds later my bikini wax technician arrived. She appeared to be Russian also, but she didn't have an accent like the lady that brought me back here. She told me to get naked from the waist down and lie on the table. There's nothing like getting right to it, I guess. I did what she said and took off my pants and underwear, and was careful to hide my underwear under my pants so they couldn't be seen. I read in a magazine somewhere that all women do this and hide their underwear when they go to the doctor or the tanning salon or something. And it was true, at least for me.

Once I was naked, I hopped up on a massage table of sorts and the bikini wax technician, or whatever her real title was, came over to me. I didn't want to tell her it was my first time, but by the frightened look on her face I could tell she knew.

'Have you ever been here before?' she asked.

'No. This is actually my first time,' I said. 'It's actually my first bikini wax ever.'

'Oh, well, don't worry. It'll be a breeze,' she said. 'What kind of wax do you want?'

'Um, a bikini wax?' I said, thinking it was quite obvious since I was lying buck-naked on a massage table.

'Yes, I know that, what kind of bikini wax?' she asked.

'What kind? Oh, sorry. I guess a Brazilian. Is that where you take it all off?'

'No, a Brazilian is where we leave a little at the top,' she said.

'Okay, well, I want that,' I said. I was nervous.

'Okay,' she said. As I laid there quietly in my cubicle, she started to pour semi-hot wax on my pubicle.

'Damn, I could pitch a tent and go camping down here,' she said, laughing.

'Well, I've never had a wax before,' I said, embarrassed.

'Ahh, I'm just giving you a hard time,' she said. 'You'll be fine, just relax.'

Just then the phone rang. And she answered it. I figured

that she'd wait until she was off the phone to continue, but she just kept on pouring. Then she took a linen cloth strip and pressed it into the wax.

'Doug, I told you that I'd be home in time to make dinner,' she said to the person on the phone. 'I just don't know what you—'

Rip!

She pulled the cloth strip up while still on the phone. And with it came half my pubicle. Oh it hurt!

'—want me to make,' she continued. She then pressed the cloth back down into the wax. 'I could make, hold on—'

Rip!

Again she pulled the cloth strip up. Holy sweet Jesus this was painful!

'—steak or something. Do you want that?' she said. I couldn't believe she was giving me a bikini wax while talking to someone on the phone about what to make for dinner.

'Okay, well, I'll call you back when I'm done,' she said. She then hung up the phone.

'Sorry,' she said to me. 'My husband isn't sure what he wants for dinner.'

'No problem,' I said.

As she continued to pour and pull, her fingers went places where only a few doctors and boyfriends have gone before. When she was done, I just laid there with my mouth slightly open, unable to talk.

'Flip over,' she said.

'What?' I asked.

'Flip over. I'm gonna do your butt,' she said.

'My butt?' I asked. 'Why my butt?'

'Oh, don't worry, everyone gets their butt done,' she said.

'Okay,' I said, kind of freaked out. 'I don't really have a hairy butt or anything though.' I turned over and laid on my stomach.

'That's what they all think. Don't lay on your stomach, get on all fours,' she said.

All fours, was she crazy? What am I a dog? But I did what she said.

'Oh, sorry,' I said, getting up on my knees.

With her two hands, she spread my cheeks apart and poured hot wax in. I seriously couldn't imagine doing what she does for a living. And just like on the front side, she pushed the cloth strip into the wax on one of my cheeks and pulled.

Rip!

Oh my gosh! It was just as painful. She proceeded to do the other cheek as well, and when she was done, she took the white cloth and shoved it in front of my face to show me.

'See, that's from your ass,' she said. 'Do you want me to throw it away, or do you want to save it to knit a sweater?' she asked, laughing again. I bet she used these same jokes on everybody.

'No, you can throw it away,' I said, completely shocked. She then wrote up a slip for me and left the room while I got dressed. I looked down at my newly waxed pubicle and wondered what the purpose of a little strip of hair, which was the signature of the Brazilian, was. It looked like a small landing strip.

While ringing me up, the woman at the front desk encouraged me to buy something called Tend Skin, which she said would stop a rash from occurring. Eww. The bikini wax was $60 and the Tend Skin was $20, and I figured I'd better tip the bikini wax technician 20 percent, so my total came to $92. Wow. Pricey.

When I got back to work, it was very difficult for me to be productive for the rest of the afternoon. All I thought about was 'down there.' And every time someone looked at me, I wondered if they knew what was going on 'down there.' And thoughts of 'down there' soon led to thoughts of sex and then it was just a lost cause. I packed up early and went home.

That evening, I went to see Sam, my trainer, who was happy at my progress so far. It was also time for me to renew my sessions, so I bought ten more. We sort of developed a brother-sister relationship, which he said frequently happens with his female clients. I asked him if he would cat-sit for me for an upcoming weekend, because I had to go out of town for my sister's thirtieth birthday party, and he said yes.

Brad came over that night, and we stayed up late to watch the premiere of *Curtis Court.* We had a really bad time slot in New York, so the show didn't air until 1.00 A.M. Brad said he liked it, but I wasn't sure if he was telling me the truth or just being nice. Later that night, however, I was *sure* he was telling me the truth when he said that he loved the bikini wax. It was a big hit! Upon falling asleep, I quietly thanked the bikini wax technician, or whatever her title was, for a job well done. Despite the bad jokes, phone calls, and slipping fingers, she did a fine job! Hail to bikini wax technicians everywhere! You are appreciated!

SIX

AMERICAN EXPRESS

® **American Express**

Karyn Bosnak
400 E. 57th St.
New York, NY 10010

Date	Payee	Amount
	PREVIOUS BALANCE	$ 4,994,00
Sep 29, 2000	Bergdorf Goodman – Jay Strongwater	$ 378.00
Oct 1, 2000	United Airlines – LAX to GRB	$ 271.00
Oct 16, 2000	Manhattan Transit Authority	$ 60.00
Oct 21, 2000	Red Salon – Hair	$ 318.00
Oct 23, 2000	Crunch	$ 900.00
Oct 24, 2000	Elena's Salon – Wax	$ 102.00
Oct 25, 2000	Bloomingdale's – Coach	$ 540.00
Oct 25, 2000	Bloomingdale's – BCBG Handbags	$ 229.00
Oct 26, 2000	Bloomingdale's – Coach	– $ 540.00
Oct 26, 2000	Bloomingdale's – BCBG Handbags	$ 253.00
Oct 28, 2000	Bloomingdale's – Fendi Handbags	$ 810.00
Oct 29, 2000	Bloomingdale's – Fendi Handbags	– $ 810.00
	PAYMENT	– $ 1,200.00
	Total	**$ 6,305.00**

American Express

Karyn Bosnak
400 E. 57th St.
New York, NY 10010

Date	Payee	Amount
	PREVIOUS BALANCE	$ 6,305,00
Nov 4, 2000	Bloomingdale's – Theory	$ 428.00
Nov 5, 2000	Bloomingdale's – Theory	– $ 256.00
Nov 11, 2000	Bloomingdale's – French Connection	$ 520.00
Nov 12, 2000	Bloomingdale's – French Connection	– $ 315.00
Nov 13, 2000	Manhattan Transit Authority	$ 60.00
Nov 16, 2000	Bloomingdale's	$ 594.00
Nov 19, 2000	Bergdorf Goodman	$ 291.00
Nov 21, 2000	Bloomingdale's – DKNY Coats	$ 1,080.00
Nov 22, 2000	Bloomingdale's – DKNY Coats	– $ 1,080.00
Nov 22, 2000	Bloomingdale's – Anne Klein Coats	$ 648.00
Nov 22, 2000	Bloomingdale's – Winter Accessories	$ 86.00
Nov 27, 2000	Crunch	$ 900.00
	PAYMENTS	– $ 1,200.00
	Total	**$ 8,061.00**

American Express

Karyn Bosnak
400 E. 57th St.
New York, NY 10010

Date	Payee	Amount
	PREVIOUS BALANCE	$ 8,061.00
Dec 2, 2000	Bloomingdale's – Karen Kane	$ 351.00
Dec 2, 2000	Bloomingdale's – Greg Norman	$ 162.00
Dec 4, 2000	Elena's Salon	$ 102.00
Dec 9, 2000	Red Salon	$ 318.00
Dec 9, 2000	Bergdorf Goodman – DKNY	$ 297.00
Dec 11, 2000	Manhattan Transit Authority	$ 60.00
Dec 16, 2000	United Airlines – LGA to ORD	$ 220.00
Dec 16, 2000	United Airlines – ORD to RSW	$ 230.00
Dec 16, 2000	Alamo Car Rental	$ 266.00
Dec 19, 2000	Saks Fifth Avenue – Movado Watches	$ 1,296.00
Dec 20, 2000	Saks Fifth Avenue – Movado Watches	– $ 1,296.00
	Total	**$ 10,067.00**

Karyn Bosnak
400 E. 57th St.
New York, NY 10010

Date	Payee	Amount
	PREVIOUS BALANCE	$ 1,835.00
Oct 12, 2000	Late Charge	$ 25.00
Oct 12, 2000	Finance Charge	$ 37.00
	Total	**$ 1,897.00**

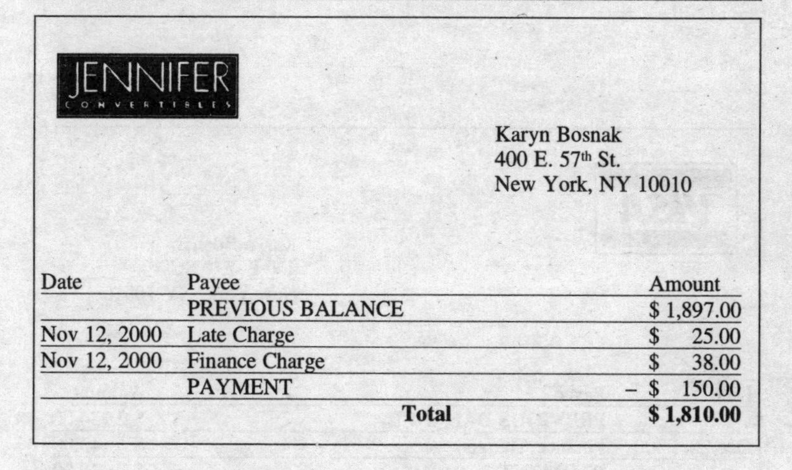

Karyn Bosnak
400 E. 57th St.
New York, NY 10010

Date	Payee	Amount
	PREVIOUS BALANCE	$ 1,897.00
Nov 12, 2000	Late Charge	$ 25.00
Nov 12, 2000	Finance Charge	$ 38.00
	PAYMENT	– $ 150.00
	Total	**$ 1,810.00**

Marshall Field's

Karyn Bosnak
400 E. 57th St.
New York, NY 10010

Date	Payee	Amount
	PREVIOUS BALANCE	$ 324.00
Dec 5, 2000	Finance Charge	$ 6.00
	PAYMENT	– $ 20.00
	Total	**$ 310.00**

MasterCard

Karyn Bosnak
400 E. 57th St.
New York, NY 10010

Date	Payee	Amount
	PREVIOUS BALANCE	$ 897.00
Dec 15, 2000	Finance Charge	$ 18.00
	PAYMENT	– $ 40.00
	Total	**$ 875.00**

VISA

Karyn Bosnak
400 E. 57th St.
New York, NY 10010

Date	Payee	Amount
	PREVIOUS BALANCE	$ 2,134.00
Dec 20, 2000	Finance Charge	$ 43.00
	PAYMENT	– $ 70.00
	Total	**$ 2,107.00**

Grand Debt Tally $15,169.00

PUFF DADDY & PUFFY ME

Despite high hopes, *Curtis Court* didn't premiere with stellar ratings. The show did okay in some markets, but poorly in the big three, which were New York, Los Angeles and Chicago. And those really were the markets that counted. *Curtis Court* wasn't a bad show by any means. I think the court show genre was just overloaded at the moment. In addition to *Curtis Court*, there were eight other court shows on the air, with *Judge Judy* leading the pack. Every day we all waited for the ratings, and every day they were the same.

In television there are periods called sweeps, which occur every November, February, and May. During these months, shows air their best episodes and the ratings are scrutinized. Since most companies decide by December if they are going to renew a show for another season, November sweeps are crucial. And with *Curtis Court* on the edge of having decent ratings, even just a slight bump up in the numbers would be good.

Despite things at work getting crazy, I went out of town the first weekend in October for my sister's thirtieth birthday party. The whole family and a few friends met in Green Bay, Wisconsin, for a Green Bay Packers versus Chicago Bears football game. Things don't get any more Midwestern than that.

My sister wore cheese on her head, and my mom wore green and yellow beads around her neck. And me, well I'm not much of a football fan, so I wore my Gucci sunglasses and people-watched. For added excitement, I gave my sister's friend Kathy a makeover during halftime. I showed her how easy it was to make her lips look fuller with lip liner. No need for collagen injections when you have a good liner!

For her birthday, I bought my sister the most beautiful picture frame at Bergdorf Goodman. I wanted to get her something special that she would always have, and the saleslady told me that this was the perfect gift. A guy named Jay Strongwater, who designed a whole collection of them, designed the frame. Some have precious stones in them, and others have enamel inlays. They look like little pieces of jewelry. The frame measured about two inches by two inches and was perfect for a small photo. At $350 it was pricey, but it was her thirtieth birthday and she deserved it. And they put it in such a cute box and wrapped it so nicely!

When I got back on Monday, the November sweeps pressure had officially begun, and work became pretty intense as the pressure rose. I started working late and put in a few weekends. I even booked a great case that got a bit of press. The case involved two girls who were suing a dance club in New York called Club New York. Club New York was the club that became famous after being the scene of the Puff Daddy–Jennifer Lopez shooting. The two girls were at the club the night the shooting occurred, and claimed that their fur coats were stolen from the coatroom after chaos erupted. All the other court shows were trying to book the case, and I beat them to the punch and they appeared on *Curtis Court*. Puff Daddy didn't come, but we got a little press nonetheless, and that made my boss happy.

The more I worked, the less I saw Brad. And one day, he just never called again. Seriously. That's what happened. There was no big blowup. There was no big breakup. One day I just realized that I hadn't seen him or talked to him in weeks. I was sad, but I pushed any feelings I had toward the back of my mind because I needed to concentrate on work.

November finally rolled around, and the staff patiently awaited the ratings every day. And each day we got the same news: there was no big improvement in the numbers. The show wasn't bad enough to be canceled immediately, but it wasn't good enough to be automatically renewed for another season either. So despite the less-than-stellar ratings, we continued to try to save *Curtis Court*, the little court show that could.

Feeling sad on my way home from work one night, I stopped by Bloomingdale's to see what I could find. I needed a little pick-me-up, and some new face lotion was just what I was looking for. Maybe I was working too many hours, or maybe it was the cool November air, but whatever it was, something was making my skin look not so radiant. And looking not so radiant made me feel not so radiant.

While walking through the cosmetics department, I stopped by the La Prairie counter. I knew their cosmetics were super expensive, but I figured that must be the case because they worked. A plump, feminine-looking man was standing behind the counter.

'Hello,' he said to me in a very high pitched voice as I walked up. 'What can I help you with today?'

'Well,' I started, 'my skin looks just horrible lately, and I don't know what to do about it. It just feels dry and is puffy and doesn't glow like it used to.'

'I can see,' he said. He could? I thought only I noticed it. I instantly became incredibly worried.

'What should I do? Do I need an exfoliant? A lotion?'

'Well, the first thing I would start with is an eye cream, because you are starting to get wrinkles,' he said.

'I am?!' I shrieked. 'Where?'

'Oh, yes, honey, fine lines,' he said, turning a magnifying mirror toward me, 'look.' I looked into the mirror and saw that he was indeed correct. I had fine lines around my eyes. This could very well be the worst day of my life, I thought.

'These are the first wrinkles I've ever seen on my face,' I said with tears in my eyes. 'I don't even lay out. I'm always really good about protecting my skin. How could this happen?'

'Oh, honey, it happens to the best of us,' he said, sticking out his hand for me to shake. 'My name is Francis.'

'Hi, Francis,' I said. 'My name is Karyn.'

'Well, Karyn, don't worry, dear. We're going to stop those wrinkles dead in their tracks and do something to help your lackluster appearance.'

'My lackluster appearance?' I asked.

'Honey, you are the one who said it, not me. I just pointed out your wrinkles. We're going to fix it all though, don't worry.'

For the next hour, I listened as Francis explained all the La Prairie products to me and told me how they'd help my skin. He even gave me a mini-facial. According to him, I needed the eye cream, the face cream, the age-defying serum, and the gentle nonabrasive exfoliant. That would be good to start anyway. I decided to go for the gusto and buy the four products, because I had to feel pretty again. Feeling pretty was important to me. It did wonders for the self-confidence. And even after the mini-facial alone, I felt better. So I could imagine how great I'd feel and look after using the products every day.

I handed over my Amex to Francis and told him I'd take the four products. It was an investment in my face. And a good face is priceless. And everyone knows that good skin when you are older starts with taking care of it while you are younger. And I was younger now. The products came to a whopping $594 with tax. I could barely look as I signed the receipt. But I was on my way to glowing again. And I needed to glow.

FLOATING CHECKS

Before I knew it, it was Thanksgiving. Thanksgiving's not a huge holiday in my family, so I decided not to go home. I actually hadn't been to a Thanksgiving dinner with my family in years. Ever since my Aunt Marge made moldy pie, in fact.

Aunt Marge is my great-aunt, and every year since I was

little, I would always look forward to her cherry pie on Thanksgiving. The whole family would. But then one year Aunt Marge cut her finger off while mowing the lawn. And ever since then, the pie making took a serious hit. Every year after that it tasted worse and worse, but I ate it. And finally one year, I bit into a nice piece of the pie and it didn't taste so good. At the same time, my mom was in the kitchen and realized that the pie was moldy. Poor Aunt Marge had made it too early and let it sit on her windowsill for a week. And poor Karyn felt ill for days. That was my last Thanksgiving with the family. Every Thanksgiving after that I spent with Naomi and her family.

But this year I decided to spend Thanksgiving with a college friend who now lived in New York. His name was Pearce, and we lived in the same dorm our freshman year. I recently got back in touch with him when I heard that he also lived in New York. Pearce is famous. Well, at least I think so. He designs doorknobs, but they are super-expensive doorknobs for the rich and famous. And recently he appeared on *Martha Stewart Living*. (Okay, maybe just the back of his head was on TV as she got a tour through the studio where he worked, but still . . .)

I was supposed to meet Pearce and a couple of his friends at a restaurant in Greenwich Village called Ye Waverly Inn. I called ahead and found out that it was a prix-fixe dinner at $75 a person. So I figured with drinks it would cost me around $125. That Monday, I went to the bank and realized that I only had about $50 in my account. I took it out and didn't know where I was going to get the rest of the money. I didn't go through the hassle of getting the Gift Cheques again, because all I needed was about $75. And I was going to get paid on Wednesday, but the money wouldn't be available for me to take until Friday, because Thursday was a holiday. So I was screwed. Until I remembered that I could write a check at the local Food Emporium grocery store for $25 over the amount of whatever I bought.

So after a little planning in my head, this is what I did: On Monday night, I went to the store and bought a pack of gum. When I got to the counter, I paid for the gum with a check for $25 over. The total came to $26.08. On Tuesday, I did the same thing. And then on Wednesday I did the same thing again, and now had $75 in my pocket. That plus the $50 from before would get me through Thanksgiving.

But I also got paid on Wednesday, and deposited my check as soon as I got it. I knew the checks that I wrote at the grocery store wouldn't go through until at least Friday, and by that time the first $100 from my paycheck would be available and would cover them. So I was set!

Because I didn't buy a plane ticket home, I splurged on a nice new outfit for Thanksgiving. And for a little change in scenery, I went to Bergdorf Goodman to buy it. It was so pretty! It was a green silk Cynthia Rowley button-down shirt-dress, and I wore it over a pair of black tight pants with my rhinestone belt. I was a big fan of the shirt-dress. It's just a dress that buttons down the front and they're just so cute! I now had two of them.

The food at Ye Waverly Inn was okay, but you just can't beat a home-cooked meal. Well, you just can't beat a home-cooked meal minus the moldy pie. The turkey was a bit dry, and the potatoes didn't have lumps in them, but it was okay.

Throughout dinner, Pearce and I reminisced about old college times. He reminded me of the time we ran naked through Frat Park, and the time my cat accidentally caught on fire while walking too close to an open flame. (I'll be honest – it wasn't a candle. His roommate was lighting a fart on fire and the cat got too close. The little bugger ended up fine though, just had some singed whiskers – so don't worry.) He also reminded me of the time that I spent my tuition money on clothes.

'Oh my gosh, I forgot about that!' I said.

'How could you forget? You almost couldn't enroll the next semester because you hadn't yet paid your tuition,' he said.

He was right. My mom sent a check made out to me (big mistake) for my tuition, which was about $1,700 a semester. My bank account just so happened to be overdrawn at the time, so I couldn't turn around and write a check to the university for $1,700 because it would have bounced, so I just left it in my checking account until I was able to pay it. But as time went by the $1,700 turned into $1,600. And soon enough the $1,600 turned into even less. Then one day shortly thereafter, I saw that one of my favorite clothing stores was having a big sale, and I spent the rest of it on clothes. I thought that I'd figure out a way to make the $1,700 back before the next semester, and even got myself a job to help do so.

But before I knew it, the next semester rolled around and I didn't have any money. So my mom sent me money for that semester's tuition, and I used it to pay off the previous semester's tuition, and it was a never-ending cycle. I finally graduated, but I was unable to receive my actual diploma because I didn't pay my final semester's tuition. When my mom asked where my diploma was, I told her that it got lost in the mail and I had to order a new one. A year later, the school finally ended up sending me to a collection agency, and I paid the $1,700 back. It was then that I, Karyn Bosnak, finally received my college diploma. You'd think I would have learned my lesson, but I didn't.

Pearce was also actually the first person who told me about how easy it was to get a credit card. I remember when we were freshmen, I wanted a pair of $250 Revo sunglasses. Remember those? Anyway, I didn't have enough money for them, and I wanted them really badly.

'Why don't you get a credit card?' he said.

'How can I get one of those?' I asked.

'Anyone can get one. You can go sign up at a booth

in the quad. You can even get a free T-shirt,' he said, laughing.

'Really?' I asked.

'Yeah,' he said. 'And then you can get them and only have to pay $38 a month or so.'

'It's kind of like layaway, but you get to take the stuff home!' I said with excitement.

'Exactly,' he answered.

So I got a credit card, and I bought the sunglasses. Well, I charged them. And since then, I've always sort of looked at a credit card as a means to acquire things that I wasn't able to afford.

The total for dinner came to about $116 each, and I had just enough money to cover it. Afterward, I bid my farewell to Pearce and his friends and decided to go home to get a nice night's sleep. I had a busy weekend ahead of me. I was completely behind in my 'Buy and Return Credit Payment Management Plan,' as I now liked to call it, and needed to do some serious catching up.

ALL I WANT FOR CHRISTMAS . . .

While the Buy and Return Credit Payment Management Plan seemed like a good idea initially, it was sort of spiraling out of control very quickly. My monthly payment to American Express got less and less, as more payments in everyday life started to pop up.

For one, I now had to make monthly payments to Jennifer Convertibles for the couch I bought. And I was a few months behind, so I had to send them almost $150 just to catch up. And while they were really eager to tell me about the no payment/no interest for three months, they forgot to tell me that the interest would be 24 percent when it did kick in. Yes, maybe I should have read it myself, but I didn't. Even after I sent in the $150 payment, the balance was still higher than it was when I bought the couch because of late fees.

And while I might have said that my American Express card was the only credit card that I had when I moved to New York, I should have rephrased that as the only credit card that I had that was open with credit on it when I moved to New York. I had three other cards, a Visa, a MasterCard, and a Marshall Field's card, and I closed them before I moved, but still owed money on them. The total balance of those was about $3,100, and the monthly payments were about $150. It wasn't much, but it was still $150. And for some reason, I had a real problem paying them all of a sudden.

And with my monthly trips to the hair salon, and my regular bikini wax visits, and weekly manicures and pedicures, things really started to add up. I also had my cell phone bill and my cable bill.

Also, I never seemed to be able to return as much stuff as I bought while on the plan. And with that problem, the whole thing seemed to do more harm than good. I would always bring things home and realize that they were just too cute to take back.

For example, on a recent excursion, I bought a $1,000 winter coat. When I got it home I hung it in my closet, and like I said I would, I took it back the next day. But the next day when I returned it, I saw a $600 coat that I really, really liked. So after returning the other one, I bought the $600 one and kept it. If I wasn't there returning the $1,000 coat, then I wouldn't have seen the $600 coat and therefore wouldn't have bought it. And then I had to get gloves and a hat to match too.

Another time when I was in the purse section buying a nice $500 Coach purse that I was going to return, the friendly saleslady told me about how Friends & Family Day was coming up. And then, just to be nice, she gave me her discount card so that I too could save 15 percent on all my purchases. And it just so happened that right behind me was a super-cute brown leather BCBG purse with fringe that I had been eyeing for $250. But with her Friends & Family Day coupon the purse was only $212, and I couldn't pass that up. It just had so much character!

So the next day, when I returned the $500 Coach purse, I realized that my Friends & Family Day coupon was still valid, and so I bought a very practical black leather BCBG bowling bag. And that was something I could use every day.

Another downfall of the Buy and Return Credit Payment Management Plan was that the salespeople at Bloomingdale's were starting to recognize me and I was afraid that any day they would catch on to my plan, and somehow I'd be forbidden to shop at Bloomingdale's forever.

But the biggest problem with the Buy and Return Credit Payment Management Plan was that it seemed to really throw my perception off about what is expensive and what isn't expensive. When you buy a coat at $1,000 and return it, one at $600 seems like a steal. The same thing happened with purses. Compared to a $750 Fendi, the $212 BCBG one was a bargain.

I needed an intervention. I needed all this buying and returning to stop. I needed someone to save me. What I needed was another credit card. Not so I could buy more stuff, but so I could take out a cash advance and pay all of this horrendous American Express balance off. A balance that had grown to over $8,000. All I could afford to pay this month was $1,000, and buying and returning $7,000 worth of stuff seemed crazy. I didn't know if even I could do it.

Yes, all I wanted for Christmas was another credit card. A normal credit card this time, not one of these 'charge cards' wannabes. I mean what really is the purpose of that anyway? If I *had* the money to pay for all the things I was buying then I wouldn't have to 'charge' them now, would I?

And just like when God was listening to me when I needed to find a place to get my hair done, God was listening to me now too. When I got my mail that Saturday, I saw it: an envelope from Platinum Discover Card with a big stamp on the outside that said 'Pre-Approved.' I opened it up and saw that it was true. I had been pre-approved with a credit line of $7,500! The letter said, 'Transfer all your balances and get an APR of only 7% for the first three months.' Thank you, God! I quickly filled out all the paperwork and sent it back to Discover. I sure hoped it worked and that the 'Pre-Approved' envelope wasn't a mistake.

A NEW YEAR'S RESOLUTION

In the beginning of December, things started to lighten up at work. The November sweeps pressure was finally off, and I started to go out a bit more. Ann Marie and I had become better friends and we started to go out sometimes after work. Through her I met a couple of guys, but nothing really panned out with any of them.

I also finally met my mom's friend Pandy's son for coffee. And my mom was actually on target with this one. He *was* good-looking. His name was Jon and he was gorgeous! John F. Kennedy Jr gorgeous! But after our brief coffee date, I never heard from him again. They can't all fall in love with me, I guess.

We also had our work Christmas party, and it was super boring. The best part of the night was my new black DKNY dress that I'd bought at Bergdorf, and watching my associate producer Betsy get drunk and sing 'Last Dance' by Donna Summer on the stage. I think she was hoping to be discovered by some big King World hotshot. But the only thing that everyone discovered was that she was a very bad drunk, and a very bad singer.

The week before Christmas I went to Naples, Florida. My mom and stepdad have a house there and Naomi was supposed to come and meet me, but at the last minute she had to cancel, so I ended up going by myself. It was actually kind of nice.

Naples isn't a big party town or anything, and all I really wanted to do was relax, so every day I did just that – relax.

Let's just say that I relaxed until I remembered that I still had $3,000 worth of stuff to buy and return. The Buy and Return Credit Payment Management Plan had really taken over my life. It was all that I did. Since I was still waiting to hear if I was approved to receive my Discover Card, I still had to keep current with my payments. Of that $7,000 I needed to buy and return, I successfully did $4,000 of it while still in New York, and had $3,000 left to go for this month. The good thing about Naples was it had a lot of malls with stores that I had never been to before.

The first place I went to was Saks Fifth Avenue. After looking around for a while, I noticed that they didn't have as many high-priced items as the Saks in New York. They didn't have a winter coat section, or a big selection of BCBG or Theory clothes. So I decided that the best thing for me to buy was jewelry. And I decided to buy a watch. A nice watch.

I found the watch counter and started to look around. And some of the watches were really nice. After deciding on a nice gold Movado watch, I flagged down the saleslady and told her that I wanted to purchase it. The total came to $1,296. I was almost halfway there. I decided that I'd do the second half of the buy and return tomorrow, and my watch and I went home. That night I rented movies and lay by the pool.

The next day I went to Saks and told the cashier that I accidentally bought the wrong watch for my boyfrind. Oops. Silly me. Screwed up. But the return wasn't as easy as I thought it would be. Apparently, when you buy a really nice watch, they have to call it in and check serial numbers and stuff. So I was at the store for almost forty-five minutes. Finally, they approved my return, and I vowed never to buy a watch at Saks again unless I intended to keep it.

After leaving Saks, I moseyed into the mall and saw a

Banana Republic store. I noticed that they seemed to be having a big sale toward the back of the store, and decided to check it out. And it was there that I saw the cutest black leather jacket ever, for only $100! Now that's a bargain! I found my size and took it up to the counter, along with some other great bargains, to pay. I'll admit that I wasn't planning on returning any of it. It was all just too cute.

After the saleslady rang up my items, I handed over my American Express card to pay. She ran it through and told me that there was some sort of a problem.

'What do you mean, some sort of a problem?' I asked. I had never had a problem with my American Express card before.

'I don't know,' she replied. 'The computer is telling me to call the company.'

'Okay, well, can you call them?' I asked. I was sort of embarrassed because there was a big line of people behind me. It was the holidays, after all. The woman then dialed the number and was put on hold immediately. Fifteen minutes later, an operator finally picked up her call.

'Hi, this is Sara at Banana Republic,' she said. 'I have a customer in front of me who just gave me an American Express and an error message came up and I was told to call the company.' I listened while Sara gave the operator the error number and my full name and credit card number. After a couple of minutes she told me that the operator wanted to talk to me.

'Okay,' I said awkwardly as I grabbed the phone. I noticed that the people behind me were watching and listening.

'Hi, Miss Bosnak?' a woman said to me on the phone.

'Yes,' I answered. I was scared. Maybe they caught on to my Buy and Return Credit Payment Management Plan.

'Right, you are over your limit and we have to cut you off,' she said.

'Over my limit?' I asked. 'But I have a Gold card. I didn't think that I had a limit.'

'Yes, you do, and it's $10,000,' she said.

'How am I supposed to know there is a limit if no one tells me? It's not on my statement. And I actually know for a fact that I'm only up to $8,000,' I said.

'No, you aren't. You were actually at $11,200 until you returned something for $1,200 earlier today,' she said. 'I don't even know how you were allowed to charge it that high because you have a limit.'

'Oh,' I said, stunned. 'I see. Well, can't you just let this one little charge go through? It's only a couple hundred dollars.' I looked at the black leather jacket lying on the counter. It was so cute and such a great deal. I'd never be able to find another one like it.

'No, I'm sorry, but I can't,' she said.

"Okay,' I said. 'Thanks.' I handed the phone back to the saleslady.

'I've been cut off,' I said to her quietly. 'I'm sorry.'

'It's okay,' she said. She was nice. 'Do you have another way that you want to pay? Another card or something?'

'No,' I said. 'I'm just going to pass on these items. Thanks, though.' The truth was, I didn't have any money. I was flat broke. I had fifty bucks in my wallet, and still had three days left in Florida. I walked out of the store with my head down. I have never been so embarrassed.

For the rest of the week all I did was lay by the pool and eat Ritz crackers that I found in the pantry. For a treat, I topped them off with a hunk of cheddar cheese that I found in the freezer. I definitely relaxed because I didn't have any money to do anything else. But I worried. I worried about what I was going to do about that bill. I owed $10,000 to American Express. What was I thinking? Seriously, I needed to get a grasp on this. I had been in New York for just over six months and I had gone hog-wild. I needed to figure something out. I needed to exert some self-control. At the end of the week, I flew back to Chicago with $5 in my pocket. My mother picked me up at the airport.

* * *

Christmas was glorious and it was nice to see my family. I tried not to think about the $10,000 and just enjoy my time home.

Since my parents are divorced, my sister and I split up the holidays between the two houses. We spent Christmas Eve at my dad's house, with my uncle, cousins, and Grandma, who was wearing her new 'Heart of the Ocean' jewelry set that she recently bought off television. And we spent Christmas Day at my mom's house. Each year, my sister and I alternate buying the gifts for my parents, and then split the cost, and this year was my year to buy. For my mom, I bought a pretty Karen Kane outfit that cost $350, and for my dad, I bought two Greg Norman golf shirts for around $150. I bought them in New York, and charged them before I was cut off. When I tried to collect my sister's half of the money, she explained to me that she was not happy with me, and yelled saying that I'm never allowed to buy the gifts again because I spent too much money.

'But Mom's outfit is pretty,' I said defensively.

'It's a pair of pants and a shirt, Karyn,' she replied. 'I can't believe you spent $350 on *that.* And Dad didn't need *two* Greg Norman golf shirts last night either. One would have been fine. I don't know what I was thinking letting you buy the gifts in New York anyway.'

'I'm sorry,' I said. 'But I really need your half of the money.' She just looked at me and walked away.

A little while later, we went to my aunt's house, where my Aunt Marge was. But thankfully, she didn't make pies this Christmas. And finally, we finished off the day at my grandpa's house. My grandpa is my mom's dad and he was born in Ireland. He has been married three times and now lives with his new girlfriend. Christmas at Grandpa's is always fun because my mom has eight brothers and sisters. In order, their names are Patsy, KC (my mom), Billy, Michael, Arty, Carol, Jimmy, Rory and Roby. And everyone comes to

Christmas at Grandpa's house. Well, everyone except my Uncle Jimmy because he's a Jehovah's Witness now. And, in typical Irish Catholic fashion, every aunt, uncle and cousin has been married and divorced at least once. So every year there are always some new relatives hanging around.

While at Grandpa's, I finally convinced my sister to pay me for half of the gifts, and vowed never to spend that much money again. She forgave me.

The following day, I flew back to New York and settled back into my apartment. While I was gone, Sam had watched Elvis for me. I was so happy to see that he was alive and well.

That night, after I put all my stuff away, I settled down to open my mail. And there buried underneath a few bills I saw a blank envelope. I tore at the corner and opened it as quickly as I could. And there it was! My new Platinum Discover Card! It had arrived! Without hesitation, I called to activate it, and then spoke to an operator to transfer over as much of my American Express card balance as was allowed, which was $7,500.

I hung up the phone and got ready for bed. But I didn't fall fast asleep. I just laid there and worried. Yes, Discover accepted my balance transfer, but what if they hadn't? What if I hadn't gotten the card? What would I have done? I couldn't believe that I'd let my credit cards get that far out of control. What would I have done in Florida if I hadn't had that fifty bucks in my wallet? How would I have gotten back to the airport? I was all alone. And what if my sister hadn't paid me for the gifts to teach me a lesson? How would I have gotten back to my apartment from LaGuardia?

I wasn't in Chicago anymore, where I could just call up my mom and she'd rush me $50 or go deposit it in my checking account. I was in New York – a huge city, all alone. I didn't have that many friends yet either who I could borrow money from. And that's embarrassing anyway – to be borrowing money at age twenty-eight.

The most horrible part of all of this was that it only was

going to get worse. At the time I would have told you no way – but it did. That night I laid in bed and swore to myself that I was going to turn this around. My New Year's resolution was to pay off the remaining $2,500 and go back to my original plan to use the card only for emergencies. But I've never been very good at keeping New Year's resolutions . . .

SEVEN

American Express

Karyn Bosnak
400 E. 57th St.
New York, NY 10010

Date	Payee	Amount
	PREVIOUS BALANCE	$ 10,067,00
Jan 19, 2001	Bloomingdale's	$ 750.00
Jan 19, 2001	Bloomingdale's	$ 103.00
	PAYMENT	– $ 7,500.00
	Total	**$ 3,420.00**

JENNIFER CONVERTIBLES

Karyn Bosnak
400 E. 57th St.
New York, NY 10010

Date	Payee	Amount
	PREVIOUS BALANCE	$ 1,810.00
Jan 12, 2001	Finance Charge	$ 36.00
	PAYMENT	– $ 40.00
	Total	**$ 1,806.00**

Marshall Field's

Karyn Bosnak
400 E. 57th St.
New York, NY 10010

Date	Payee	Amount
	PREVIOUS BALANCE	$ 310.00
Jan 5, 2001	Finance Charge	$ 6.00
	PAYMENT	– $ 20.00
	Total	**$ 296.00**

MasterCard

Karyn Bosnak
400 E. 57th St.
New York, NY 10010

Date	Payee	Amount
	PREVIOUS BALANCE	$ 875.00
Jan 15, 2001	Finance Charge	$ 17.00
	PAYMENT	– $ 40.00
	Total	**$ 852.00**

VISA

Karyn Bosnak
400 E. 57th St.
New York, NY 10010

Date	Payee	Amount
	PREVIOUS BALANCE	$ 2,107.00
Jan 20, 2001	Finance Charge	$ 42.00
	PAYMENT	– $ 70.00
	Total	**$ 2,079.00**

DISCOVER
FINANCIAL SERVICES

Karyn Bosnak
400 E. 57th St.
New York, NY 10010

Date	Payee	Amount
Jan 1, 2001	Balance Transfer	$ 7,500.00
Jan 1, 2001	Finance Charge	$ 44.00
Jan 1, 2001	Over Limit Fee	$ 25.00
	PAYMENT	– $ 250.00
	Total	**$ 7,319.00**

Grand Debt Tally $15,772.00

A LAST-DITCH EFFORT

To go along with my New Year's resolution, I decided I'd start paying cash for things like my manicures and pedicures and getting my hair done. So my financial future was looking a bit brighter.

The future of *Curtis Court* was also looking a bit hopeful. King World decided to give the show one more chance during February sweeps. Even a slight increase in ratings would have been enough to make them reconsider renewing it. So once again the pressure was on the producing teams to book the best.

During a recent producer brainstorming meeting, someone came up with the bright idea to book celebrities as experts for appropriate cases. For example, Dee from *What's Happening* was now a veterinarian and could give an expert opinion in a case involving an animal. Darva Conger from *Who Wants to Marry a MultiMillionaire?* fame was an emergency room nurse and could give her expert opinion in a medical matter. Ideas like these could often be called 'last-ditch efforts' to save an ailing show, which is exactly what they were.

We may have been reaching, but all we needed was a slight improvement. Just a little bump up in the numbers would do. So we decided to go ahead with the plan and book a celebrity week. In addition to Darva and Dee, 'Bull' from *Night Court* stood in as a celebrity bailiff one day, and Susan from the original *Survivor* acted as a postverdict reporter another day. When you are an ailing court show whose ratings are in the can, it's kind of difficult to get celebs like Tom Cruise and Julia Roberts, so these folks would just have to do.

Because of both my crazy work schedule and my lack of funds at the moment, I called to cancel any remaining training sessions with Sam. By now, I was pretty familiar with the routine anyway, and if I wanted to do it on my own, I think

I could. When I hung up, my phone rang again, and it was my landlord's office.

'Hello, Karyn?' a woman's voice said.

'Yes,' I answered.

'This is David Frankel Realty. We haven't received your rent check yet, and were wondering when you mailed it,' she asked.

'Oh, gosh, I mailed it two weeks ago,' I said. I was telling the truth. 'I'm surprised you haven't received it yet. Should I send over another one?'

'That would be great if you could,' she said.

'Okay, sorry,' I said. I really did mail my rent check. I dropped it in this mailbox by my apartment, but I've had other people not receive things that I've dropped in that mailbox. I'd have to make a note not to use that one again. With that, I made out a new rent check and sent it on its way, noting this was the second time I'd been late with my rent.

Later that day, I booked a case involving a girl who was suing her ex-boyfriend and father of her son for spraying her in the eyes with mace. The defendant said she deserved it because she pulled his new wife's hair in a jealous rage. The plaintiff was suing him for the medical bills that she incurred after having her eyes flushed out. The ex-boyfriend said that the can of mace was old and he therefore didn't think it would harm her. He said she was fine afterward and didn't need her eyes flushed out, but went to the hospital anyway just to mess with him.

After briefly reviewing the case, the judge asked me to book a mace expert to find out if a can really can go bad, and a medical expert to find out if having your eyes flushed out after being sprayed with potentially bad mace is necessary. After locating and booking the president of a mace manufacturing company, I decided to claim Darva Conger, the woman who wanted to marry a multimillionaire, who was already booked and needing a home, as mine. She would be the perfect medical expert.

While sitting at my desk getting ready for the case, my phone rang. It was my friend Greg, a guy that I grew up with who now lived in New York. He was the same guy who set me up with the Pet Store Guy.

'Karyn,' he said, 'what's up? How's the show doing?'

'Hey, Greg,' I said, 'not very well. But thanks for asking.'

'Listen, we have to go out,' he said. 'I have this new guy I want to set you up with.'

I paused. A new guy? Not another Pet Store Guy, I hoped. 'It's so funny, that's what I am to people in New York,' I said. 'I'm the set-up girl. I'm the girl who everyone wants to set up with their friends.'

'Well, you're cute and funny,' he said.

'Thanks. Okay, what's his name?' I asked.

'Well, his name is Dan and he drives a Mercedes,' he said.

'How do you know him?' I asked.

'Well, Samantha's cousin bought a car from him before,' he said. Samantha was Greg's wife.

'What do you mean bought a car from him?' I asked warily.

'He manages a Mercedes-Benz dealership,' he answered. Oh, he *drives* a Mercedes because he *works* for Mercedes.

'He's a car salesman?' I asked.

'Not really,' he said, laughing. 'Well, yeah, kind of. But he's a manager!'

'Oh, I don't know,' I said. 'Does he wear bad ties and have coffee breath?'

'No, he's totally normal and really nice. C'mon . . . it's a free dinner on Friday night,' he said, trying to convince me.

'Okay, fine,' I said. 'What are the plans?'

'Well, you should be at my apartment by 8.00 P.M. on Friday, and we'll share a cab downtown to meet him and Samantha at a sushi restaurant called Bond Street.'

'Okay, 8.00 P.M. on Friday at your place,' I said. 'I'll see you then. But if this one tells me that he waxes his back in the first five minutes of meeting him like the last one did, I'm outta there,' I said.

Greg started laughing. 'Yeah, sorry about that last one,' he said. 'I'll see you Friday.'

THE LOST RENT CHECK

Friday turned out to be a rainy and cold January day. I have never minded snow so much, but I have never been a big fan of rain. It always messes things up, like hair and shoes. I decided to leave work a bit early that night because I had to get some cash for my big date with the car salesman. So around 5:45 P.M., I grabbed my stuff and went to the corner deli to use their ATM.

After rummaging through the gum wrappers and lip gloss in my purse, I finally found my card and inserted it into the machine. I decided to take out $100 because in addition to needing some cash for the night, I also needed to pick up the outfit that I was going to wear at the dry cleaners. A few seconds later, the machine spit out a receipt, but no cash. Hmm.

I wasn't sure what the problem was. I knew that I had money in my checking account because I had recently deposited a paycheck. I looked at the receipt and it said 'Insufficient Funds' on it. Insufficient funds? How could that be? I looked at my watch. It was almost 6.00 P.M..

I decided to run back to the office because it was closer, and went online to look at the details of my checking account. After logging in, a screen popped up that said I had negative $95 in my checking account. How could I have been overdrawn? I should have had the entire last paycheck of $1,700 in there. I clicked a button on the screen to get more details. I saw that my rent check for $1,800 had just cleared, and then the check that I wrote for the phone bill cleared, and then another rent check for – oh my gosh! The lost rent check suddenly was found. And cashed! I quickly logged off and called my landlord.

'Hello, can I please speak to the accounts payable woman?' I asked the woman who answered the phone. I hoped that she was still there. A few seconds later she picked up.

'Hi, this is Karyn in apartment 4E. Do you remember me? You called me last week that you hadn't yet received my rent check?' I asked.

'Oh, I remember,' she said.

'Well, I sent you over a new check and you cashed it, and then the old one must have found its way to you and you cashed that one too. How could you do that? I told you that it was lost in the mail, and now my checking account is overdrawn,' I said frantically.

'Well, let me take a look,' she said. After a few minutes she figured out what had happened. 'Yes, you are right. We cashed both checks.'

'Yes, I know that. That's why I'm calling you. But the second check that I sent to you was a *replacement* check, not an *additional* check. Common sense would tell you after cashing the replacement check not to cash the original one if it arrived.'

'You know we have so many apartments that it's hard to keep track. Maybe whoever cashed it thought that you were paying early for February.'

'Early?' I said. 'Look at my history. Do I ever pay early? I don't think so.' This was the one time when I thought that actually paying my rent late might help me.

'I'm sorry,' she said, 'but if you didn't want the original check cashed then you should have stopped payment on it.' Stop payment? Oops. I forgot to do that. She might have been right, but I wasn't going to let her know that.

'Don't blame this on me,' I said. 'You should have made a note or something to not cash it if it showed up. I now have absolutely no money *and* I have a date tonight. *And* I don't get paid for another week.' I was near tears.

'I'm sorry for the mix-up. Look at it this way, next month's rent is already paid,' she said cheerfully.

'That doesn't help me right now at this moment,' I said. 'Good-bye.'

I hung up on her and decided to call my bank to see if there was anything they could do. Maybe they were planning on returning the check for insufficient funds. They did it to me once before, why wouldn't they do it again? And this time I needed them to do it.

I talked to an operator who told me that although I didn't have enough money in my account to cover the check, they were going to honor it because the amount that I was short was less than $100. When the check for $1,800 was presented, I had $1,705 in my account, which made me $95 overdrawn. Had I had $1,699 or less in there, then they would have sent it back because I would have been at least $101 overdrawn. All these little bank rules that I didn't know about never worked in my favor!

I sat at my desk and didn't know what I was going to do. It was now 6:15 P.M., and I had to be at the cleaners by 7:00 P.M. to pick up my clothes for that night. And I didn't have any money. But I wasn't too worried about that because I could always write a check and figure out how to cover it tomorrow.

I was more worried because I didn't have even one dollar in my pocket. And even though I was going on a date, I should still bring some money. This wasn't like a one-on-one date either. Greg and his wife would be there, so it was more like I was just meeting this car salesman. What if he expected me to pay for my own dinner? I mean, it could happen. And how was I going to get home?

I finally just broke down in tears. I was so irritated. I thought about going to the local Food Emporium to do my $25 float-a-check thing, but even that would give me just $25. And I didn't really have time to do that anyway. Ann Marie and Jodi had already gone home, and I didn't know anyone else well enough at work to borrow money from them. Just then, Gwen walked up to me.

'Are you okay?' she asked.

'Yes, I'm just irritated. I have this date tonight and my landlord's office deposited a check that they shouldn't have and now I don't have any money. I don't even have a dollar,' I said, slobbering.

'Oh, that sucks. I've been there. I know how you feel,' she said. 'With this divorce and two kids, things have gotten quite tight.' She then picked up her purse and started going through it.

'All I have is twenty dollars, but you can have it and pay me back whenever you can,' she said.

'Really?' I asked, looking up at her.

'Really, take it, please. And go. You are going to be late,' she said.

'Oh, Gwen, thank you,' I said.

'No problem. And stop crying or you'll look like shit when you get there,' she said. I smiled and laughed a little, and wiped the tears off my face.

I quickly got my stuff together and again left work. Since I only had $20 in my pocket, I thought it was best that I took the bus home. The dry cleaners was only one block from my apartment and closed in exactly forty minutes, so I should be able to make it there.

Now Friday-night crosstown traffic is pretty bad, and when it rains it's even worse. And the bus that I climbed on was at an absolute standstill. After ten minutes, I jumped off and decided to jog the rest of the way home. Fifteen minutes later, I finally got to the block of the dry cleaners. I looked at my watch, and it was 6:50 P.M. Phew! I'd made it!

As I approached the door, I noticed that it looked awfully dark inside. They must be getting ready to close, I thought. As I got closer, I started to make out the outline of a metal gate that was pulled down over the windows and door. They can't be closed! It's not 7.00 P.M. yet!

I walked up to the door and cupped my hands around my eyes and pressed them to the glass to see if I could see anyone inside. There was nothing. No one was inside. Everything was still. I backed up and looked at the outside of the door and saw the sign that said they closed at 7.00 P.M. They'd closed early. Of all the nights!

'Fuck!' I screamed and jumped up and down. What horrible customer service! Kings Dry Cleaners on 57th Street in Manhattan shouldn't be in business! In addition to having the outfit that I was going to wear tonight inside, they had everything else I owned as well! I thought about my closet and knew I had nothing to wear. I had to be at Greg's in exactly one hour. Then on a whim I decided to quickly run to Bloomingdale's to buy something; it was only three blocks away and I was sure I would be able to make it back in time.

I got to Bloomingdale's at 7:05 P.M. and ran up the escalator to the second floor. In a mad panic, I grabbed a long black BCBG cardigan and a pair of tight black pants. I also grabbed a white T-shirt to go under the sweater that said 'LIVE LOVE and be FABULOUS' in big gold letters on the front. I didn't have a chance to try it on. But I was sure it would look cute. I hoped. But what if it didn't?

Just in case, I decided to get an alternative and return the one I didn't wear. Across the aisle I saw the Theory section, and I grabbed a cute sheer black blouse with rhinestone buttons and a pair of gold velvet pants with a big rhinestone buckle that were hanging on one of the outer racks. I had been eyeing the pants for a while anyway. They were adorable!

I took my items up to the counter and gave them to the girl to ring up. One of them had to work. The total came to $750 and I handed over my American Express card to pay. I had vowed to use it only for emergencies, and this was an emergency! I looked at my watch and it was 7.15 P.M.. Now that's power shopping!

I ran toward the down escalator and realized that I didn't have any shoes to wear with my outfits. Boots would look too bulky. A pair of gold lamé heels would be perfect! So instead of leaving, I turned around and ran to the shoe section.

After briefly scouring the section, I found the perfect pair of gold lamé pointy heels. They would add just the right amount of funk to either outfit. As quickly as I could, I grabbed the nearest shoe guy and asked him to bring me a size 6½. I wasn't even going to try them on.

I patiently waited for the shoe guy to bring me the shoes. And patiently waited. And patiently waited. Where was that shoe guy? Almost ten minutes later, he still had not returned. I was really antsy. Just then, another shoe guy walked by, so I asked him to bring me the shoes too. I was irritated and frantic and started to feel really hot. It was so warm in the store, and I still had my coat, hat and scarf on. Just then I saw the first shoe guy walk by. He didn't have my shoes in his hands. I grabbed him by the arm.

'Excuse me, sir?' I asked, irritated. 'Where are my shoes? I asked you for them over ten minutes ago.' He just stared at me blankly. From the look in his eye, I could tell that he had forgotten all about me! Didn't he know what kind of a hurry I was in? I felt like a crazy mad woman. I had to be at Greg's apartment dressed and ready to go in exactly half an hour.

'Oh,' he said, trying to cover up his mistake, 'I had them and looked for you but couldn't find you. You must have moved.'

'No, I didn't move, and you didn't look for me. I have been standing in the same place since I asked you for them,' I said confrontationally. 'I am in a hurry and I need them now!'

'Well, I'll go get another pair. What shoes were they again?' he asked. I thrust the display shoe that was still in my hand toward him. I wanted to hit him over the head with it but stopped myself. I was so irritated, but I decided it was better to have two shoe guys looking for them than one shoe guy. He looked at the shoe and turned to walk away. He had no business being a part of the Bloomingdale's sales team. I'd have to make a note of his name and write a letter.

As he walked away I started to murmur under my breath. 'Hurry the fuck up this time, idiot,' I said quietly. I'm usually very nice to salespeople because I was once a salesperson, but this guy was an idiot and I was in a hurry. Just then he stopped in his tracks and turned around. Oh, crap, I think he heard me.

'Excuse me?' he asked.

'Excuse me what?' I said. I decided to pretend like I didn't say anything.

'I heard what you said, miss. Did you just tell me to hurry the fuck up, idiot?' he asked.

'Well,' I said, stuttering, 'you're awfully slow.'

'Miss, you're going to have to leave. Please leave the shoe department right now.' Was he kicking me out of the shoe department? Was I really being asked to leave the shoe department of my favorite store?

'No, I want my shoes,' I said. My heart started to beat fast. 'You were supposed to get me my shoes and you screwed up.'

'Please turn around and leave the department,' he said again, walking toward me. Oh my gosh, it was really happening. I was really getting kicked out of the shoe department. Doesn't he know how much money I spend here? Just then, the other shoe guy walked up with my gold shoes in a size 6½. I grabbed them out of his hand.

'I'll leave after I pay for these,' I said to the first shoe guy. 'And by the way, it took him less than five minutes to get these.' I turned around and brought my gold shoes to the nearest register. I tried not to look back while the girl rang me up because I didn't want to be escorted out in the middle of my transaction. As soon as she was done, I grabbed the bag and made a mad dash out of the shoe department. It was 7.35 P.M. I could be home by 7.40 P.M., change, and still be at Greg's by 8.00 P.M. if I hurried. He only lived two short blocks away.

As I hurried home, I realized how obnoxious I'd acted in the shoe department. I kind of felt like a druggie looking for a fix, or like an alcoholic trying to lick the inside of an empty bottle to get the last drops. I literally was shaking while shopping. The more I thought about it, I was embarrassed that I'd yelled – especially sworn – at the man in the shoe department. But I was more embarrassed at my lack of self-control. I promised myself that I would only use my American Express card for emergencies, and let's be honest – this was hardly one. But when I was shopping, the amount of money I owed completely did not matter. The only thing that mattered at that moment was making sure I had something to wear that night.

THE CAR SALESMAN

Despite my greatest effort, I showed up at Greg's fifteen minutes late. He was waiting outside. Because I was in a hurry, I'd run out of the apartment unprepared and had forgotten my umbrella and had to walk there in the rain. I was a mess, but I tried not to let it get to me. I decided to wear the LIVE LOVE and be FABULOUS tee under the BCBG sweater with tight black pants. And my gold shoes looked just as lovely on as I'd imagined.

On the way to the restaurant, I told Greg all about my lack of funds and the dry cleaner and Bloomingdale's, and was worried that Dan might not pay for dinner. He told me not to worry, that he was sure Dan would pay.

'Just butter him up and flirt endlessly during dinner,' he said, laughing. 'Give him a little knee rub under the table.' I laughed back.

When we got to the restaurant, Samantha and the car salesman were already waiting for us by the bar. Bond Street is a sushi restaurant and is the ultimate in New York chichi. The whole place is filled with model-type women and hot men. It was very cool. It was a scene. And I felt right at home in my new outfit.

Dan seemed like a very nice guy. He was tall and a bit on the thick side, but I never let that bother me much. I kind of like chunky guys. They're manly. Greg might have been joking in the car, but I decided to take his advice and flirted endlessly. I needed to make sure that I was in the clear when the bill came, so I laughed at all Dan's jokes and affectionately touched his arm whenever I talked to him.

Toward the end of the evening, I began to get irritated that all of Dan's stories had to do with Mercedes. It was Mercedes this and Mercedes that. But I continued laughing at all his stories because a girl's gotta do what a girl's gotta do. Just then, Dan told Samantha and me that he had a small gift for each of us. He then reached down in his coat and pulled out two black-and-gold Mercedes special editions of the new 2001 *Zagat* guide. It was here that he won my heart! A new *Zagat* guide! And a Mercedes one at that! As much as I was irritated that he kept dropping the Mercedes name during dinner, I had to admit that these were kind of cool.

So I decided to give him a chance. And gave him a kiss on the cheek to say thank-you. After dinner when the check came, Greg and Dan split it down the middle and paid. Phew! I was in the clear! All of my heavy petting worked! As Greg was signing his credit card receipt, he looked over at me and gave me a wink.

As we walked out of the restaurant, Greg and Samantha decided to call it an early night and went home. But Dan and I went out for a drink. He took me to a new place called Underbar, which was just opened by Cindy Crawford's husband, Rande Gerber. There was a line to get in, but Dan was sure his Mercedes-Benz umbrella would assure us entry. I tried not to look as he blatantly shoved the logo into the doorman's face. I was embarrassed. It was like he was screaming, 'Look at me! I drive a Mercedes and I'm cool.' The sad thing was that it actually worked.

Part of me was starting to hate this New York scene, but part of me still loved it. I mean, I hated the fact that something like a Mercedes-Benz logo on an umbrella meant that we were cooler than other people in line. How shallow. But just as I was thinking this, I looked down at my Prada purse and my BCBG outfit and realized that I was just as bad as Dan. Looking fashionable wasn't just important to me, it had become a necessity. And just like Dan shoving his umbrella in the doorman's face so he could see it, I was carrying my Prada purse with the logo proudly displayed so everyone could see too. It was as if I too was saying, 'Look at me! I carry Prada and I'm cool.'

But the truth is that people judge you by what you look like on the outside. And I'm not talking just doormen here. But also coworkers, friends, dates – everyone. The way people dress says a lot about them. It makes an impression. And I always want the impression I make to be a good one. So I like to look good. I like to dress to impress.

Once inside, we checked our coats and got a drink. As I looked around I started laughing. It was such a scene! One woman was completely decked out in head-to-toe, waaay over the top Versace. She even had a pair of sunglasses on. In a bar. At night. And the bar was called Underbar because it was underground – meaning there was no outside light coming in whatsoever! It wasn't sunny. As I looked at her I had to laugh. I may be a slave to fashion, but at least I wasn't that bad. She was a fashion victim. There's a difference. God, please strike me down if I ever get like that.

Dan and I chatted for a short while, and after one drink we shared a cab home. By the time we got to my apartment, the rain had stopped, so we decided to take a walk around the block. We ended up at Sutton Place Park, which was at the end of 57th Street on the river. We sat on the bench and looked at the 59th Street Bridge and felt groovy together. I think it was the same park where Woody Allen and Diane Keaton sat and looked at the bridge in *Annie Hall.* We talked for almost an hour.

As Dan walked me back to my apartment, he asked to see me again. I said yes. And unlike the Pet Store Guy, I wasn't planning on canceling. After a kiss good night, I said good-bye and went up to my apartment.

That night as I lay in bed, Elvis sat on my lap and purred. I pulled out my brand-new *Zagat* guide, found Bond Street and circled it. Next to it I wrote, 'Greg, Samantha, Mercedes Dan & me – a fashion slave maybe, but still FABULOUS nonetheless.'

GUESS WHO'S HERE TODAY?

Each year at the end of January, a big television convention occurs called NATPE, which stands for the National Association of Television Program Executives. Basically, it's a weeklong schmoozefest where television executives try to convince television program directors from television stations around the world to buy their shows. Years ago, almost all the television deals were made during NATPE, but that wasn't really the case anymore. But still, the stars and/or hosts of the shows go and everyone there tries their best to sell their programs.

For *Curtis Court*, a show that our bosses said was on the brink of renewal, NATPE should have been a big deal this year. But King World decided not to bring James Curtis to the convention, which was not a good sign. The staff was a bit upset. We had all worked so hard during January to try to keep the show on the air, and even before February sweeps began, we felt like they were giving up. Instead, King World seemed to be focusing their attention on a new talk show they had coming out in the fall, *The Ananda Lewis Show.* Ananda was at NATPE, and King World was really promoting their new host.

At the end of the week, a bit depressed because I felt like I was on the brink of losing my job, Dan called and asked me to go to a New York Rangers game. It really cheered me up.

'Who are the Rangers?' I asked.

'It's hockey. They play at Madison Square Garden,' he said, laughing at me.

'Oh yes! That sounds fun! I like hockey!' I said. Hockey *is* fun. My friend Jeff played hockey in high school, and I always went to cheer him on. I didn't pay attention that closely or anything, but I always seemed to have a good time. So I liked hockey!

'Sounds good. Why don't I pick you up at work around 6.30 P.M., and then we'll share a cab to Madison Square Garden together.'

'Perfect,' I said.

That Friday night, Dan met me in front of my work building and we went to the hockey game together. I had not been to Madison Square Garden yet and was excited. Sports aside, Madonna and Cher had performed there!

Dan and I sat down in our seats, which were 'Mercedes seats,' he said, and therefore really close to the ice. Other than men in masks hitting a puck with a stick, I wasn't too sure what was going on, so during the first quarter Dan did his best to explain it to me. He reviewed the basic rules, and told me that the Rangers were playing a team called the Islanders, which was also a New York team. I paid attention to the game as long as I could, but lost interest about five minutes later. I quickly moved on to my favorite thing to do when I'm stuck at a sporting event and bored, I played the 'Guess who's here today?' game.

Naomi and I like to think that we were the originators of the 'Guess who's here today?' game. We developed it while bored out of our minds one night at a Chicago Bulls game. When you live in Chicago and you come across Bulls tickets, you have to go, even if you don't like sports. Well, I mean you had to go when Michael Jordan was still there and they were good. And that night he was there, and they were good, but we were still bored. So we developed this game to pass the time. The premise of the game is simple. You find people in the crowd who look like famous people, and then say to your friend, 'Hey, guess who's here today?'

Your friend then says, 'Who?'

And then you point out the person and say, 'The Queen Mother,' or whomever it is that the person looks like. It's good for a good belly laugh or two. And once you get started it's hard to stop. And that damn Queen Mother always shows up at the same places I am. She's everywhere! A slight variation to the game is to tell your friend who's there, but not point them out, and instead make your friend find them. That'll even get you a bigger laugh sometimes.

Tonight, after scouring the crowd, I discovered that Richard Simmons was there and decided to let Dan know.

'Hey, guess who's here today?' I said.

'Who?' he asked, looking at me, thinking I was serious.

'Richard Simmons,' I said, laughing and pointing to a man a few rows away with big puffy curly hair wearing a hot pink T-shirt. Dan looked at the guy and let out a little fake laugh and then continued to watch the game. He didn't seem to like my game. Or maybe he just didn't get it. I decided to try again.

After scouring the crowd again, I discovered that none other than Michael Jackson himself was among us as well.

'Hey, look. Michael Jackson's here too today,' I said, pointing to a pretty white woman with a pointy nose and jet-black hair sitting next to us. This time Dan just nodded and continued to watch the game. Ugh. I was bored. And he was no fun.

By halftime I was all hockeyed out. I sat in my chair and looked down at my manicure and realized that I needed a new one. And I was cold. It was cold in there. Maybe I shouldn't have worn my sheer Theory shirt to a hockey game, but it was so darn cute that I couldn't resist. And I thought velvet pants would be warmer than they were. I know the plan was to return the other unworn outfit from last weekend to Bloomingdale's, but once I tried it on, I just couldn't. And besides I already had the perfect shoes, so what was the point?

Just as things were getting painful, the end of the third quarter finally came and I was excited that there was just one more to go. I tried my best to look like I was having fun, but I just wasn't. Just then, Dan stood up and grabbed his coat. Oh, I was so excited that he wanted to leave early!

'Oh, are we leaving early?' I asked.

'No, Karyn, the game's over. There's only three periods in hockey.'

'Oh, really?' I said with excitement. I knew hockey was my favorite sport for a reason! It's fast!

After the game, Dan and I went to a local bar to listen to a band and had a nice time, but I knew that he wasn't the one. I mean, he didn't like the 'Guess who's here today?' game. And seeing as that's one of my favorite pastimes, I just couldn't see how things could work out. At the end of the night, I hopped in a cab and went home by myself.

YOU ARE DISMISSED

As the February ratings began to come in, any hope we had for a renewal flew out the window. There was no change in the numbers at all. Although King World wouldn't tell us immediately that the show was going to be canceled, all the signs pointed to yes. Our show budgets were cut in half. The secretary even started receiving faxes confirming time slots for the upcoming *Ananda Lewis Show* that was going to air in the fall, and several of those time slots happened to be existing *Curtis Court* ones. Soon, our boss stopped coming into the studio during tapings, and our senior producer, Jodi, began to take over.

Most producers for daytime talk shows are under contract for a certain amount of years with the show they work for. For example, I was under contract with *Curtis Court* for two years. That meant I couldn't quit and get another job at a competing talk show while that contract was valid.

But those two years are broken up into periods called 'option periods.' An option period gives the company I work for a chance every so often to cancel my contract. At *Curtis Court*, my option was up on April 6, and the company had to let me know if they were renewing it at least one month in advance of that date. But by March 7, they claimed that they still weren't sure if they were going to renew *Curtis Court*. So, our bosses asked the staff if we would give them two more weeks to decide. I said yes, but not everyone did. If *Curtis Court* wasn't renewed, then I wanted to work at *Ananda*, so I wanted to stay in good with the bosses.

Finally, two weeks later, in the middle of taping cases, our boss called an emergency meeting in the conference room. Just like when the initial less-than-stellar ratings came back, there weren't any balloons or cake at this meeting either. The news probably wasn't good.

Everyone came upstairs to the conference room, including James Curtis. The crew told the litigants there were technical problems so they patiently waited in the studio, having no idea that the show was getting canceled upstairs.

Mary came in and broke the news to us. She said that despite a strong effort, the numbers just weren't good enough. It was sad. I looked around at our small staff and knew that we had all worked so hard. I think that when you put that much effort into a show and it doesn't succeed, you feel defeated. And it was hard not to feel sorry for James Curtis. He was so nice that we all wanted the show to succeed, if not for ourselves and our jobs, then for him.

James Curtis, the crew, and a few producers went back to the studio to finish taping for the day. And at the end, after the last case, he made his ruling and banged his gavel one final time.

'You are dismissed,' he said.

Later that afternoon, everyone on the staff tried to figure out what to do next. People started faxing out their resumes and calling friends. And some people, including me, talked to Mary about the possibility of working at *The Ananda Lewis Show*.

On the money front, I would thankfully be getting my tax return back any day, which would help me out for a couple of months. But $1,800 a month rent was steep and I couldn't afford to be unemployed for too long. Later that afternoon I knocked on Mary's door.

'Hey, come in, Karyn,' she said, still kind of melancholy. I sat down and we started to talk.

'You know, it's upsetting about this show,' she said. 'I really thought it was good.'

'I know, I did too,' I said.

'You are a very good producer, Karyn. Better than some at this show that have been doing it for years. You are creative and pay attention to detail. You have a good eye,' she said.

'Thank you again,' I said. 'I've learned so much from you in this past year, and I just want to let you know that I'd be really interested in working on *Ananda*.'

'I'd love to have you there too. I think it's going to be a very high quality program. First class all the way. Think about the old *Oprah* show. Not as celebrity driven as it is today, but when she tackled issues. And then mix that in with some fun shows. That's what I think we are going for.'

'That is so much what I want,' I said. 'I want to make a difference. I like the court genre, but I hate the fact that everyone is always at odds with each other. There's always conflict. I want to make feel-good television. I want to make people smile!' I said, laughing.

'I love that about you! You are so refreshing. And you have great ideas,' she said. I felt very honored to have Mary compliment me. 'I'd love for you to be a producer at *Ananda*. However, I'm not going to be the executive producer of the show, a man named Jose is. So you'll have to meet him too.'

'Sounds great! I look forward to it,' I said.

The following week, Jose flew into New York from Los Angeles and started to meet with potential staff. Jose was also semifamous in the talk show world. Like Mary, he was old school, and had been in daytime talk for a while. That week,

I met with him briefly. He told me that he heard a lot of good things about me, and I was pleased. The possibility of a job at *Ananda* looked good, but I wouldn't find out if I definitely had a job there for a few more weeks.

The following week we had our wrap party, and that Friday was my last day of work. As I packed up my desk and headed out the door, I turned around and said good-bye to my short cube, a place that had felt like a second home since I'd moved here.

That weekend, Naomi came to town for a bachelorette party and invited me to come along as well. A friend of hers who lived in New York was getting married. Since our Plaza slumber party, Naomi had come back to New York for business on several occasions, but always chose to stay at a different hotel each time. We had slumber parties in some of the nicest hotels in the city! This time, however, she had to stay with me.

The bachelorette party was more like a bachelorette weekend. On Friday night we all went to see a play called *Naked Boys Singing*. And it was just that – a bunch of boys singing buck-naked onstage. It was so funny! They were completely naked. From head to toe! We could hardly control our laughter as they sang songs like 'The Bliss of a Bris' and 'Perky Little Porn Star.'

On Saturday night we went to dinner at a restaurant called Ruby Foo's, and then went out dancing. I've never been one for cheesy bachelorette parties, but I had so much fun! All the girls were so nice, and I had some new friends. And I even made some money! By the end of the night we were all dancing on top of the bar at Hogs & Heifers, and guys were giving us money! I felt like a go-go dancer. And I liked it!

It was so nice to let loose. I'd just lost my job, and while I was hoping I'd get another, nothing was for sure. The girl who organized the party was named Jane, and she was very cool. And at the end of the night she asked me if I wanted to be a part of a share in a house on Fire Island for the summer. A share! Yes! This is what all New Yorkers do! And I had heard about Fire Island and how much fun it was supposed to be. I'd have to figure out a way to come up with about $1,200, but I could do it. I quickly said yes!

That Sunday I slept all day. Naomi got up and packed up her stuff and went home and I barely moved. We hadn't gotten home until six in the morning. When I woke up Monday, I had a voice mail message. I didn't even hear the phone ring. I pushed the button to listen.

'Hi, Karyn, this is Jose. I just want to tell you that we'd like to offer you a position at *The Ananda Lewis Show* as a producer. So congratulations, and give me a call so we can start negotiating your contract.' I got the job! I did it! I was on to bigger and better things! And a bigger paycheck, which I needed.

That morning I just lay in bed and smiled for a while. I felt like my whole life was starting to come together. I felt like I was on the brink of something big, but I just didn't know what it was. And I couldn't wait to find out!

THE FALL

June 2001

THE PREPARATION

It's funny how something that you expect to be one of the best experiences of your life can turn out to be one of the worst. I was really looking forward to working at *The Ananda Lewis Show*. It was going to be the new fresh show in daytime – the new *Oprah*. And I was getting in on the ground floor – the launch.

The two months after *Curtis Court* prior to *Ananda* were my preparation months. Since I had never produced a solid hour of daytime television before, I was a bit nervous, to say the least. So I made it a primary concern to use the two months to relax and focus.

Every day I woke up and read three papers, the *New York Times*, *USA Today*, and of course my favorite, the *New York Post*. I wanted to make sure I knew what was going on in the world. And, to get more acquainted with the city, I made sure to eat at least one meal a day at a restaurant in my *Zagat* guide I had never been to. I don't know exactly how this prepared me for work, but somehow I thought that the more city savvy I was, the better a producer I would be.

In addition to becoming news and food savvy, I also decided to upgrade my life, so to speak. In the electronics department, I got rid of my old desktop computer and bought a new laptop. I also got rid of my old cell phone and bought a new fancy Motorola StarTac. It looked so important, and I was going to be important! I also replaced my stereo, which I thought had broken. But when I gave it to my doorman Edson, he told me that he got it to work just fine. But it was too late to return the new one, so I just let him keep it.

In the apartment department, I finally finished painting my walls a lovely shade of yellow. I also had Spiro the super hang a white wrought-iron-and-crystal chandelier that I'd bought.

It looked just like the people's across the street. It was fancy! And I finally broke down and bought a pretty blue floral quilted fabric shower curtain for $120 that I saw in the Ballard Designs catalog. I had been wanting it for a long time.

In the beauty and health department, I left the nazi bikini-wax lady and instead opted to try the infamous J. Sisters salon. The price was the same, the wax was the same, and the pubicle cubicles were the same, but I didn't have to get on all fours for them to get 'that area.' I just had to lie there and stick my leg up high in the air. It seemed a little more 'user friendly.' I also got a few massages and facials, which in addition to my La Prairie products made my skin glow! Furthermore, I did a weeklong colon cleanse and even had a professional colonic. A colonic is a procedure I read about in a magazine where a technician flushes out your colon with water. It's really gross actually. Apparently Princess Diana used to get them done on a regular basis. But once was enough for me. I also upgraded in the hair department, and left Red Salon for Louis Licari.

In the wardrobe department, I upgraded my big plastic Gucci sunglasses to a more streamlined pair of metal-rimmed Gucci sunglasses. I also cleaned out my closet and gave a few bags of clothes to Catholic Charities. I replaced what I gave away with some new casual clothes that I bought at Abercrombie & Fitch. I also bought a few new suits and some nice pairs of shoes to wear on show days.

But my favorite upgrade of all was in the purse department. As soon as I saw the new Gucci bucket purse at Bergdorf Goodman, I just knew I had to have it! The outside was covered with the signature Gucci Gs, and it had a black leather bottom and two black leather straps. It was the upgraded version of the Gucci bucket purse that my mom bought me in high school after I made the cheerleading squad! In my opinion, it was the mother lode of Gucci purses! Sure it was $500, but the price was justifiable because I could fit a folder in it. So it was kind of like I was getting a purse for $250 and a workbag for $250 – except they were just combined into one. And two purses for $250 each wasn't that bad.

I also got a lot of visiting out of the way. I flew back to Chicago to see my family, took a trip to Minneapolis to see my sister and her husband, and made a trip to Los Angeles to see my friend Tracy. I was a busy, busy fifth B those two months.

Yes, I spent a lot of money, but I had just worked out a contract for my new job and had negotiated a pretty decent salary of $2,000 a week. I was pretty happy with it, even though it was kind of low for a talk show producer. Most make about $2,300 a week and upward. But it was my first talk show and I was a new producer, and once again I decided to take the lower salary for the experience. But even taking the lower salary got me a $26,000 a year raise, and that was enough to cover a few months of being frivolous.

But since I wouldn't actually start getting that new salary until June, and wasn't getting *any* salary during the two months in between, I had to charge a few things. And since the new Discover Card I got was still maxed out, that just left my American Express card – until I got another Visa and another MasterCard. So I used those until they were filled up and then had to reinstate the Buy and Return Credit Payment Management Plan again to offset my Amex payments until I could actually afford to pay the money back. But since I wasn't working, it was pretty easy to do because I had all the time in the world. All I did was shop, shop, shop – day in and day out. My doormen actually started to make fun of me for coming and going with so many shopping bags. Edson was the worst. Sometimes after shopping, I would wait around the corner for him to get off work just to avoid the teasing.

The closer I got to starting work, the more I saw my career path in front of me. I would be a producer for a few years and then I'd become a senior producer, and then supervising producer, and then executive producer. And by that time, I'd be making so much money that any money I owed to Discover or American Express or any other cards for that matter would seem like mere pennies, or so I thought . . .

EIGHT

American Express

Karyn Bosnak
400 E. 57th St.
New York, NY 10010

Date	Payee	Amount
	PREVIOUS BALANCE	$ 3,420,00
May 1, 2001	The Wiz – Computers	$ 1,824.00
May 3, 2001	Gift Cheques	$ 1,025.00
May 3, 2001	Bloomingdale's Shoes	$ 233.00
May 5, 2001	Abercrombie & Fitch	$ 342.00
May 5, 2001	Bloomingdale's – Gucci Sunglasses	$ 243.00
May 9, 2001	The Wiz – Cell Phones	$ 120.00
May 12, 2001	The Wiz – Stereo Equipment	$ 648.00
May 13, 2001	Bergdorf Goodman	$ 534.00
May 13, 2001	Levi's	$ 208.00
May 13, 2001	Saks Fifth Avenue	$ 303.00
May 16, 2001	Marie's Colonics	$ 120.00
May 20, 2001	Catherine Atzen Day Spa	$ 224.00
May 21, 2001	Bloomingdale's – BCBG	$ 432.00
May 22, 2001	Banana Republic	$ 270.00
May 22, 2001	Fresh	$ 96.00
Jun 1, 2001	J. Sisters Salon	$ 80.00
Jun 1, 2001	Louis Licari	$ 389.00
Jun 1, 2001	Tiffany Nail	$ 64.00
	Total	**$ 10,575.00**

JENNIFER
CONVERTIBLES

Karyn Bosnak
400 E. 57th St.
New York, NY 10010

Date	Payee	Amount
	PREVIOUS BALANCE	$ 1,274.00
Jun 12, 2001	Finance Charge	$ 25.00
	PAYMENT	– $ 40.00
	Total	**$ 1,259.00**

Marshall Field's

Karyn Bosnak
400 E. 57th St.
New York, NY 10010

Date	Payee	Amount
	PREVIOUS BALANCE	$ 93.00
Jun 5, 2001	Late Fee	$ 25.00
Jun 5, 2001	Finance Charge	$ 3.00
	Total	$ 121.00

citi MasterCard

Karyn Bosnak
400 E. 57th St.
New York, NY 10010

Date	Payee	Amount
	PREVIOUS BALANCE	$ 422.00
Jun 15, 2001	Late Fee	$ 30.00
Jun 15, 2001	Finance Charge	$ 8.00
	Total	**$ 460.00**

Capital One VISA

Karyn Bosnak
400 E. 57th St.
New York, NY 10010

Date	Payee	Amount
	PREVIOUS BALANCE	$ 711.00
Jun 20, 2001	Late Fee	$ 25.00
Jun 20, 2001	Finance Charge	$ 14.00
	Total	**$ 750.00**

Karyn Bosnak
400 E. 57th St.
New York, NY 10010

Date	Payee	Amount
	PREVIOUS BALANCE	$ 7,090.00
Jun 1, 2001	Cash Advance	$ 300.00
Jun 1, 2001	Finance Charge	$ 148.00
	PAYMENT	– $ 150.00
	Total	**$ 7,388.00**

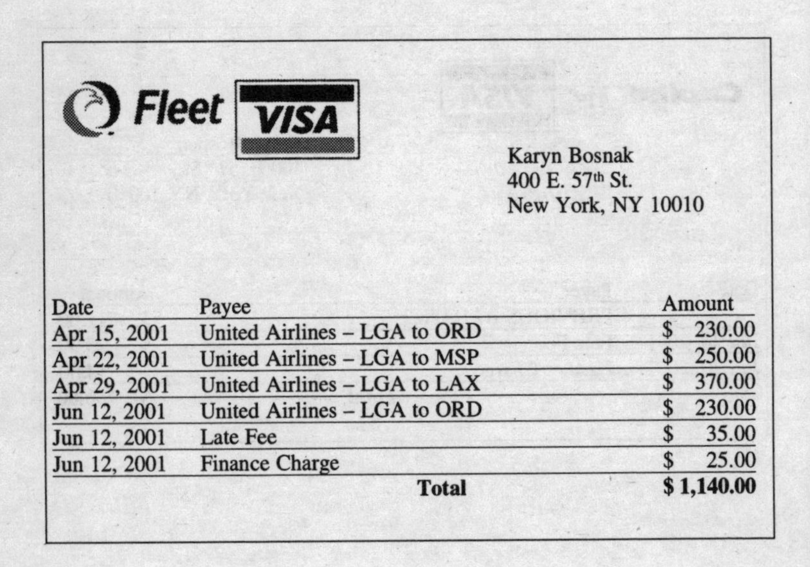

Karyn Bosnak
400 E. 57th St.
New York, NY 10010

Date	Payee	Amount
Apr 15, 2001	United Airlines – LGA to ORD	$ 230.00
Apr 22, 2001	United Airlines – LGA to MSP	$ 250.00
Apr 29, 2001	United Airlines – LGA to LAX	$ 370.00
Jun 12, 2001	United Airlines – LGA to ORD	$ 230.00
Jun 12, 2001	Late Fee	$ 35.00
Jun 12, 2001	Finance Charge	$ 25.00
	Total	**$ 1,140.00**

DIRECT MERCHANTS BANK

Karyn Bosnak
400 E. 57th St.
New York, NY 10010

Date	Payee	Amount
Apr 13, 2001	Kenneth Cole	$ 174.00
Apr 13, 2001	Nordstrom – Rhinestone Belt	$ 189.00
Apr 13, 2001	Banana Republic	$ 271.00
Apr 14, 2001	Blind Faith Café – Evanston, IL	$ 32.00
Apr 15, 2001	Virgin Megastore	$ 78.00
Apr 16, 2001	Bloomingdale's – Michael Stars	$ 140.00
Apr 17, 2001	Saks Fifth Avenue – Burberry Handbags	$ 190.00
Apr 18, 2001	eBay Purchase – Prada Shoes	$ 145.00
Apr 27, 2001	The Standard – Dining	$ 65.00
Apr 27, 2001	Bloomingdale's – La Prairie	$ 326.00
Apr 27, 2001	Fancy Nails – Los Angeles, CA	$ 45.00
Apr 27, 2001	French Connection	$ 298.00
Apr 28, 2001	Relax the Back	$ 50.00
Apr 29, 2001	Bloomingdale's – Shoes	$ 245.00
May 15, 2001	Cash Advance	$ 500.00
May 17, 2001	Bike Heaven	$ 324.00
May 18, 2001	The Wiz – CDs	$ 78.00
Jun 22, 2001	Late Fee	$ 30.00
Jun 22, 2001	Finance Charge	$ 65.00
	Total	**$ 3,245.00**

Grand Debt Tally $24,938.00

TEAM ANANDA

The staff for *The Ananda Lewis Show*, including myself, started work the first week in June. The week prior to that Naomi, my sugar mama, came into town for work and we had one last slumber party at the W Tuscany before I was off to the races. It was my last hurrah. For my first day, I chose to wear a gray Banana Republic suit with a lovely pair of DKNY black strappy heels. As I headed out the door, I grabbed my Gucci purse and took one last look in the mirror. I looked so professional!

The offices for the show were in the King World building – in the same space where the *Curtis Court* offices had been. I wasn't too thrilled about it, but I'd survive. The studio, however, was in the CBS building, which I was very excited about! It was the same place where they taped the *CBS Evening News with Dan Rather* and *60 Minutes.* I knew there were no cute guys in the King World building, and now I had a whole new building of male possibilities to explore.

The whole first week was an orientation of sorts that took place in a conference room at CBS. Everyone gave presentations, from the sales team to human resources. We learned what kind of show *The Ananda Lewis Show* was going to be, which was a fun, fresh daytime show that was geared toward women. *The Ananda Lewis Show* was going to be different from the other daytime talk shows. It was going to be better.

After all the speeches and presentations, everyone introduced themselves to each other. I was happy to discover that the staff wasn't made up of the usual talk show junkies who seemed to move from show to show. Everyone had a different background. Some people came from news, others came from morning shows. It was very diverse. Everyone brought something unique to the table.

On the boss front, there was Mary, my boss from *Curtis Court*, who was the senior executive producer of the show, and Jose, the executive producer. There was also a woman named Alexandra, who was the supervising producer, and another named Elise, the coordinating producer. It went like this: Mary, Jose, Alexandra, Elise – Mary was in charge of the big picture, Jose was in charge of the show, Alexandra was more hands-on and dealt with the producers, and Elise was in charge of the technical stuff.

In addition to me, a few other *Curtis Court* people were also hired, including the senior producer, Jodi, who was heading up a department called Futures. The idea behind the Futures department was that they would book shows that took more than a week to produce. They were like an advance team. It seemed like a great staff and a great setup.

Toward the end of the orientation week, everyone finally got to meet Ananda. While we all sat in a stuffy conference room in suits, she showed up in a purple hippie skirt with her two Chihuahuas in a bag. It was funny. She told us all about herself and where she was from. She grew up in San Diego, went to Howard University, and after that hosted a show on BET called *Teen Summit*. From there she went on to become a VJ for MTV. She had won awards, and had even interviewed Hillary Clinton. She was smart, she was young, but most of all, she was refreshing.

Ananda was my age, and I felt like I could identify with her. As much as she was about to embark on a new journey, so was I. And I couldn't help but think that maybe we had some of the same self-doubt running through our veins. Fear of the unknown, so to speak.

By Friday we were finally out of orientation and in our offices – I mean cubes. Yep, cubes again. And I got to sit one whole cube away from where my last one was. That day each producer was assigned a team, which consisted of one associate producer and one production associate. My team consisted of a girl named Molly, who was my AP, and a guy named Mike, who was our PA.

Each day that first week I wore a new suit and carried my Gucci purse. I felt together. I felt on top of things. And I was excited that I was going to work on a show that was going to make a difference. I wanted to make feel-good TV, and I felt like I was at the right place to do that.

To the outside world, and even to me at the time, everything looked great. But ever so slowly, things started to crumble. In a few short months, my whole world would be turned upside down.

The pace picked up pretty quickly during the second week. Our 'in time' was moved to 8:00 A.M., so we could get ready for a news meeting that was held at 8:30 A.M. Not being a morning person, this was not the easiest thing. So each morning I counted on an Iced Venti Americano from Starbucks to give me the jump start I needed. With four shots of espresso, it seemed to do the trick.

That Tuesday, each producing team was assigned their first show. Mine was called 'A Teen Girl's Guide to Style.' It was a big hodge-podge of stuff relating to finding your own fashion style, like shopping at thrift stores and Be-Dazzling your own clothes. It wasn't exactly a life-changing kind of show, but it was definitely fun.

After coming up with a plan of action, my team and I began booking our show. While Molly and Mike were going to start finding the girls, I was going to work on the Be-Dazzler guy. I had always wanted a Be-Dazzler and was excited at the possibility of getting my very own.

For the next few days my team and I worked hard. The Be-Dazzler guy was a cinch to book, but we didn't seem to be having the same luck with the teen girls. When most shows produce shows like this one, they rely on 'carts' or fan mail to pull the guests from. Carts are like advertisements for guests that you see during shows – 'If you are a so-and-so and would be interested in being on the show, then call us at this number' kind of thing. But since the show was new, we didn't have any of those, so we had to find everyone by just being resourceful.

Basically, we were looking for teen girls who dressed like Britney Spears and Christina Aguilera who needed help with finding their own style. And we needed them to have mothers who were sick of spending a lot of money on new clothes, and were worried that their kids were confused slaves to fashion lacking their own identity. Our bosses didn't want it to be a 'my teen dresses too sexy' type of show, but more of 'please help my teen daughter find her own style' type of show. We needed a very specific type of girl with a very specific type of mother.

So for the past week, my team had spent almost every day roaming shopping malls and combing through *TRL* groupies in Times Square to find guests. And it never failed that once we found the perfect girl, she had a mother who wasn't concerned about how she dressed. Or once we found the perfect mother, she had a daughter who dressed conservatively and was in no way a slave to fashion. By the end of the week, we had about a hundred girls – but not one of them was good enough. It was proving to be a very difficult type of show to book without carts.

But the following week, we kept at it. Day after day we continued to look for the perfect guests, and day after day they never showed up. My show, which was supposed to be a hodgepodge of fashion, was quickly turning into a hodgepodge of a mess.

THE 'LOST' CHECKBOOK

By now it was the end of June, and I had been working for over three weeks. And as much as I tried to concentrate on booking Britney Spears wannabes, I began to freak out about my finances a bit, which were beginning to unravel at the seams. You could say that at the moment I was a bit 'cash poor.' All of the money that I spent over the two months before *Ananda* wasn't money at all – it was credit. I did have some cash, but I used it to pay rent for April and May. I hadn't yet paid June. Well, I did pay it but I stopped payment on my check.

You see, one day at the end of last month after balancing my checkbook, I mailed off my June rent check and all of my bills. Electric, phone, credit cards – you name it. But soon after I dropped them in the mailbox, I realized that I had made a huge error, and that I didn't have enough money to cover all the checks I'd written. So I had to do something or some major check bouncing was going to happen.

So after thinking about it for a while, I decided to stop payment on my rent check. I had enough in my account to cover all my bills, just not enough to cover all my bills *and* my rent. And one $25 stop-payment fee was a heck of a lot less than eight $30 insufficient funds fees. So it seemed like the only logical thing to do. I figured that by the time my landlord got the check back marked 'stop payment' I would have enough money and would be able to pay it. And I'd just make up some lame excuse to tell them like 'I lost my checkbook and I had to stop payment on a bunch of checks' or something. I figured it would look better to my landlord if I stopped payment on the check myself rather than having the bank tell them that I didn't have any money to cover it.

But things didn't go exactly as planned. Things had become kind of crazy at work. I would get there every day at 8.00 A.M., and wouldn't get home sometimes until 9.00 P.M.. I was exhausted. And it seemed that the more exhausted I became, the more money I spent. After a long day, I'd be too tired to wait for the bus, so I'd take a cab home, which cost $7 a night. And then the next morning I'd be too tired to get out of bed, so I'd push snooze until absolutely the last minute. Then I'd have to rush to get ready and would take another cab back to work to get there on time, which cost another $7. And of course I wouldn't have any time to make breakfast at home, so I'd get some coffee and a muffin at Starbucks, which ran around $5.

Then during the day, I'd be too busy to go out and get lunch, so I'd order in and spend another $15. And in the afternoon when that 'lull' hit, I'd spend $5 on some more Starbucks and gummi bears to bring my energy back. And I never made dinner. I'd pick it up on the way home or order in. And that always cost around $15 too.

I was into convenience. It didn't matter if something cost more; if it was more convenient then I did it. I didn't do it at the time, but after adding it all up, I realized that I was spending about $54 a day on this crap. And I didn't just work five days a week – I was working the weekends too. So all this money was just flying out the door – over $350 a week.

I received my first paycheck on June 21, and had planned to use it to pay my June rent. But after a few days when I checked online to make sure it had cleared, I realized that I still didn't have enough money to pay my rent. All because I was being frivolous. I was just burning through my cash.

The next payday was July 5, and by that date another month's rent would be due again. And to make matters worse, my rent had increased to $1,950 a month. On top of that, every day when I got home I received another bill in the mail, asking for another monthly payment. So here it was, June 27 – my show wasn't coming together, I owed $3,900 to my landlord, and I had a huge pile of bills that I couldn't pay sitting at home on my table. Just then my phone rang.

'*Ananda Lewis Show*,' I said, slurring all the words together. Try saying it fast five times. It's kind of like a tongue twister.

'Hi, Karyn?' a woman asked.

'Yes?' I answered, thinking it was a show guest.

'This is the bookkeeper from your landlord's office.' Ugh. It was the dreaded phone call. 'Um, we have a check here that you wrote for June's rent that came back from the bank with a letter saying that you stopped payment on it,' she said. She sounded concerned.

'Oh gosh!' I said, trying to sound overwhelmed. 'You'll never believe it, but I lost my checkbook and had to stop payment on a few checks. I totally forgot to call and tell you.'

'Oh, okay,' she said. 'I knew there must be a reason. Because no one just stops payment on their rent check,' she said.

'Yeah, I know. I'm so sorry. It totally sucks! I had to stop payment on all sorts of checks. I'll put another one in the mail to you today,' I said. 'I totally meant to call you, but I forgot.'

'Well, okay then,' she said. 'As long as you mail another one today.'

'Absolutely,' I said. I wasn't exactly going to mail it today, but the mail was always so screwed up that I doubted they would know the difference. This was my third infraction with the realty company.

As I hung up the phone, I looked at a calendar. As I looked at the weeks laid out before me, I saw that after the check on July 5, I would get my next one on July 18, and the one after that on August 1. I could use the ones on July 5 and 18 to get caught up with my rent, but doing that meant not paying any of my bills until August 1. But on August 1, I'd owe my landlord another $1,950 – so I couldn't use that one to pay my bills either. The check after that would come on August 15. Fueled by a panicked work environment, a cycle had started that I was afraid was about to spin too far out of control. I didn't know if I'd ever be able to catch up. Just then the phone rang again.

'*Ananda Lewis Show*,' I said, slurring all the words together again.

'Can I please speak to Ms Bosnak?' a woman asked.

'This is,' I said.

'Hi, Ms Bosnak, this is American Express,' she said. Oh

crap. 'I'm calling to find out when you plan on making payment to your account.'

'Um,' I said. 'How much is my monthly payment?' I asked, meaning 'How much do you *think* I owe you because I'm enrolled in the brilliant "Buy and Return Credit Payment Management Plan."'

'Well, your total balance is over $10,000,' she said.

'Yeah, but how much do I owe you right now?' I asked. As she said her next words, I realized it: I had been so busy working that I'd forgotten to do the whole Buy and Return Credit Payment Management Plan thing for June's bill.

'You owe over $10,000 right now,' she repeated. The words just echoed in my head like she'd said them in slow motion or something. *$10,000, $10,000, $10,000 . . .*

'$10,000?' I asked. 'Are you sure it's not like I only owe $1,000 this month and $9,000 next month?'

'No. You owe $10,000 today. Right now. All at once,' she said rudely, and then added, 'Your account has been frozen too because you are over your limit.'

'Huh,' I said, thinking about the amount. *$10,000, $10,000, $10,000 . . . Frozen, frozen, frozen. . .* 'Um, I'm gonna have to give you a call back.'

'When do you plan on paying it?' she asked. She was persistent.

'I'm going to have to call you back,' I said again and then hung up.

I leaned back in my chair and started to freak out. How stupid could I have been!? How did I just forget to buy and return $10,000 worth of stuff!? There was no way I would be able to come up with $10,000 to pay American Express. But instead of trying to figure out what I was going to do, I decided to get back to work. Because if I messed up and got fired or something, then I'd be *really* screwed.

Being a producer there's always that feeling that you are only as good as your last show. The term 'job security' doesn't always apply. So far in my career I had been lucky, and my bosses always really seemed to like me. But I was embarking on something different here, and needed to make sure that they were confident that I could do my job. I needed to make sure that they trusted me. So I needed my first show to be great. I felt that if for any reason they thought it was bad, then I'd be out the door.

So every day for the rest of that week, I threw myself into my job. American Express continued to call, but thankfully they either got my voice mail or I convinced them that I was someone else, and Karyn was unavailable at the moment. In all my craziness I completely blew off my first weekend in Fire Island – a weekend for which I had already paid.

NINE

AMERICAN EXPRESS
® American Express

Karyn Bosnak
400 E. 57th St.
New York, NY 10010

Date	Payee		Amount
Jul 1, 2001	OVERDUE		
		Total	**$ 10,575.00**

JENNIFER
CONVERTIBLES

Karyn Bosnak
400 E. 57th St.
New York, NY 10010

Date	Payee		Amount
	PREVIOUS BALANCE		$ 1,259.00
Jul 12, 2001	Finance Charge		$ 25.00
Jul 12, 2001	PAYMENT		– $ 40.00
		Total	**$ 1,244.00**

Marshall Field's

Karyn Bosnak
400 E. 57th St.
New York, NY 10010

Date	Payee	Amount
	PREVIOUS BALANCE	$ 121.00
Jul 5, 2001	Late Fee	$ 25.00
Jul 5, 2001	Finance Charge	$ 3.00
	Total	**$ 149.00**

citi MasterCard

Karyn Bosnak
400 E. 57th St.
New York, NY 10010

Date	Payee	Amount
	PREVIOUS BALANCE	$ 460.00
Jul 15, 2001	Late Fee	$ 30.00
Jul 15, 2001	Finance Charge	$ 10.00
	Total	**$ 500.00**

Capital One VISA

Karyn Bosnak
400 E. 57th St.
New York, NY 10010

Date	Payee	Amount
	PREVIOUS BALANCE	$ 750.00
Jul 20, 2001	Late Fee	$ 25.00
Jul 20, 2001	Finance Charge	$ 16.00
	Total	**$ 791.00**

DISCOVER
FINANCIAL SERVICES

Karyn Bosnak
400 E. 57th St.
New York, NY 10010

Date	Payee	Amount
	PREVIOUS BALANCE	$ 7,388.00
Jul 1, 2001	Finance Charge	$ 148.00
	PAYMENT	– $ 150.00
	Total	**$ 7,386.00**

Karyn Bosnak
400 E. 57th St.
New York, NY 10010

Date	Payee	Amount
	PREVIOUS BALANCE	$ 1,140.00
Jul 12, 2001	Late Fee	$ 35.00
Jul 12, 2001	Finance Charge	$ 25.00
	Total	**$ 1,200.00**

DIRECT MERCHANTS BANK

MasterCard

Karyn Bosnak
400 E. 57th St.
New York, NY 10010

Date	Payee	Amount
	PREVIOUS BALANCE	$ 3,245.00
Jul 22, 2001	Late Fee	$ 30.00
Jul 22, 2001	Finance Charge	$ 65.00
	Total	**$ 3,340.00**

Grand Debt Tally $25,185.00

RAZZLE BEDAZZLE 'EM

The next Tuesday, I finally mailed my June rent check and prayed to God that it wouldn't clear until I got paid on Thursday, which was July 5. Unlike last year, I was actually happy to work the day after the holiday. In order to avoid my bank's whole 'five-day-check-clear' rule, I planned on taking my paycheck directly to the bank that it was drawn from to cash it, and then planned on depositing that cash into my checking account.

As much as I needed to focus on my bills – especially American Express – my primary concern was my show, which was scheduled to tape in one week. By now we had our guests for the show locked in, but I wasn't completely convinced they would be good. I was very worried. The more I worked that week, the more I began to realize that I didn't really like my new job that much. I knew it would be hard work, but I didn't expect it to be *this* hard.

Because I was a new producer, I thought maybe my producing skills were to blame for the chaos in my show, but as I looked around the office, I realized that every producer seemed to be having the same problems that I was. Sometimes with a launch, things go smoothly, and sometimes they don't. And things definitely weren't going smoothly at *The Ananda Lewis Show.* It's hard for me to say exactly what the problem was. Because if I knew, or if anyone knew, for that matter, then we would have fixed it and things would have gotten better. Everyone on the staff seemed to be overworked and overstressed. We were all wiped out, and the show hadn't even aired yet.

Later that week I awoke with a sore throat and was worried that I was getting a cold. The last thing I needed was to be sick for my big day. So I swallowed echinacea and guzzled orange juice and went back to focusing on getting my show in order. I had chyrons to write (chyrons are words that you see at the bottom of the screen that move the story along – names of guests, etc.), tape pieces to edit, a script to write – there were a lot of loose ends that needed to be cleared up. The last thing I could take was a sick day.

While I could count on my AP Molly to help take care of things, I couldn't say the same for my PA Mike. He wasn't the sharpest knife in the box, if you know what I mean. For example, last week I had asked him to get me some safety pins for the show, and about an hour later he came over to my desk empty-handed – except for a list.

'Karyn,' he said.

'Yes, Mike,' I replied, knowing that I was in for a big treat with whatever he had written on his notepad.

'I've done some research on the safety pins that you asked for, and I found out that they come in three sizes. They have small ones, which measure about three-fourths of an inch, medium ones, which measure about one and one-eighth inches, and large ones, which measure about one and a half inches.'

'Mike,' I said, 'they're safety pins. I don't really care. I just need them to hold up someone's BeDazzled outfit if it falls down.' I felt like I was talking to a two-year-old every time he asked me a question.

'So,' he asked after pausing for a moment, 'which ones should I get?'

'Mike, I don't really care,' I said with irritation. 'Just get the medium ones.'

'About how many?' he asked.

'Just get a package, dude! This is not brain surgery! It's safety pins!' I had a hard time being patient with Mike.

'There's an art supply store down the street that I can go to to get some,' he said. 'I called ahead and they have them in stock.'

'Mike, you can get them next door at the drugstore. There's no need to go all the way to an art supply store,' I said.

Molly thought it was funny when I lost my patience with Mike, but it was impossible not to. Every simple task turned into a huge project with him. And with a script to write, and tapes to edit and all the other stuff that I had to do, I didn't need to hear a 'State of the Safety Pin Address.'

Before I knew it, the day of my show arrived. After having a morning meeting, my team and I headed over to the studio at CBS. If you've ever been in the CBS building, you know it's like a big ole maze. And it's enormous. If I got lost once that day, I got lost a hundred times. Molly too. And Mike – by the time the show started, Mike wasn't allowed to leave the backstage area. To make matters worse, most shows that had been taped so far only had a few guests on them – maybe six or seven at the most. But my show today had twenty-four. So just keeping track of them all was a show in itself.

After a couple hours of preparation, script and chyron changes, the show finally began taping. I took my place on the side of the studio, and Mary stood next to me just like at *Curtis Court.* The show started off a bit slowly, which I wasn't too thrilled about, but after a while it seemed to pick up. Some of the guests were good, and as I expected some of them were bad. By the end of the show, I thought it was just okay. Just okay isn't the end of the world, but after all of the work that went into producing it, it wasn't exactly what I was hoping for. I couldn't help but feel disappointed.

After all the guests left the studio, I gathered up some of my stuff so I could go back to the office. On my way out, I saw Mary in the hallway. I was exhausted, I was still sick, and she could tell.

'Are you okay?' she asked, noticing the disappointed look on my face.

'No,' I said. Then I burst into tears. She walked over to me.

'What's wrong?' she asked.

'I don't think my show was very good,' I said. 'I think it sucked.'

'It didn't suck, Karyn,' she said. 'It was a big show. A lot went into it. It was good.'

'It sucked. I know it sucked. You can say it. It's okay.' I was still crying. 'I mean, I'm fine with the fact that it was bad. I can accept it.'

'You did a really great job. I know how you feel though. It's just kind of like a release. You've been working on that damn show for a month! And now it's finally over,' she said. It was.

'Yeah, thank God,' I said.

'Here's five bucks,' she said, reaching into her pocket and handing me a five. 'Go get a cup of coffee, relax, and regroup. And then get back up to your desk, because you have another show to start working on for next week, sister!' She started laughing. She was right. I did have another show in exactly one week. And another show exactly one week after that. It felt like my life was going sixty miles an hour at the moment, and there wasn't an exit in sight for miles.

'Thank you, Mary,' I said. She was so nice. I didn't want to disappoint her. With that, I left CBS and walked to get some coffee and gummi bears. And after a short break, I got back to work.

For the rest of that week and the following week my life continued at the same pace. My social life had become completely nonexistent. Because of work, I was too busy to go away to Fire Island for my second weekend – another weekend for which I had already paid. The more I worked, the more I began to despise the job. I wanted to quit, but I couldn't. I owed so much money to credit card companies – I didn't even know how much at this point. I just completely shoved all my bills in my closet like they didn't exist. And I was still a month behind in my rent. And even if I did catch up, I'd never be able to pay $1,950 a month without this job. I felt trapped, and essentially, I was – there was no one to blame but myself.

THE CEO OF YOUR OWN LIFE

By the beginning of August, I finally paid July's rent and continued my life of work hell. By now I had completely stopped going to the gym and continued to eat horribly. And the cold I had still had not gone away. Now I even had bumps in the back of my throat.

The previous weekend, my dad had turned sixty, and there was a small surprise birthday party for him in Chicago. My work schedule was still crazy, but I managed to sneak home for one whole day. My sister and her husband were there too, and my friend Naomi even managed to come as well. I was so overtired that I got tears in my eyes when I saw them.

That day at the party, I tried to put on a happy face for my dad and pretend that my new job was great. But I was so stressed out and sad inside that it was difficult. My sister knew how unhappy I was, and so did Naomi. But my dad had no clue. As I watched him open presents, he looked at me and seeemed so proud. As much as I wanted to quit my job, I didn't want to let him down.

Later that day, Naomi let it slip out that she had just talked to Brad. Potentially Gay Brad. Brad who never called me back Brad. The one guy that I actually liked since moving to New York.

'Did he say anything about me?' I asked.

'Well, yeah,' she said. 'I asked him what happened between you two, trying to make it sound casual so he wouldn't think that I would run back and tell you,' she said.

'And,' I said.

'And he said that he stopped calling you because you worked too much,' she said.

'Are you kidding me?' I asked.

'No, that's what he said,' she said.

I worked too much. Gosh, if he thought I was bad then,

he should see me now. 'Wow,' I said. I had just finished telling her how much I hated my job.

'I think you should quit your job,' she said.

'I can't quit my job,' I said. As much as she was my best friend, I couldn't tell her that I couldn't quit my job because I owed butt-loads of money and was an entire month behind in my rent. I was embarrassed.

'Why not?' she asked.

'Because I'm under contract,' I said. 'If I break my contract and quit, I can't go work at another television show.' It was true.

That night after the party I flew back to New York. I cried on the plane the whole way home. I didn't just cry because Brad stopped calling me. I cried because I always said I'd never become one of those people whose job is their whole life. I didn't want to be one of those forty-year-old women who is successful but single and childless. I always thought that I wanted a career. But now that I had one, I wasn't so sure anymore. This job was horrible. But because of my financial obligations, I was trapped.

The next Monday, instead of rushing off to work, I decided to call in and tell them I'd be late. I needed to go to the doctor. On my way there, I felt a sense of relief. I felt like I was playing hooky.

I arrived, and after a brief exam, I met the doctor in his office for my diagnosis. He sat down at his desk and I sat down in the chair across from him. I was ready to hear that I had developed an incurable disease from too much work.

'You are fine,' he said. 'It's not strep throat or anything. Just a cold.'

'Good,' I said. I was relieved.

'But, Karyn, if you've had it for weeks, then why did it take you so long to come and see me?'

'I've just been really busy at work, and it's been hard for me to find the time,' I said.

'Well, working a lot is no excuse for you to neglect your health,' he said. He was right.

'Yeah, I know,' I said. Just then I started to tear up again. I was so embarrassed because there was no reason for me to cry. But lately I seemed to be crying at the drop of a hat.

'Why are you crying?' he asked.

'I'm just really stressed out. I'm not really that happy at my job,' I said.

'Well, get a new one,' he said.

'It's not that easy,' I replied, surprised at his frankness. I wanted to scream 'I can't quit my job because I owe a gazillion dollars to credit card companies!' but I didn't.

'You just don't understand,' I said instead.

'What don't I understand? If you hate your job, get a new one,' he said again. 'To be honest, Karyn, you are fine and healthy. People come to see me every day who are dying. If the worst thing that's wrong with you is that you have a bad job, well then, just get a new one,' he said unsympathetically.

I know my doctor had a point here, but I was too upset to realize it. And being a doctor he should have been a little sympathetic to my problems, considering I was having a complete breakdown right in front of his eyes.

'Excuse me?' I asked, shocked.

'Seriously, your problems aren't that bad,' he replied. 'You seem to be making a mountain out of a molehill. Just get a new job.'

'Sir, I'm not trying to be rude here, but people kill themselves over bad jobs, so don't downplay my problem,' I said.

'Are you having thoughts of suicide, Karyn?' he asked, looking at me pathetically.

'No, sir, I'm not. But how dare you be so insensitive as I'm sitting in front of you having a breakdown. You're my doctor.'

'Well, I'm sorry,' he said. 'Do you want me to prescribe you anything to help deal with the stress?'

'No, I don't,' I said as I rose to leave. 'I'll be fine.' I walked out of his office and paid the lady in the front. After walking out the front door and jumping into a cab, I vowed never to go back to that doctor again.

Later that afternoon, as I was going over my next show with Alexandra, the supervising producer, she asked me if I was feeling better.

'Yeah,' I said. And then it happened again. I broke into tears.

'Oh no. Not another one,' she said.

'Huh?' I asked, confused.

'You're the second producer to cry in my office today,' she said.

'I'm sorry,' I said, wiping the tears from my face.

'Don't be sorry. I know how you feel. You are frustrated and tired. I feel the same way.'

I confided to Alexandra about how much I hated my job, and she just listened and listened. She seemed to understand where I was coming from. I told her what my doctor said and explained how irritated I was by his insensitivity.

'You know, Karyn, as sad as it was that he was so insensitive, he did have a point. This is just a job.'

'Yeah, I know,' I said. But just like I didn't tell my doctor, I also didn't tell Alexandra why it was so difficult for me to just walk out the door.

'What you need to do is go home. You need to regroup,' she said. 'You are a very good producer. You care a lot about what you do. The problem is that you might care too much. You need balance in your life.' She was right. I did care too much. But I only cared too much because I needed the job – more importantly the big paycheck that came along with the job – because I needed to pay off my bills.

'You need to have control over all the areas in your life. When you put everything you have into just one area, like your job, for example, then you jeopardize the rest of you.

Your body breaks down, you break into tears for no reason – these are all signs that something is out of whack.' I kept listening.

'What you need to do is become the CEO of your own life. Pretend that "Karyn" is a business, a company. There's the personal department, there's a love department, there's a family department, and there's a professional department. And know that if any of these areas are out of whack, then all the other areas won't be able to function properly either, and the whole business will go under.'

She was right. I had been completely avoiding my credit card bills for the past month because I needed to concentrate on working so I could pay off those bills – which was why I was taking my job so seriously. And in taking my job so seriously, I'd started to ignore my health, my personal life – everything. I needed to gain control.

COMPANY OVERHAUL

Later that afternoon, I decided that I needed to confront my debt. I couldn't avoid it forever. It wasn't going to go anywhere. The first thing I needed to do was figure out exactly how much I owed. After checking the balance of every card and adding everything up, I realized that I owed over $25,000. In my mind I always thought it was around $17,000 or so, but I was way off. It was twenty-five thousand fucking dollars. Holy shit.

I heard about this thing called a debt counseling program from a girl I used to work with. She had a bunch of credit cards and told me how she enrolled in a program like this and said it was the best thing she ever did. The company canceled all of her cards, lowered all of her interest rates and consolidated all of her debt.

After poking around on the Internet for a while, I found the name of a company that seemed to be the same thing called CreditGUARD of America. On the top of their website it said, 'Every three seconds another person falls behind on their bills.' I decided to call them up. As the phone rang, I felt nervous.

'CreditGUARD of America,' someone answered.

'Hi,' I said. 'I think I want to enroll and I guess I need to talk to someone.' I didn't know what exactly to say.

'Sure, no problem,' she said. 'About how much money do you owe?'

'Um . . . around $25,000,' I said. I felt so ashamed.

'Is it all credit card debt?' she asked.

'Yes,' I said, embarrassed. I expected her to yell at me and tell me that I was an idiot. But she didn't.

'Okay, how many cards do you have?' she asked calmly.

'Um, eight,' I answered.

'Are they all overdue?' she asked.

'All of them but two,' I said. I had just sent payments in to Jennifer Convertibles and Discover.

'You can only enroll the cards that are overdue,' she said. As much as I wanted to enroll all of them, I was still relieved. The one that worried me the most was American Express. As long as they took that one, then I'd be okay.

'Okay,' I said. 'Wait, how does this work?'

'Well, if you choose to enroll in the program, you'll give me all of the account numbers for the credit cards that you have that are overdue. Then, we will call the companies, close the accounts, and negotiate a lower interest rate for you. After that I will work with you to figure out how much you can afford to pay each month, and then once a month, we will debit your checking account for that amount and send the payments to the companies for you.'

'Does it look bad on my credit report?' I asked.

'It looks worse to constantly be late on your payments. We don't report anything to credit reporting agencies, but the credit card companies of the cards that you enroll may say something like you enrolled in a debt management plan. That may turn off some people when they see it, but it obviously looks better than filing for bankruptcy.'

'Okay,' I said. 'How do you make money?'

'We are a nonprofit organization,' she said.

'Really?' I asked, surprised.

'Really,' she said.

'Okay,' I said, 'I'm in.'

For the rest of the afternoon, I filled out paperwork that she faxed me, and by the end of the day I was a member of CreditGUARD of America. On the fifteenth of every month, they would deduct $432 right out of my checking account and disperse the appropriate payments to my creditors.

In addition to canceling all of the cards, the woman on the phone was able to lower all of my interest rates. They lowered most of them to around 10 percent, and there was actually no interest rate on my American Express and Marshall Field's bills. Really! Zero! She also told me that if any of my creditors called me in the next week looking for payment, all I had to do was give them her number. I felt so relieved! I was being the CEO of my own life! I was taking control!

The next thing I needed to take care of was my rent. And simply catching up wasn't the best option here. I needed to move. $1,950 a month was a lot of money. Almost half of the money I took home was going toward my rent. I needed to find a cheaper place to live. Just then, my phone rang.

'Hi, Karyn, it's Scott!' a guy's voice said. Scott was a guy I used to work with in Chicago at *The Jenny Jones Show*. He now also lived in New York and worked for the *Sally Jessy Raphael Show*.

'Hi!' I exclaimed. I was happy to hear from him.

'How's the bike treating you?' he asked. Scott and I had bought bikes together one day during the two months I had off. It was actually kind of funny, because one day he called me up and asked me to go bike riding.

'Oh, I'd love to, but I don't have a bike,' I'd said.

'Me neither, let's go buy some,' he'd said.

'Okay!' I yelled. And so about a half hour later, I met Scott at the local bike store by my apartment and we each spent about $300 on a bike just so we could go bike riding. But the difference between Scott's purchase and my purchase was that he'd wanted a bike for a long time and had been saving up for one. So he paid cash. But I just wanted to go for a bike ride that day, so I charged mine.

'Great, the bike is treating me great,' I said. The truth was that I hadn't taken it out since we last went for a ride.

Anywho, just as God was listening to me when I needed to find a hair place for cheap, and just as God was listening to me when I needed that Discover Card, God too was listening to me worry about finding a cheaper place to live.

'Cool,' he said. 'Listen, the reason I am calling is that I remember the last time we talked you said something about your rent going up to almost $2,000 a month. And I found a great huge two-bedroom apartment that I want to move into, but my current roommate doesn't want to move. So I was just wondering if you'd be interested in moving in with me and having a roommate.'

'Yes, absolutely!' I said without hesitation. 'How much is the rent?'

'It's $2,300 a month, so it would come out to $1,150 each,' he answered. $1,150 a month? That would save me $800 a month on rent alone! Almost $10,000 a year!

'Oh my gosh, I'll take it,' I said immediately. 'I don't even need to see it.'

'Wait, wait, let me tell you about it. It's huge. You'll die when you see it. It's two bedrooms, two bathrooms, two floors. And it's brand new. It was built only a year ago, so everything in it is new. Oh yeah, and it's in Brooklyn.'

'Brooklyn?' I asked. I hesitated. I thought about my 'near Brooklyn' experience when I'd forgotten to get off the train on the way to get my hair done.

'Yeah, Brooklyn,' he said. 'It's in a neighborhood called Boerum Hill, which is right past Brooklyn Heights and Cobble Hill. It's only three stops on the subway from Manhattan. It's in an awesome neighborhood. Brooklyn is a very cool place to live. It's kind of like Bucktown was in Chicago,' he said. Bucktown in Chicago is an area that used to be considered 'dangerous' until all the yuppies started to move in and take it over. So it still had a gritty city feeling to it, with pockets of bad areas. But for the most part it was safe. In the rent department, you got a lot more for your money in Bucktown. And it seemed to be that that was the case with Brooklyn too. But even when I lived in Chicago, I was never a Bucktown kind of girl. I was a Michigan Avenue kind of girl. So I doubted I was a Brooklyn type of girl either, but the price was just too good to pass up.

'Okay, I'm in,' I said. 'I seriously don't even need to see it. I trust your judgment. Just sign me up.'

'Cool,' he said. 'It's available 1st October. I'll call the landlord and tell him that we will take it, but I still think you should see it. So let's go this weekend.'

'Okay, sounds like a plan,' I said.

As I hung up the phone, a huge smile crept across my face. I was going to be okay. I was going to get out of this horrible mess and move into a cheaper apartment. Everything was going to be okay. I just needed to call my landlord and make sure that they would let me out of my lease. And seeing as I was a month behind in my rent, I didn't see why they wouldn't.

The next day Scott called to tell me that the landlord was getting the lease ready, but would also have to run a credit check on each of us. I had Mary type up a note telling him that I made over $100,000 a year because I knew he would probably freak out when he saw that I owed about $25,000. I faxed it to him along with the credit check consent form that Scott had told me to fill out.

On Wednesday morning, I called my landlord to ask if I could break my lease. No one was available for me to speak to, so I just left a message. That day, the King World sales team was having a big sales luncheon for the show at Chelsea Piers, and the entire staff had to attend. And of course when someone from my landlord's office called me back, I was right in the middle of lunch.

'Hi, Karyn? This is the attorney from your landlord's office. You called about a question on your lease?' she said.

'Yeah. Thanks for calling me back,' I said nervously, making my way outside. 'Um, as you probably know, I am a month behind in my rent, and I was just wondering if there is any way that you would let me out of my lease. I've just had some problems paying my bills lately. I honestly just can't pay the rent anymore.' No more excuses. No more 'I lost my checkbook.' I had to be honest.

'Oh, I'm sorry,' she said. 'If we find someone to rent your apartment we'll let you out of your lease. But if we don't then you'll be responsible for the rent until we do.'

'Okay,' I said. 'I'm looking to move out by October 1st.' I didn't want to move. I loved my apartment, but I didn't have a choice. I started to cry again.

'Well, that gives us a little over a month,' she said. Just then, she could tell that I was crying. 'Listen, don't worry, honey. Between us I'm pretty sure we'll be able to find someone.' She was so nice.

'Thank you,' I said.

'And you know what? Since we have a security deposit from you, why don't you just pay August's rent, and I'll use the security deposit for September's. It'll be easier rather than having you pay September, and have us do an inspection, and then reimburse you.'

'You'd do that?' I asked.

'Yes. I'll just have Spiro the super assure me the apartment is in good condition.' she said.

As I hung up, I wiped my eyes dry and went back inside to

the party. That call, and the one that I'd made the day before to the credit counseling service, were two of the most humbling calls I had ever made in my life. It was embarrassing to own up to the fact that I had been so irresponsible. But I was doing the right thing. Everything was going to be okay. I was going to get my finances cleared up, move into a cheaper apartment, and if I was still unhappy at my job, then I wouldn't feel so trapped to stay and I could quit. I was going to be okay.

TEN

CREDITGUARD
OF AMERICA

Karyn Bosnak
400 E. 57th St.
New York, NY 10010

Date	Creditor	Payment	Balance
Aug 15, 2001	American Express	– $ 218.00	$ 10,357.00
Aug 15, 2001	Capital One Visa	– $ 29.00	$ 762.00
Aug 15, 2001	Citibank MasterCard	– $ 21.00	$ 479.00
Aug 15, 2001	Direct Merchant's Bank MC	– $ 76.00	$ 3,264.00
Aug 15, 2001	Fleet Visa	– $ 48.00	$ 1,152.00
Aug 15, 2001	Marshall Field's	– $ 20.00	$ 129.00
Aug 15, 2001	Service Charge	– $ 20.00	$ 40.00
	Total		**$ 16,143.00**

JENNIFER CONVERTIBLES

Karyn Bosnak
400 E. 57th St.
New York, NY 10010

Date	Payee	Amount
	PREVIOUS BALANCE	$ 1,244.00
Aug 12, 2001	Finance Charge	$ 25.00
	PAYMENT	– $ 100.00
	Total	**$ 1,169.00**

DISCOVER FINANCIAL SERVICES

Karyn Bosnak
400 E. 57th St.
New York, NY 10010

Date	Payee	Amount
	PREVIOUS BALANCE	$ 7,386.00
Aug 1, 2001	Finance Charge	$ 148.00
	PAYMENT	– $ 150.00
	Total	**$ 7,384.00**

Grand Debt Tally $24,696.00

THE LAUNCH

After three months of preparation hell, *The Ananda Lewis Show* finally premiered on Monday, September 10, 2001. Despite my exhaustion and utter hatred of the show, I couldn't help but feel excited. I hoped it did well. When you work that hard on something, you want to be proud of the final product. I wanted it all to be worth it.

As for my big Fire Island share, I eventually had a chance to go one weekend, but it was just not my scene. It was nice, but it was just a little too college-ey for me. I hated it. And I had paid for four weekends of it. What a waste.

As planned, I went to see the apartment in Brooklyn with Scott, and he was indeed correct. It wasn't that far from Manhattan, the neighborhood was kind of cool, and the apartment itself was huge. In addition to being two floors, it also had a backyard!

The landlord, however, was reluctant to rent it to us after he saw my credit report. He couldn't understand how I made so much money but still had so much debt. After Scott assured him that I was a trustworthy person, he finally approved our application. He did, however, make us give him two months rent as a security deposit, which I didn't have. So, vowing to never do it again, I called my mother and begged her for the money. And like she always helped me with my Marshall Field's bill at home, she helped me out in this situation too – but told me it was the last time.

That Monday, as I finished up some last-minute changes for my show that was set to tape the following day, I couldn't help but feel excited. I was moving into a cheaper apartment, I was on a credit card repayment schedule, and the show was finally premiering. All these things meant that life would hopefully get easier. Everything was coming together.

That night, there was a big launch party for the show that

took place in the penthouse suite of the Hudson Hotel. The Hudson Hotel was one of the hippest hotels in the city. It was an Ian Schrager hotel, which meant that it was super cool. The last two times that I had been to the bar there, I'd seen Harrison Ford and Claudia Schiffer. Separately, but I saw them. And he is just as sexy in person, ladies. And she was just as pretty too.

As the day wound down and the party grew nearer, I began to feel a bit of pressure because I hadn't yet finished writing my script for tomorrow's show. But being the CEO of my own life, I knew that I needed balance. So staying and working while everyone else went to the party was not the answer. So even though I wasn't finished, I left work around 7.00 P.M. to go to the party, and vowed to come in early in the morning to finish the script.

The penthouse suite at the Hudson took up the entire top floor of the hotel. The suite was shaped like a U, with each leg of the U being a huge outside deck. One side was completely open with tables, and the other side was covered with a tent. There were open bars and people passing hors d'oeuvres. The inside was decorated with all-white furniture, metal chairs and Lucite tables. It was one swanky party! Now *this* was what I imagined the life of a New York City television producer was like!

Shortly after the party started, it began to rain. Then pour. A huge thunderstorm started. As hotel staffers tried to close the sides of the tent, a powerful gust of wind blew across the deck and plates and glasses went flying. A few minutes later, my AP, Molly, got a call from Jennifer in the travel department. All of our guests that were going to be on the show tomorrow were flying in that evening, and because of the heavy rain, their flights were canceled. So Molly had to return to the office to reschedule all of them on morning flights.

About an hour later, the rain finally stopped and the hotel staff reopened the sides of the tent. I don't know if it was the after effects of the storm, but there was not a breeze in the air. The night was perfectly still and the sky had become perfectly clear. It was a beautiful night.

After mingling and mixing with everyone at the party, I walked over to the edge of the roof and took a good look at the beautiful Manhattan skyline. A smile crept across my face because it was *my* city. New York was now my home and I wasn't going to let it eat me up. I was going to get through this rough financial time and survive here. I couldn't let a bad couple of months get me down.

After the party, a few other staff members and I went out to another place. And after rescheduling all of our guests' flights for the morning, Molly joined us as well. That night we stayed out until 3.00 A.M. Because she lived in Queens and didn't want to go all the way home, Molly ended up staying on my couch.

The next morning we both woke up in a daze and hurried back to work to finish the script for our show. The show was about women and heart disease, and all of the guests were women who had suffered heart attacks at early ages. Sarah Ferguson, as in the Duchess of York, was the spokesperson for the American Heart Association, and was also scheduled to be a guest. I was so looking forward to meeting her.

Because of the party the night before, the morning meeting that usually took place at 8.30 A.M. was moved to 9.00 A.M. Since all of our guests were rescheduled to arrive that morning, I had Molly check on the flights to make sure they would be on time.

Around 8:45 A.M., as I was putting the finishing touches on the script, I heard someone say something about a plane crashing into the World Trade Center. As I looked up from my desk to the television in the corner of the office, I saw the news feed of smoke coming out of the side of one of the buildings.

'What happened?' I yelled to Kirk, our news producer, who was standing by the television.

'A plane crashed into the World Trade Center,' he said.

'How horrible,' I said. 'Like a commuter plane?' I asked.

'They're not sure,' he said. I turned around and looked out the window to see if I could see smoke, but I couldn't. The World Trade Center was all the way down in the Financial District, which was about four miles south of me. As the news started reporting more details about what happened, more staff members gathered around the television, including me. All of a sudden, as we were watching, Kirk jumped up.

'Oh my gosh, did you see that?' he screamed.

'See what?' I asked.

'Another plane just crashed into the other building!' A few minutes later, the news started to replay the second crashing over and over again, and everyone in the office started to get incredibly worried.

'That's not an accident,' Kirk said. 'Two planes don't accidentally fly into the biggest buildings in Manhattan. That was very deliberate.' Just then I thought about our guests who were flying in that morning. I knew Sarah Ferguson was already in town, but we had three other sets of people scheduled to land around 8.30 A.M. I turned around and saw Molly at her desk.

'Molly,' I said, yelling in the direction of her cube. 'Did our guests land?'

'I'm already on top of it,' she said. 'I've called Jennifer in travel and she's checking.'

As time went by, people started pacing and panic began to set in. A lot of people had friends who worked in the building and weren't sure of their whereabouts. I, fortunately, did not know anyone.

Around 9.15 A.M., my boss called our show meeting. We still didn't know what was going on, and therefore didn't know if we would be taping. But by the end of the meeting, news came in that Manhattan had been locked down, and we soon began to realize the magnitude of what was happening. We would definitely not be taping any shows today.

When I returned to my desk, Molly confirmed with

Jennifer that all of our guests had landed safely. The only problem was that we couldn't find them. They were either still at the airport or in cars on their way to the city, but with all the panic we couldn't figure it out.

'Molly,' I said, starting to freak out, 'these women have heart conditions.'

'I know, I know,' she said, looking at me.

I picked up the phone to call Sarah Ferguson's PR agency to let them know that we weren't taping, but I kept getting a busy signal. Then finally, after several attempts, I got through. After talking to a woman on the phone, I found out that Sarah Ferguson had already left Manhattan.

As news flashed on the TV about another plane crashing into the Pentagon, Jennifer told Molly and me that one of the drivers from the car company that we used had one of our guests in his car in Queens. He was unable to bring her into Manhattan though because of the bridges and tunnels being closed, so Jennifer was setting up for him to take her to a hotel around where they were.

Just then, Molly's phone rang, and another one of our guests confirmed that she and her husband were just dropped off at her hotel down the street. Since I didn't really know what was going on, and felt responsible for bringing these people into New York, I asked Mike to bring them money so they weren't stranded there penniless.

'I don't want to go,' Mike said. 'I want to go home.'

'Mike, I know, and I want to go home too. But please just do this one thing for me. The hotel is just down the street. It's a half a block away. We are responsible for these people. We brought them here, and we can't all just leave and go home. We have to make sure they're safe.'

'I know but I want to go home,' he said again. 'I want to be with my family.' He seemed to be on the verge of tears. For as much as Mike bugged me, I felt bad.

'If you just bring them the money then you can go home. Please,' I begged. Just then Molly's radio went off.

'You have two more guests that just arrived downstairs,' she said. They were our final missing guests.

'Please, Mike,' I said. 'If you go to the hotel, I'll take care of the people downstairs.'

'Okay,' he finally said reluctantly.

Mike and I walked downstairs, and as I stopped to take care of the people in the lobby, he kept walking to the hotel. The guest was the mother of an eighteen-year-old girl who died from a heart attack. The daughter was perfectly healthy and had been on her way to a Dave Matthews Band concert with her friends. Just yesterday, her family and friends had held a prayer service to mark the one-year anniversary of her death. I introduced myself to her and her sister, who she'd brought along as a traveling companion. They were from Georgia and were both so sweet.

'Hi, Karyn,' she said. I could tell she was terrified.

'Hi,' I replied. 'Everything is going to be fine.' I tried to sound calm.

'You know, Karyn, I want so badly to be with my daughter – but not like this,' she said. This poor woman was still so fragile, and I'd brought her to New York during one of the biggest terrorist attacks ever.

'I know, I know,' I said. 'But we are all going to be fine. And as much as you want to, you are not going to be seeing her anytime soon.' I had no idea if this was true.

After giving them $100 in cash, I put them into a cab to go to their hotel. As the cab pulled away, I looked across the street at the CBS building. People were running in and out of the revolving doors. I imagined that they had probably just called almost every employee in to work. It was a frightening sight. It was chaotic.

Shortly after I returned to my desk, Mike too returned and gathered his stuff to go home. Soon after that, news came in about the two towers collapsing. This time when I turned around to look out the window behind me, I saw a big white cloud. It didn't look like smoke. It just looked like a cloud.

After calling my parents and telling them that I was okay, I called my sister Lisa at work. She cried when she heard my voice.

'I'm so glad you are okay,' she said, sobbing. 'I was so scared. I tried to get through to you, but the line has been busy.'

'I'm absolutely fine. What you are seeing on television is southern Manhattan. I'm about four miles north of that. I'm okay.'

'You should go home, why aren't you home?' she asked.

'We had to make sure all our guests were in their hotels and safe. I'm totally fine. I'm in a short building on the third floor. I'm going to be okay. I'm not even at CBS.' As I said these words to my sister, I was shocked at how strong I was. Me, the biggest crier of all, didn't cry.

For the rest of the day, I stayed at work and watched as the rest of the day's events unfolded. Everyone did. No one really went home. We didn't work, but we stayed. I think we all felt safe in our short office building.

That night after watching President Bush's speech, I finally packed up and left. As I walked out onto 57th Street, I was shocked to see how quiet it was. I was one of the only people outside. That same calm that I felt after the storm last night was again present. I hopped onto the crosstown bus and the driver gave me a free ride home.

That night I stayed up until the wee hours of the morning watching the live news coverage. I wondered if the storm from last night had just occurred twelve hours later if this would have all happened. What if the flights were delayed? Even canceled?

One by one I listened as people played voice mail messages from loved ones that were trapped in the towers. Message after message I listened. Around three in the morning a woman called up in tears to say that her brother was in a tower. She said he left her a voice mail message and she wanted to play it for everyone to hear. She wanted everyone to feel the pain that she was feeling. She wanted everyone to hear the fear in his voice. Just then, a frightened man's voice came through my television set.

'Hi, it's me,' he said. 'I just want to tell you that I'm in the World Trade Center and I'm going to die. And I just want to tell you that I love you. And if there's anything that I ever did to hurt you or Mom and Dad, then I'm sorry. I'm so sorry if I've ever done anything to disappoint you. I love you.'

It was then that I finally cried. I cried for him and I cried for all the other voices that I heard that night. Voices that were scared. Voices that knew they were going to die any moment. Voices that put so many things in my life into perspective. He was going to die and he knew it. And the only thing that mattered to him was his family. Not his clothes or his shoes or even his job. At the end of the day, at the end of your life – the most important thing really is the relationships that you have with the people in your life. Nothing else really matters. Everything can change in a moment. And life is too short to be unhappy. And my doctor was right – if the worst thing that was happening to me at the moment was a crappy job, then I didn't have it too bad.

For the next few weeks as I went to work, I saw Army men with rifles on every corner. Tanks would drive down 57th Street – past Bergdorf Goodman, past Otto Tootsie Plohound. New York was like a different city. I felt like I was living in a war zone.

As for *The Ananda Lewis Show*, it was preempted by news every single day for almost two weeks. And as much as everyone tried to get back to work, how do you even begin to do that when what you do for a living really doesn't matter in the long run? How do you justify trying to produce a fun lighthearted show? What do you do? How do you pick up a phone and try to book a makeover show when honestly, the cut and color of someone's hair really doesn't matter? So for a few weeks following the eleventh, we produced some shows relating to disaster, and slowly we tried to get back to producing some upbeat shows. When the show did finally start airing again toward the end of September, the ratings weren't that good. Ratings in all of daytime television seemed to take a dive because more people were tuning in to news stations like CNN and MSNBC, including myself.

It was then that our executive producer, Jose, announced that he was leaving the show to move back to Los Angeles to be with his family. He had planned on going back and forth betwen the two cities, but after everything that had happened, it seemed like Los Angeles was where he needed to be. And Mary also announced that she would be moving on and up into development for King World. We were going to be getting new bosses. The plan was to relaunch *The Ananda Lewis Show* in November during sweeps.

So, just as I was getting ready for this big change at work, I also was getting ready for a big change at home. October was approaching, and it was time for me to pack up my bags and leave Manhattan for Brooklyn. A new chapter in my life was about to start.

EXILE TO BROKELAND

Thankfully, as planned, my landlord was able to sublet my apartment for October 1st, so I didn't have to worry about trying to pay double rent for a couple months. So I started to pack up my apartment, and being the CEO of my own life I even took a day off work to move.

Even though my new apartment was much larger than this one, my new bedroom was much smaller. I knew it wouldn't hold my cherry wood sleigh bed – or armoire, or nine-drawer dresser – so I had no choice but to get rid of it. I really wanted to sell it because I could have used the money, but since my mother bought it for me as a gift, she wouldn't let me. She instead paid to have it shipped to my sister. She wanted to 'keep it in the family,' she said.

The week prior to my moving, some of the doormen saved boxes for me so I wouldn't have to buy any. They were all so nice and I was so sad to go. I kind of felt like they were family. They were the people that I saw when I came home from work every day.

On moving day, as I was packing up my apartment, I was amazed at how much stuff I had accumulated over the past year. I had knick-knacks on every table, pictures on every inch of the walls, and vases full of silk flowers. I was truly amazed at how much stuff a 475-square-foot apartment could hold.

To make things easier on myself I hired a moving company. I don't drive U-Hauls, and I didn't really have any friends who were too eager to help me move, so it seemed like the logical thing to do. It cost me $400, but it was worth it. In less than an hour, they packed up my entire apartment. My entire New York City life – from my bike to my shoes to my nighties – was out of my Manhattan apartment and on its way to Brooklyn. I even took my lock. Damned if I was gonna let the super sell it back to the next sucker. After they left, it was just Elvis and me.

With a tear in my eye, I said good-bye to my short fridge, good-bye to my three big windows, good-bye to the chandelier people across the street, and good-bye to my two empty closets. One last time, I took the elevator down to the first floor, and said good-bye to all my favorite doormen. Sam, Osei, Edson – they were all there that day. And as I jumped into a cab and headed downtown toward Brooklyn, I said good-bye to 57th Street.

Elvis and I got to my new apartment much quicker than the movers, who were stopped and searched before they crossed the Brooklyn Bridge. So for about an hour, the two of us cleaned the apartment. Well, I cleaned and Elvis hid in the corner. He wasn't too happy to not be at home. I tried to explain to him that this was our new home, but he wouldn't listen.

I looked at the apartment so quickly last time that I seemed to have missed a few details. It seemed that I was now living catty-corner from the Brooklyn Penitentiary, as in *a jail,* as well as down the street from a boys' home – a delinquent boys' home, where the bad kids lived. I also lived a few blocks away from a rather large housing project. Now nothing is wrong with living in a housing project, but we all know that they aren't the safest places to be. Sure, the neighborhood was up-and-coming, it just wasn't quite there yet.

But other than that, it was great. The building that I now lived in housed six apartments. Three of them, including ours, consisted of the first floor and the basement. But the basement had windows, so it wasn't your typical dark, yucky basement. It was only halfway in the ground. The other three apartments were on the second and third floors. Some people that Scott and I knew from Chicago, which is how he found out about the apartment in the first place, occupied the apartment on the second and third floor directly above us.

The first floor of our apartment was a large living area and open kitchen. Past the kitchen was where my bedroom was located. It had a bathroom in it, as well as a door that led outside to the backyard, which was all ours. It measured about sixteen by twenty-five feet and had actual grass! After one year in Manhattan, I couldn't believe how impressed I was by grass! Our two downstairs neighbors had small yards just like us, and a short wrought-iron fence separated each one. The fence was big enough to keep each separate, but short enough to keep it social. The downstairs floor of the apartment was really just one big bedroom and another bathroom, which was Scott's. It was a bigger space than my bedroom, but I didn't really want it because it was too dark for me.

The movers arrived the same time the 1-800-Mattress guy did. Not thinking, I accidentally sent my mattress and box spring along with my bed to my sister. When I realized my mistake, I was disappointed, yet somehow strangely proud of myself for remembering the 1-800-Mattress number from the commercial. Just dialing the number alone made ordering a mattress fun!

After all of my stuff was unloaded, I slowly started unpacking. Just then Scott showed up with his stuff in a U-Haul. I was kind of freaked at the thought of having a roommate, because I had lived alone for over five years. But the more I thought about it, the less worried I became. Scott was pretty cool.

As he jumped out of the driver's seat, I noticed that he seemed to be fidgeting with something down by the ground. A few seconds later I saw the most spastic dog rip around the corner. Her name was Veda, and she was an eight-month-old Jack Russell terrier. You know, the kind of dog on *Frasier*. Except the one on *Frasier* is calm and Veda was a maniac.

With her tongue hanging out of her mouth, she kept trying to run forward but was stopped short by her leash. So her front legs were flailing wildly in the air while her back legs were still planted firmly on the ground. Her head was thrashing in every direction, and I think that her eyes were crossed. But the funniest thing was that she had a smile on her face. Dogs smile, they do. And she had a huge one! She seemed to be having the time of her life just hanging out on her leash! She wasn't at the zoo. She wasn't at the dog run. She was just on a leash in Brooklyn.

'She gets *realllly* excited,' Scott said, laughing.

'Um, I can see that,' I said. Poor Elvis wasn't gonna know what hit him.

'She's a big partier,' he said.

'Apparently so,' I replied.

For the rest of the afternoon, I helped Scott unload his

truck and Veda and Elvis partied. Well, Veda partied, but Elvis wanted no part of it. Every so often we would hear the sound of Veda's paws running across the floor, then a *hissssss* sound come from Elvis, and then a *pop, pop, pop* – which was the sound of Elvis whacking her in the head with his paw. He would do it repeatedly back and forth – kind of like on the *Three Stooges.* After a while, Elvis finally found a hiding place in the back of the closet and didn't come out for the rest of the day.

That night we met our neighbors, a married couple who had moved to Brooklyn one year ago from Texas. Their names were Allan and Diane, and they were in their early thirties. They both worked in the hotel business. Diane worked in sales at the Waldorf and Allan was a manager at the Hudson Hotel, the same place we'd had our launch party. And I do mean he *was* a manager, because he recently lost his job due to layoffs that occurred after the eleventh.

Allan and Diane had two big-ass dogs, a Doberman named Uwe (pronounced OOO-vay) and a wolf named Jazzy. Jazzy really was a husky, but she looked like a wolf to me. Every time Veda ran outside that night, Jazzy stared through the fence and licked her chops and slobbered a bit. So did Uwe, but Uwe did it because he had a crush on Veda. Jazzy did it because she wanted to eat her. Allan said she would chill out once she got used to her.

For the rest of the weekend, Scott and I finished unpacking. Well, I didn't exactly finish unpacking. I decided that I wanted to live a simple lifestyle. I didn't want knickknacks everywhere and a bunch of stuff out cluttering up my life. So I only unpacked what I needed, and shoved the rest of my boxes in a huge front closet. So my bedroom consisted of a mattress on the floor and clothes in my closet – that was it.

Since I now lived in Brooklyn, I had to take the subway to work every day – the *stinky* subway. The *let's see how many people can cram into one car at eight in the morning* subway. The *I know I didn't put any deodorant on this morning, but I'm gonna lift my arm and shove my pit in your face* subway. As a precautionary measure, I started to carry around antibacteria gel with me and frequently applied it to both my hands and the area underneath my nose. The thinking that went behind the 'area underneath my nose' part was that I hoped it would kill any yucky germs before they passed through my nasal passage.

As much as I didn't want to move to Brooklyn, I decided that it wasn't that bad. And for some strange reason, I felt like I had been there before. I am a big believer in déjà vu. You know, when you all of a sudden think you've been in the exact same situation, that you are in at that moment, before. Every time I have déjà vu, I feel a sense of relief and security. Because for some reason, I think it'a sign that I'm supposed to be where I'm at. No matter when or where the déjà vu takes place, I think it's a sign that I'm on the right path, that I'm doing the right thing. And almost every day since I moved to Brooklyn, I had déjà vu. So I thought that it was God's way of telling me that I was going to be okay and I was doing the right thing. In some strange way, I felt like it was part of a larger plan. I felt a sense of relief. Maybe it was just the cut in rent that relieved me – but I like to believe it was something else.

Oh, and also since Brooklyn began with the letter B, I felt it was only appropriate that I end up there. I was the fifth B in the sixth B, so to speak. I know it's kind of schizophrenic of me to think that way, but whatever made you think I was sane? I just charged up $25,000 in clothes and bikini waxes in a year. I have a tendency to act a little crazy at times.

F#S^#@!!

Shortly after Scott and I moved in, we had a sidewalk sale, and I pulled out some of the stuff from my boxes and sold away! I was planning on using the new money to buy myself a bed frame. I wasn't a huge fan of sleeping on the floor. All was going well until we hit a bit of a snafu and Scott had to close the sale down early. It seemed that I'd gotten a little carried away and sold the microwave.

'You sold the microwave?' he asked. 'Why did you sell the microwave?'

'I don't know,' I said. 'I think I just got a little overzealous. Someone offered me money for it.'

'Yeah, great. Um, but now we don't have a microwave, Karyn,' he said. 'And we're going to need to buy a new one.' Oops. He was right.

So he closed down shop early and that was the end of my sidewalk sale days. I did however make a few hundred dollars, and used it to buy myself that new bed frame. It was nothing fancy, but it was very low and modern. It was simple and it matched my new simple lifestyle.

Around the middle of October, the big management change finally took place at work. As Mary moved up, and Jose moved home, two guys named David and Ed moved in. David was a very young executive producer in his early thirties, who also came from the world of talk. Ed did as well, but his big claim to fame was creating the show *Fanatic* for MTV. Because of that, he never had to work another day in his life, and only came to the show because he was a friend of David's – David needed all the help he could get to try to save the sinking ship of *The Ananda Lewis Show*.

As sad as I was to see Mary and Jose go, I was excited that we had new bosses who would give the show a fresh start. Despite the fact that I still hated my job, I decided to stick it out. For one, the job market in New York was at a standstill. No one was hiring. And for two, I finally felt like I had a firm grip on my finances, so I would be able to concentrate on work. And with my rent being lower, and the paycheck that I was bringing home still pretty high, I would concentrate on paying down my debt as quickly as I could.

By now most television shows had gone back to their

normal selves as best they could. David Letterman was back on the air, so was Jay Leno, and people started to feel like it was okay to laugh again. It was okay to have fun. We would always be changed people, but it was still okay to watch silly daytime shows. It was still okay to give someone a makeover, because sometimes people needed a lift.

Because of the initial low ratings of the show, we had to perform big in November sweeps. So just like the beginning of the season, the pressure was on to perform again.

The first show I was assigned from the new management was called '*Cosmopolitan*'s All About Men.' Each year, *Cosmopolitan* magazine came out with an 'All About Men' issue that dished dirt on men's likes and dislikes, and picked one hot bachelor from each of the fifty states. So to promote the magazine, we were going to produce a show along the same lines as the issue. And I was the lucky producer to be assigned the show. And it was a big show.

For the next week my team and I worked feverishly. We had lifesize pictures of the bachelors in the issue blown up to hang in the studio. We created games to play like 'Name the top five erogenous zones on a guy' (see answer below).* We set up a girl on a date with three guys and had each one tell her what she did wrong. It was a hoot and a holler, and a whip and a slap.

As the show grew nearer, the pressure became greater. I worked more closely with Ed than with David, and I really liked him. He expected me to work hard, but was very easygoing and approachable. He reminded me of a big cartoon character that you just wanted to put your arms around and squeeze. I wasn't attracted to him or anything (he wasn't on my team anyway), I just liked him a lot.

The day before the show, Ed and I started to work on the script and ended up pulling an all-nighter. As in *I got home from work at six in the morning, changed my clothes and was back at work*

*Inner thighs, nape of the neck, ears, chest, and nipples

by eight all-nighter. It was obviously not by choice, but we hadn't taped such a high-production show yet and had to make sure everything was set so it would run smoothly.

Now let me tell you, it's a sad day in New York when a cute, single producer such as myself doesn't have time to take a shower or even sleep the night before fifteen hot, young bachelors were on her show. But that's what happened. Yep, poor ole Karyn didn't look too cute that day. But despite my lackluster appearance, the show ran relatively smoothly, and that's really what was important. And at the end of the day I packed up and went home to get a good night's sleep.

Since David and Ed had come on board, most of the shows were running pretty smoothly. Work seemed to be getting back to normal until anthrax showed up at CBS, and once again tapings were halted. November sweeps were just around the corner, and all the canceled tapings really began to take their toll.

It was then that the big snafu happened. Just like my *Curtis Court* contract, my *Ananda* contract was broken up into option periods. Everyone's contract on the staff was drawn up that way. The current option period expired on November 30, and King World needed to let each person know whether they were going to pick up their next option thirty days prior to that expiration date, which was by October 31.

But since David had only been executive producer of the show for two weeks and had really only gotten to see each producer work on just one show, King World didn't think it was fair to him or to us to make him decide whose options he was going to renew by that date. So once again they asked us to sign an extension, which would give them two more weeks to 'judge' whether they wanted to keep us.

They didn't make a big announcement about the extensions or anything. Our production executive just started calling each employee into her office one by one to explain what was going on. But word got around, and everyone knew what was happening.

Finally, on Thursday of that week, it was my turn to be called into her office. After she explained the situation, my understanding was this: I could sign the extension and give King World two more weeks to decide if they liked me and wanted to keep me. Two more weeks of working until midnight, possibly pulling all-nighters. Two more weeks of working my ass off to produce shows for November sweeps. And if those shows didn't run so smoothly, after all that they could still tell me 'no thanks.' I kind of felt like this option was a 'dazzle me for two weeks to prove that you are worth keeping' option. Or I could not sign the extension, in which case King World would have to honor my initial contract and let me know by October 31 whether or not they wanted to keep me.

I felt like I had already proven myself to this show, and was pretty sure that David and Ed liked me, but you can never really be sure. Television is a very fickle business.

So I had a choice to make, to sign or not to sign. The expected thing for me to do would be to sign because I have always been a go-with-the-flow type of girl. And everyone else was signing it, so why shouldn't I? But when I opened my mouth to tell her my decision, those words didn't come out.

'I'm not going to sign it,' I said to the production executive. What? I don't know why I said it. It just came out of my mouth. I didn't even think about it.

'Okay,' she replied.

And with that I got up and left her office.

Again, I don't know why I decided not to sign it. I guess I felt like I had worked my butt off for the show during the past five months, and actually for the company for the past year and a half. I put my heart and soul into this job. And if they couldn't show me the decency of giving me four weeks' notice, like it was stated in my original contract, to let me know if I had a job come December, then I wouldn't show them the decency of doing what they 'considered' fair to David and fair to me. And let's be honest, the extensions were really only for the benefit of them. How did I, or any employee, benefit from having two weeks' notice as opposed to four to find work if they chose not to keep us? It gave them more time to decide. And since every employee knew they were deciding, they would work their butts off to produce the best shows they possibly could for November sweeps. Their livelihoods depended on it.

Later that evening David called me into his office.

'Hey, Karyn,' he said as I was sitting down.

'Hi,' I said in my usual cheerful voice.

'I heard that you didn't sign the extension and was wondering why,' he said.

'I just want to know sooner rather than later if you are going to pick up my option,' I said. 'That's all.'

'Are you not happy here?' he asked.

'It hasn't been easy, but I'm totally on board,' I said. 'I think that you know that, and I just don't want to feel like I have to prove it to you for two more weeks. In my initial contract, it says that you have to let me know thirty days in advance, which is by next Wednesday, and I just want to know by then.'

'Oh, okay,' he said. He hesitated for a moment. 'I just wanted to know. You have a great attitude, and I was kind of shocked when I saw that you were one of only three people who didn't sign it. And I know the other two are not happy and don't want to stay.'

'Well, I want to make it work and you know that. I just would rather know sooner than later,' I said.

'Okay, thanks,' he said. I think it only seemed fair.

Before I knew it, it was Wednesday the thirty-first. Halloween. Option renewal day. Or Option nonrenewal day. I went to work, and worked away. And waited to see if I got a renewal letter. I figured if they didn't want to keep me they would have probably said something to me by now. And since no one had, I expected that I'd get the letter. But by five o'clock, it still hadn't come. Since I was sick of waiting, I decided to find David and ask where it was. But he was still in the studio taping a show, so I sought out the production executive and asked her.

'You aren't getting one,' she said. Huh?

'You mean they decided not to pick up my option?' I asked.

'King World made the decision to not pick up anyone's option who didn't sign the extension,' she said. 'It has nothing to do with you. It was an across-the-board decision.'

Since I didn't sign the piece of paper they shoved in front of my face one day last week, I lost my job – it was as simple as that. I stared at her blankly for a few seconds and then went back to my desk. I didn't really believe what had just happened.

In a daze I packed up my stuff and left. If I did indeed lose my job, then there was no sense staying past six. By the time I got home reality had set in and I started to cry. What the fuck was I going to do? I owed about $25,000 and I'd just lost my job. And ultimately it was my fault for not signing that stupid piece of paper. All of a sudden, I became really angry and started to feel really betrayed. I had worked for this stupid-ass company for a year and a half and devoted so much of my time to them, and I felt completely screwed over. So I picked up the phone to call David, knowing that he would be out of the studio by now. When I got him on the phone, I very calmly asked him what happened.

'You didn't pick up my option?' I asked. 'I worked my fucking ass off for this stupid show since it started and *you* didn't pick up *my* option.' I was calm. I really was. Okay, maybe not.

'It was a King World decision and I had nothing to do with it,' he said.

'So that's it?' I asked. 'You didn't even fucking tell me? I had to go and ask someone?' (Using the 'f' word helps me to get out my aggression.)

'I told you that it wasn't my decision, and I honestly didn't even know that it was official,' he said.

'What if the production executive wasn't there to tell me? And I showed up tomorrow, and then next week, and the week after still thinking I had a fucking job? Huh? Was I just supposed to guess that I was fired? Because usually when people are fired, David, someone tells them. They don't have to fucking ask.' It *really* helps me get out my aggression.

He was silent.

'Whatever,' I said and hung up the phone. I was livid. I was fucking let go. Fuck!

The next day I woke up and went to work. I didn't even want to go and don't know why I did. As soon as I sat down in my short-ass fucking cube, Ed called me into his office.

'What happened?' he asked.

I told Ed the whole story of what happened and he listened intently and nodded exactly when he was supposed to, meaning that he understood what I was saying. Of course I cried, cuz I had been having a problem keeping those fucking tears in my eyes since I started working at this damn show. I told him that if I knew that by not signing the piece of paper I would lose my job, then I might have signed it.

'Karyn,' Ed said to me with his big cartoonlike puppy eyes, 'can I be honest?'

'Please do,' I said.

'Get the fuck out of this place. It's a fucking disaster. It's going to do nothing for your career. If you went into David's office right now and asked, he'd probably take you back. He likes you. But I suggest you take this opportunity to get out of your contract. Move on. You hate it anyway.'

He was right. I would be totally out of my contract at the end of the month, and could work wherever I wanted and do whatever I wanted to do. It was kind of a freeing feeling. So that was it. I *did* lose my job. But maybe it was for the better. I'd get another job. I had a month to do so, which was plenty of time. I wasn't worried because I had never been without a job in my whole life. Never.

Alexandra, the 'CEO of your own life' boss, was one of the other two people who didn't sign her extension either, so she was leaving as well.

Anywho, I produced one more show about stepfamilies in crisis and realized then that I had made the correct decision. It was one of those 'conflict shows' where everyone that was on the show hated each other, and I just despised working on it. The whole thing fell apart at the last minute too, but I didn't care that much. I still left at six every day.

I am a firm believer that everything happens for a reason, so I thought that somehow this fiasco must be part of a bigger plan. David and I made up, and I realized that it really wasn't his decision to not pick up my option, and by my last day there, I kind of thanked him for it.

I threw myself headfirst into a job search, and called everyone I knew looking for work. David even lined up a couple of interviews for me. The jobs didn't pan out, but it was nice that he tried to help. I soon started to realize that the market wasn't looking too good. Everywhere I called told me the same thing: budgets were being cut and they were on a hiring freeze. As my last day of work quickly approached, I began to worry that I might not be able to find a job as easily as I thought I could.

I told Ananda about my leaving the show, and when she asked me why, I told her that I just wasn't happy there. It was the truth. Contract fiasco or not – I had never been so miserable in my whole life.

'What do you want to do?' she asked.

'I don't know,' I said. 'I really don't know.' That was the truth also.

Someone once told me, 'When what you do makes you hate what you do, it's time to get a new job.' And that was exactly what happened to me at *Ananda*. My experience at the show made me so miserable that I wasn't sure if I ever wanted to work in television again. I couldn't figure out if it was the show that I hated or the career.

On my last day of work, a bunch of people had a party at a bar to say good-bye to Alexandra, me and a couple other people who were leaving as well. After about an hour, Ananda showed up and gave me a going-away card. On the inside she wrote, 'Good luck with ?' She couldn't have hit it more on the nose. Four months of '?' was exactly what was about to happen.

ELEVEN

CREDITGUARD OF AMERICA

Karyn Bosnak
123 Broke Street.
Brooklyn, NY 11201

Date	Creditor	Payment	Balance
Dec 15, 2001	American Express	– $ 218.00	$ 9,485.00
Dec 15, 2001	Capital One Visa	– $ 29.00	$ 646.00
Dec 15, 2001	Citibank MasterCard	– $ 21.00	$ 395.00
Dec 15, 2001	Direct Merchant's Bank MC	– $ 76.00	$ 2,960.00
Dec 15, 2001	Fleet Visa	– $ 48.00	$ 960.00
Dec 15, 2001	Marshall Field's	– $ 20.00	$ 49.00
Dec 15, 2001	Service Charge	– $ 20.00	
	Total		**$ 14,495.00**

JENNIFER
CONVERTIBLES

Karyn Bosnak
123 Broke Street
Brooklyn, NY 11201

Date	Payee	Amount
	PREVIOUS BALANCE	$ 950.00
Dec 12, 2001	Finance Charge	$ 19.00
	PAYMENT	– $ 100.00
	Total	**$ 869.00**

DISCOVER
FINANCIAL SERVICES

Karyn Bosnak
123 Broke Street
Brooklyn, NY 11201

Date	Payee	Amount
	PREVIOUS BALANCE	$ 7,377.00
Dec 1, 2001	Finance Charge	$ 147.00
	PAYMENT	– $ 150.00
	Total	**$ 7,374.00**

Grand Debt Tally $22,738.00

THE UNEXPECTED ROOMMATE(S)

I woke up Monday morning and just lay in bed for a while. I didn't have anywhere to go, so I didn't see the point in rushing to take a shower. As I lay there in bed with Elvis sleeping on my pillow, I thought about my last two months in Brooklyn. I was happy to discover that I was adjusting relatively well to roommate life. However, I couldn't say the same for Elvis. He did eventually come out of his hiding space in the closet, but Veda continued to harass him, and as a result he continued to repeatedly whack her in the head with his paw. His favorite place to seek refuge was on top of the kitchen table, which was just out of the little freak's grasp. Sometimes when eating, Scott and I would find remnants of those tabletop visits in the form of cat hair and dirty paw prints. I wasn't thrilled that he had been up there, seeing as he shat in a box of rocks on a daily basis, but what was I gonna do? The little bugger had to escape somewhere.

Unlike myself, Scott was relatively normal. But he did have his little quirks, as we all do. For example, he was really into lighting. Our apartment, like a lot of New York apartments, came equipped with really ugly 'boobie' lights on the ceiling. I'm not exactly sure what the correct name of that style of ceiling light is, but we called them boobie lights because they resembled big breasts. Scott insisted on removing them and replacing them with more appealing fixtures. He also put dimmers on all the switches in the apartment, because we all know how important good lighting can be.

He was also really into cleaning, and more importantly straightening. If I cleaned a table or the floors, he'd clean them again even after I told him that I already did it. And I think an internal buzzer went off inside of him any time the placemats on the table became crooked. Even if they were just one centimeter out of whack, he would be over there straightening them up. I think it was one of his favorite pastimes. That same internal buzzer that went off with the placemats also went off when the ice cube bin in the freezer fell below a certain critical level. But when it did, he would be over there crackin' trays and filling it back up so that it was just on the verge of overflowing.

But as clean and meticulous as he was, there was one thing that I just couldn't understand: he drank out of a big Brita machine in the fridge. Now, I'm not a tap water person myself. In fact I'll admit that I'm a bottled water junkie. Evian bottles littered my desk at work, and jugs of the stuff filled the fridge as well. And sure I've been tempted to buy a Brita to save on all the plastic that I wasted, but have you ever looked closely inside one of those things? I know I'm not the only girl to notice all that crap that floats around. It's yucky crap. It's black crap. And people think that's clean? No thanks.

I eventually got up around 10.00 A.M. and made my way to the kitchen. The first thing I did was sit down to call the unemployment office. My bosses at King World told me that since I was in fact laid off, I could do this. After a short conversation with a woman at the New York State Department of Labor, I was set. I then decided to make some breakfast, but after opening the fridge and noticing its sparse contents, I decided to get dressed and go to Starbucks instead. I put on jeans and a sweater and headed out the door.

I paid $5 for my usual Café Americano and a muffin, and then sat down and thought about my plan of action. I had called tons of places in the last month looking for work, and no one was hiring. Every single person I talked to told me to call back in January. So I kind of didn't know what to do.

My financial situation was this: I would be making $405 a week in unemployment, which came to $1,620 a month. My rent was $1,150 and my payment to CreditGUARD of America was $432, which left me just $38. But I also had a Discover Card payment of $150, a Jennifer Convertibles payment of $40, a gas, electric and phone bill that were each around $30, and a cell phone bill that was around $60. I thought about canceling the cell phone, but since I had a yearlong contract I would have been charged $250. I instead changed to the cheapest plan they had, which was $40. So after all those payments, I would be negative $282 a month before I even bought food. I did however have about $1,500 saved, which would help pay that extra money, but I knew it wouldn't last that long. I didn't want to be out of work, but it looked like I didn't have a choice. So I just sat there and drank my coffee.

Later that night while Scott, Veda (who needed to be in the middle of whatever you were doing) and I were watching QVC, we heard a funny noise come from inside the wall. Since we'd moved in together, both Scott and I were delighted to discover that we had a mutual love for QVC. We're not big orderers or anything, we just liked to watch the program. In our opinion, QVC is far superior to all of the other shopping networks by a long shot. First of all, they have a counter meter, so you can see how many people are getting in on the 'fabulous offer' that you are watching. Second, they have a countdown clock that tells you how much time you have to get in on that 'fabulous offer.' And third they take 'call-ins' – just regular people like you and me who partook in that 'fabulous offer' and purchased the product that you are learning about. With those three things combined, how can one not order?

On that particular night, we were listening to Betty Sue tell us all how great her 'Breezies' brand underwear were, and were excited at the fact that over two thousand people had ordered themselves some Breezies brand underwear too. And then it happened. With only a minute and a half left on the Breezies brand underwear countdown clock, we heard a funny scratching noise coming from inside one of the walls.

Scratch Scratch Scratch!

Even Veda turned her head away from the TV to figure out where it was coming from.

'Did you hear that?' Scott asked me while turning down the volume.

'Yeah,' I said. A few seconds later, we heard it again.

Scratch Scratch Scratch!

Scott looked at me.

'It sounds like it's coming from inside the wall,' he said. He got up and walked over to it to listen.

Scratch Scratch Scratch!

'It sounds like a mouse,' he said. Huh! A mouse?

'Oh, please don't say that,' I said.

New York may be famous for having a rodent problem, but so far I hadn't had any. In fact, I've never had a mouse in any of my apartments. But my friend Tracy once had one that fell out of an air vent by the ceiling and got tangled in her hair while she was sleeping. Seriously. Just then we heard what sounded like little feet running across the ceiling above us.

Trot Trot Trot!

We immediately looked up and then looked at each other.

'That didn't sound like a mouse,' I said. 'That sounded more like a bear or something.' I got goose bumps all over my body.

'Maybe it's a rat,' he said. 'Seriously, I just saw a news special where there was a rat so big in a house in the Bronx that it actually took down a two-year-old and wrestled it to the floor,' Scott said.

'Oh, my gosh!' I said. 'I saw one about a rat that was so big it ate a baby! It swallowed him whole, I swear!'

'I believe you,' Scott said.

As we continued to listen, we again heard noises in the wall . . .

Scratch Scratch Scratch.

. . . and again heard something run across the ceiling . . .

Trot Trot Trot!

'I'll call the landlord tomorrow,' Scott said. And with that, we went back to watching QVC.

Later that night, as I lay in bed unable to sleep, I started to worry about my finances. I had only been unemployed now for all of one day, but I had never been in this situation in my whole life. I've always had a job or had a job lined up, and had never been out of work. And after all the calls I made in the past few weeks, it looked more and more like this situation was probably going to last through the month of December. Because no one, especially at television shows, seemed to be hiring in New York at that time. Before I knew it, it was two-thirty in the morning and I was still lying in bed wide awake. Just then I heard a noise come from inside my closet.

Scratch Scratch Scratch!

Oh no. I hoped it was just coming from inside the walls again, but then it got louder.

Scratch Scratch Scratch!

I quickly jumped up and stood on my bed. But since my bed was a 'low bed' it only stood about six inches off the ground. So I imagined if there was in fact a mouse or a rat in my closet and he did come out to play, he'd run right out and into the bed. I needed to act quickly.

As I stood there wondering what to do, I again heard more noises. By now I was pretty sure they weren't coming from inside the walls. Which meant that whatever was making the noises was on the loose. And of all the places to be! My closet! Near some of my most prized possessions! As thoughts of a rodent climbing all over my clothes filled my head, I decided that I needed to do something, but since I was too afraid to do anything alone I decided to wake up Scott. With one big leap, I jumped off my bed and into the living room, thinking that if my feet touched my bedroom floor, the rodent would jump out and attack me. I then ran down the stairs and opened the door to Scott's bedroom. It was dark and he was sleeping.

'Scott,' I said loudly enough to wake him.

'Uhhh,' said a groggy voice. 'What?'

'I think there's a mouse in my closet,' I said, terrified.

'So what? Just close the door and go to sleep,' he said.

'I can't. I'm afraid,' I said. 'I'm not a rodent kind of girl.'

'Well, I'm not a rodent kind of guy either, but it's not gonna come out and get you. Go to sleep.' Go to sleep? Who was he kidding? How was I going to go to sleep on a low bed with a rodent in my closet? Aggravated and realizing that he was not going to come help me, I went back upstairs and decided to arm myself with a broom for protection.

When I got back in my room, I saw that by now Elvis was staring intently inside the closet toward where the noise was coming from. Feeling brave, I decided to use the end of the broom to poke around by my shoes to see what would happen. Maybe I'd scare him enough to make him go back in the hole that he came out of.

Just then, something happened. A scuffle of some sort. But I'm not sure what because I immediately closed my eyes and started jumping up and down on my bed screaming. A few seconds later, I opened them up and saw that Elvis was now by my bathroom door looking as if he was ready to pounce on something.

'Elvis, come here,' I said frantically, trying to get him away from whatever creature happened to now be in my bathroom. He wouldn't listen and didn't even flinch. He just kept staring.

'Elvis,' I yelled louder. Tears started streaming down my face because I was terrified and I didn't want Elvis to get whatever it was. He's my baby. He's not a rodent eater. He sleeps with me and cuddles and stuff.

'Elvis,' I said for a third time. Just then, another scuffle occurred and I saw something gray run from one side of the bathroom to the other. With the broom, I jumped off the bed, ran into the living room and started to scream at the top of my lungs. A few seconds later Scott walked upstairs with Veda in his arms. Both of their eyes were half closed.

'He's in there!' I said frantically. 'In my bathroom! He's in there!'

'Okay. Shh, shh, shh. Settle. Just settle. It's just a mouse. There's no need for all the ruckus,' he said.

'But it's a big one. I saw it,' I continued. 'Just get Elvis, please. I don't want Elvis to get it. I don't want him to touch it. He sleeps with me!'

'He's a cat, just let him get it,' Scott said.

'No!' I screamed back. 'Rodents are dirty and I don't want him to get a disease.'

'Okay.' He handed Veda over to me. 'Hold her and give me the broom.'

'He's big. You're gonna need a pistol,' I said.

'A broom will do,' he replied.

While Scott made his way to the bathroom to rescue the cat, I held Veda tightly in my arms. Before I knew it, he grabbed Elvis by the scruff of the neck and handed him over to me. Unable to hold both pets, I put Elvis in the front hall closet and closed the door. Scott then made his way back to the bathroom and looked inside.

'Eww,' said Scott.

'Eww, what?' I asked.

'Eww, he's big,' he answered.

'I told you,' I said. 'What's he doing?'

'He's hanging out in the corner kind of staring at me. Maybe I should let Veda down to get it,' he said, laughing.

'No! That's gross,' I said.

'I'm kidding,' he replied.

'Is he a mouse or a rat?' I asked.

'Um, either a super-big mouse or a baby rat. I can't tell.'

'Yuck!' I yelled.

'Okay, here goes,' he said.

A few seconds later I heard the bang of the broom and a *squeak, squeak, squeak* noise come from the bathroom. I then heard the clatter that sounded like my $50 metal bathroom garbage can hitting the floor.

'What's going on?' I asked. 'Did you get him?'

'Umm, yeah,' said Scott from inside the bathroom. 'But he's not dead. He's just sort of stunned. I covered him with your garbage can. I'm going to need something flat to slide underneath it so I can trap him and run him outside.'

I opened the front closet to find something and saw that Elvis was sitting right by the door dying to get back out, not understanding why he had to be in there. 'It's for your own good,' I told him as I grabbed a large flat mirror that was leaning against the wall. I closed the door and gave it to Scott.

Still waiting in the living room, I heard him slide the mirror under the garbage can. He then walked out of the bathroom, through my bedroom, holding his 'trap' in between his two hands. As he made his way into the living room, he realized that he didn't have any shoes on.

'Oh crap,' he said. 'Can I borrow your slippers?' They were white and fluffy.

'Sure,' I said, taking them off. I put them in front of where he was standing, and he tried to wiggle his feet inside. Just then, the rodent seemed to get a burst of energy and started to move around underneath the can. Scott lost his balance a bit. Just then, I saw a big fat tail sneak out of the side of the can and for a moment I was afraid that he was going to get away. He started making noises.

Squeak Squeak Squeak!

'Hurry, open the front door!' Scott yelled.

As quickly as I opened it, Scott ran outside, slippers barely on. He then put the garbage can and mirror down on the sidewalk. He'd made it! He then turned back around toward me.

'What should I do with it?' he asked.

'I don't know,' I said.

'Should I just leave it here for someone to find?' he said.

‘No, you can’t do that.’

‘How about over there?’ I said, pointing to a Dumpster across the street.

‘Oh yeah,’ he said, ‘good idea.’ He picked up the garbage can and mirror and walked them both across the street still wearing my fluffy white slippers. He lifted up the can and dumped the rodent into the Dumpster. He then brought both back with him.

‘I don’t want those,’ I said as he was walking back into the apartment with them.

‘Oh just clean them,’ he said. ‘We might need them again.’ He did have a point. I did however dispose of the slippers. With that, Scott took Veda and went back downstairs to go to sleep.

‘Now don’t wake me if you see another one,’ he said on his way down. Another one? What if there was another? They always say where there’s one there’s more. And come to think of it, how did that little bugger get in? Was there a big hole in my closet? And if so, were there more living in there right now?

I decided to seal off my bedroom and set up camp on the sofa. I got Elvis out of the closet and placed him next to me for protection and tried to go to sleep. Tried, but was unsuccessful. The next morning around 8.30, Scott came upstairs and found me sitting upward still wide awake.

‘What are you doing?’ he asked.

‘I haven’t got to sleep yet,’ I said. ‘I’m afraid that there’s more in there.’ I pointed to my room.

‘Oh, you need help,’ he said. ‘There aren’t more in there.’

‘How do you know?’ I asked.

‘Because I doubt there are,’ he said.

‘I’m going to mouse-proof the house today. I looked under the radiators that are against the walls, and there’s a huge gap where the floor just drops off. I’m going to go buy cement and fill them up.’

'Do not pour cement into those holes,' he said. 'Just wait until I call the landlord to see what he says.'

'Okay,' I said. 'I am going to disinfect my mouse-ridden room though and look for holes.'

'That's a good plan,' he replied. 'Let me know if you find anything.'

Later that day, after I disinfected my room, Scott called to tell me that he had talked to the landlord and had told him about the rodent.

'He asked me if we saved the body,' Scott said.

'No he didn't,' I said.

'Seriously, he did,' he replied. 'I just wanted to say, "Yeah, dude, we caught him, killed him, and then wrapped him in a bread bag and put him in the freezer."'

'What a weirdo,' I said.

'When I told him that we didn't, he tried to convince me that it was a figment of our imagination, and said that the noises we heard were probably just coming from the dishwasher. I was like, "We didn't just hear it, we caught it. Let it loose. Remember?"'

'Anyway, what's he going to do?' I asked.

'He's going to hire an exterminator or something,' he answered.

'Well, that's good,' I said.

That evening Scott came home and we both continued to hear *Scratch Scratch Scratch!* from inside the walls and *Trot Trot Trot!* from inside the ceiling. I imagined that a small army of rodents lived inside the walls and were kicking back on sofas, just hanging out.

Toward the end of the week, our landlord did show up with a guy who put poison in the walls and in the ceiling. And by the following week, a rotting corpse smell filled the apartment, signaling that the poison had indeed worked.

How could it be that this was now my life? A couple of months ago I had a job that paid six figures and was living alone in a nice apartment in Manhattan. And now I was unemployed and was living with a roommate and dead rodents in the walls in Brooklyn.

By the time Christmas rolled around, the smell had gone away, but I still hadn't found a job. I did however find a cheap ticket home for just $140. I had never seen a fare that low in my life. But it was still right after September 11, so I guess people weren't too eager to fly.

Instead of taking a cab to the airport, which would have cost me around $25 each way, I decided to take the subway to Harlem, and then transfer to a bus to the airport. It would only cost me $1.50. Before this, the closest I had ever been to Harlem was the northern part of the Central Park bike path on the day that Scott and I bought our bikes. So I didn't really know what to expect.

But despite my fear, Harlem wasn't that bad. The worst thing that happened to me was that I had to wait an hour for the bus – in stiletto boots. And that was hardly Harlem's fault. I got angry and wanted to kick some ass, but seriously whose ass was I gonna kick? No one's.

Just to make sure I was at the right stop, I asked a man standing next to me.

'Excuse me?' I asked. 'But am I at the right bus stop? I'm looking for the bus to the airport.'

'Yeah, duh,' he said rudely, motioning down to the bags lying next to him. The *plastic* bags lying next to him.

I wanted to say, 'Oh, I'm sorry, sir, I didn't realize that the garbage bags at your feet were your suitcases.' But I didn't, because he might have beat me up.

Shortly after, the bus finally arrived and took me to the airport. With a half hour left, I got the plane and my flight took off and landed safely. When I arrived in Chicago, I put on a happy face for everyone to see. That year, my sister bought all the presents and, knowing that I didn't have a job, didn't even ask me to pay her back. Big sisters are good like that. I tried to remain hopeful that the job market would pick back up in January, but things weren't looking so good. It was a different economy out there. Things weren't the same as they used to be. I had always thought that I was okay, but now I was beginning to think that that wouldn't be the case.

I AM WOMAN, HEAR ME ROAR . . .

Even though I didn't exactly ring in the New Year in 2002, I was determined to start it with a bang. On Monday, January 7, I started my job search. The previous weekend, I used some of my $1,500 to buy a five-in-one fax machine/laser printer/copier/scanner and . . . well, I couldn't figure out what the fifth thing was. I didn't have much money, but in the long run it was better to invest in one of these and save myself the time and hassle of going to a Kinko's. There wasn't a Kinko's anywhere near my apartment anyway. Anywho, it was an investment in my future.

Since my big purchase, I realized that I was a bit low on funds, so I decided to stop my morning trips to Starbucks, and instead bought a pound of their coffee for $10 and made it at home. It would save me some money. And I needed to conserve as best I could.

For a few days I worked hard on updating my resume on my trusty laptop computer, which I'd named Claire. Of all the things that I regretted charging, the laptop wasn't one of them. It was actually one of the few smart purchases I made. I gave it the name Claire because every time I went online to find a job, a woman's voice from MSN Internet Access said 'Good morning' or 'Good evening' or 'Goodbye.' She sounded so nice and was always so courteous, so I decided that she deserved a name. So with my updated resume, Claire and my new five-in-one, I was off to the races.

The first thing I did every morning was play Helen Reddy's 'I Am Woman' for inspiration.

She'd tell me how she was a woman who liked to roar, and

then said something about how she wasn't going to let the meanies keep her down. I didn't know the words that well, but it didn't matter. I sang them from the top of my lungs!

That Helen sure knew how to motivate.

I started by calling everyone I knew for a job. Again. And again they all told me that their shows weren't hiring anyone. Damn! I then called *Live! with Regis & Kelly* and faxed my resume to Gellman. But neither Gellman nor Reege called me back. I also called *Martha Stewart Living* and not only faxed my resume but also sent a hard copy on special handmade paper. I'm not kidding. I really did that. But I didn't hear back from the Martha either. I then gave good ole Babs and the ladies at *The View* a ring – even after they'd snubbed me once before. When I was still in Chicago and was looking for a job in New York, I'd sent them my resume *and* a frozen Lou Malnati's pizza (my favorite Chicago pizza) with a note that said, 'A little slice of Chicago is coming to New York.' Yes, maybe it was a little 'cheesy'; ('scuze the pun) but I thought it would at least get me a return phone call. But I got nothing. Not even a thank-you note. And I didn't get anything back this time either. Day after day I didn't get anywhere, but I didn't let it get me down. Every day I played that Helen Reddy song. She told me how she could bend a little bit but never be broken.

I could never be broken too. She motivated, that Helen. Yes she did.

I then moved on to the nighttime talk shows and sent my resume to *David Letterman, Conan O'Brien* and *Last Call with Carson Daly*. I knew they were probably a long shot, but what did I have to lose? I was funny. I was creative. I'd be an asset to any one of their staffs. But again, I got nothing. Nothing, I tell ya!

I also sent it to every news station from CNN and MSNBC to FOX News Channel and Court TV. And after that, to the folks at CBS, NBC, ABC, and FOX. And eventually, to the people at MTV and VH1. And again nada. Nothing. Zilch.

And even though it's a completely different type of producing, I sent it to all the primetime series from *Law & Order* and *Ed* to *Sex and the City* and *The Sopranos*. And every soap opera from *As the World Turns* and *Guiding Light* to *One Life to Live* and *All My Children*. I even told them I'd be interested in an entry-level position. An entry-level position, for goodness sake. And nothing.

Before too long I moved on to those websites like HotJobs.com and Monster.com. And between you and me, I think those things are a big sham because I never got one phone call back. And I didn't just apply for television jobs – I applied for everything. From marketing and PR jobs to magazine and publishing jobs – they all got my resume. And still nothing. I even sent my resume in for jobs with positions that I didn't even understand. One was for an 'Act. Mgr./Bus. Dev.' What the heck is that? Could they be more vague? But I sent them my resume and told them that I'd make a swell 'Act.Mgr./Bus.Dev.' And still, no one called me back. A couple weeks had gone by and I still hadn't gotten anywhere. But every day I played Helen for motivation. I told myself I was wise, just as she did in the song. I also told myself I was strong and incredible – or was it invincible? Whatever it was, it didn't matter. I was a woman just like Helen was. OK, maybe a jobless woman – but I was still a woman nonetheless. By the end of January I had bookmarked fifty-four job search sites on Claire the computer. Fifty-fucking-four. And I visited them all every single day. How could this have happened to me? Since when did I become a bad hire? After a while I started to get a few courtesy letters in the mail. I don't know why people called them that, because everyone knows they are really 'we will never call you ever' letters.

TeleVest

January 28, 2002

Karyn Bosnak
123 Broke St
Brooklyn, NY 11201

Dear Karyn:
Your resume has come to my attention. Unfortunately, we do not have a position available at this time for someone with your credentials. I will be pleased to keep your resume in our active file in the event that a suitable opportunity presents itself in the near future.

In the meantime, I thank you for your interest in Procter & Gamble Productions and wish you success in your future endeavors.

Sincerely,

Stephanie Marsh

Stephanie Marsh
Manager, Human Resources and Administration
Daytime Programs
As the World Turns and *Guiding Light*

I received so many of those that I wanted to start writing back to each person. I wonder what they would do if I did . . .

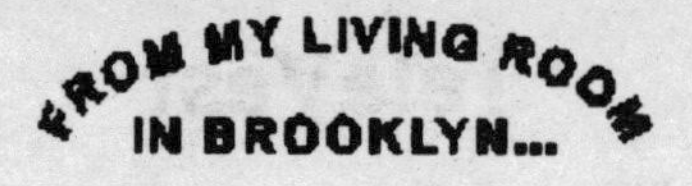

January 28, 2002

Stephanie Marsh
Manager, Human Resources and Administration
Daytime Programs
As the World Turns and *Guiding Light*

Dear Steph,
First of all, I didn't send *you* my resume, I sent it to your boss. So please thank his lazy ass for me for passing on his dirty work to you. And second of all, what do you mean there's nothing open for someone 'with my credentials'?

Sure I've never worked at a 'fancy' soap opera before, Steph, but how hard can it be to fluff hair all day and make sure that Billie Joe doesn't look fat in her outfit? I'm a jack-of-all-trades. I'm telling you, I could do the job. Working in daytime television, I made miracles happen every single day, Steph. I got a guest some teeth an hour before showtime, Steph. I gave the clothes off my back to some sorry sap who showed up in an Alf T-shirt, Steph. I CAN DO ANYTHING! DON'T YOU UNDERSTAND?

Obviously not. So go ahead and keep my resume in your 'active' file. I won't wait by the phone for your call. And by the way, I didn't know that your company was owned by Procter & Gamble. But now that I do, I just want to let you know that Secret deodorant sucks.

Sincerely,
Karyn Bosnak

PS – I'm a big fan of Downy though.

And can you believe that in the middle of all the letters, I got a 'courtesy' postcard? How cheap can you seriously be? A postcard? You can't fork over the extra sixteen cents for a letter stamp?

Dear Sir/Madam;

Thank you for your interest in a position with Court TV.

We have reviewed your resume and find that while your experience is impressive, it does not match our current needs. However, we will keep your resume on file. We will contact you should an appropriate position open in the future.

We wish you success in your job search.

Sincerely,

Veronica Lange

Veronica Lange
Vice President, Human Resources

At least good ole Stephanie had the decency to personalize and sign her letter. But Veronica, on top of the 'Dear Sir/Madam' part, Veronica's signature was even stamped. Not even stamped actually. It was just run through the printer like the rest of the postcard. I wanted to drop good ole Veronica a note too . . .

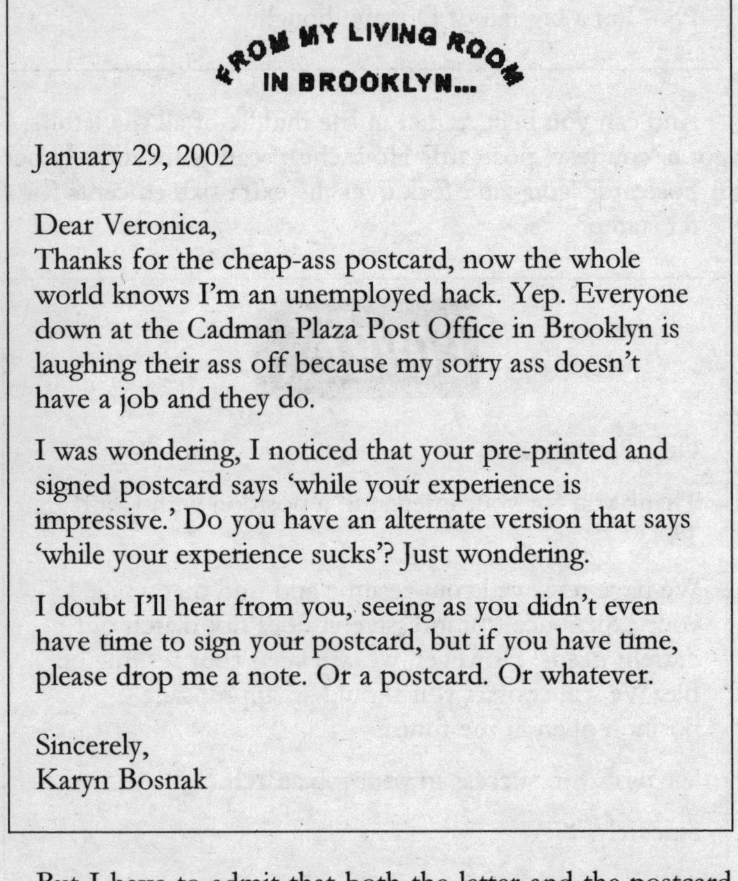
FROM MY LIVING ROOM
IN BROOKLYN...

January 29, 2002

Dear Veronica,
Thanks for the cheap-ass postcard, now the whole world knows I'm an unemployed hack. Yep. Everyone down at the Cadman Plaza Post Office in Brooklyn is laughing their ass off because my sorry ass doesn't have a job and they do.

I was wondering, I noticed that your pre-printed and signed postcard says 'while your experience is impressive.' Do you have an alternate version that says 'while your experience sucks'? Just wondering.

I doubt I'll hear from you, seeing as you didn't even have time to sign your postcard, but if you have time, please drop me a note. Or a postcard. Or whatever.

Sincerely,
Karyn Bosnak

But I have to admit that both the letter and the postcard beat the e-mail response. The e-mail response was truly the worst. It was the 'We are too cheap to send even a postcard' response. It made poor Veronica look like a Rockefeller.

DATE: January 31, 2002
TO: Karyn Bosnak
FROM: Pop Sustainability
RE: Resume

Dear Ms Bosnak:
We regret to inform you that we have recently filled the position for which you applied. However we'd like to invite you to an open house that we are having, as we'd love to hear your ideas on ways that we can bring our company into the next millennium . . .

After reading that I wanted so badly to hit the Reply button . . .

DATE: January 31, 2002
TO: Pop Sustainability
FROM: Karyn Bosnak
RE: Re: Resume

To Whom it May Concern:
Let me get this right . . . You aren't going to hire me, but you want me to come to an open house and give you all my ideas for free? Is that it? Do I have that correct?
Here's an idea . . . fuck off! Yep! You and your company can go fuck yourselves all the way into the next millennium!
You're gonna have to pay me,
Karyn Bosnak

Yep. By the end of the month I had gone mad. I had gotten mad. I was angry – partly with myself because I felt responsible for my situation, and partly with everyone else for not wanting to hire me. And after I was done being mad, or angry, or whatever I was, I became sad. I felt like a loser.

I got up from the kitchen table and walked into my bathroom and looked at myself in the mirror. My hair had two months of roots exposed. My brows were overgrown. I was a hot mess. And I was fat. I'd gained almost ten pounds while working at *Ananda*, and since I'd left I gained another five. My 'fat jeans' didn't even fit anymore. For Christmas my mom gave me a gym membership to the New York Sports Club in Brooklyn and I hadn't gone once since I'd joined.

Just then I felt sick to my stomach when I thought of the $3,600 that I spent in personal training fees at Crunch. And that was on top of the $75 a month that I paid in dues. And for what? I was a fat pig now. Fatter than when I started.

And I could barely fit into any of the clothes that were hanging in my closet. And I didn't even want to think about what I'd look like in the lingerie and nighties that I'd bought,. I wanted to think about them less after I remembered that I hadn't had a bikini wax in months. What was all that really for? It didn't get me anywhere. Except jobless, single, and fat in an apartment in Brooklyn.

JUST A THOUGHT . . .

Later that afternoon, I decided that I needed to go to the gym. Yep. I needed exercise. Every day as I was looking for a job, I loaded up on sandwiches from the deli. Like my doormen, I had grown to know and like the guys at the corner store. Their names were Sam and D. Sam owned the joint and D made the sandwiches. And D made some mean sandwiches! They were good, and I seemed to put on a few pounds from scarfing them down every day. I was sure that I'd feel better if I got in shape. So I squeezed into my gym clothes, grabbed my Walkman, and headed out the door.

As I was walking to the gym minding my own business, three neighborhood hoodlum boys came up behind me and started to push me. By the looks of them, I'd guess they were thirteen or fourteen years old. I was on a busy street, and there were a lot of people around, so I just guessed they were being silly, and didn't get too terrified.

'Hey, lady,' they said, laughing.

'Hey what?' I said back to them, trying to sound friendly. By now, two of them had gotten on either side of me and started to push me to the left and then pull me to the right, and then back and forth and back and forth again like I was a wishbone. They kept doing it and they kept laughing. They thought it was funny.

'Hey, lady, where's the train?' they asked. Now, I knew these boys knew where the train was. And I realized that they were just trying to harass me. But obviously I couldn't help but get a little freaked out.

'It's over there,' I said, pointing in the direction of the subway.

Just then the third boy came up behind me and started to hit me over the head with a plastic soda bottle. Yes he did! A plastic soda bottle! It might have been plastic, but it still hurt and it still freaked me out even more.

'Hey, lady,' they kept saying. I tried to pull away, but the two of them each had a firm grip on both of my arms, so I didn't have much luck. And the third one kept whacking me on the head!

Just then, a man was approaching us and looked at me, realizing that I was uncomfortable. When he stopped in front of us, they let go of me and started harassing him. They pulled his glasses off his face and threw them into the street. And then did the same with his briefcase. And all the while they laughed. They thought it was so funny to harass people. A few seconds later, a police car pulled up and they ran away. At which point the police left too.

I thanked the man for stopping and helped him gather his things. I know what happened wasn't horrible, but all I wanted to do was work out! And I got harassed by the hoodlum boys in the neighborhood! So I cried. Yep, me the eternal crier. I wasn't hurt, but once again I just felt like a loser. So I turned around and went home, put on my pajamas and crawled in bed. It was the middle of the afternoon.

The next thing I knew Scott was standing over me shaking me.

'Karyn, get up,' he said. I was still lying in bed.

'No,' I said, pulling the covers up over my head.

'Yes,' he said, pulling them back down.

'Why?' I asked.

'Because it's two o'clock in the afternoon on Saturday and you've been sleeping for almost an entire day now. You need to get up.'

'I don't want to,' I said.

'Why not?' he asked.

'Because no one likes me,' I said.

'Like who?' he asked.

'Like everyone I sent my resume to. Even the neighborhood hoodlum boys hate me,' I said.

'Huh?' he asked. I told him what had happened. He tried not to, but he laughed.

'Okay, I know it's not funny, but the plastic soda bottle part is kind of comical,' he said. I didn't laugh. 'Okay, maybe not. But you still need to get up.'

'I don't want to. Look at me,' I said, pointing to my roots and my eyebrows. 'And I don't even want to show you what's going on down there.' I motioned under the covers.

'Thanks for sparing me,' he said.

'I need a job so badly. I don't have any money,' I said. Scott was the only person that I'd told about my debt. I had to because of the whole apartment credit check thing. He was really supportive and nice about it though.

'Veda doesn't have money either,' he said, pointing to his delirious dog, who was standing on my bed next to where I was sleeping, staring at me square in the eye with her tongue hanging out of her mouth. I let out a bit of a laugh.

'She doesn't have any money,' he continued, seeing that I was amused. 'Not one penny, not a dime to her name.' I looked at Veda, who was panting deliriously with her eyes crossed again.

'Yeah,' I said back, 'she doesn't have any money though because she doesn't have any pockets to put it in.' Just like I liked to give Elvis human characteristics, Scott liked to give them to Veda too.

'You could always just hang up a sign,' he said.

'What do you mean?' I asked.

'A sign. I was just at the grocery store and I saw a sign hanging up on the bulletin board that said, "I need $7,000. If you can help me, let me know. I just need seven grand." And at the bottom there were a bunch of those tear-off things with a phone number on it.'

'That's not a bad idea,' I said. I pictured myself hanging up a sign at the local Brooklyn grocery store. 'I need $20,000!' Yeah, right. That couldn't possibly work. No one would just give me $20,000.

'It's a thought,' he said. Yes, it was. Just a thought.

A few minutes later, I pulled myself out of bed and took a shower. I needed to get a job because I needed to pay off my debt, because no one was just going to give me $20,000. And with that, the thought was already out of my head.

TWELVE

CREDITGUARD OF AMERICA

Karyn Bosnak
123 Broke Street.
Brooklyn, NY 11201

Date	Creditor	Payment	Balance
Feb 15, 2002	American Express	– $ 218.00	$ 9,049.00
Feb 15, 2002	Capital One Visa	– $ 29.00	$ 588.00
Feb 15, 2002	Citibank MasterCard	– $ 21.00	$ 353.00
Feb 15, 2002	Direct Merchant's Bank MC	– $ 76.00	$ 2,808.00
Feb 15, 2002	Fleet Visa	– $ 48.00	$ 864.00
Feb 15, 2002	Marshall Field's	– $ 20.00	$ 9.00
Feb 15, 2002	Service Charge	– $ 20.00	
	Total		**$ 13,671.00**

JENNIFER CONVERTIBLES

Karyn Bosnak
123 Broke Street
Brooklyn, NY 11201

Date	Payee	Amount
	PREVIOUS BALANCE	$ 786.00
Feb 12, 2002	Finance Charge	$ 16.00
	PAYMENT	– $ 100.00
	Total	**$ 702.00**

DISCOVER
FINANCIAL SERVICES

Karyn Bosnak
123 Broke Street
Brooklyn, NY 11201

Date	Payee	Amount
	PREVIOUS BALANCE	$ 7,371.00
Feb 1, 2002	Finance Charge	$ 147.00
	PAYMENT	– $ 150.00
	Total	**$ 7,368.00**

Grand Debt Tally $21,741.00

26: PROFESSIONAL GAMBLING

By the beginning of February, I had really hit rock bottom. I still was unable to find a job and pretty much just felt like giving up. Early in the month, my dad came to visit me for about a week. When he asked me how I had been surviving for two months without working, I told him that I had savings. I didn't want him to worry so I didn't tell him that I was nearly flat broke. I paid for my February rent, but by the looks of my checkbook I wouldn't have enough to get through March. I needed money badly.

During his visit, he wanted to go to Atlantic City for a day, so the two of us took a bus there from Penn Station early one morning. I didn't feel that well and had a bit of a cough, so I took some cough syrup before we left. Then I followed it with a cup of coffee. Then I got on a hot bus. Then I barfed.

Yep, I've always tended to get carsick, even without the cough syrup and coffee. But let me tell you that the three of them mixed together is just a recipe for disaster. Thankfully, I made it to the bathroom on the bus before I let loose. Bus bathrooms are kind of like Porta Pottis. They don't flush. And they stink. And as I leaned over and watched whatever the liquid was that was in the bottom of the toilet slosh around, I once again wondered how I'd ended up such a loser.

After a couple of hours, the bus finally arrived in Atlantic City, and as I got off and looked at my pants in the sunlight, I realized that I had missed the toilet a few times. Little specks of throw-up seemed to be sprinkled all over the bottom of my pants – my black stretchy pants because my butt wouldn't fit into my jeans anymore. But I just wiped it off. I was in Atlantic City, after all – not exactly the runway of a fashion show.

The night before we left, I'd had a dream about the number

26, so I decided to only play games that involved that number. Aside from the $10 free token that they gave me on the bus, I had twenty bucks in my pocket – and that was all I planned on spending. After looking around for a while, I found a fifty-cent slot machine that had a total of $2,600 in its jackpot. Perfect! With my dad taking the machine next to me, I sat down and put my $10 inside. I pulled the lever and *spin, spin, spin* – nothing. I pulled it again and *spin, spin, spin* – nothing. I pulled it again, and *spin, spin, spin – ding ding ding!* Lights started flashing and I didn't know what had happened.

'What happened?' I asked my dad.

'Honey, you won!' he said.

'I did?' I asked. Really!?

'Yeah!' he answered, checking out the machine. I was so excited! I'd just won $2,600!

'Oh, wait,' he said. 'You didn't bet the maximum though.'

'What does that mean?' I asked.

'That means you won, you just didn't win the jackpot,' he answered. Damn! Just my luck!

'How much did I win?' I asked.

'Let's see,' he said, looking at the machine. 'It looks like you won $550.'

'Five hundred fifty? Really?! That's good enough for me!' I exclaimed. I never won anything! Raffles, contests – you name it. I never won. But I won today! And I had only been in the casino for all of ten minutes. I was so excited! Good ole number 26. Yep, God was watching out for me once more.

That day, I left Atlantic City with $700 in my pocket. I may have still had barf on my pants, but by now it was dry and I was a rich woman! It's funny how all of a sudden I realized how much money $700 was. I felt like I'd struck gold or something. I needed that money. And I won it so easily that I couldn't help but want more.

If I came here once a week and won $700 each time, then I'd be in the clear. But was becoming a compulsive gambler really the answer to my problems? I believed it was! It was then that I decided to embark on a gambling career. Yep.

So shortly after my dad left, I made plans for my second trip. I would leave right after Scott left for work, and take the same bus that my dad and I took. I'd gamble for a few hours and turn my $10 into $700. And then I'd hop on the 3.30 P.M. bus back to Manhattan, and be back in Brooklyn before he was home from work. He'd never know. Not like he kept tabs on me or anything, but I didn't want anyone to know about my new venture until it was successful.

The night before I left, I prayed to God to send me another number. But when I woke up the next day I was disappointed to realize that he hadn't. But I went anyway. That day, everything went according to plan, except the 'turn my $10 into $700' part. That part didn't quite pan out. And my $10 investment ended up to be more like $100. And it was then that I decided being a professional gambler maybe wasn't the best career choice for me.

WORK PART-TIME AND MAKE FULL-TIME MONEY

After things didn't pan out in the gambling department, I realized that my future looked bleak. Every day I woke up later and later, and let's just say I didn't shower as frequently as I should have. What was the point? I didn't have anywhere to go.

Day in and day out I just watched TV and clicked my way through life. The Mercedes-Benz Fashion Week happened the second week in February. All the fancy fashion shows in New York took place in a tent in Bryant Park. One cable channel televised all the shows and had '24-hour fashion coverage.' So I watched and watched. I bet Dan sure used his umbrella during fashion week. I bet that umbrella was like a golden ticket at every bar in the city.

Every day I woke up around one o'clock or so, plopped down on the couch and tuned in to watch the fashion shows. Everyone looked so glamorous. All the fashion models and celebrities pranced around in the prettiest clothes. I wished I was fabulous like that.

One night around three in the morning, I was a little fashion showed out and decided to flip around to see what else was on. Since I've always been a big fan of the infomercial, I stopped on Krystle Carrington trying to sell her hockey-mask thing. Rejuvenique, it's called. With its electronic waves, she assured me that it would take years off my face! If I got one of those, Francis from La Prairie wouldn't know what hit him. But I didn't have any money, so I couldn't buy one.

'I loved you on *Dynasty* though, Krystle!' I yelled at the TV set. Yep, I was addicted. Infomercials are good. I mean, they are *good*! They basically tell you that if you buy their product, your whole life will come together. Your whole life will be perfect. Their product will make your life so much easier.

'*Try the Showtime Rotisserie!*' one said. '*With our automatic timer you can spend less time cooking and have more time for your active lifestyle! Just set it and forget it!*' My active lifestyle? I hadn't left the couch all week. Oh, no, wait, I did – to go to the kitchen.

'*Try the Inside-the-Shell electric egg scrambler,*' another said. '*No more runny egg whites! Automatically homogenizes the yolk and white to a perfect consistency in seconds!*' I know I wasn't exactly a vision of energy, but how lazy can you be? As if scrambling eggs is that difficult.

But I appreciate the infomercial as an art form, so I kept watching Krystle trying to hawk her hockey mask. Then, when she was done, another infomercial began to air. One I had not seen before.

'*With* Winning in the Cash Flow Business,' a man on TV named Russ said, '*you can work part-time and make full-time money.*' Really? Wow.

'*With* Winning in the Cash Flow Business,' he added, '*you can make your money like the banks and the insurance companies do.'* Huh. Really? Wow.

'Winning in the Cash Flow Business *really works*,' he promised. '*And I'm going to prove it to you. I'm going to introduce you to regular folks like you and me who were successful selling real estate notes.*' Real estate notes? What are those?

One by one I watched as person after person told me how successful they were selling these so-called real estate notes.

'*I made $8,000 on my first deal*,' a man said. He was sitting by a pool that I assumed was his.

'*We made $5,000 just last week on two deals*,' a couple said. They were sitting on a boat that I assumed was theirs.

'*I can't deposit the checks fast enough*,' a woman said. '*Just last week I closed another deal for $4,000.*' She was wearing diamond earrings that I assumed were hers.

'*And you did all of this with no money down?*' Russ asked.

'*I did*,' she answered. '*With no money down.*'

No money down? Huh? I didn't have any money, so did that mean that I too could make $4,000 with no money down? According to Russ, I could! All I had to do was buy his real estate note-selling program for $150. And then I, too, could work part-time and make full-time money! I, too, could make my money like the banks and insurance companies did!

With that I picked up the phone and ordered my program! I even paid extra to have it rushed to me. It was an investment in my future!

A few days later, the program arrived in the mail. I listened to the audiotapes, I watched the video, and I read the book – from front to back I read that book. And after I was all done, I still didn't know what in the heck a real estate note was.

But I wasn't going to let that stop me. No. I was going to sell these things called real estate notes. And in order to do so, I needed to buy something called mortgage leads.

Mortgage leads were names and addresses of people who would sell me their real estate notes. In his book, Russ gave me the names of a couple of companies who could sell me some mortgage leads. He told me that I needed to ask for something called 'seller carry back loan leads.' So I did just that.

After calling one of the companies, I got some guy named Frank on the phone and told him that I was interested in 'seller carry back loan leads.' The good thing was that Frank knew exactly what I was talking about – even though I didn't. But the bad thing was that the leads were going to cost me $75 a month. And I had to sign a six-month contract if I wanted those leads. After thinking about it for a while, I decided to do it. I had already bought the program, so I might as well buy the leads. So I paid my $75, and signed my six-month contract. And with that, I now had the leads – the names and addresses.

According to Russ, the next thing I needed to do was mail all these folks a postcard asking them to call me about their mortgage. That was it, just a little note to ask someone to call me. So after buying a bunch of blank postcards, and buying $100 worth of postcard stamps, I sent out five hundred postcards to the addresses that Frank had given me – just like the one good ole Veronica sent to me, except I signed my name to mine. I thought it would look more personal. And then I waited. And no one called me.

But in my book Russ told me that I might have to mail people up to five times before they'd call me back. So a week later, I mailed another five hundred postcards to the same people. And I waited. And nothing. And then someone called. A man who lived in Tennessee was interested in hearing what I had to say. Crap! I mean cool! What the heck was I going to say to him though?

I looked in my book and found a phone script that Russ told me to use when someone called me back. So after studying it for a while, I was confident that I could do it, and picked up the phone. All I needed to do was gather a few key details about the man's real estate note. After dialing, I waited for someone to answer.

'Helllow,' a man answered in a southern accent.

'Hi, is Jim there?' I asked.

'This is Jiiiim,' he said.

'Hi, Jim, this is Karyn,' I said nervously. 'I sent you the postcard about your real estate note.'

'Oh, hi. Well let me tell you what I got here,' Jim just started talking. 'I got an eight-year note with a face value of $87,000 and a balance of $84,000. It has an interest rate of 8 percent, and a . . . blah blah blah . . . blah blah blah blah . . . What can you do for me?' he asked.

I didn't know what the heck to say. Because I didn't have a clue what he was talking about! I had read that damn book a million times and I still didn't know what the heck a real estate note was! I immediately hung up the phone. I didn't know what else to do!

What was wrong with me? I had just spent almost $400 on crap I didn't need!

Broke. That's what I was. Dead broke. And apparently dumb too.

MY SIMPLE LIFE

By March, I was a basket case. Since I had been unemployed I was slowly running out of all my beauty products. My Clarins self-tanner disappeared. My La Prairie ran out. Face lotion, shampoo, you name it – all of it was quickly disappearing. I even had to downgrade to Maxwell House coffee. I was able to scrape together enough money for my rent, but again I didn't think I'd be able to get through April. I still hadn't gotten my hair done, and I had actually tried to cut it myself, which was just a big mistake. I looked like I belonged in a loony bin.

Without a job, and without being able to pamper myself like I was used to, I slowly started to lose grasp of who I was. It might sound stupid, but I began to realize how much I identified who I was with where I worked and what I looked like. I was 'Karyn the spunky audience girl at *Jenny Jones.*' Or I was 'Karyn the court show producer with the cute clothes.' I was 'Karyn the girl who always had the greatest lip gloss and great highlights.' I was 'Karyn the successful sister/daughter who lived in New York.'

I always seemed to have it together, and now I didn't. I had turned into 'Karyn the girl with the bad roots and last season's lip gloss and fashions.' I turned into 'Karyn the chick with no money who couldn't go to that new restaurant that everyone's talking about.' I turned into 'Karyn the gal who needed a manicure and a bikini wax so badly that she didn't know what to do with herself.' I was now just some chick who lived in Brooklyn. My job and my clothes and always having it together gave me confidence that I all of a sudden didn't have.

I still had a closet full of clothes, but I didn't have anywhere to wear them because I didn't have any money to go anywhere. And even if I did have somewhere to go I probably wouldn't have gone anyway because of my bad roots. I felt like the person I used to be, the person who I had always been, was hanging in my closet. And I looked in the mirror and felt like I didn't know the person staring back at me. Or if I did, I didn't like her. I didn't accept her.

Sure my problems were mild. I wasn't in some horrible car crash that left me disfigured. I didn't lose a limb. Thankfully. I just had bad roots, outdated clothes and no job. But the feelings that I had were still valid. If you have blond hair and then dye it brown, you too would feel differently about yourself when you looked in the mirror, because it's not the person who you are used to looking at every single day. The same is true for weight. When you gain ten pounds and then look at yourself in the mirror, you don't have that same self-esteem that you once did. And when you lose that weight again, you feel great. You feel on top of the world.

I had always been one of the happiest girls everywhere I went. I was always smiley. I was always friendly. I was always so carefree, always living for the moment. I took chances that were sometimes foolish – but I took them. And all of a sudden I lost that zest for life. I felt worthless.

Whether it's wrong or right to feel like this wasn't the issue, because I did feel it. It was there and I needed to deal with it. And the last thing I was going to do was hate myself for hating myself. And although people might not admit it, I'm sure they sometimes feel the same way.

I hate to say that I'm a victim of anything. I never play that card. Even as much as I pitied myself at that moment, I wasn't going to sit back and play the victim role, because I made some choices in life that put me in the situation that I was in at that moment. However, I would say that if I am a victim of anything, it was a bad economy. That was something that I hadn't planned for. Being without a job was something that I never thought would happen to me.

But the last thing I was going to do was pack my bags and move home. The last thing that I was going to do was call my parents and beg for their help. That would have meant that somehow I had failed – and I'm not a failure. I was going to get through this on my own.

I needed to make some decisions. So I decided to sell some of my stuff. I had purchased stuff on eBay before, so I was familiar with how it worked. I actually got the cutest pair of Prada pumps on there for like $100! But now was not a buying time. Now was a selling time.

One by one I pulled out the boxes still full of my belongings from my old apartment and slowly began auctioning stuff off. I had lived without it for four months and somehow survived. So maybe I didn't need it. I started with the small stuff and sold some picture frames and vases that I 'had to have.' I also sold some antique dishes and some books. Some things had memories and were hard to part with, but I sold them anyway. As soon as I was done with the small things, I moved on to the larger items.

I thought that if I sold my great deal of a rug and survived, then somehow I'd be okay. So I sold it. And I lived. And then I sold my chandelier, and I lived too. And I realized that I didn't need all these things in my life. That I had been surviving just fine without them. I wasn't completely happy or anything, but every day I woke up and I was alive. And the more stuff I sold, the better I felt. It was like therapy. I was unloading. I was getting all of the clutter out of my life.

And then I realized that this was why I had moved to New York – to figure out who I was. I didn't like being defined by my friends, my family or my job in Chicago. And all of a sudden I wasn't being defined by these things anymore. I didn't know who the person staring back at me in the mirror was, but wasn't that what I wanted? I felt like maybe this was all supposed to happen.

Toward the end of March my tax return showed up, so I was able to pay my April rent and sent the rest of the money toward my Jennifer Convertibles bill. By the time April arrived, I slowly started to pick myself back up. I read in my *Allure* magazine about how L'Oréal Preference hair color was the same stuff that the salons used, so I decided to try it to lighten up my roots a bit. And it actually wasn't that bad. Okay, it wasn't that good, but it wasn't that bad. It was a bit orange, but at least it wasn't two-toned anymore. And I broke down and bought a pumice and gave myself a pedicure – a much-needed pedicure. I also bought Dove soap for my face. No more expensive department store products. I was drug-store girl now.

One day in early April I woke up to the phone ringing. I had been unemployed for almost five months. I leaned over and picked it up. It was Ed and David, my old bosses from *Ananda.*

'Hey, wake up!' they said. I was on speakerphone.

'Okay, I'm up. What's up?' I asked.

'Good – we're cutting to the chase. We have a job lead for you and you need to stop what you are doing right now and call our friend because she needed to hire someone like yesterday, and needs someone immediately.'

'Oh my gosh, thank you so much!' I said.

'Before you call though, we have to tell you that it's for a cable show that doesn't pay well. It's in casting or something and you are way overqualified for it, but we thought we'd call you anyway because the show sounds right up your alley. It's a reality show about New Yorkers and their dogs.'

'Oh my gosh, thank you!' I said. 'I'll call right now.' They gave me the number and I immediately hung up the phone and called about the job.

The position was indeed a supporting position in the casting department for a show called *Dog Days* that was being produced for Animal Planet by a production company called CameraPlanet. And Ed and David were correct in saying that it didn't pay well. It paid $900 a week before taxes, which was a 55 percent pay decrease from my last job – less than half of what I was making at *Ananda*. But I was desperate and needed to work, so I interviewed on a Thursday, got the job on a Friday, and was scheduled to start work on that Monday. It was freelance, which meant no insurance, and would last fourteen weeks, which would bring me through the middle of July.

THE RAT RACE

That weekend, I got ready for my new job. I needed new clothes badly because in a bad washing machine mishap I had accidentally dyed all of my white clothes from last summer yellow. Every T-shirt, we are talking everything. Bright yellow. Ruined. So I really didn't have a lot of stuff to wear.

The good thing was that I wouldn't have to dress up. This show was in the casting department for a show with dogs, and at least one day a week was going to be spent at an open casting call at different dog runs all over Manhattan. I needed jeans and T-shirts and stuff like that.

Since I had exactly $200 in my checking account, I couldn't exactly go to Bloomingdale's and buy a bunch of Michael Stars T-shirts at $40 a pop like I did last summer (which were now all yellow, by the way). No. I needed quantity. I needed bulk. So I decided to head down to the Brooklyn Old Navy.

Now I had been in an Old Navy before, but I never bought anything there. But I had high hopes, because how much can you screw up a T-shirt? It's cotton stitched together, right? And I was presently a big fat pig, and was about fifteen pounds heavier than when I started at *Ananda*, so I wasn't about to go spend $100 on a pair of jeans that would hopefully be big on me in a couple of months. I've always made a vow not to spend a lot on 'fat' clothes. That's like being an enabler. When your clothes don't fit, it's time to go on a diet. So anyway, I headed down to the local Old Navy to see what I could find.

After browsing around, I was a bit impressed with the clothes – but very impressed with the prices. The T-shirts were like $10 and weren't that bad either. They even have a sale rack at Old Navy. Seriously. I got a $24 skirt on sale for $8. I mean it was already a bargain at $24 – there was no need to mark it down. So after about an hour at Old Navy, I walked out with a pair of jeans, three skirts and ten T-shirts and a pair of sandals, all for under $150. Now that's power shopping! I also touched up my roots and painted my nails. I needed to look presentable.

On Monday I went to work for the first time in almost five months. My alarm went off at 7.00 A.M., and I showered and left for work by eight because I didn't want to be late for my first day. After a short train ride, I got there a bit early, so I went to Starbucks. I hadn't had Starbucks since – gosh, who knows? It seemed like forever. The cup was so good. Finally, around 9.00 A.M., I left and went to meet my new boss, Molly.

CameraPlanet's offices were located on the top two floors of a loft building in the Flatiron District of Manhattan, right by Madison Square Park. The inside of the office was mostly a big open space with a few private offices. The staff for *Dog Days* would be housed in an open area with open desks. I didn't even get a cube here. Just a chair pulled up to a table that was shoved against a wall. No frills, to say the least.

After a brief meeting, Molly introduced me to the guy I'd be working with, Manny. Manny was the casting director and I would basically be working for him. He was in his early thirties and wore big thick black glasses and didn't have any hair. He wasn't naturally bald or anything, I think he just shaved his head. Michael Jordanitis – except he was white and Jewish. Being a producer I was used to leading a team and not answering to anyone. And when I interviewed I was told that I'd be in a department of three people, with no titles. Now all of a sudden he was the casting director, and I came to find out that I was a casting associate. But because I needed work so badly, I didn't say anything.

Manny explained to me that we had one open casting call a week that took place in one of the many dog runs around the city. We were looking to cast people for a reality show about New Yorkers and their dogs. It was an eight-part series, and new cast members would constantly be added, so the casting process would be ongoing. On the off days, the department needed to concentrate on getting word out about the casting calls as well as line up some experts like doggie psychics and stuff that would be implemented into the series.

For the next few weeks it was kind of hard to take a backseat to Manny, but I did it. I swallowed my pride every day. I seriously had to put my tail between my legs (no pun intended) to do this. He was nice – it was just kind of hard to not be in charge. I felt stifled. The job was kind of limiting. I couldn't be that creative. Sometimes I sat at my desk and wanted to scream out loud. But I did what I was told and trudged on.

Molly ended up leaving when production began, and I moved on to solely booking experts and working more closely with the field producers. The change was kind of nice because I now kind of ran my own ship and didn't have to take a backseat anymore.

About one month before production was scheduled to end, I started to look for another job again. And just like when I was in my apartment, I was once again having trouble finding something. I had some leads, but I either had too much experience or not enough experience. As time grew closer to my last day, I began to worry more and more. Every night I just lay in bed and agonized about how much money I owed. I felt so stupid that I charged up all those things. I felt like I was the only person with debt – like the only person who could have done something that foolish.

My mom and stepdad came to visit for a weekend, and I tried to have fun but I couldn't. I felt like the debt had paralyzed me. My mom had always bailed me out in the past, but I just couldn't ask her again.

On Monday, June 10, I scrounged up $1.50 to get to work. I didn't have any more money and wouldn't be getting paid for two more weeks. I sold some stuff on eBay and expected a couple of payments to arrive in the mail any day, so I went to the local Food Emporium on my way home from work to write a check for $25 over the amount, just so I could have some cash to buy a subway card so I could get to work. I thought by the time it cleared I would have received the checks. To make a long story short, those checks didn't arrive in time, and I bounced that Food Emporium check. Yep, like a rubber ball, that puppy bounced all the way to a collection agency. I had a closet full of clothes, but I bounced a check for food and cash so I could get to work. It was pathetic.

The next week, the staff found out that production was ending two weeks early and the company laid off over half the staff. All the cameramen, field producers, etc – they were all out of a job. The supervising producer of the show, Lori, asked me to stay on board in post-production as an episode producer for an additional six weeks because of my 'chipper attitude.' Despite my inner turmoil I put on a smile for everyone to see. Glad to see that they bought it.

Despite my promotion, I didn't get a raise. I didn't ask. I knew that budgets were tight, and I felt if I did, then I too would have been laid off. A normal episode producer should have been making twice what I was making. But I just kept my mouth shut because I was grateful to be kept on, and even more grateful to get a promotion as a producer again.

Every day that last week of work before moving into the post-production department, I just walked to work and wondered if this was going to be what the rest of my life would be like. Going from job to job unable to pay my bills, bouncing checks at grocery stores, worrying about being laid off early – this couldn't be it. Could it?

In a few short weeks my episode would be edited, and I'd have to find a new job again. And after that job ended, another new job again. And then another. And then another. I felt like I was in a rat race. And I hated it. I felt so defeated. I felt like I had been through the wringer. I was simply existing, and was not making any kind of mark in the world. A breaking point had to happen, because I was at my wits' end.

THE REBIRTH

June 2002

LYING IN BED AND DREAMING . . .

One night, while lying in bed wide awake for the umpteenth night in a row, I again started worrying. Bouncing that check at that grocery store made me realize that I needed to make a change. I needed to get rid of this debt. I still owed over $20,000 and that was a lot of money. I *had* a debt payoff plan – I moved to Brooklyn, I canceled my cards and turned them over to a debt consolidation agency – but then I went and lost my job. And, well, that screwed everything up.

And look at me now. I didn't get my hair done anymore, the last time I shopped was at Old Navy. I even plucked my own eyebrows. And I used Pantene – a grocery store-bought shampoo. I was a changed woman!

I thought about Donald Trump, Bill Gates – all the richies in the world. To them, I bet $20,000 was a drop in the bucket. But to me, it was as big as the ocean. Even if just two of those richies gave me $10,000, my debt would be gone. Or if five of them gave me $4,000, then my debt would be gone. And that money would probably mean nothing to them. Come to think of it, if twenty thousand people gave me just one dollar, then all my debt would be paid off.

The more I thought about it, the more I believed that there had to be at least twenty thousand people out there who had been in my situation before and felt my pain. Frivolous debt – that's what I had. If twenty thousand people gave me just one dollar, all that frivolous debt would be gone. Just a buck. Almost everyone can afford a buck, and all I needed was twenty thousand people to give me one. The more I thought about that, the more obtainable it felt. There are millions of people in New York alone. If just twenty thousand of them gave me a dollar, then I'd be home free!

I then thought about that sign that Scott had seen at the grocery store. It really wasn't a bad idea. What if I made a sign asking for $20,000? It might work, it might not – but what did I have to lose by trying it? What did it really hurt to ask? Seriously. If someone didn't want to help me, then they didn't have to. But if just one person saw it and they did . . . and then another person saw it and *they* did . . . and so on and so on, then great! I'd be paid off! So I decided to make my sign.

THIRTEEN

CREDITGUARD OF AMERICA

Karyn Bosnak
123 Broke Street.
Brooklyn, NY 11201

Date	Creditor	Payment	Balance
Jun 15, 2002	American Express	– $ 238.00	$ 8,344.00
Jun 15, 2002	Capital One Visa	– $ 29.00	$ 472.00
Jun 15, 2002	Citibank MasterCard	– $ 21.00	$ 290.00
Jun 15, 2002	Direct Merchant's Bank MC	– $ 76.00	$ 2,580.00
Jun 15, 2002	Fleet Visa	– $ 48.00	$ 720.00
Jun 15, 2002	Service Charge	– $ 20.00	
	Total		**$ 12,406.00**

JENNIFER
CONVERTIBLES

Karyn Bosnak
123 Broke Street
Brooklyn, NY 11201

Date	Payee	Amount
	PREVIOUS BALANCE	$ 201.00
Jun 12, 2002	Late Fee	$ 25.00
Jun 12, 2002	Finance Charge	$ 5.00
	Total	**$ 231.00**

DISCOVER
FINANCIAL SERVICES

Karyn Bosnak
123 Broke Street
Brooklyn, NY 11201

Date	Payee	Amount
	PREVIOUS BALANCE	$ 7,860.00
Jun 1, 2002	Late Fee	$ 30.00
Jun 1, 2002	Over Limit Fee	$ 30.00
Jun 1, 2002	Finance Charge	$ 159.00
	Total	**$ 8,079.00**

Grand Debt Tally $20,716.00

POSTING THE LETTER

On Wednesday, June 19, I made that sign. I waited until after work and pulled out good ole Claire the laptop from the closet and put her on the kitchen table – the same place I'd sat for months trying to find a job. After thinking about it for a while, I realized that I didn't want my letter just to say 'I need $20,000.' I felt that with an amount that high, I needed to give people a reason why I owed the money. I wasn't going to lie about it though. I needed to be truthful. I also needed to laugh at myself about what I did. And I needed to make it sound fun to help me pay it off. I wanted my letter to sound kind of fun and campy – kind of like an infomercial. So I just started typing.

After a while, I came up with what I thought was an appropriate letter. But the more I thought about it, the more I opted *not* to hang it at the grocery store. I mean, how many richies really hung out at the local Brooklyn Met? Not many, I bet. I needed to go more global with this project. I decided to turn to the Internet.

Now I'm not very Web savvy, but I was familiar with a webside called Craigslist.org, which is kind of like an online classified paper or bulletin board that you can post things on for free. There are several editions of Craigslist online – almost twenty, actually, one for each major city in the United States. There's a Craigslist Chicago, a Craigslist New York, a Craigslist San Francisco, etc. Each of those editions is broken down into different sections. There's a For Sale section, a Help Wanted section, a Wanted section, a Community section, etc., just like the classifieds. I had become pretty familiar with it during my unemployed days and thought that it would be the perfect place for my letter.

After poking around the site for a while, I decided that the Wanted section seemed like the right place to post it, because

I wanted $20,000. I mean, it only seemed logical. And I decided to start with the New York edition. In order for people to repond to my letter, I needed to provide an e-mail address, so I signed up for a free one at hotmail. After thinking about it for a while, I came up with the name 'savekaryn@hotmail.com,' because I was looking for someone to save me.

After going through all the 'posting' motions, my letter was up. There, sandwiched between someone wanting a dresser and someone wanting an air conditioner was my listing. The headline said: WANTED: $20,000. And when you clicked on it, you got my letter.

Hello!
My name is Karyn, I'm really nice, and I'm asking for your help! Bottom line is that I have this huge credit card debt and I need $20,000 to pay it off. All I need is $1 from 20,000 people, or $2 from 10,000 people, or $5 from 4,000 people – you get the picture. So if you have an extra buck or two, please send it my way! Together, we can banish credit card debt from my life!

HERE'S THE DEAL . . .
I'm a 29-year-old girl who moved to New York a few years ago from Chicago. I now live in Brooklyn. Over the last few years I've run up quite a credit card bill . . . let me tell YOU! $20,221.40 to be exact. OUCH! Maybe it was too many morning lattes that pushed me over the edge, maybe it was the Prada pumps that I bought on eBay (They were only $100 – a STEAL!) Who knows! My debt just got larger and larger, and here I am today with a huge monthly payment.

TOGETHER WE CAN MAKE A DIFFERENCE!
You see, I'm done with my frivolous ways. I've stopped buying designer clothes. I've stopped using department store products. I decided that I really Do like Oil of Olay. It really DOES work just as well . . . And Old Navy is actually kind of cool . . . I've

done my part, now I need you to do yours. I believe that this world is a good place, and if someone needs help, then they should ask for it.

SO I'M ASKING . . .

Please help me pay my debt. I am nice. I am cheery. I am the girl at the office that MAKES YOU SMILE. I didn't hurt anyone by spending too much money. I was actually HELPING OUT THE ECONOMY. Give me $1, give me $5 – Hell, give me $20 if you feel like it! I promise that everything you give me will go toward paying off my debt.

WHAT'S IN IT FOR YOU, YOU ASK?

It's normal that one should ask this question. I'll be honest . . . nothing is really in it for you. But I do believe in Karma. If you help me, then someday someone might help you when you need it. SO HELP ME, and maybe someday, I'll be able to help you.

AND TO THE IRS . . .

Yes I'll report everything I make as income. I'm honest – sometimes too honest, but I believe in honesty! If you'd like to help me, please e-mail me at savekaryn@hotmail.com.

XOXO,

Karyn

When I was done I told Scott what I did, and although he'd given me the idea, he thought it was a bit strange. He didn't think it would work. But I didn't want to feel down about it, I needed confidence. So I decided to call Naomi and tell her.

'Hello,' she said, answering the phone.

'Hi,' I said. I paused.

'Hi,' she said. 'What's up?'

'I have to tell you something,' I said quietly.

'What?' she said.

'I feel really stupid telling you,' I said.

'Tell me,' she said. 'What?'

'Well, I owe some money to credit card companies,' I said.

'Okay,' she said and paused. 'How much money?'

'I don't want to tell you that part,' I said. 'But I'm trying something creative to get rid of it and I need your opinion.'

'Okay, how much though?' she said. 'You can tell me.'

'$20,000,' I said, whispering. I thought if I said it quietly, it would sound like a smaller amount.

'Shut up,' she said.

'No, it's the truth. I owe $20,000,' I said. 'I kinda feel like I'm gonna barf.'

'Okay,' she said calmly. 'What's your creative plan?'

'Well, I've drafted up a nice letter and posted it on a website asking for help to pay it off. And I want to know if you think it will work.'

'Okay, where do I go? What's the website?' she asked.

I told Naomi about Craigslist and how to find the letter, and explained the whole story about how I consolidated most of my debt, and how I thought I'd be able to pay it back and that's why I was so freaked about losing my job. I also told her about how Scott saw the sign at the grocery store, and that's how I came up with the idea.

After reading the letter and laughing, Naomi thought it was a good plan.

'I think it's good,' she said. 'It's funny.'

Somehow, knowing that my best friend knew and validated my effort, I felt better. When we hung up the phone, I continued to post my letter to the Wanted section of every Craigslist across the country. The more the merrier, I thought. By the time I was done, it was past midnight. I was so tired and had to be at work early, so I fell right to sleep.

THE RESPONSE

The next morning I got up early because I was dying to see if anyone responded to my letter. I pulled my laptop back out of the closet and fired her up on the kitchen table again.

'Come on, Claire . . .,' I said as I patiently waited for her to turn on and log online.

'Good morning,' she finally said in her usual cheerful voice, signaling to me that the connection had been made.

'Top of the mornin' to ya,' I replied.

I logged in to my new savekaryn e-mail account and pushed the button for my inbox. After taking a few seconds to load, the page finally appeared before me. I had twelve e-mails! I stared at the computer because I didn't know what to do. I was kind of afraid to open them. I didn't know what to expect. But then I decided to go for the gusto and clicked the first one from someone named Lenny. I closed my eyes while it opened. After peeking out of the corner of my eye and realizing it wasn't going to explode in my face, I read it.

> Stop by my place in Hoboken, NJ, and we can talk about me helping you. Someone helped me once so it only seems fair! My place is amazing and I'm an attractive guy. A picture of me is attached.

Oh my gosh! Are you kidding me? A picture of him *was* attached, and he was kind of attractive, but I didn't reply. I just moved on to the next one from Fred . . .

> What would you do for larger donations?

Um, nothing, actually, but thanks for asking. I clicked on the next one from Lori . . .

Has anyone sent you money? From one Brooklyn transplant to another . . .

Nope. Not one dime, Lori. But I still didn't answer her. I just moved on to the next one from Alex . . .

I was wondering what type of response you have had. I'm in a similar situation in that I went on a one-month vacation to New Zealand with brand-new credit cards . . . well I came back seven months later with veteran credit cards. I've now got so much to pay off I'm stuck. I've even thought about writing the president. He likes to spend money, maybe he can relate. And instead of 500 million for this and that, he can spend 499.970 million.
Cheers

Oh, I'm so sorry, Alex! I know how you feel. But I again moved on to the next one from Wookoo . . .

Don't bother to tell the IRS anything. You've done no work and you've sold nothing. So any monies you receive, up to $10,000 from a single donor, are gifts and not reportable or taxable as income.

Of course this information is useful to you only if someone is enough of an idiot to pull you out of the pig wallow you've managed to make for yourself.

Don't have to report it? Good to know! I then clicked on one from Naomi . . .

Sorry you're in debt, but at least you look good.

Oh, it was Naomi, my friend! That was nice of her. Then I clicked on one from Hardy . . .

Unusual that the exact amount of your debt is such an even number . . . Consider me skeptical.

Not unusual, just correct. Then there was another from Scout . . .

Go bankrupt – it's easier and even less degrading than begging. But anyway, good luck. I hope things work out. Peace.

I don't want to go bankrupt, because I felt like that was just like giving up. I then opened another from someone named A . . .

Get a life!

You get one, loser! I clicked off that one fast, and opened up one from Crummy . . .

Work for a living.

I do work for a living! I opened up three more e-mails from people just asking me if I have received any money, and then clicked on the last one from a girl named Nikki . . .

Hi: Today for you tomorrow for me. Don't forget to help someone else as soon as you are able to. Where do you want the $5 I am going to send you mailed?

Good luck and be careful with your credit card :)

Oh my gosh! She wanted to send me money! This actually could work! I mean the letter had been up for only like six hours or so. This could work. But I needed to think it through. Where would I have her send the money? Just then another e-mail popped up in my inbox. It was from Craigslist . . .

> We have removed your posting as we found it to be inappropriate for our site.

Inappropriate? Huh? Maybe it couldn't work. No – it could! I knew it could! I just needed to think some things through. I didn't e-mail anyone back because I didn't know what to say, so I logged off and got ready for work.

By the time I got to work, I decided that the best thing for me to do was to set up a website. Because no one could tell me that my letter was inappropriate for my own website except me. And I didn't think it was inappropriate. I thought it was kind of funny. And besides, a website would give people a central place to go. It could be like 'Save Karyn' central. Yes, a website. I was going to create a website and call it 'savekaryn.com.'

SETTING UP THE BASICS

The more I thought about it, the more it seemed appropriate. The whole idea actually seemed appropriate. Because of two reasons:(1) It could actually work and I could pay off my debt; and (2) Even if it didn't work, the few e-mails that I received so far were kind of funny, and I could take my whole 'getting out of debt experience,' chronicle it, and write a funny 'How I tried to get out of debt' kind of book. Then I'd sell the book and *that's* how I'd pay off my debt. Yep. I could include my plea letter to ask for help, I could volunteer for some funny medical studies that I saw being advertised on Craigslist – stuff like that. And a website would be a great central place to organize everything. So I decided to do it.

As soon as I arrived at work, I did a few Internet searches to figure out how to make a website, because I didn't have a clue. I found out that the first thing I needed to do was register my desired domain name, which was savekaryn.com. There were a lot of domain name registration websites to choose from, and I decided to go with one called Register.com. It seemed like the biggest one out there, and it was only $35 to register it for a whole year. So after going through all the motions, I used my banking card to pay. I didn't really have the extra money, but I felt like if I wanted it to work, then I needed to do this.

Now that I had that done, I needed to create my website. Another reason that I chose to use Register.com was because they offered a step-by-step website-building wizard. All I had to do was enter the information that I wanted online into a template, and with one click of a button, it would be published to the World Wide Web. And it was cheap – only $14.95 a month for a twenty-page site. The only drawback was that the templates they had to choose from were pretty basic and looked low-budget, to say the least. But obviously I didn't have the money to put together a fancier site. And I thought a low-budget website was kind of funny anyway.

Since I was at work, I couldn't exactly start building it, so I moved on to the next step. I needed to figure out a way for people to give me their money. I didn't want to give people my home address, so I decided that I'd get a PO box over the weekend. But since I wasn't so sure people would remember to mail a buck to me after they read my website, I decided that I also needed to provide an instant online payment option.

Through using eBay, I was familiar with PayPal, which is a website that allows people to send money to anyone who has an e-mail address. All you have to do is sign up for an account, and fund it by using a credit card or checking account. I already had a PayPal account associated with my normal e-mail address, but I didn't want to use that one. I wanted one just for my Save Karyn project. So I set up a new account associated with the e-mail address savekaryn@hotmail.com.

When it asked me for my first and last name, I entered 'Save Karyn.' To test it, I used my real PayPal account to send a dollar to my Save Karyn PayPal account, and it worked.

Since I had been successful at selling my stuff on eBay, I decided to link my website to my eBay auctions and vice versa. So I set up a separate eBay user name, aside from my normal one, because again I wanted the whole Save Karyn effort to be separate. By linking to my auctions it would show people that I was in fact serious about eliminating my debt.

After getting that all out of the way, I decided to get back to work. I had to clean up my desk and get ready to move into an edit suite on Monday, and I only had today and Friday to tie up any loose ends.

On Saturday, I went in search of a PO box. The first place I decided to go to was a local shipping place right down the street from where I lived. It was privately owned and I had used them to ship my rug and my chandelier, and I saw that there were mailboxes inside that I could rent. It was called Pack-Man Boxes, and the guy who owned it was Pack-Man. I didn't know his real name, and I didn't want to find out, because to me he was Pack-Man.

I walked in and up to the desk.

'Hi, how much is a PO box?' I asked.

'They aren't post office boxes,' he snipped back. 'They are *personal* mailboxes – PMBs.' Huh. Someone's grumpy.

'Okay, how much are the *personal* mailboxes?' I asked again.

'They are $25 a month,' he said.

'Really?' I asked. I expected them to be like $10. 'If I get one, how long does it take before I can start receiving mail?'

'Immediately. You'd just pay, fill out some paperwork and you'd be all set,' he said.

'How much are the ones at the post office. Do you know?' I asked.

'They're much cheaper, like five or ten dollars a month, but there's always a waiting list,' he said.

'Okay,' I said.

I decided to explore the cheaper option just to make sure he was indeed correct. So I left Pack-Man Boxes and walked all the way to the post office, which was kind of far. Once I arrived, I waited in line for forty-five minutes, was told that I had to fill out an application and then wait, because there was in fact a waiting list. But I couldn't wait, so I went back to Pack-Man.

'Hello again,' he said.

'Hello,' I said. 'I'm back and I'd like to get a PMB box please.'

'Okay,' he said. Pack-Man proceeded to have me fill out a bunch of paperwork, and then asked me what the box was for.

'What's it for?' I replied. 'Mail.'

'Yeah, but *what* is it for?' he asked. 'A business?'

'Not really,' I said. 'More like a project.'

'Who or what is the mail going to be addressed to?' he asked.

'Save Karyn,' I answered.

'Okay,' he said, looking at me funny, as if to say, 'Why do you need to be saved?'

After ringing it up, he told me that I had to pay for three months at a time, and my total came to $75. I paid with my banking card.

LAUNCHING THE WEBSITE

Later that night, I went home and started to set up my website. I decided that if I expected other people to give me money, then I needed to put forth a huge effort as well. On the top of each page I created, it said, 'Save Karyn – Help her pay off her credit card debt!' It sounded fun! I decided that the front page needed to get to the point and grab people's attention! It said:

WANTED: $20,000
CREDIT CARDS ARE BAD!

Hello!

My name is Karyn, I'm really nice, and I'm asking for your help!

You see, I have this huge credit card debt and I need $20,000 to pay it off.

So if you have an extra buck or two, please send it my way!
All I need is $1 from 20,000 people, or
$2 from 10,000 people, or
$5 from 4,000 people . . .
You get the picture!

Together, we can banish credit card debt from my life!

I liked the 'Together we can banish credit card debt from my life!' It sounded like a bad infomercial to me. On the next page, I posted the initial letter that I had created, but I changed a couple of details. I decided to change my age from twenty-nine to twenty-six, and to take out the 'I moved from Chicago' part. What if for some reason my parents saw it? I didn't want them to know that I owed $20,000. I was embarrassed about it. Not the website, but the debt.

In addition to that I also created a page called the Grand Debt Tally that I planned on updating on a weekly basis so people could watch my debt shrink. It showed that I had a goal, and I thought that if people could actually watch my debt go down on a tally, then they'd be more likely to want to help. After adding up all of my bills, I figured out that I owed just over $20,000. It said:

GRAND DEBT TALLY . . .

Keep track of my progress!
WATCH MY DEBT SHRINK WITH EVERY DONATION!

(updated weekly)

$20,221.40 TOTAL DEBT June 23, 2002

I planned on subtracting the amount of money I received from eBay sales and people's donations, as well as the money that I paid myself. After that I created the all-important 'Give Karyn Money' page, which instructed people on how to send me money if they wanted to. It said:

GIVE KARYN MONEY . . .

Together we can make a difference!

If you feel my pain – feel free to give me a dollar!

If you don't feel my pain, think I'm a moron, but get a kick out of my low-budget website – you too should feel free to give me a dollar!

NOTE: I AM NOT A CHARITY. I REPEAT: YOU ARE NOT GIVING YOUR MONEY TO A CHARITY, BUT RATHER A CHICK WHO SPENT TOO MUCH MONEY.

So this is where you can make miracles happen. It is this lovely page that will help you, help me. There are two ways to send me money. You can pay via PayPal or send me cold hard cash or a money order or cashier's check to my PO Box.

Now realize when you pay via PayPal that I am only getting about 70 cents to the dollar because of fees. But it's still a fine choice for those of you who don't want to go through the hassle of mailing a letter.

If you choose to send me cash or a cashier's check/money order through the mail, then you've made a fine choice as well. Make the checks payable to 'Karyn,' and send it to my PO Box.

Thanks!

At the bottom of the page, I added a link to PayPal and listed my new PMB address. For everyone that indeed gave me money, I created a page called Karyn Thanks, where I planned on listing everyone's name.

I then created a 'Buy Karyn's Stuff' page. After thinking about it, I decided to auction off one 'Big Ticket Item' each week, which would be a purse or a pair of shoes – something big. In addition to that one big item, I'd list a 'bunch of crap' as well.

That was my plan. Each week, I'd part with one of the frivolous items I had bought. Yes, I had parted with some of my stuff, like my rug and my chandelier, but I hadn't yet sold anything like my sunglasses or shoes or anything like that. At this point all I wanted was to be debt-free. I didn't care if at the end I was sitting naked in an empty bedroom. I just didn't want to owe any more money. So, in addition to the frivolous item, I'd sell some more of the crap that I'd accumulated.

To further show people that I was serious, I created another page called the 'Daily Buck,' which would contain daily anecdotes about what I did to make a buck or save a buck. And of course I would keep my website visitors up-to-date with the happenings at SaveKaryn on a page called the 'Weekly Update.'

So people could get hold of me, I created a 'Contact Karyn' page with a link to my e-mail. I liked the initial twelve e-mails I received and wanted to hear what people had to say. It said:

CONTACT KARYN . . .

Let me know what you really think!

So before I started this website, I put a posting up on Craigslist.org and I got 12 e-mails in the first few hours that the posting was up. For some reason, the folks at Craigslist didn't think my posting was worthy of their site and took it down. (I posted it under the 'Wanted' section and the heading was 'Wanted: $20,000.' It seemed okay to me.)

But anyway, I got 12 e-mails. Some dude told me that I don't have to report what I make as income. He said you only have to report monetary gifts if they are over $10,000 from one single person. Good to know. So if you are feeling generous, please make the check out for no more than $9,999.99 to be on the safe side.

Some other dude told me that I do have to report it, because it IS considered income. So I'm gonna check with an accountant to be on the safe side. Don't want to end up in jail . . . Some other dude sent me his photo and wants to meet over dinner to discuss the issue . . . Um, I think I'm gonna pass on that one . . . And, guys, there's not much of an issue to discuss here. I need the cash. End of story.

Seriously, I would like to hear from you. Drop me a line. Write me a letter, send me an e-mail. Tell me a story. I'm sure you've been in some sort of mess like this before. Share.

After I was done, I didn't push the button to publish my site on the Internet. I wanted to wait until I chose and listed my first weekly Big Ticket Item on eBay, and had something to put down for the Daily Buck. So, I saved my changes and went to sleep.

On Sunday, I woke up and insted of going directly back to the computer, I decided to have another sidewalk sale because I needed some material for the Daily Buck. And I needed to make some money. So I hauled some of my boxes out from the front closet and put them on a table outside and waited for people to show up. But unlike last time, no one did. So after a few hours, I hauled all of it back inside and went back to my computer.

In addition to writing my first Daily Buck, I also listed my first Big Ticket Item on e-Bay. It was a pair of rubber Prada ducky boots, which I said were perfect for rain or snow! I also wrote my first Daily Buck.

Sunday, June 23, 2002

Today I had a sidewalk sale. I only made $4. I sold mostly crap. I seem to have a lot of crap. It's the kind of crap that I had to have when I saw it in the store. Anyway, at the last minute some guy swooped in and bought a planter I had for $10. So I really made $14.

I decided to keep them simple. But the website was still missing something. Pictures. My website needed pictures. I didn't have a digital camera, but Scott did. It took kind of fuzzy pictures, but it had worked just fine for my eBay auctions so far. So I decided it would be good enough for my website too! Scott was lying on the couch watching TV, so I asked him to help me take them.

'Scott,' I asked, 'will you take pictures of me for my website.'

'Huh?' he said. He didn't sound too excited.

'My website,' I said. 'Will you take pictures?'

'I'm tired,' he said.

'Please wake up. I'm almost done,' I pleaded. 'You have to!'

'All right,' he finally said, pulling himself off the couch. I handed him his camera.

'Do you want your face to show?' he asked.

'No,' I said. 'I don't want wackos there to know what I look like.'

'I agree,' he replied. 'How about you hide behind your computer and I just get like the top of your head.'

'Yeah!' I said. 'It'll be kind of like the guy on *Home Improvement* – the neighbor that you see only half his face.'

'And we can make some fake bills and scatter them all around you,' Scott said.

'Yes!' I agreed. With that I pulled out a stack of blank envelopes and wrote things on the top of them like 'To: Bloomies' and 'To: Saks' in big red letters, and scattered them all around my computer.

Scott directed me where to sit and how low to duck my head, and proceeded to take a few pictures. When he was done we looked at them and both burst into laughter.

'Oh my gosh!' I said. 'They're so funny! You can only see from my eyebrows and up!'

I then asked him to take one more picture, but this time I pulled out my checkbook and pretended to write a check to pay a bill. After scattering the bills all around me again, Scott stood on a chair and took the photo behind me, so all you could see was the back of my head. They again turned out hilarious!

I added the picture of me behind the computer to the front page, and the picture of me writing in my checkbook to the Grand Debt Tally page. Then, I wrote my first weekly update. When it was all said and done, I pushed the Publish button, and savekaryn.com was now up and running.

WEEKLY UPDATE – FIRST DAY OF WEBSITE LAUNCH
June 23, 2002

Hello! Welcome to my first weekly update! I'll keep it brief . . . I have been busy launching my low-budget website and planning my marketing strategy. Each week I am going to auction off something that I just 'had to have' on eBay. You can click on the 'Buy Karyn's Stuff' tab at the left to get more information on that. This week's 'Big Ticket Item' is a pair of rubber Prada boots that I got on sale at Neiman Marcus. I think I wore them once. Check 'em out! All the money I raise from the auctions will go toward paying off my debt! You see, I'm doing my part!

I have also created a section called 'The Daily Buck,' This section will be updated daily and will contain tidbits of information on what I did that day to save a buck or make a buck. You may greatly benefit from some of these things. Please accept these daily morsels as free tips to help you be thrifty like me!

So, check out the website, and let me know what you think. Click on the 'Contact Karyn' link and send me an e-mail! Also, please help spread the word about savekaryn.com. Send website links to your friends, talk about me in bars (it wouldn't be the first time . . .), dream about me at night. Together we can make a difference!

FOURTEEN

DATE: July 12, 2002
FROM: Sully
TO: Karyn
SUBJECT: You are not alone

Hi, Karyn: I just wanted to let you know I enjoyed your website. I am an ex-Brooklynite myself, and had to chuckle to myself that only a Brooklynite would have the chutzpah to do what you are doing.

There is no way, of course, for me to know whether you're actually paying off your debt with the money you receive or just throwing it away frivolously, but you come off as a pretty honest person, so I am going to send you a couple of bucks.

Thanks, and good luck!

FROM: Karyn
TO: Sully
SUBJECT: Re: You are not alone

Thank you! You'll have to take my word for it. I grew up Catholic and have this HORRIBLE Catholic guilt! All the years of private school . . . If I say I'm paying my credit card bills with what you give me, then I'M PAYING MY CREDIT CARD BILLS WITH WHAT YOU GIVE ME! If I lied about it, heaven wouldn't let me in.

WEEK I: GETTING THE WORD OUT

On Monday, June 24, I started in a new position at my job. I was now an episode producer and was assigned to work with an editor named Randy, who was foxy! He had ice-blue eyes and jet-black hair and was a hunk of burning love.

But anyway, Randy and I were assigned to work on the series finale for *Dog Days:* the doggie wedding. Yep. A Jack Russell terrier named Cherry found her true love to be a Great Dane named Atticus. And Randy and I were in charge of the episode from the proposal on the Brooklyn Bridge to the doggie wedding, where Cherry wore a $1,200 Elizabethan doggie wedding dress. We even had to edit the doggie honeymoon at the Loews Hotel. Seriously, this was my job.

The first day that Randy and I were put together was also the first day that we were able to look at field tape. Usually the field tape is logged and the producer, who was me, would have a chance to look at it before being put with an editor. But the turnaround time from when the tape was due was so fast that there wasn't time to do it. So Randy and I sat in a room with thirty or forty hours of unlogged footage and picked out the best clips to create one forty-six-minute episode. It was quite a challenge, to be honest.

So, for the next two days that was all I did. I got to work at 9.00 A.M., and left work around 9.00 P.M. By the time my CreditGUARD of America charge, website charges and PMB box charges cleared, I was again dead broke. And I wouldn't be getting paid until July 8. But despite how busy or poor I was, I updated my site and added my Daily Bucks.

Monday, June 24, 2002

Today I entered a contest in the NY Post to win a motorcycle. I don't know how to drive a motorcycle. But I figure if I win it I'll sell it and use the cash to help pay off my debt. I'll let you know how it turns out.

Tuesday, June 25, 2002

Today I was so poor that I bought a turkey sandwich on bread with mustard and ate half of it for lunch and half of it for dinner. I was hungry, but I could stand to lose a few pounds. Maybe I could be a supermodel.

Wednesday, June 26, 2002

Today I called about an ad that I saw on a website looking for volunteers to participate in a PMS study. I left a message. If they approve me, I can make $500 AND I'll get a free exam. Since I don't have health insurance, the free exam would save me around $200! So technically, if they accept me, I'll come out $700 ahead!

By the time Wednesday rolled around, I e-mailed the initial twelve people back and asked them to visit my new low-budget website! I tried to keep all the responses light and funny, because I thought they'd be more likely to donate. I also asked them to forward the website to all of their friends.

On Thursday morning I woke up early and checked my e-mail, and Nikki did indeed send her $5 through PayPal! I was so excited! Attached to her e-mail was a note.

> I hope my $5 gets the ball rolling. I used to be in a similar situation. My advice is to lose the extras. Ditch the cell phone, cancel the long distance, buy phone cards, and stop eating out.
>
> At least you admit that you have to do something about it. Good luck! I will be checking your website for updates!
>
> Nikki from Chicago

After I read it, I stood up and jumped up and down! And she was from Chicago! A good ole Midwesterner to the rescue! I sent her a thank-you e-mail, and then shut Claire down and went to work. When I arrived, Randy was already there, eagerly awaiting my presence.

'Hey, did you know Atticus went engagement-collar shopping for Cherry?' he asked.

'I actually did know that,' I said. 'Did he pick out a nice one?'

'No, he was too cheap to buy one,' he said, laughing. 'The collars were like $60 and stuff. I wouldn't buy one either.'

'They were that much?' I asked.

'Yeah,' he said. 'They had like doggie breath mints at this place, and something called "poochie sushi," and apparently they're having a doggie ice cream social soon.'

'They had it already,' I said, as if I had major gossip. 'And Cherry and Atticus both went. It was when the in-laws got to meet.' This was true. Cherry's mom and Atticus's dad set up the wedding, so they had to make sure that Cherry's dad and Atticus's mom approved of the other dog. Seriously, this was my job. Randy and I got back to work, and I realized that he was really nice. We had worked in a ten-by-ten-feet room for the past four days and would continue to do so for the next four weeks.

I thought about my website as I worked all day. Yes, I made five bucks. But did I really think it would work? Not really. In my mind, I thought that maybe, just maybe some richie would get a glimpse of it and give me a large sum of money, maybe someone who had once been in my position. To me it was a joke. It was funny. It was kind of fun to poke fun at myself and the cheap-ass life that I was now living. Especially in the Daily Bucks.

Friday, June 28, 2002

Today I answered an ad that I saw in the Wanted section on

Craigslist. Some guy was looking for a fake Rolex. He collects them. I just happened to have one fake Rolex and two fake Cartiers. He is going to take them all, and pay me $50!

Over the next few days I received about fifteen e-mails or so, from different people than the original twelve, so I knew that they were forwarding it to their friends. Like my initial response, some people were nice, and others were mean. I got a couple of e-mails from people telling me that they were going to mail me money, which was cool! And I got some other e-mails from people telling me to drop dead. One guy wrote, 'Given the viral nature of the Web, I am sure you will likely succeed in convincing many to give up their cash.' I hoped he was right. Another woman offered me a 'free session of spiritual energy healing' that she said would help me reduce anxiety and help bring insight into why I spent so much in the first place. So I was already coming out the price of one Reiki session ahead!

Since I had been busy at work, I didn't have a chance to figure out how I was going to publicize my website. I didn't know how people got others to visit a website. So I just made sure to respond to everyone's e-mail. Mean or nice, they got a response – a chipper response. I always made sure I was friendly. I always made sure I asked them to send the link to all their friends, and then I just crossed my fingers and hoped they would.

Aside from my initial Craigslist posting, the only other way that I think people were finding my website was through my eBay auctions. You can create this thing on eBay called an About Me page that basically tells a little bit about you and summarizes your current auctions. At the bottom of the page, there is a place where you can link your favorite websites. So I used my About Me page to tell people about my new website and provided a link at the bottom. I was hoping that normal eBay users that were looking at my auctions would also visit my website.

Saturday, June 29, 2002

My cat peed on my bed last night. Fucker. Don't know why. I'm going to have a talk with him later. I needed new sheets because you know how cat pee smells. So I took a shirt that my mom bought me that I never wore and returned it to the store that she bought it at and exchanged it for some new sheets. Sheets can be expensive . . .

After that I checked my PMB box and didn't get any mail, but I had just launched my website, so I tried not to get too down on myself. It might take a while.

Before I knew it, it was already Sunday, which meant it was time to list another Big Ticket Item. After going through my closet, I decided to part with my burgundy Gucci sunglasses – the pair that I'd bought right when I moved to New York during my first trip to Bloomingdale's. As sad as it was to part with them, it had to be done.

By the end of the week, I had received 174 hits and $6. Well, really I received $5, but I decided to count the dollar that I'd sent myself during my test as a donation. So as it stood after Week 1, my Grand Debt Tally was . . .

$20,221.40 TOTAL DEBT June 23, 2002
-$90.35 my money
-$5.22 your money
-$68.47 eBay sales
$20,057.36 TOTAL DEBT June 30, 2002 – WEEK 1

WEEK 2: GOING HUNGRY

I wanted to make sure that I was completely honest about what I did with the money I received. If I said I was using it to pay my bills, then I was going to use it to pay my bills. The thing was, I didn't even know if what I was doing was legal. I didn't check with anyone. And the last thing I wanted to do was to get in trouble for misleading people. So like I said I would, I used the money that I received to pay off my debt. The cool thing about PayPal was that they offered a service called Bill Pay, which meant that I sent the money in my PayPal account directly to certain creditors – Discover Card being one of them. So, since the woman who won my Prada boots paid using PayPal, and Nikki sent me her $5 through PayPal, I had already made a payment to Discover.

Monday, July 1, 2002

Today I drank some really bad instant coffee that I found in the back of a random cabinet at work. I mean it was REALLY REALLY bad . . . Not just your average run-of-the-mill bad, but REALLY REALLY bad. You really have no idea. I figure I saved at least 3 bucks. It was BAD bad.

The bad thing was that I was still broke. So, while at work trying to focus on dogs and weddings, all I could focus on was my growling stomach. The worst part about it all was that Randy showed up to work every day with a bag full of food that he got at a health food store on his way there. And once he arrived, he'd take all the food out of the bag and put it on a shelf in our office so I could stare at it all day. And our office was small – so small that not only could I not help but stare at it, I could smell it.

He had granola bars, sandwiches, fruit, juices – you name it – all just sitting on a shelf. In the middle of his mad gaggle of food was an apple that had been sitting there for almost a week. To me, it didn't look like that apple was going anywhere. In fact, in my opinion it was about to go bad. So, while Randy left work for a few minutes to run an errand, I ate that apple. Yep. I scarfed it down, almost ate the core. And that night, I wrote about it on my website.

The next day I got e-mails from people calling me an apple thief, telling me that they weren't going to give me money if

I stole things. So, I fessed up to Randy about his apple, and he didn't really seem to care, to be honest.

Tuesday, July 2, 2002
Today I ate a coworker's apple. I saw it sitting on their desk at work for a couple of days now. It was going to go bad! If they ask where their apple went, I'll just tell them that I bet the cleaning man threw it away because he doesn't want mice in the building. UPDATE: I fessed up to eating the apple on Wednesday. The person really didn't seem to care. And I bought them an apple of my own on Friday, but once again, they didn't eat that apple either. So I brought it back home and ate it Saturday. I'M NOT A THIEF!

Anywho, as the week wore on I continued to get a few e-mails and even got five more bucks from a guy named Ryan. He said that he had his own problems with the plastic, and sending $5 to a stranger probably wouldn't help. And he didn't believe my karma theory either. He said the problem with that was that 'too many assholes in the world had it too good.' He said the reason he was sending me the money was that my 'site was so brilliant that he couldn't resist.' Brilliant! Wow!

Wednesday, July 3, 2002
Today my cat barfed on my new sheets. (See Saturday, June 29th's, Daily Buck to understand the story of the sheets.) I'm not gonna get new sheets again, because cat barf comes out of sheets. I can't afford the $3 to wash them because I don't get paid until Friday, so I just cleaned 'em up real good with some Woolite. No one will ever notice.

The hours at work were still crazy, so I had less time to figure out how I was going to promote my site. But I really felt like I needed to get the word out there. I thought about having stickers made and sticking them on light posts all over

New York, but that just seemed like too much work, and it would cost money anyway. The only place that I knew of to advertise it online for free was Craigslist, so even though they told me not to, I posted my web address one more time, but this time in the Community section. I figured maybe they removed it last time because they didn't think it was appropriate for the Wanted section. So after going through all the motions and posting it everywhere, I got another e-mail from them, saying, 'We are trying to discourage this type of thing . . . can you please not post this?' Huh. Whatever.

Over the last week and a half, I was so poor and hadn't been eating that I lost five pounds. Normally this would not be a good thing, but in my case, it was. I still hadn't lost that extra *Ananda*/unemployed weight that I put on.

Allan and Diane next door had a barbecue for the Fourth of July. But I didn't have anything to bring, so I didn't go. I didn't want to be that neighbor who showed up to the party with nothing and then eat all their food. They didn't know that I was dirt poor, and I was too embarrassed to admit it. So I sat inside and listed a bunch of stuff on eBay. In addition to the Gucci sunglasses that I listed on Sunday, I added some lampshades, silk flowers, a leather day planner, and one of my all-time favorites: the movie *Clueless* on VHS.

When I was done, I did eventually join the barbecue, but I pretended like I wasn't hungry. It was really hot out that day and I wore a denim skirt with a slit up the front and back, and the only undies that I had that were clean were hot-pink lace thong underwear – not exactly the kind of undies you want to be wearing while sitting outside on a hot day at a barbecue. While trying to climb over the short fence that separated our two yards, I accidentally tripped and one of my legs went flying in the air, giving everyone a wide-open pink-panty shot. People pretended not to see, but it was quite obvious that they had. Allan kept offering me food, and I finally did accept. So the pink-panty shot was worth it after all.

I had to work on Friday, and since I was freelance, I had to work Saturday too just so I could get paid for a full week because of the holiday. Aside from my unlimited-ride subway card that I used to get to work, I had $2 in my pocket to last me until I got my paycheck. So I ate one Ramen soup in a bowl thing for seventy-nine cents each day. That's it. I hadn't eaten one of those since college. And since I put lukewarm water in it instead of 'hot scalding water' like they suggested, the dried peas that were supposed to soften didn't. And I got a headache from the MSG. That night I found other cheap entertainment.

Friday, July 5, 2002
Let me just say that I LOVE magazines. There's nothing quite like a new fresh Bazaar to enjoy on your train ride home from work. However, magazines can be quite expensive. And they are NOT something that should be purchased if you are watching your budget. These last few weeks have been difficult for me. There's a new InStyle with Britney on the cover . . . a new Allure . . . too many to name. So tonight, I went to my local bookstore, plopped down in the corner, and read all of my favorite magazines for free. The more I read, the more money I saved. I even read the pricey European ones with the extra thick, glossy pages. Those are like $8. Fashion magazines are like therapy. They make me want to be a better person.

Saturday, July 6, 2002
Today I colored my own hair. Don't tell anyone, but I'm not a real blonde . . . shh!!!! I've been getting my hair colored since I was in grade school. The myth is true – gentlemen DO prefer blondes . . . At least for me anyway. I bought a bottle of L'Oreal Preference. At $8, it's a bargain. And Allure magazine told me that it was the same stuff that the salons use. Getting your hair colored at a salon is pretty expensive – a color and highlight will run you about $150. So I figure I saved $142.

On Saturday, after doing laundry, I went to check my PMB box and Pack-Man was there. No one else worked there but him. I went to my mailbox, inserted my key and opened it up. And inside were two envelopes! I got mail! I grabbed them from inside, closed my mailbox and headed out the door to open them up. When I got home, I sat down at the kitchen table and started.

The first one was from a guy named Dan who had e-mailed me a couple of times already. He addressed it to Learn how to save! Karyn. And inside was a $20 money order!

The other envelope was from Naomi's parents. I almost died when I saw their name! She must have told them! Inside was a $100 check with a short note that said, 'We happened purely by accident to stumble upon your website, and we would like to help "Save Karyn" with the enclosed check. We love you! Good luck and love! PS – Can't Elvis Help You?' Naomi's parents also liked to give Elvis human qualities. I couldn't be angry at her telling them. They were so nice! I had tears in my eyes!

By Sunday, I had received 341 hits that week, twice the amount from the week before. In addition to writing my weekly update, I added a disclaimer to my Give Karyn Money page on the advice of two separate accountants that e-mailed me. They told me to make sure I told people they could not deduct their donations on their tax returns. I accepted all the free advice people gave me. I also updated my Daily Buck.

Sunday, July 7, 2002

Today I needed to do laundry, but I'm out of detergent. That can be quite pricey. That is unless you've discovered THE DOLLAR STORE!!!!! *Oh my gosh! What an emporium! Everything in the whole store is just $1. One buck. Seems appropriate that I talk about it in my 'Daily Buck' column. And you don't need to go anywhere else. They have everything! Shampoo, toilet paper (pretty decent quality too – doesn't scratch your booty), mops, even food! It's truly amazing.*

I also added a Frequently Asked Questions page because people seemed to always ask me the same questions, like 'Do you have a job?' etc.

FREQUENTLY ASKED QUESTIONS

You know, I have been getting a TON of e-mail and people have asked a lot of the same questions. Is your site for real? Do you work? Why don't you file for bankruptcy? Will you pose nude for cash? Stuff like that . . . So I've taken the time to answer some of those questions.

IS YOUR SITE FOR REAL?

Very good of you to ask this question. My site is for real. I am a bit elusive as to exactly who I am for personal safety reasons. You gotta be careful in this day and age. This is the Internet, after all.

HOW COULD YOU HAVE GOTTEN YOURSELF INTO SUCH A 'PIG WALLOW'?

Again another good and well-worded question. I just couldn't stop buying things. It's as simple as that. I'm going to be honest here . . . I wasn't out saving the world. I was just at Bloomingdale's.

DO YOU WORK? AND WHY DON'T YOU GET A PART-TIME JOB?

Yes, I do work. And I actually work about 65 hours a week. I am always working. That's why I can't get a part-time job. I have had a job since I was 15 years old.

I was actually working and making good money for a while, which is when I racked up most of my debt. But then I became unemployed for four months, which really set me behind. When you don't have a job and you can't for the life of you get a job because the economy SUCKS, it kind of throws a monkey wrench into your great elaborate debt payoff plan. I am now working, but am making less than half of what I used to make (but getting the best experience), and am therefore having problems paying my bills.

DO YOU EXPECT US TO PAY ALL OF YOUR DEBT WHILE YOU SIT BACK AND DO NOTHING?

No, I do not. I am simply asking you to help if you can. If you can't – no big deal. I am making monthly payments on my own. I break down how much you pay and how much I pay on my Grand Debt Tally page. It actually may look like I'm paying less than I actually am, because I'm showing exactly what I'm getting from you, and not showing the addition of finance charges. Those finance charges are coming out of the amount that I pay.

WILL YOU POSE NUDE OR GO ON A DATE WITH ME FOR MONEY?

No, sorry. I'm not about selling myself or my body for money.

WHY DON'T YOU CONSOLIDATE YOUR DEBT AND BUY A BOOK ON FINANCE?

I already consolidated my debt, except one credit card. I was going to send that one to the same consumer credit counseling service that all my other bills are at, until I realized that I could pay it through PayPal. So I'm leaving it open and all of the PayPal payments I receive, whether it be from an eBay sale or just a donation, will go directly toward paying that bill and never even see my checking account.

And I've read a book about how to organize my finances, but all it did was make me realize how much I screwed up and how behind I am on saving for my future. It depressed me.

WHY DON'T YOU FILE FOR BANKRUPTCY?

In the long run, just who exactly is paying for me filing for bankruptcy – you! But not by choice. Your finance charges will go up, your taxes, etc. If you help me pay off my debt, you'll be VOLUNTARILY giving me a dollar.

It's like the bootleg CD theory. They are all over Manhattan, but you just shouldn't buy them. Because if you buy them, then you'll run up the cost of CDs in the future. It's like stealing. Someone's gonna pay, and it will be the consumer.

So you can voluntarily give me a dollar, then I will avoid bankruptcy, and we will all save on interest rates and taxes in the future.

I NOTICED SOME SPELLING MISTAKES.
ARE YOU STUPID?

No, I am not stupid. AND I was actually a 'super-speller' in grade school. You know, I got a different, more-advanced spelling test than everyone else. But I type really fast, and as I've gotten older, I have come to rely on SpellCheck to catch my errors. And there is no SpellCheck on my low-budget website. So if you see something that is spelled wrong, please drop me an e-mail!

I thought that pretty much covered it. Afterward, I chose to list a nice pair of pink-and-red patent leather Prada Mary Janes as my Big Ticket Item. They were adorable! I was sad to part with them, but once again I didn't have a choice. Thinking about the previous week made me realize how badly I wanted this debt to be gone. I hardly ate anything. I had a closet full of clothes, but no food in the fridge.

As I was updating my Grand Debt Tally page, I decided that I wouldn't deduct the eBay payments until I received them. So even though my sunglasses auction closed, I didn't receive the $75 that they went for, so I sadly wasn't able to apply it against my debt.

$20,057.36 TOTAL DEBT June 23, 2002
-$113.45 my money
-$124.55 your money
-$0.00 eBay sales
$19,819.36 TOTAL DEBT July 7, 2002 – WEEK 2

WEEK 3: THE VIRAL NATURE OF THE WEB

I woke up really early Monday morning because I had to check in at the PMS study that I found out about on Craigslist. The office was located on the Upper West Side, which was completely past where I worked, but I would make $500 if I got accepted.

After checking in at the lobby of a medical building, I went upstairs to meet with a nurse. It wasn't an exam or anything, she just explained to me that I needed to keep track of all my moods for one month in a daily journal that she gave me. If my PMS turned out to be what they considered to be 'severe,' then I'd be accepted to the study, which was about calcium and cramps or something like that. So the plan was for me to call her in one month to go over my daily entries.

I still had the two checks that I received sitting at home because I didn't want to deposit them until I had my own money. I'm not sure if you know this or not, but I'm not always really careful with my money, and my fear was that if I deposited them into my checking account, then I would spend it. So I left them at home until I figured out what to do.

When I got to work, I checked my e-mail like I did every morning and saw that I had three. One was from someone named Janitor. It said:

Dearest Karyn,

I am terribly sorry about your financial difficulties. There is, however, some good that will come of your financial incompetence: you have inspired me to add a special section to my website (www.whitetrashrepublic.com) called 'Retard of the Month!' I have selected you to be the inaugural recipient of the 'Retard of the Month' honors.

Unfortunately for you, there will be no trophy for you to sell on eBay, nor a cash prize for you to pay your Neiman Marcus bill.

I know it must be tough for a Brooklyn princess such as yourself to live on the income that you pull in as secretary or bathroom attendant or whatever it is that you do, but that's one of the harsh realities of the world. If you want easy money, I suggest that you suck it up and look for a job as a hooker and/or selling narcotics. Hell, I'll even be your pimp if you like.

On your site it says, 'My name is Karyn, I'm really nice and I'm asking for your help.'

What it should say is 'My name is Karyn, I'm a dumb cunt who doesn't know how much money I have and in the process of emulating the wardrobes of the whores on Sex and the City, I've run up a $20,000 credit card bill. So, if you are responsible with your money, unlike myself, and have some extra cash to give away, instead of giving it to some worthwhile charity like the September 11th Fund, or the Fresh Air Fund, give it to me, cuz, gosh, I'm just plain old stupid and if my Prada pumps got repossessed, that would be like, totally lame, and my other Brooklyn princess friends won't hang out with me anymore! Thanks!'

Thanks for the material.

Oh my gosh! What an ass! I clicked on the link to his website, and was brought to the front page. And there underneath big bold letters that read 'Retard of the Month' was Janitor's e-mail to me and a link to my site.

My initial response was a bit of fear actually, because his website seemed to be mean and anti-everything. Being the 'Retard of the Month' was kind of funny, yes, but at the same time, I didn't want to be featured on what was in my opinion a yucky website.

As much as I wanted to e-mail him back and defend myself, I knew that's what he was probably looking for. I wanted to tell him that I would never expect someone to give me money before they gave money to charity, which is why I never positioned myself as being seriously needy. I made fun of the fact that the worst things that were happening to me were that I had to read my favorite beauty magazines at Barnes & Noble. What made me angrier, though, was the fact that this guy, who was an obvious 'hater,' wanted to lecture *me*. But my mom always told me to 'kill them with kindness,' she that's what I decided to do. I sent him an e-mail back and said, 'Thanks!' And that was it.

I didn't know how the Internet worked that much. I had never been to a chat room. I didn't know that sites like this existed. Before this, I used it to shop, check my horoscope and send e-mail. That's about it. But I slowly started to realize that there's a whole other universe out there in cyberspace.

Later in the day, I got another scary e-mail from a man who said he could track me down in seventy-two hours, and asked me how I would like it if I opened my door and found myself 'staring down the barrel of his gun.' He finished his e-mail saying that if I didn't take my site down, that these things could happen.

I knew by putting myself out there I was opening myself up to criticism, but this was a little extreme. I didn't think people would be so offended by what I was doing. To me it was a silly website that was funny. Why send *me* e-mails like that and not websites that promote hatred?

From working in television, I knew that sometimes people who put themselves out there received e-mails and letters like this. And maybe I should have, but I didn't take them that seriously. It did obviously make me realize how important being anonymous was, so after I was done reading them, I made sure that all my accounts from my eBay to my Register.com were registered to just the name 'Save Karyn' and had a bogus address.

Later that day, I opened four or five more e-mails, all of which were nice. One woman told me I should be a comedienne, another told me that she got in trouble at work for laughing so hard at my Daily Bucks. Two other people told me how much they identified with what I was going through. One of them told me that she owed $25,000 and her husband didn't know. It was weird that the site seemed to evoke such different responses in people. It either completely offended them or made them laugh. People seemed to either love it or hate it.

Tuesday morning was my mom's birthday. And after mailing her some lame gift that I bought with a store credit at Banana Republic, I checked my e-mail. When I logged on, I saw that there were almost twenty e-mails in my inbox. I was shocked because so far every morning there had only been a couple. After clicking through and reading each one, I found out that my site was being talked about on a website called Metafilter.com. I didn't know what it was, so I clicked on the link and it said that the site was a 'community blog.' In reading I figured out that a 'blog' was almost like a big message board. People could post things and discuss things. It wasn't a live chat, but it was like a conversation. I started to read what people were saying . . .

'She needs to go to church.'

'Y'know, I clicked the link expecting to hate it and I ended up enjoying the whole site;-)'

'She's in the shit & she's doing something about it . . . sounds cool to me. She seems to be having fun doing it, which is also cool. As someone who has been up to their arse in debt in the past [following burglary] I'll applaud her approach . . . just stay away from the economy-brand foodstuffs . . .'

'She could at least do the decent thing and set up a juicy webcam for those who contribute.'

'She's selling a Clueless VHS tape on eBay. Isn't she lovely?'

'The WHOIS for Karyn's domain lists:
Save Karyn
Save Karyn
Main St.
Brooklyn, NY 11201
US
Phone: 123-456-7890
E-mail: savekaryn@hotmail.com
Suspicious? Slightly.'

'Smart? Definitely. I wouldn't be too surprised if a 26-year-old woman who owes a wedge might not want to give out her address . . .'

'She says, "Fashion magazines are like therapy. They make me want to be a better person." That is so beautiful.'

'If you can get past the brazen shamelessness of the site, it's pretty funny – especially in regard to how little she offers in return for strangers paying her debt. Quote: "Not all my e-mails are as friendly. Some guy named Crunz is pretty pessimistic. I don't think he likes me very much. And since I'm such a PLEASER, my main priority is to WIN HIM OVER. Crunz wanted to know what he would get from giving me money, and I told him not much."'

Wow! People were talking about my site! I was so glad that I'd entered a bogus address the day before at Register.com. I didn't know people could actually look that stuff up, but I figured there must be a way. But how dare they make fun of *Clueless*! I couldn't wait to see what they said when I listed my *Darrin's Dance Grooves* VHS.

When I was done reading, I went back to my inbox and opened more e-mails. One of the next ones told me that my site was also being discussed on another blog called Paintball-resource.org. I clicked on the link.

> 'She's selling stuff on eBay as well. Furthermore, I don't see what the fuck all you care what she does to get money. Did she break into your house, rape your little brother, and make off with your bank? Don't donate if you don't want to. However, with a little exploration of her site, it's easy to see she's not entirely serious, and I would doubt she had any debt at all.'
>
> 'Regardless if she's in debt or not, I think we can all agree she's got terrible taste in shoes.'
>
> 'No shit!'
>
> 'You're tellin' me you wouldn't wear those?'
>
> 'I'd wear em . . . . if I could wear the polka-dot jumpsuit and drive a tiny little car full of my 25 best friends . . .'

They were making fun of my Prada shoes? My pink-and-red Prada shoes! How dare they! I immediately went back to my e-mail. After opening more e-mails from people telling me that I had terrible taste in shoes, I decided to get back to work.

Randy and I were working on the proposal scene, when Atticus proposed to Cherry in the middle of the Brooklyn Bridge. Well, since dogs can't talk, his dad asked her mom if the dogs could get married. Cherry said yes. I mean her mom did. Seriously, this was my job. While trying to concentrate on dogs, I kept an eye on my e-mail. Every couple of minutes I'd get another. It was awfully hard to concentrate. Around one o'clock or so, I saw one that said 'Reporter requesting interview' in the subject line. I opened it.

Hello, Karyn,

I am a newspaper reporter in Toronto, Canada, and we are considering doing a story about your site. However, we (my editor and I) are concerned that it is (a) a joke or (b) a front for some company or something else. Can you help us out? How can we know you're legit? Would I be able to do a phone interview with you?

Your site is hilarious, by the way.

'Oh my!' I gasped.

'What?' Randy said, turning around looking at me.

'Nothing,' I said. I didn't want to tell him.

'No, what?' he asked again.

'Okay,' I said. 'I kind of created this website, as sort of a joke, and all these people are starting to go to it.'

'What is it?' he asked.

'Okay,' I started. Once again, I was embarrassed about owing the money so I didn't want to tell him. And after my death threat I really wanted to remain anonymous. But I didn't think Randy would actually beat me up or anything if he knew, so I decided to tell him. 'I owe $20,000 to credit card companies that I racked up by shopping, and I started a website asking people to help me pay it back.'

'No way,' he said, not believing me.

'Way,' I said. 'Obviously I set it up because I wanted it to work, but I didn't really think it would. And I got all these e-mails today, and I just got a request for an interview from a reporter.'

'Are you going to do it?' he asked.

'I'm kind of nervous. She said she thought my site was hilarious, but what if she's just telling me that to get an interview? I've gotten a lot of really mean e-mails from people.'

'Let me see your site,' he said.

I proceeded to go to savekaryn.com and show Randy

all the pages. He laughed out loud at some of the Daily Bucks.

'Hey,' he said, reading the one about the apple. 'That's my apple. I'm the "guy at work!" You didn't steal anything else from me, did you?' he asked jokingly.

'No,' I said. 'And I felt guilty so I fessed up! You know that!'

'Do the interview,' he said. 'You need to get traffic. How much money have you gotten?'

'About $130 dollars,' I said, laughing.

'Do the interview,' he said. 'You owe $20,000. You need a lot more than $130.'

With that, I e-mailed the reporter back and assured her that I was legitimate and we set up an interview for Sunday at noon. I decided that if she came across as mean, then I would just hang up on her. What did I have to lose? I wouldn't give her my phone number, though, because I know how reporters can be, and I didn't want my full name published.

That night I worked until 9.30 P.M. When I got home, I answered as many e-mails as I could. I got an e-mail from a guy named Dan in Britain. As in London, England.

> News of your worrying plight has reached the shores of this scepter'd isle (Britain that is) and we would like to help (although I cannot genuinely say that I represent all 57 million of us). Good luck with it all. I will distribute the link to your site around Europe, to see if they can help.

I also updated my Daily Buck.

Tuesday, July 9, 2002

Today I drank water from the Brita. I'm gonna be honest here. I'm afraid of tap water because of the whole anthrax and chemical warfare thing. Not because I'm too good for tap water – it wasn't anything like that. And because I live in New York and everyone was freaked out after the 11th because of what it could have done to the water supply. I haven't exactly gotten over that fear. It's kind of like a phobia.

So my roommate has one of those 'clean your water' Brita things in the fridge, but I don't really think it works. It always has crud in it. Even when you clear it, there is still stuff floating in the water. It's kind of creepy.

Anyway, I was really thirsty and I just came to the realization that I have to stop buying bottled water and I drank the Brita for the first time. And I'm okay. I really jumped over a hurdle today by doing that. I used to buy about three jugs per week, so that's a savings of about $4 a week!

Before I logged off, I checked the daily traffic and saw that I'd received over 4,000 hits in that day alone. The entire previous week I'd only received about 300. Wow! It was two in the morning and I was so exhausted. I fell fast asleep.

On Wednesday, money from my paycheck was finally available for me to withdraw, so I deposited the Save Karyn checks into my checking account. I then turned around and wrote a check for the exact amount and mailed it to Jennifer Convertibles. That day, I proceeded to get more e-mails from people, and found out that the site was being talked about in another blog called Livejournal.com. And the money started coming in. Not a lot, but more. The people that were giving me money were saying things like, 'Your site is funny. It's worth a buck,' and 'You are brilliant and courageous.' It felt really good to make people laugh. I loved it!

Wednesday July 10, 2002

Today I bought my cat Friskies. If you don't already know about my cat, he has a problem digesting his food and frequently barfs on my sheets (See Wednesday July 3rd's Daily Buck). Like, we're talking daily here . . . So anyway, I have been buying him 'Science Diet for the Sensitive Stomach' and he seems to have improved a bit. Recently he's been only barfing once a week or so. But it's really pricey. And he's just as happy when he eats Friskies. I've taken him to the vet and they always tell me he's fine – he just likes to barf. So, oh well. Back to Friskies we go. He eats it back up anyway after he regurgitates it, so it's not like I have to buy twice the amount.

Later that night, determined to get more chuckles, I decided to add a section called the Daily Me-MAIL. On it, I would share some of the wacky e-mails that I started receiving from people – and my responses, of course.

THE DAILY Me-MAIL

E-MAILS TO ME ABOUT ME –
UPDATED DAILY!

DATE: July 10, 2002
FROM: scarlett_munchkin
TO: Karyn
SUBJECT: money to help you out

Hi, Karyn,

A friend sent me your website and I read your story. It sounds like you're a nice person in a bad situation. It's soooo easy to let credit cards get the best of you. So, I'd like to send you $100 in exchange for sex. That's right SEX. If you have enough balls to ask for money, then I guess I have enough to ask for this. I know that $100 is kind of low, so I don't want to be insulting, but you didn't have a picture on your site, so I can't tell if you're cute or not. If you send a picture and you're really cute, I may be willing to go as high as $1000. Let me know.

FROM: Karyn
TO: scarlett_munchkin
SUBJECT: Re: money to help you out

First of all, I'm cute – let's get that out of the way. I've also been referred to as HOT on countless occasions.

You see, I am hard up for cash. So I started a website called 'Save Karyn' in which I ask people who can feel my pain to give me a buck – because bucks are what I need. In return they really get nothing.

But you seem to be hard up for some good sex, because you just offered to pay me for some. You didn't even ask me if I'd do it for free. I told people straight out that they weren't going to get anything in return for giving me a dollar. The most exciting thing they can do is watch my debt shrink, read some Daily Bucks, or perhaps this e-mail from you.

So my advice to you is this: start a website. It's helped me, maybe one can help you too. Call it, 'Save the Scarlett Munchkin' and just straight out ask people for sex. I've gotten some bucks – you just might as well get yourself a nice piece of ass!

Anyway, gotta run and pay a bill. Take care! Good luck! Tell all your friends about my website! Maybe we can put links from mine to yours and vice versa!

XOXO,

Karyn

Oh, I forgot . . . PS – Send a buck if you can!

After adding that page, I asked Scott to take more pictures. He took one of me leaning into the empty fridge pouring water from the Brita into a glass. I put that one on the Daily Buck page. He also took one of me from the back updating my website. It was supposed to look like I was answering e-mails. My big Gucci purse was in the background and Elvis was perched on my shoulder. That one would go on my Daily Me-MAIL page. But before I put it up, I decided to put a big black bar across Elvis's eyes. If I felt it was important for me to remain anonymous, then I had to give him the same courtesy. He looked like a big 'Glamour Don't.'

On Thursday, the responses to the Me-MAIL section were great! Before I knew it, I had another interview request. But this time it was from a Canadian radio station asking me to call in to their morning show the following day. I obliged, and again not wanting to give out my number, I took their number to call.

That night after work, I went out with Randy to hear a band play. When I got to the bar, I was delighted to find out that he had a lot of cute guy friends. He introduced me to some. I had lost a little over five pounds and was starting to get some of my confidence back.

'This is Karyn,' he said.

'Hi, Karyn,' a guy said. 'Oh, wait, you're Save Karyn!'

'Randy!' I said, turning to him. 'You weren't supposed to tell anybody!'

'Sorry,' he said. 'It was funny though.'

All of a sudden, all of his friends wanted to know what Save Karyn meant. So I explained my whole website idea. And they all told me that it was very refreshing to hear someone be so honest.

I sort of adopted the theory that every time I didn't spend money it meant that I was saving it. It made me feel better. So that night, Randy bought me a beer for $5, but I also didn't eat dinner. Thinking dinner would have run me about $4, I decided that I came out $9 ahead. And I wrote about it in my Daily Buck.

Friday morning I woke up a bit groggy because I'd stayed up late. Not just because I went out, but because I tried to answer as many e-mails as I could. When I got to work, I checked my e-mail and was shocked to see that my inbox was almost full. There were tons! I clicked on a few and realized that people were starting to respond to everything I wrote. I got all sorts of e-mails from people saying how backward my way of thinking was in regards to me 'saving $9.' In response to my cat barfing, I got e-mails telling me that he may be diabetic. In response to my Brita experience I got e-mails telling me that the black crap floating inside was carbon. I got another e-mail from an occupational safety guy assuring me that New York City water was safe to drink. I got more advice from accountants and attorneys telling me that I didn't have to claim the money on my income tax. Someone else told me that a Baltimore radio station was talking about my site. It was so exciting!

Around 10:40 A.M. I told Randy that I was going out for coffee, and armed with my cell phone I went downstairs to a park next door to call in for my first radio interview with the Canadian station. I dialed the number that I'd scribbled on a Post-it note, and someone answered.

'Hi,' I said. 'I'm Karyn and I'm calling in for an interview.'

'Hi, Karyn,' the person said. 'Hang on and we'll be on the air in a second.'

I sat down and waited on hold. I was nervous. I was shaking. I didn't know what to expect. Would the host be nice or mean? All of a sudden I heard a bunch of radio commercials and then the host introduced me and I was on the air . . .

'Hi, Karyn, how's it going so far?'

'It's going okay!' I said in a really high pitched voice. My voice tended to get higher when I became nervous.

'How much have you collected so far?'

'I've collected about $180,' I said.

'How long has the website been up?' he asked.

'About three weeks,' I replied.

'For people just tuning in, tell us about your website,' he asked.

'It's called savekaryn.com – that's Karyn with a y,' I said, clarifying it for people. 'And basically, I racked up $20,000 in credit card bills while buying really stupid things like Starbucks, shoes and purses, getting my hair done, and manicures and pedicures – stuff like that. And now I'm asking people that if you feel my pain, if you've been in my situation, if you could give me a dollar to help pay it off, then that would be great! You can help me pay my debt!' The host laughed.

'Karyn, why should people give you money because you went nuts with a credit card?'

'You don't have to,' I said. 'If you don't want to, then don't go to the website and don't give me a dollar. But you know what? I know I spent too much money, and I know that all you out there at one time or another in your life bought something that you couldn't afford before.'

'I've done it, I've done it,' the host piped in agreeing with me.

'Yeah,' I said, 'one too many power tools! So if you feel my pain and have been in my situation and want to give me a buck, then great! I'll accept it.'

'And you're selling stuff on eBay?' he said.

'Yeah, I have a nice pair of Prada shoes up this week, and in the coming weeks I'll list some other things like some purses. And I have a pair of Gucci sunglasses that will make you look like a superstar!'

'I'll tell you what,' he said, still laughing, 'I'll go ahead and put it out there for you. It's www.savekaryn.com – that's Karyn with a y, and maybe some of our listeners will help you out. I have to say that you have a lot of gumption, girl!'

'Thank you!' I said. And with that I was disconnected.

It went well! I was so excited! With a huge smile across my face, I went back to my desk. I immediately checked my e-mail to see if any Canadians gave me money. And by God, the whole inbox was filled up again! I then checked the traffic of my website and was shocked to see that almost three thousand people had already visited it, and it wasn't even 11.00 A.M. Surely one Canadian radio station couldn't be the cause for this. I started going through my e-mails to find the explanation. While scanning through the subject lines I saw one that said 'You've hit the big-time now . . .' and clicked on it to see what that meant.

> As I'm sure you're now aware, your site was linked on USAToday.com's Web guide 'Hot Sites.' Could be the start of something interesting, for sure.

I wasn't aware! I clicked on the link that he provided and was brought to *USA Today*'s website. There at the bottom of a page called Hot Sites, under Kermit the Frog and Muppets.com, was one of the pictures from my website of me leaning over my checkbook. Next to it, it said:

> Save Karyn
>
> There's something touchingly human about Karyn. The 26-year-old New Yorker ran up a $20,000 credit card debt, and is now asking the online community to help her pay it off. What's in it for you? 'I'll be honest,' she admits. 'Nothing is really in it for you.' Yes, there's something touchingly human about Karyn.

'Oh my gosh!' I gasped. Randy turned around.

'What?' Randy asked.

'Oh my gosh, I'm on *USA Today*'s website!' I said, freaking out.

'No!' he said. 'Why are you freaking? It's what you wanted, right?'

'Yeah, I didn't expect it! I'm not ready for this. I'm freaked! I didn't expect for this many people to see my website. I don't even know if it's legal. Is it legal?! I don't even know what I'm doing! I didn't even tell my family! What if someone finds out it's me?!'

'Okay, just chill out,' he said. 'You'll be fine. Do you *not* owe the money or something?'

'No, I owe the money!' I said. 'But I am lying about my age. I'm not twenty-six. I'm twenty-nine. I did that just to throw off anyone that knew me.'

'You're twenty-nine?' he asked.

'Yeah,' I said.

'You don't look twenty-nine,' he said.

'Thanks,' I said. 'I don't lie in the sun.'

'Niiice,' he said. 'All right, so just change it to say you are twenty-nine and I don't see how it could be illegal if you are telling the truth.'

Randy made me feel better momentarily, but the more I thought about it, the more freaked I got. I truly was frightened. I didn't think many people would go to my website. I wasn't ready for this. It was a hot mess. There were spelling errors on it, mistakes – things that I needed to fix.

As the day went on I continued to get more e-mails from people. So for $20 a year, I upgraded my hotmail account to accommodate the volume. People told me I was in more blogs. Someone told me that I was being featured as the 'Cruel Site of the Day' on another popular website called Cruel.com. When I clicked on it I noticed that they had over 15 million visitors to their website. It was very popular. 'My Yahoo!,' which was the opening page for yahoo.com, also had a blurb about my website on it. I didn't even know these websites existed. In addition to those e-mails, other people gave me advice, told me to read books, and yes, some people *did* point out my spelling mistakes.

And the money started rolling in. Attached to PayPal payments were notes that said things like 'It's so simple it's funny,' and 'You should write a column,' and 'Please be real and don't make me a sucker.' They sent me five bucks, ten bucks – I even got twenty from someone. People sent me the balances of their PayPal accounts, so I started getting odd amounts too like $1.48 or $1.79.

By about one o'clock, I got five more requests for interviews from radio stations. One was in Austin, another was in Denver, another in Atlanta, one in Wichita – and the last one was even in the Virgin Islands. I e-mailed all of them back and set up interviews for the following week.

After that I got an interview request from *Business Week* magazine. *Business Week*! The editor who e-mailed me said that she wrote about credit cards and debt, and thought my site was hysterical. She wanted to interview me for a possible story. Me! In *Business Week*! I'm the biggest financial screwup in the world, and someone from *Business Week* wanted to talk to me about it! I set up an interview with her for the following day.

As excited as I was, I thought I was going to barf. I didn't eat lunch. I really felt sick. I couldn't work, and thankfully Randy picked up the slack. Later that day, I opened an e-mail from someone saying that I was in a Norwegian newspaper. They even gave me a link. When I clicked it, a picture from my website was again up, with an article that I couldn't even read.

'Nå kan du betale Karyns kredittkortgjeld
Av: Bjorn Tore Oren (12. jul 2002 13:08, ny 13:10)
Karyn var litt vel hissig med kredittkortene sine for et par måneder siden. Nå trenger hun din hjelp for å bli kvitt problemet.

Ved hjelp av nettstedet Savekaryn.com håper hun å samle inn så mange småsummer at gjelden blir nedbetalt. Hun oppfordrer alle som kommer innom til å sende henne penger via betalingstjenesten Paypal, eller ved hjelp av en gammeldags sjekk.

Siden Karyn skylder $20 000 til kredittkortselskapene, trenger hun å appellere til de generøse aspektene ved svært mange nettbrukere. Hun konkurrerer dessuten med en rekke ideelle organisasjoner, som fortjener pengene nesten like mye.

Uansett, på Savekaryn.com kan du følge (den foreløpig trege) nedtellingen mot gjeldfrihet, og lese om hvordan Karyn selv hjelper til ved, for eksempel, å drikke vann fra springen i stedet for flaskevann. Eventuelt kan du se på noen av de raffe klærne som landet Karyn i en myr av trøbbel.'

All I could read was 'savekaryn.com' and 'Karyn.' Quickly enough though, I had a translation of it in my inbox from a nice Norwegian named Haavard. It was like a snowball effect. The e-mails kept coming in. By the end of the day I had over two hundred. As I packed up my stuff to go home, I checked my e-mail once more and saw one that said 'Movie Rights' in the subject line. I opened it up.

I'm a Creative Executive for a film production company in Los Angeles. I think your story is really interesting. I was looking at your website and I think you have a really funny take on this whole thing. I'm wondering if the film rights are available. Have you given any thought to your story being a movie? Any good stories that aren't on the website?

I looked at his e-mail address and saw that it ended in '@spe.sony.com.' I typed www.spe.sony.com into my browser and was brought to the home page of Sony Pictures Entertainment.

'Randy,' I said, showing it to him. 'Look at this e-mail. Do you think this is a joke or something?'

'Sony Pictures? No fucking way!' he said. 'What do you mean a joke?'

'You know how you can get free e-mail addresses at places like hot-mail and stuff? Do you think you can sign up for one on some Sony site somewhere where your e-mail would end in @spe.sony.com?'

'I doubt it,' he said. 'E-mail him back.'

With Randy sitting next to me, I e-mailed him back and we set up a time to talk the following week.

That night I did go home and barf. I was freaked out. I called Naomi and had her ask her husband, who is an attorney, if lying about my age would be considered misleading and fraudulent. He laughed. I also asked her to ask him if the fact that I said I was a 'nice girl' was misleading, because I have been known to steal a boyfriend or two. He again laughed and assured me that what I was doing wasn't illegal.

Later that night, I called my sister, Lisa, and told her. She was disappointed about the debt, but thought the website was hilarious. She thought that my mom would understand and suggested that I tell her, but wasn't so sure about my dad. We agreed that he would probably think the website was funny, but not the debt. My dad has always been very careful with his money, and I didn't want to let him know I was a big mess.

Friday, July 12, 2002

Tonight, I decided to talk to my neighbor's tomato plants to help them grow more quickly. He's got like ten of them, and he isn't going to be able to eat all those tomatoes. So I figure if I talk to them and he sees me, and then the tomatoes grow more quickly and get really, really big, he'll give me some for free. It was an investment.

Saturday, July 13, 2002

Today I was digging through my closet pulling out stuff to sell on eBay, and I came across an old laundry card. You know, one of those things that you put money on to do your laundry. So I marched down to the Laundry and checked the balance and I had $3.25 on it still! AND the card is worth $2 if I turn it in, so I just scored $5.25 today!

On Saturday, I checked my mailbox but I didn't have any letters. But once again my inbox was full. I received some e-mails from people in Venezuela and Australia, both telling me that radio stations were talking about savekaryn.com. I also found out that I was on another blog called Memepool.com, and was also listed on a website called Majorgeeks.com. I was flattered to be considered a geek!

I spoke with the editor from *Business Week*, who told me that I could be the face of consumer debt today! She said I was exactly what millions of Americans in debt looked like. Not physically – but the profile. I was educated and worked hard, but I spent too much. She assured my anonymity, and I faxed her a copy of my bills to prove to her that I did indeed owe the money. She said that she needed it to show her boss.

And finally I had my interview with the journalist from Canada, who told me that her article was being written for the *National Post*, which was like *USA Today* in Canada. She said it had one million readers. She was very friendly and seemed to understand my plight. I was careful not to tell her my last name, and she understood why I wanted to remain anonymous. Afterward, I gave myself a pedicure to celebrate.

Sunday, July 14, 2002

Let's be honest here . . . gnarly feet suck. And no matter how poor you may be, there is no excuse for gnarly feet. Especially in sandal season, when not only you, but everyone has to look at your feet. So, today I decided to give myself an at-home pedicure. I soaked, scrubbed and moisturized. I trimmed, filed and painted. And voila! Purdy feet. I did it for myself, I did it for my coworkers, I did it for the strangers on the train. AND I saved about $30.

That night, while writing my weekly update, I made the decision not to write about any of the radio stations or the interview with the *National Post*, or *Business Week*, or the movie guy – or anything like that, for that mattter, because I didn't want to jinx anything. I had a feeling that if I started bragging about it on my website it would all go away. So I decided to keep it as simple as possible, and kept to my formula.

During that week, I got 21,932 hits on my website and I made $132.90 in donations. I was so happy when I was done that I decided to spread the joy. So at the end of my weekly update I wrote:

> *Say hello to a stranger this week, smile to your bus driver, be nice to your doormen (if you have them), and take in the sunshine! Life is too short for anything less.*

I was starting to believe that.

$19,819.36 TOTAL DEBT July 7, 2002
-$125.00 my money
-$157.90 your money
-$2.74 eBay sales
$19,533.72 TOTAL DEBT July 14, 2002 – WEEK 3

FIFTEEN

THE DAILY Me-MAIL

E-MAILS TO ME ABOUT ME – UPDATED DAILY!

DATE: July 14, 2002
FROM: Low
TO: Karyn
SUBJECT: yer site . . .

How about this, you put on a pair of panties and a t-shirt, have a friend take a photo of you from the neck down, and then mail me the same panties that are in the picture. I'll give you some money for that . . .

FROM: Karyn
TO: Low
SUBJECT: Re: yer site

Dear Low:

I got a better idea . . . instead of the undies, how about I send you my flip-flops? You see, it's summer and it's hot. And you know what that means? I sweat. Yep. Sweat. From head to toe. And you know what happens to your flip-flops when your feet sweat and you are forced to wear them day in and day out because you are on a budget and can't afford another pair? Well – they stink. Like old vinegar, ripe cheese – they stink. So if you'd like to see what I smell like, I'd rather send you my flip-flops than my panties. Let me know . . .

Karyn

DATE: July 15, 2002
FROM: Donna
TO: Karyn
SUBJECT: question

Since I've been in a similar situation I'd really like to know, where is your pride?

FROM: Karyn
TO: Donna
SUBJECT: Re: question

I left it at Bloomingdale's.

DATE: July 17, 2002
FROM: Diane
TO: Karyn
SUBJECT: hey

this is so cool i am probably going to be like you when i get older but oh well i have one dollar in my name one uno unus hahahaha i don't have anything to do with it so might as well give it to you i like doing weird things well anyway i do not know how to get it to you but it is right there do you see it i see it just gotta keep my cat from eating it she does things like that bad cat bad

FROM: Karyn
TO: Diane
SUBJECT: Re: hey

Dear Diane,

Crack is bad.

Best,

Karyn

WEEK 4: I LOVE THIS WORLD!

The momentum that seemed to start the previous week only picked up in Week 4. On Monday and Tuesday, I did six radio interviews – all from the park next door while 'getting coffee.' And I did okay. The hosts weren't all that friendly, but I always kept my cool. I made a vow not to be mean back to anyone. 'Kill them with kindness.'

And every time I went back to my desk when I was done, there was money from listeners. So it seemed to be worth it. News of my website made it to Iceland, there was blurb in the *Detroit Free Press*, and news of the website even made it to the *South China Morning Post*. Seriously. I started getting money from Hong Kong. In addition to that I got another interview request from the *Wall Street Journal*. Me, in *Business Week* and the *Wall Street Journal*? Seriously. How screwed up was that?

Tuesday evening I called the 'movie rights' guy. He did in fact work for a production company under the Sony umbrella. I didn't know what to say or even if I should talk to him. You always hear stories about people getting screwed over and stuff, and I just didn't know what to do. So I briefly told him my story and at the end of the conversation, he just said that he would keep in touch with me.

I started getting e-mails from all sorts of people identifying with what I was going through. I got a 'good luck' from some sorority girls because 'they felt my pain!' I got more e-mails from people who owed the same amount of money, some even more. I think that people started to identify with who I was. I think they saw a bit of themselves in my story and me. Some of the money that I got came with notes that said 'I'm giving you this so you can buy some normal food,' and 'Here's three for the cat.' People *loved* the cat. In four short days, Elvis had acquired many admirers.

And with a passion, every day, I kept updating my Daily Buck:

Monday, July 15, 2002

I only have $3 'til Friday, so today I ate a half a bag of stale Baked Tostitos and some old bread and butter pickles. I ate Tostitos for breakfast, Tostitos for lunch, and Tostitos for dinner, followed by the pickles.

Tuesday, July 16, 2002

Tonight I went to the grocery store and bought a box of macaroni and cheese. It was 99 cents. It wasn't Kraft. As I was paying, the lady handed me one of those foot-long coupons that they always give you nowadays, and I won a free turkey! I seriously won a 13-pound free turkey, which retails for $15.47! Holy smokes! 3 bucks 'til Friday and I win a free turkey! I don't know how to cook a turkey, but I'm guessing this puppy's going to feed me for weeks.

Wednesday, July 17, 2002

Today my minidisk player ran out of batteries on the train on the way to work. Since I don't have any money for new batteries, I sat there and stared at the man across from me. I saved myself about $2, but have really started to wonder why men jam themselves into pants that are too small and then sit with their legs wide open on the train.

That week in addition to listing my gold-rim Gucci sunglasses for the week, I listed my *Winning in the Cash Flow Business* program. Maybe someone else would be able to figure out what a real estate note was.

On Wednesday, the *National Post* article came out. Since I didn't live in Canada and couldn't get my own copy, I went online to read it. I was still nervous because I still didn't know what slant the reporter would take. I located it in the Arts & Life section. The headline said, 'Karyn wants you to help pay off her credit cards.' It started out:

'In every work of genius we recognize our own rejected thoughts,' wrote Emerson. Judging from the number of times I heard friends say 'I thought about doing that, but . . .' when I put them on to www.savekaryn.com, 'Karyn' is something of a genius . . .

No way! She just called me a genius! I kept reading . . .

While Karyn tries to answer all her e-mails – coming from as far afield as Norway and Australia – she is also trying to hang on to her anonymity. At this point, her parents don't know about the site ('They're not very Web savvy') and only a handful of close friends do. Her mother, she says, would find it funny, but she isn't so sure about her dad . . .

Ain't that the truth! All in all, it was a really friendly article. That same day, a Canadian freelance journalist who lived in New York and wrote for the *New York Times* requested an interview. I mean, the *Wall Street Journal* was one thing, but the *New York Times* was another. It was much more widely read. Could you imagine if they did a story? So we set up a time to talk that evening. She happened to be friends with a reporter who wrote for the *New York Post* and told her, so we also set up a time to talk that evening.

The *New York Post* is my favorite newspaper. It's a bit gossipy, but that's why it's my favorite. So the thought of being in the paper both excited me and frightened me. Yes, I thought it was funny when they printed stories about Hillary Clinton and showed her walking outside with no makeup on, but did I want to be portrayed like that? No. So I was nervous.

By the end of the night, after I'd talked to both reporters, I felt a little bit better. They were both New York City women and knew where I was coming from. I made sure to tell the *New York Post* girl that it was my favorite paper and I read it every day. I thought maybe this would assure they would be somewhat nice.

By the time Friday rolled around, I did three more radio interviews, and had received over eight hundred e-mails. Exhausted after work, because I still had a job to do during all of this, I went to the corner store. Pack-Man was there.

'You have a lot of mail,' he said.

'Really?' I asked.

'Yeah, they all want to Save Karyn!' he said really loudly.

'Shh!' I said, looking around because I didn't want him to blow my cover.

'What time do you open tomorrow?' I asked.

'I'm actually going to go there right now. If you want to come and get it, you can,' he said.

'Please!' I said.

We left the corner store and Pack-Man and I walked two doors down to his store. He unlocked the front door and I went in. I opened the mailbox and it was almost full!

'Oh my!' I said.

'What is this project?' he asked.

'It's a secret,' I said. 'I can't tell you.'

'Okay,' he said. 'It's not illegal, is it?'

'No!' I said. I hoped it wasn't.

'Okay,' he said.

With that I left Pack-Man and ran home.

'Scott!' I yelled, coming through the front door. 'Look!'

I put all my mail on the table. There had to be over thirty letters.

'No way!' he said.

'Yes!'

'Are you going to open them?' he asked.

'Yeah, but I need gloves and goggles and stuff,' I said. I wasn't about to get no anthrax.

'I agree,' he said. Scott pulled out a pair of big yellow cleaning gloves from underneath the kitchen sink, and I got a pair of plastic electrician's goggles that I'd bought once when I was going to make a mosaic table (it was a quickly abandoned project). I put them on and started opening.

Every letter was like the nice e-mails. They said things like 'I've been there!' and 'Good luck!' But there was something a bit sweeter about them. To take the time to pull out paper, write a note – someone even put glitter hearts in their letter – that meant a lot. All for some girl they didn't know! A girl named Katie who lived in Florida even made me a mixed tape. The envelopes had a lot of singles, a few fives and tens. One even had a twenty-dollar bill inside with a note that said:

Don't pay your credit cards with this. Do something frivolous but worth it. I've done the mac and cheese three times a day thing, it's a long road and every once in a while you need a break. Go get a caramel mocha frappe latte thingy, see a movie, buy a couple of cheesy magazines – just spend it.'

All I want is for you to do something completely anonymous for someone someday, where they have no chance of figuring out who did it.

XOXO

Nice. They were all so nice! I felt blessed.

In addition to all the people I received money and kind words from during the week, more wackos started coming out of the woodwork too. Some crazy guy bid on my eBay items as a joke. He entered a top bid of $10,000, so anytime anyone else would bid, his bid would top theirs. Then he refused to pay after he won them all, so I had to relist everything.

I also started getting a lot of requests for advertisers. Since the goal was to pay off my debt, my initial response was to jump on the bandwagon and get as many as I could. But the more I thought about it, I decided not to. I didn't want to sell out. If this actually worked, and I actually was able to pay off my debt from the kindness of strangers, then what a great story. People all over bonding together to help some random chick on the Internet get out of debt – that would say a lot about humanity. Also, I didn't want a bunch of blinking advertising all over my site. I didn't want to change a thing.

On Sunday, a woman from the *New York Post* came over to take pictures of me for the article. Since I still wanted to remain anonymous, I agreed to allow them to take photos only if they hid my face. So after talking with the photo editor of the paper, we came up with the idea to take all of the money that I had received and fan it out in front of my face. Both the reporter and she told me that the article would be fun, so I was game to play.

That day, the photographer asked me to get out all of my purses and shoes and stuff to cover myself with to add to the picture. And when I pulled them out, she asked me where the rest of it was.

'That's it,' I said.

'That's $20,000 worth of stuff?' she asked.

'Sadly, yes,' I said. 'That compounded with eating out and getting your hair done equals $20,000.' It was true. I had a lot of purses and shoes, but I didn't have a *lot* of purses and shoes. I wasn't Imelda Marcos or anything.

Later, as I was updating my site, I decided to apply the full amount of the money I received from my eBay sales to my debt and pay for the shipping on my own. So, if someone bought something for $50 and I charged them $10 for shipping, instead of applying just the $50 to my debt, I applied all $60 of it and paid for the shipping by myself. If I didn't do this, then I would have started to take money out of PayPal and divvy it up and stuff, and I didn't want to do that. So, I actually paid more each week than what it looked like.

That week, I received 44,585 hits and $455 in donations. I didn't think it could get any better or any bigger. I had no idea that it would. I found that while I could use the Daily Buck to be fun and silly, I could use the weekly update to be more serious and heartfelt. That week after telling everyone the website stats, I added:

From me to you, things have been really weird this last week. I really didn't think anyone would go to my low-budget website initially. I've gotten money, which is great because it is what I asked for. But more than that, I've gotten letters and e-mails from people who have been, or are currently, in the same situation as me.

Debt sucks for sure. It makes you feel bad about yourself because it's an idiotic thing to do, and you know that you are the one responsible for doing it. Whether it be lack of self-control or an emergency that landed you in debt, it's embarrassing. For me, the most embarrassing part of this ordeal isn't the fact that I'm asking you to give me a dollar – heck, that's the easy part! It was actually admitting that I owed the $20,000. I felt like I was the only person in the world who could have done something this stupid. But I AM NOT ALONE. And to all the people who e-mailed me and are in the same situation, YOU ARE NOT ALONE either!

And one more thing, you know what's amazing? All of these people that gave me a dollar . . . they don't know me. They just decided to help out some anonymous girl on the Internet who maybe made them laugh for a few minutes. Thank you! I love this world because people like you exist in it. It makes all the badness go away, even if for just one moment . . . So until next week . . . peace!

$19,533.72 TOTAL DEBT July 14, 2002
-$432.00 my money
-$455.95 your money
-$214.72 eBay sales
$18,431.05 TOTAL DEBT July 21, 2002 – WEEK 4

WEEK 5: THE DEATH OF CLAIRE

On Monday, *Business Week* came out and I started getting a different kind of e-mail because the people who read *Business Week* were businesspeople, I assumed. A lot of them sent money as well, but it was to celebrate my 'entrepreneurial attitude' and 'great marketing ability.'

Dying to see the article, I ran to a bookstore during lunch, and there on page 12, in a section called Shopaholics, was a color photo of the Grand Debt Tally page of my website in the middle of an article titled 'Sister Can You Spare Me a Buck?' It was short, but it was still positive. The article ended saying:

> *Not all the responses have been kind. Karyn says half her e-mail is critical. 'I didn't hurt anyone by spending too much money,' she protests. 'I was actually helping out the economy.' She has a point. Consumer spending, which grew 3.1% in 2001, helped prevent the economy from cratering.*

Aha! I'd made that part up about helping out the economy! It just sounded good. Good to find out it was true! I bought four copies and went back to work. I planned on telling my parents eventually, and I'm sure they would want a copy, so that's why I bought so many.

Later that day I spoke with the *Wall Street Journal* guy, who told me that they would not do a story without a last name, so they didn't do a story. I didn't mind, though, because I was going to be in the *New York Post* on Tuesday and the *New York Times* on Thursday.

It really was hard to work because what was going on was so exciting! I sat at my desk and tried to concentrate on Cherry and her mom scoping out places to have their doggie wedding, but I just couldn't. And I could see that

Randy was kind of getting irritated so I focused to the best of my ability.

That night I decided to tell my mother. I called her on the phone after work and swore her to secrecy. And as I expected, she wasn't too worried about the debt, and thought the website was hilarious.

'People owe that much money on a car,' she said.

'I know, but I don't have a car, Mom,' I said.

'I know, but you are going to be okay,' she said. 'Grandma told me.'

'Really?' I asked.

'Of course,' she said. 'I wouldn't lie about that. When are you going to tell your father?' she asked.

'I don't know,' I said. 'I'm afraid.'

'Well,' she said, 'I do agree that he probably won't be happy about the debt. But I do know he would find the website funny as well.'

'Yeah,' I said.

'You better tell him before it hits a Chicago paper that he reads,' she said.

'Yes,' I said. 'I will.'

Later that night, I kept updating my site. I added more Daily Bucks . . .

Monday, July 22, 2002

Today I stole the top off of some girl's water bottle at work because I lost mine. She's one of those girls who throws her bottle away when she's done, one of those girls I USED to be. Except she wears her sunglasses at her desk and I would never do that. Because I stopped buying bottled water and have been refilling my bottle from the Brita, the top is really important. The top helps me get the water from home to work. The top helps me to not spill my water on every pedestrian on the train. Since I've been reusing this bottle for about two weeks, the top has saved me about $28. So I really needed the top. And I bet she didn't even notice hers was gone. (See Tuesday, July 9th's, Daily Buck for the story behind the Brita.)

And I added more Me-MAILS . . .

DATE: July 18, 2002
FROM: Stan
TO: Karyn
SUBJECT: My DVD addiction sent me into credit card hell, and I am still there

Hi, my name is Stan, and I owe $1,400 to Mastercard. There I said it and I feel better :)

I have been buying DVDs almost every week for the last 5 months. My DVD shelf has begun to dwarf a small child, and I am worried it will soon overflow and consume my very being. It all began with my love of movies, a movie here and a movie there. Some of my favorites at first, and then movies I didn't like a whole lot, but felt I needed anyway. Then the problem took a nasty turn as I investigated movies I HAD NEVER SEEN BEFORE, but had to have.

I have 15 DVDs on order right now, with no hope of paying for them. I truthfully cannot stop. I would donate a dollar to your cause, but I can't even donate enough to my credit card bill! I have begun contemplating selling off . . . my Stanley Kubrick collection, the crown jewel of my collection. I don't know if you are into movies or not, but this is the big momma of DVD collections, it has Clockwork Orange, Eyes Wide Shut, The Shining, 2001 Space Odyssey . . . I am getting teary-eyed thinking of losing it right now.

Well, just thought I would let you know that there are other 20-somethings who have serious debt problems. Any advice as to how to stop the downward spiral?

Thanks, Stan

FROM: Karyn
TO: Stan
SUBJECT: Re: My DVD addiction sent me into credit card hell, and I am still there

Dear Stan,

I am sorry to hear about your addiction to DVDs. I don't know too much about DVD addiction, but I'm guessing it could get really ugly. I feel your pain.

If it makes you feel better, I too had a horrible addiction that I had to overcome. Even saying the word sends shivers up my spine . . . so I am gonna whisper it to you . . . shh . . . I was addicted to . . . lip gloss. There I said it. I, STAN, WAS ADDICTED TO LIP GLOSS. Gosh, it pains me just to think about it. There was Mac, Givenchy, Prescriptives (the mother lode!), T. LeClerc, Nars, Bobbi Brown – the list goes on. I even bought Bonnie Bell once or twice. But I overcame it, and you can too.

Stan, I have received hundreds of e-mails from 20-somethings just like us in debt. So, YOU ARE NOT ALONE. And $1,400 is not that bad. Just don't let it get any higher and start paying it back now.

What I am about to suggest may sound crazy, but I ask you to please NOT press the back button on your browser. I think that you should sell all of your DVDs. Even the Stanley Kubrick collection. You may find something strangely satisfying about not having any of those damn DVDs around to clog up your thinking space.

However, I am NOT really in the position of giving advice. After all, I am a woman who ran up $20,000 in debt by buying a bunch of designer crap.

Take it one day at a time, Stan, baby steps . . . baby steps . . . it'll be okay . . .

Karyn

And sometime around three in the morning, I did an interview with a reporter from the *Sunday Herald Sun* in Melbourne, Australia, which was the second largest national newspaper in Australia. I was exhausted!

On Tuesday, I woke up at 7.30 A.M. and rushed to the corner store to get myself a *New York Post*! And wouldn't you know it? The deliveryman was late! So I took a shower and left for work, and checked again on my way to the subway. And still nothing.

I hopped on the train and worried the entire way to work. Despite covering my face with dollars, I'm sure people that knew me would be able to figure out that it was me, and for that reason alone I wanted the article to be friendly.

I finally arrived and stopped by a newsstand to pick up a copy. Flipping through the paper I finally found the story. And oh my gosh! It was in color and was located on the cover of the New York Pulse section – which is like the cool entertainment section of the paper. Past all the news and stuff! It's the part that I read! It was the entire page!

In big bold letters it said 'Angel of Debt: Damsel in distress seeks $20K bailout from strangers.' This is why I like the *New York Post*! Could they make me sound any more desperate!? It was purely brilliant! In addition to the picture and the title, they had 'A Week in the Life' at the bottom of the newspaper that they pulled from my Daily Bucks, and also had a rough breakdown of where all the money went.

Later that day I showed Randy, who agreed that it was a great article. The e-mails started pouring in, and I found out that the *San Francisco Chronicle* had also run a short story that day saying:

A lot of people will be infuriated that the creator of www.savekaryn.com has $20,000 worth of credit card debt and is begging for others to bail her out. More will be infuriated because they didn't think of it first.

And *USA Today* also ran the same thing that was on their website in their newspaper. So there in the Life section underneath the Muppets again was the small blurb about my website. But this time it had a title that read 'From Kermit to Karyn: It's not easy being green, or in the red.' I wanted to just die! It was so exciting!

By noon, I had so many e-mails that I didn't know what to do. And people I knew in New York were starting to call me after they read the *Post*, just to 'see what's up.' They pretty much figured it was me, but wouldn't say anything. They were waiting for me to spill the beans, but I didn't. The anonymity thing, which I'd started to ward off the wackos and throw off my parents, seemed to create more excitement. So I just kept going with it.

Later that afternoon, I got an e-mail from *Good Morning America* asking me to be a guest and talk to Diane Sawyer. After thinking about it for a while, I said no. Yes, it would be great publicity. But I kind of felt like it was just too early to 'come out of the closet,' so to speak. I was in the *New York Post* and would be in the *New York Times* on Thursday, but I just felt like maybe I should wait to reveal myself until the debt was paid off or something.

The Sony pictures guy called after seeing the story in the *Post* and loved it. I also got a few e-mails from publishers and literary agents asking me if I'd thought about writing a book. I had, but I didn't know what I needed to do.

So I called my friend Jodi. Jodi was the girl I worked with at *Curtis Court* who was also in the Futures department at *Ananda*. When the show got canceled she became an agent, and she worked at an agency that mostly represented sportscasters but also had a television department and a literary department. I called her up and told her the whole story. I didn't know what to do about the Sony guy, the publishing inquiries – none of it. So I made an appointment to meet with her on Thursday.

By the end of the day, the reporter who wrote the story for the *New York Times* called to tell me that they pushed it from running on Thursday to running on Sunday. I was going to be in the Sunday *New York Times.* Oh my gosh. I couldn't believe it!

I was so overwhelmed with the responses I was getting. Every day I didn't think it could get bigger than it was getting. And I started to feel unworthy about what was happening. I started to believe that maybe I didn't deserve all the attention, and at this point the praise that I seemed to be getting in every article. I felt that despite the website being what it was, people expected the girl behind it to have her shit together, and I didn't. I kind of felt like a fake, like I was pretending to be on top of the world, but I wasn't. And I thought that at any moment, everything was going to come crashing down around me. Somehow people would realize that I wasn't as funny or as fabulous as I was appearing to be. I felt like any moment someone was going to take it all away from me and tell me that I didn't deserve it. I felt like I didn't deserve something good to happen to me.

And after thinking about it, I felt this way because I owed all that money. I started to realize how much I had beat myself inside for the last year for being that far in debt. The truth was that I hadn't gone out in about a year. I had completely stopped living. And not just because of the money. There are free things that I could do in New York. The truth is, I had denied myself because I felt like I was inadequate. My self-esteem had gotten so low that I didn't think anyone would ever like me – both just as a person and romantically. And if they did like me, then something was wrong with them because I was a loser. That's what I felt. So these same self-doubts were nagging at me now too, telling me that I was still a loser and that once people realized it, it would all end.

So to make sure that didn't happen, every night I worked until three in the morning or so to keep my website up-to-date.

Tuesday, July 23, 2002
Today I ate dry toast for breakfast due to lack of butter and jam in the fridge. It got stuck on the way down and kind of made me 'hiccup' a bit.

Wednesday, July 24, 2002
Today I fell off the wagon and ate Taco Bell and Hostess Cupcakes for lunch. I spent $7.

But I choose to look at it in a more positive manner. By giving in to my temptation, I am giving myself something to write about in my journal for the PMS study. This entry alone will show the ladies who run the study that I have REALLY, REALLY *bad PMS, rather than just* REGULAR *bad PMS. Once they realize this, they will no doubt accept me to study and I'll make $500.*

So if you subtract my splurge today, I still come out $493 ahead. Oh, and I also got really cranky with the dude I work with. That's one more step toward PMS study acceptance. *(See June 26th's Daily Buck for the story behind the PMS study.)*

Thursday, July 25, 2002
Tonight I decided to explore the condiments in my fridge, and found some spray butter. I also found some soy cheese that's been hiding in the butter compartment for months now. To me, that equals grilled cheese. Kick butt.

I had to take the top off the butter and dab it on in spots around the bread because there wasn't a lot left. When I grilled the sandwich, only those spots turned brown. But the fake cheese melted really nice.

On Thursday, I was a guest on five more radio shows, as well as a call-in guest on a show called *Curtis & Kuby* on MSNBC and *Fox 5 News* at 10.00 P.M. in New York. I met with Jodi and the literary agent at her company named Jennifer to talk about the possibility of writing a book. I told them both about the movie people, and they told me that if it came down to it to not sign anything before talking to them. Another high note of the day was that my *Winning in the Cash Flow Business* program sold for $70!

On Friday, I received an e-mail from the *Howard Stern Show* asking me to be a guest. Anyone's initial response would be yes, but I didn't want to. For one, they wanted me to come into the studio, which I didn't want to do because I was anonymous. And I know that they tape all the shows to air on *E!* When I said no, they offered to 'mask my face' with a hockey mask. Seriously. They still wanted me to be a guest, *E!* would still tape it, but my face would be covered with a mask. Like Jason from *Friday the 13th*. I had to decline. They finally agreed to allow me to call in, but changed their mind after I refused to give them my phone number. I didn't want it to end up on air. I didn't want them to do a search and say my first and last name or something. So that was it. Oh well.

Friday, July 26, 2002

Tonight I scored on my neighbor's tomato plants. Just as I suspected, he was growing too many tomatoes for one guy to eat, and brought some over. They were good. All you need is a little salt, and you got yourself a meal! (See Friday, July 12th's Daily Buck for the story behind the tomatoes.)

Everything seemed to be going great. Until it happened.

Beep, beep, beep, and nothing. My computer went blank. I pushed the Start button.

Beep, beep, beep, and nothing. It wouldn't turn on. I pushed the button again.

Beep, beep, beep, and nothing. The screen stayed black.

Yes, it seemed that Claire had bitten the dust. Two days before the Sunday *New York Times* article was going to be published, good ole Claire died. In a panic, I ran over to Allan and Diane's apartment to borrow their phone book.

'My computer died,' I said. 'I need to find a computer fix-it place.' By now, I had explained to them what was going on. I had to tell after the *New York Post* article, I loved it so much.

Allan pulled out his phone book and lent it to me. After searching through it, I found a place to call that said they had weekend hours. Since it was almost 10.00 P.M., I decided to call in the morning.

On Saturday, I woke up and called the computer place. An answering service took my phone number and said someone would call me back in about an hour. Because I was getting antsy waiting, I decided to run to Pack-Man and pick up my mail. When I got there, Pack-Man was proudly holding up his *New York Post* opened to the article about the website.

'So, Save Karyn . . .,' he said.

'Yeah, it's me,' I replied. 'It's a secret, though, so you can't say anything.'

'I won't,' he said. 'But you have to sign my copy.'

'Okay!' I said. Cool. My first autograph! When I was done, I opened my box, and lo and behold, Pack-Man had jammed forty-six letters into my PMB! I quickly gathered them up and took them home.

The computer dude still hadn't called, so I opened up all my letters. After reading them all, and adding the money up, I'd received $285 that week alone! Not even including the PayPal money! One woman gave me a $100 bill, with a note that said 'Hope this helps! Never buy retail!' When I was done the phone rang.

'Hi, is Karyn there?' a man's voice said.

'This is,' I said.

'Hi, this is Steve. You called about a computer?' he said.

'Yeah, my computer won't turn on. It's just making these beeping noises,' I said.

'Beeping like a long beep, like a "beeeeeeep"?' he asked.

'No, more like a "beep beep beep,"' I responded.

'And you've tried to reboot it and turn it on?' he asked.

'Yes, but nothing is happening,' he said.

'Sounds like I'm gonna need to take a look at it,' he said.

I wrote down the address of the place Steve told me to meet him at, grabbed Claire, and headed out the door. He told me that it was going to be about $90, plus the amount of any parts he had to buy to fix her. Luckily, I had the money in my checking account. It was for my rent, but I had it. About forty-five minutes later, I arrived at a midtown building and waited for Steve to show up. A few minutes later, he did, with a woman.

'This is my cousin,' he said. 'We were just eating lunch.'

'Oh, I'm sorry,' I said.

'No, I'm on call,' he replied. 'It's okay.'

I followed Steve and his cousin into the building, and after checking in with security we took an elevator to the offices on the twentieth floor. Steve was probably in his thirties and was incredibly friendly. Quiet, but friendly. His cousin was a woman in her fifties. Steve took Claire into a special room to work his magic and I hung out with his cousin and talked.

After about an hour, Steve delivered the terrible news: Claire had indeed passed. The day before the *New York Times* story was scheduled to run, with a few thousand e-mails inside of her, she died. She was only a year old too. Just a young comp.

Of course I, the eternal crier, cried because I had so much stuff on my hard drive. When Steve asked me what was wrong, I told him the story of the website, and the *New York Times*, and how Claire had all sorts of stuff inside her belly. I needed that computer to update my website, to check my e-mail – for everything. And I definitely couldn't afford a new one.

'Well, I can probably retrieve most of the hard drive for you,' he said.

'How much is that going to cost?' I asked.

'Nothing,' he said. 'I'm not going to charge you for today either. People need to help each other out in this world.' I cried again.

How nice was that? For the next hour, I waited as Steve sewed Claire back up and put all her screws back where they belonged. All the while I talked to his cousin. We had a nice conversation about debt.

The following day, the *New York Times* article came out both in print and online. And of all the stories in the whole paper, the story about my website was the fourth most e-mailed story of the day by Monday. The story also came out in the *Sunday Herald Sun* in Australia. Allan and Diane offered to pay for a new laptop for me until I could afford to pay them back. That Sunday, I was so emotional because I felt so grateful and indebted to all these people, from Steve the computer guy to Allan and Diane to all the people who gave me money. I felt very lucky.

That week, I received 40,493 hits and $617. I received over one thousand e-mails. On Scott's computer, I did my weekly update and wrote all about Claire's passing. But I think there was a reason for why it happened. I wrote the following in my weekly update:

You know I've heard the saying 'Things happen for a reason' before, and today as I dropped Claire off at Steve's I think I know why Claire went kaput. While at Steve's, I met his cousin, a woman in her 50s. We talked for a good two hours, and couldn't be more different. She has been married, is now separated, has two kids, etc. We got to talking and I told her about the website and why Claire is so important to me right now.

The woman proceeded to tell me that she too has debt. At one point she said she owed $35,000 to about twenty credit card companies. She too joined a credit counseling service, and it's actually the same one that I belong to. She said now that her children are grown, she wants to go back to school, but feels like she can't get on with her life until her debt is paid off. Debt has paralyzed her and is preventing her from moving forward and that is bad.

I think if I take anything away from this website ASIDE from the money, I hope that it's the understanding that we all make mistakes in life. Some mistakes are big, some are little, but no matter the size, they can paralyze your life, make you feel not worthy, and can stop you from living. I'm not going to let my mistakes do that to me. There comes a point when you need to forgive yourself for the stupid mistakes that you make, and today with the help of that woman, I forgave myself. I think Claire went kaput because I needed that woman, and she needed me.

So 'til next week, forgive someone who did you wrong, apologize to someone you did wrong, and quit being so hard on yourself for doing yourself wrong. Peace.

Once again, I believed what I wrote. Just a few days prior to this, I was feeling like the person behind the website wasn't the person that people expected her to be. I began to realize that I was wrong.

People liked my website because they liked what I said. It was only a bunch of words. It didn't have a fancy outfit to hide behind, or Gucci purse to make it seem cooler than it was. It was a cheap low-budget website that made people laugh. *I* made people laugh. I wasn't 'Karyn the girl with the cool lip gloss and highlights' or 'Karyn the producer with the cute clothes.' I was becoming 'Karyn the funny girl with lots of crazy shit running through her head' and 'Karyn the emotional wreck with very human flaws and humorous view of the world.' I was really revealing myself, and people were accepting me for who I was. I put all my words and thoughts out for others to see, and they were accepting them. I'd moved to New York to figure out who I was, and I was slowly figuring that out through this website.

$18,431.05 TOTAL DEBT July 21, 2002
-$100.00 my money
-$617.51 your money
-$156.00 eBay sales
$17,557.54 TOTAL DEBT July 28, 2002 – WEEK 5

SIXTEEN

THE DAILY Me-MAIL

E-MAILS TO ME ABOUT ME – UPDATED DAILY!

DATE: August 6, 2002
FROM: Matthew and Victor
TO: Karyn
SUBJECT: I'll send money

Dear Karyn,

I am sending this all the way from Down Under, if ya put a picture of your breasts on your website I'll send ya $50.00 and a pet kangaroo.

Regards,

Matthew and Victor

FROM: Karyn
TO: Matthew and Victor
SUBJECT: Re: I'll send money

Dear Matthew and Victor,

While the idea of receiving $50 excites me, I am going to have to pass on the offer to 'show you my breasts.' However, I do want to applaud you on your choice of words. You see, I've received numerous requests to see my 'tits,' 'jugs,' 'boobies,' 'hooters,' 'rack' and 'bazoombas.' If I were going to show my breasts to anyone, it would be you two nice boys from Down Under, because of your fine choice of words. So kudos to you! And in regards to the kangaroo . . . I'd LOVE to have a pet kangaroo, but I've had a talk with the cat and he says it's a no-go.

Karyn

WEEK 6: NOT EVERYONE WANTED TO SAVE KARYN

I should have realized that the death of Claire was an indication that things were about to change. First of all, I lost my job. Yep. It ended on Friday. The *Dog Days* series finale, Cherry and Atticus's doggie wedding, was finally edited and Randy and I were out of a job. From engagement-collar shopping, to the proposal on the Brooklyn Bridge, to finding a place to have the wedding, to the $1,200 Elizabethan wedding dress, to picking a doggie maid of honor and doggie best man, to the ceremony, to the honeymoon at the Loews Regency Hotel – it was finished. Yes, that was my job. It was supposed to go another week, and then there was talk about moving me to another project, but it ended early and that second project didn't happen. And I found all of this out two days before my last day.

So in addition to all of the excitement of the previous week, I had also been looking for a job on Thursday and Friday. I didn't want to file for unemployment because I wasn't sure if what I was doing would be considered income, so I started doing random things to make some cash. My friend Judi the psychic (she really is a psychic – a celebrity psychic) was having a séance to bring Marilyn Monroe back from the dead at an ice cream shop called Serendipity 3 on Friday, which was the twentieth anniversary of her death. It was also twenty-five years after Elvis died and she was going to try to talk to him too. There was a Marilyn look-alike contest planned and everything. But anywho, she asked me to do a bit of publicity work for her, so I did and made some extra cash.

It was actually kind of good to be home, though, because I had a lot going on with my website. I used Scott's computer until Allan and Diane bought the new one. And every day there was more traffic, more e-mails, and more interview requests. I got television requests from CNN and CNNfn, but only agreed to be a call-in guest. I also started getting a lot more international requests from journalists all over Europe.

The nature of the rest of the e-mails stayed the same. Every time I'd open a nice one, I'd get a mean one.

> 'You're brilliant! I wish I thought of this!'
>
> 'You are so fucking stupid! You idiotic moron!'
>
> 'You go girl! I'm rooting for you!'
>
> 'How dare you make a website like this!'

Then I opened some more . . .

> 'I'm going to call the FBI on you!'
>
> 'I can't wait until you go to jail for fraud!'
>
> 'You should be arrested because what you are doing is illegal!'

And then another one . . .

> 'I'm a producer for a film company in LA and am wondering if you've sold the movie rights to your story?'

Another movie company! It was like a roller coaster! And the truth was, I still wasn't sure if it *was* legal. A ton of attorneys gave me free advice and told me that I was fine, but I was still kind of nervous. One day I ran to the corner store to get something to eat, and when I came out there was a police car parked outside my apartment and I was sure they were there to arrest me. So I waited around the corner for forty-five minutes until I realized they were just 'hanging out.'

I also finally made a decision that week about the checks I received. Most of them were made payable to just 'Karyn' so I just wrote in my last name. I didn't know if that was legal either, but since the doctor's office always wrote in their name, I didn't see the harm. And I thought that if someone liked me enough to send me money, then I doubted they would out me.

On Wednesday, I met with my friend Jodi the agent again, but this time about a possible job for a style show on cable. I didn't know what was going to happen with my website, and if all the hype died down the following week, I wanted to be prepared.

When I left Jodi's, the reporter from the *New York Post* called again because they were going to do a follow-up story about the site the next day. Apparently, someone created a website called Savekarynnot.com, which discouraged people from donating to me, encouraging them instead to give to charity. She asked me what I thought about it, and since I hadn't seen the website I said it sounded like a lovely idea because it raised money for charity. How could it not be? After I hung up, I ran some errands and ate.

Wednesday, July 31, 2002

I'm trying to get my life on track, so today I went to a grocery store that I recently bounced a check at to 'make good on the money.' I didn't bounce the check on purpose. When I wrote the check I actually had money in the account. But when the check got to my bank, that money was gone. Oops. I thought their bank would send the check through twice, like the phone company does when you bounce their checks. But they didn't, so I had to go and find out how to make good on the money.

While at the grocery store, I decided to partake in the free samples, and counted it as dinner. I had bread, olive oil, cheese, and a small piece of a deli sandwich. While at the deli counter, I asked if I could sample a few salads as well. I opted for the vegetable salads because aside from my neighbor's tomatoes, I haven't eaten any veggies in a while. The salads were good, but I pretended that I didn't like them so I wouldn't have to buy any.

NOTE: I do not make a habit of bouncing checks. I do not owe anyone else any money anywhere for a bounced check. It was an accident.

Later that night, while reading more e-mails, I opened one that said 'You've hit the Midwest!' in the subject line. I clicked it.

I just read about your story in the Chicago Tribune and want to tell you that I know how you feel.

Chicago Tribune? Oh my gosh! My dad! I still hadn't told my dad and the story ran in Chicago! I knew that he preferred to read the *Chicago Sun-Times* over the *Tribune*, but what if for some reason he read the *Tribune* that day? I had to call him. I had to tell him before someone else did. After procrastinating, I finally called him later that evening.

'Dad?' I said when he answered.

'Honey!' he said.

'Hi!' I said. 'How's it going?'

'Good,' he said. We continued to talk for a bit because I was nervous about telling him. It wasn't just the 'I owe $20,000' part that was difficult. On top of that, I had to add, 'And I have this crazy website.' Finally, after about five minutes, I spit it out.

'I have to tell you something,' I said quickly.

'What?' he said, realizing I was serious.

'It's a secret,' I said.

'Okay,' he said.

'This is kinda weird . . .,' I said. 'Um . . . I owe some money to some credit card companies. But before I tell you how much I want to tell you that I think it's going to be paid off soon. So I don't want you to worry.'

'Okay,' he said, a little leery. 'How much money?'

'I don't want to tell you yet,' I said. 'Basically I owed all this money, and I didn't know what I was going to do, so I got creative and made this website.'

'What kind of website?' he asked.

'It's not like a porn site or anything,' I said. 'It's like a funny website. And it's all a big fluke what happened. Basically, it's called savekaryn.com and I asked people to help me pay off my debt, and I didn't really think many people would go to it, but they are and now it's getting all this press. They just did a story about it in *Business Week* and the *New York Times* and all sorts of other papers too.'

He was silent.

'How much do you owe?' he asked again.

'Dad,' I said to his question, 'the lady from *Business Week* told me that I was the face of consumer debt today,' I said. 'I kinda feel like a poster child.'

'Karyn, how much?' he asked flatly.

'I owed – past tense – $20,000. But now I only owe $17,500. I didn't want to tell you until I paid it all off, but now it's kind of getting fun and I want to share it with you.'

He was silent.

'Hello?' I asked. 'What are you doing?'

'Pacing,' he said. 'What did you buy?'

'Clothes,' I said quietly. 'And shoes,' I said quieter. 'And purses,' I said even more quietly. 'And I got my hair done,' I said in almost a whisper.

He was silent. Again.

'Hello?' I asked again. 'What are you doing?'

'Still pacing,' he said.

'Don't freak, though, because I'm going to pay it off.

Because you see, now a big movie company might want to buy the movie rights to make it into a movie, and publishers have contacted me to write a book. It's going to get all paid off.'

He was silent.

'What are you thinking?' I asked.

'I'm thinking that you still owe $17,000.'

'Yeah,' I said. 'But my website seems to be working, so that hopefully will all go away pretty soon.'

'What if tomorrow it doesn't work and it doesn't go away?'

'Then I guess I'll continue to pay it back myself.'

He was silent.

'Dad, it's going to be okay,' I said again. 'I'm going to e-mail you some of the articles, okay? And I'm going to send you a link to the website so you can check it out yourself. I'm not naked on it or anything. It's a fun silly thing.'

'Okay,' he said quietly. I think he was in shock.

When I hung up, I e-mailed my dad the text to all the articles that had been written so far, from *Business Week* to the *New York Times*. And then I left him alone. I think he needed to digest what I had just told him.

Thursday I woke up, and after doing a few radio interviews I checked my e-mail. Another story had run in the *Post* again, so I was already flooded with them. After reading through a few, I stopped on one that said 'Have you seen this?' I clicked on it.

Have you seen www.dontsavekaryn.com?

I hadn't, and thinking that it was the same one that the *New York Post* journalist had told me about, I clicked on the link. But I quickly realized that it was a different one. It was called 'Don't Save Karyn,' and the layout was *exactly* like mine. They used the same template program that I had, so it was identical.

The welcoming page said, 'Don't Save Karyn – Help us to waste your hard earned money!' Below it, just like my website but with different words, it said 'Wanted: Your Money.' Underneath that was a picture of a leech, with a caption that read 'Leeches of society are bad!' This was not a charity website, this was a different one!

Our names are Bob and Ben. We're really nice, and we're asking for your help!

You see, there's this other website run by this chick who has no concept of 'fiscal responsibility,' and wants you to pay her bills! And people actually give her money! . . .

It went on to say . . .

If you give us money, in the true spirit of Karyn, we are going to waste it all on stupid stuff!

So if you have an extra buck or two, please send it our way! We promise to waste your money in inventive and creative ways, like lap dances at the local strip club, and not use it to pay any bills or help starving children in Africa or stuff like that!

On the left were links to pages that were similar to mine. In addition to the 'Letter from Bob and Ben' and weekly update pages, they had a 'Grand Spending Tally' and something called the 'Daily Fuck.' I clicked on the letter from Bob and Ben.

Hello Everyone,
Thank you all for visiting our website! Our names are Bob and Ben. We're really nice, and we're asking for your help! Bottom line is that we aren't fiscally responsible, and we don't know how to live within our means!

Yada yada yada. They were making fun of me. The letter continued . . .

TOGETHER WE CAN MAKE A DIFFERENCE!
OK, so we're not fiscally irresponsible, and we do live within our means. So what? We can still waste money like the worst of 'em! There's plenty of things we could be buying that we don't need . . . like expensive imported beer, or lap dances from strippers, or old cars that we could buy and then trash with sledgehammers, or Meat Lover's pizza deliveries to PETA . . .

They were being mean! But I kept reading . . .

Why not give to us instead of Karyn? At least we're up-front about what we're going to do with it! Show the world that you'd rather waste money on something semi-cool than do a selfless deed to help someone who doesn't deserve it! Of course we don't deserve it either . . . but that's beside the point!

Huh. I can't believe they wasted their time writing all this baloney! But I kept reading . . .

WHAT'S IN IT FOR YOU, YOU ASK?
What kind of question is that? You get to see pictures of us wasting your money – isn't that more than enough reason?

We love wasting your money!

Bob and Ben

Oh my gosh! I couldn't believe it! I never thought that what I did would spark this kind of a response. I quickly thought about the other website that the reporter had told me about, Savekarynnot.com, and went to it. And oh my gosh! It completely bashed me! 'WHY save Karyn?' it asked in big bold letters. Then it went on to list dozens of reasons why not.

The creators then posted e-mails that people had sent them, every one of them bashing me, comparing me to like the devil's spawn and stuff. Basically, they created a mean website and masked it as a nice website that collected money for charity.

As angry as I was, I couldn't dwell on them because I needed to get back to answering e-mails. Since Monday, I had been a call-in guest on almost fifteen radio shows. So I tried to put negative websites in the back of my mind and get on with it.

Later that evening, I scheduled an interview with a radio show called *The Tom Leykis Show*. I didn't know who Tom Leykis was, but apparently he had a syndicated afternoon drive-time show that aired in about one hundred cities across the country.

I went to the post office to mail some of my eBay items that sold, and I brought my cell phone with me because I knew I wouldn't be home in time to call from there. When I was done, I sat down on a park bench and called. I thought it would take about five or ten minutes like all the others had.

They put me on the air, and the host seemed kind of nice. He just asked me what the deal with my website was and I told him. Then he asked me if I would take some calls from listeners, and I agreed. A few seconds later, they connected a male caller.

'Hey, Karyn,' he said.

'Hi!' I said in my usual chipper voice.

'I just want to tell you that you are a dirty twat! You are nothing but a whore! Why don't you go sell your body somewhere, you slut!' he said.

'Um . . .' I said, shocked. I didn't think that you could talk like that on the radio. I waited for the host to disconnect him, but he didn't.

'Karyn, are you going to answer him?' Tom Leykis said.

'Um, because I decided to start a website instead,' I said.

'I'd like to punch you in your face! I bet you are a big fat pig!' he yelled again. Still no one disconnected him.

'Karyn?' Tom said again. 'Are you still there?'

'Yeah, um,' I said, stuttering, 'I'm sorry you feel that way.'

I didn't know what to do. I didn't want to hang up because I didn't want to let someone get to me. But I also wasn't going to fight and argue back because I'm sure that's what the host and the producer wanted. So for the next few minutes, I just continued to take this guy's crap, and still didn't hang up when they connected another male caller.

'You are nothing but a whore. What the hell is wrong with you? You money-grubbing bitch!' he said.

I continued to listen and answer calmly. I refused to stoop to their level. I just said, 'Hun, can you speak more slowly? I can't understand you when you scream.'

During the first break, the producer came on the phone and said, 'Oh, you are doing a great job!' trying to butter me up. I told him that I had to go, but he kept saying, 'Oh, just one more segment.' So I continued to take more calls because I didn't want to be 'the girl who couldn't take it' and hung up. I just kept thinking that maybe a nice person would call in.

But I was wrong; one after another for the next hour, every caller slammed me. They weren't just like 'You suck.' They were brutal. But I kept my cool.

When it was finally over, I hung up the phone and just dropped my head. I was mortified. I was so upset. I began to think that maybe I *should* take my site down. I thought it was all in good fun. I didn't mean for anti-Karyn sites to pop up. I didn't mean for people to call me a whore. The whole way home, I walked with my head down. I felt like a loser. I felt like giving up. I felt so beat up. I should have hung up the phone at the beginning. I should have never let so many people bash me for an hour. I was so embarrassed. Just to think that that had aired in over one hundred cities.

When I got home the first thing I did was check my e-mail. When I clicked on my inbox, I was astounded to see so many new messages. And almost every one said 'You have received money through PayPal.' They were all donations! As I opened them up, the attached notes said things like 'You did a good job, girl!' and 'Way to go not stooping to their level!' Another said, 'I hate Tom Leykis and I don't know why I listen to him! I hope you succeed!' I even got pity money. More than one person said things like 'I felt so sorry for you that I had to give you a few bucks!' What I didn't know before I called into the show, which people filled me in on through the e-mails, was that Tom Leykis apparently challenged his listeners to be as mean to me as they could. Whoever was able to make me hang up the phone would win something. All of a sudden, I was proud of myself for not hanging up! Yay! By the end of the night, I received almost $300! So ha, Tom Leykis! Thanks for the publicity!

The next morning I woke up and got ready to go to Judi's séance. Before I left, I checked my e-mail. Maybe it was because of the radio show the night before, but some of the e-mails seemed to take a different tone. In addition to some more lighthearted ones saying that I had been subscribed to over one hundred porn sites, I also got e-mails that were really, really mean. They said things like 'I hope you die of cancer' and 'I hope you get a venereal disease, preferably AIDS, and die, bitch.' In addition to those, I got 'I hope a terrorist flies a plane into your house' and 'I hope someone rapes you.'

It was kind of unbelievable how some people could be so nice and generous, and others could be so hateful. I finally clicked on an e-mail that said 'I would take my site down if I were you' in the subject line.

This is floating all over Internet chat boards. I would hate to be you.

Karyn E. Bosnak is pathetic. She is the epitome of the average 'run of the mill,' poor excuse using, same as the rest, poor slobs that give this country a bad appearance. You know why? She is weak. She was given the opportunity to use money loans from established businesses and in return she signed her name stating SHE would pay them back. Then poor little Karyn decides she just can't control her urges and she just can't stop buying things until all the money lent to her, is gone. She obviously has no self-control. She will probably end up filing bankruptcy in the long run anyway because this pathetic attempt at paying back the creditors is not doing a damn thing.

On her site she lists a small list of her balances, her eBay funds and the donations and then her payments. Then she deducts that from her credit balance? Well first off now we know why she is in the position she is in. She must be forgetting about the interest accumulating each month? She can't be that naïve, can she? For instance if she really did put $1102.67 towards the balance of $19,533.72 total debt from July 14, 2002, her new balance would be around $18,543.37. Here is why. We don't know what her interest rate on the credit is, so even if we give her a low rate of even 6.900% for the whole amount, which would be good, her balance would be reduced by about $990.00. The interest would still eat up over $100.00 each month, so even if she could make these kinds of payments towards her overall credit debt each month she is still going to end up paying a lot more than she thinks she owes in the long run. Even at a 6.900% interest rate it would take years to finally pay off. I don't believe that she cares about the interest rates and taxes in the future, (like she says on her site) simply because she was careless with her OWN financial being, so why would she care about people she doesn't know? This little yuppie-gone-bust is not honest.

On her site you will notice her sitting in front of her laptop. Laptops are not cheap. If she was hard up for cash

wouldn't it be wise to sell the luxury laptop and just work on a decent cheap desktop while she pays everything off. She is broke but she can pay for her domain name and have it hosted monthly too? I believe she is taking advantage of people in this country because we are giving people. The sick thing is, that she lives in the same state where one of the biggest tragedies of all time happened to the people of our country. Yes she lives in New York and she wants to take advantage of the people. She won't even show her pathetic face on her poorly designed website. I despise this poor excuse she is using to get donations. It is very sad. She is not broke by any means. Yet she continues to tell people she is. She is lying. She says on her website, 'Maybe it was too many morning lattes that pushed me over the edge, maybe it was the Prada pumps that I bought on eBay.' So I'm going to give you guys a little info on this little scam artist. Here's her story . . .
Name:
Karyn E. Bosnak
Address:
(insert my real home address here)
BROOKLYN, NY 11201
Phone:
(insert my real home phone number here)

Karyn E. Bosnak lived in Chicago, IL, Champaign, IL, and now in New York, NY, ripping people off. Karyn ran in the 'Race for the Cure' Chicago 5K on September 18, 1999, her running number was 1584 and she came in 135th and it took her 29:04 minutes. She was only 26 at the time. She currently resides in NY with her boyfriend. Give 'em a call!

It's sick what things you can find on the net, aint it? THE TRUTH

After my 'yuppie-gone-bust' ass stopped freaking out because my full name, home address and phone number were floating around the Internet, I gathered my thoughts. Breathe. Okay. First of all, I had no idea how anyone figured out my name. But if they did, then it would be easy to find out where I lived and my phone number because I was listed.

In regards to the interest, there was none on the $10,000 American Express bill. And on the other cards it was pretty minimal. So rather than figuring it all out every single week, I just decided to scrap it from the website altogether, and if at the end I ended up owing an extra $500 or something, then I'd just finish paying it off myself. That did not make me *not* honest. If anything I would end up undercollecting, not overcollecting.

Also, in regard to my laptop, assuming she didn't just DIE on me and I did in fact sell her, I seriously might have gotten $400. Maybe. And I wouldn't be able to get a desktop for that price. And what kind of idiot would sell their computer anyway? Having one is a necessity in today's society. I cannot live without one. It's kind of like under-eye cream. It's something that everyone needs.

And as for paying for my domain name, by this point some dude from Register.com had contacted me and refunded my initial $35 fee, and my $14.95 monthly charge, and said they would continue to waive the fees. They liked my website. So it was free. But I didn't want to put that on my website because I didn't want people to send them hate mail for fear that they might change their mind.

But it was kind of funny that whoever wrote the e-mail performed an Internet search on me and the only thing they found was that I ran a race for the cure. It was a race to raise money for breast cancer research – a race for charity. That's the only thing they could find and they wrote it like they were revealing that I was an ex-con or something.

'That Karyn is a *bad* person! She ran the race for the cure! Can you believe her? Let's get her!'

And they posted my time! Which some might say was pretty good! And they actually did. I got a few e-mails from people who saw the posting on message boards that said 'Nice time on your race, by the way!' and 'You can join our running league any time!' Some other people who saw it e-mailed the webmasters of whatever sites they found it on and asked them to remove it because of my personal information. And a lot of them did. They kind of had to because it was a safety issue. But all in all, for someone to do that because they didn't like my website was just wrong.

Aside from my name, address and phone number, the only other thing that I was bummed about was my age, which I was still lying about. I had decided to use this as an opportunity to take three years off!

When Scott – who is *not* my boyfriend – woke up, I told him about the e-mail and called the phone company to have our number changed to a nonpublished number. I also told my neighbors in case weirdos started lurking around.

By the time I got to Judi's séance, it was over. I was supposed to meet Randy there and he was waiting outside. We instead went to get something to eat.

Later, when I got home, I was a call-in guest in FOX News Channel with Rick Folbaum. He was nice, and he did play the devil's advocate a bit, but unlike the radio show the night before, he didn't call me a twat.

Saturday, August 3, 2002

Today I did laundry. I went to the dollar store to get some more detergent and picked up some fabric softener while I was there. Got some toothpaste too. While at the Laundromat, I started wondering why and how things end up at the dollar store. Is something wrong with them? I then realized that the fabric softener was in Spanish, and it didn't have one of those fancy 'no drip' caps. It spilled all down the sides and all over my hands. It kinda sucked. Maybe that's why.

Sunday, August 4, 2002

Today I used some really gnarly shower gel that I got as a

Christmas gift. I was out of soap, and found the gel under my sink, way in the back. It was way in the back for a reason.

By Sunday, 92,518 people had visited my website that week alone – the total hits so far had been over 200,000. And I received $1,352 in donations that week alone. Steve the computer guy had also been able to retrieve all my e-mails and sent them to me.

Since our phone conversation, I'd called my dad a few times, but he hadn't called me back. I didn't know if he was angry or what. So I just kept updating my website.

While doing my weekly update, I decided not to acknowledge the anti-Karyn websites anywhere on my website. I honestly didn't want to give them the traffic. And I also didn't want to give them what they were looking for, which was a reaction.

The thing was, they may have been started to squash what I was doing, but all they did was make the story bigger. They created controversy. It made the story funnier in a way, and it made more newspapers want to do stories and more radio stations want me as a guest. That meant that more people would visit my site, and more people would give me money to help me pay off my debt. The only way I acknowledged them in my weekly update was this:

I've said it before and I'm going to say it again. I know there are a lot of other people who need money more than me. I'm not a selfish idiot unaware of human suffering. I may be frivolous and have a shopping obsession, but I'm not blind to the world's problems. And if you are offended by what I am doing, then by all means, go to a different website, please. I'm sorry that I don't have some sob story to justify my debt, but I'm not going to make something up to somehow justify me asking for your help. And if shopping is the worst thing that I did, then lighten up. I wasn't out killing people, robbing people, selling drugs, etc. I just bought too many shoes. That's it. I like to look pretty.

You know, there are all sorts of people out there. And everyone has a story. This is mine. People do what they need to do in life to get by. I try not to pass judgment. And you shouldn't either. People are who they are. It's where they came from. It's what they know.

So this week, don't be so judgmental toward others. Look at them in the eye, see their soul, and accept who they are. That's what makes this world a GREAT place. And learn YOUR story. Pick a mantra, say it aloud! My name is Karyn and I like to shop! Ahhh . . . I feel better already . . . Peace.

And again I believed it.

$17,557.54 TOTAL DEBT July 28, 2002
-$50.00 my money
-$1,352.98 your money
-$286.31 eBay sales
$15,868.25 TOTAL DEBT August 5, 2002 – WEEK 6

SEVENTEEN

THE DAILY Me-MAIL

E-MAILS TO ME ABOUT ME – UPDATED DAILY!

DATE: August 11, 2002
FROM: Malcolm
TO: Karyn
SUBJECT: money

U ACTUALLY EXPECT PEOPLE TO BUY YOUR STUFF FOR. THAT IS WHAT THEY ARE BASICALLY DOING. WHY DON'T U START LOOKING IN YOUR COUCH FOR CHANGE. I HEARD YOU ON THE RADIO (101.5) AND I CANT BELIEVE THEY WASTED THEIR AIR TIME ON U. U SPENT YOUR MONEY ON A RETARDED $500 GOOCHI BAG. HOW FREAKING LAME. YOU GOT YOURSELF IN DEPT GET YOURSELF OUT OF IT.

FROM: Karyn
TO: Malcom
SUBJECT: Re: money

Dear Illiterate Asshole,

1) Yes, I actually expect people to buy my stuff. Not 'my stuff for.' It's nice stuff, so why shouldn't people buy it? So you are right, that is what they basically are doing.

2) I've looked in my couch for change, and there is none.

3) I enjoyed being on 101.5, and as much as you think they might have wasted their time talking to me, you wasted

your time listening to it, logging on to the Internet, going to my website, looking through my auctions, figuring out how to e-mail me, drafting your lame illiterate letter to me (I can't imagine that actually took you that long), and pushing the send button on your e-mail. Now that seems like YOU wasted a lot more time on me than they did.

4) 'Goochi' is spelled 'G-U-C-C-I'

5) I got myself in 'D-E-B-T' not 'Dept,' unless you think I got lost in a department of some sorts – a department STORE maybe, but not a department.

6) And I AM getting myself out of D-E-B-T.

So thanks for the advice.

I actually enjoyed wasting my time writing you back, and I sure hope you can read it. Have your grandma help you sound out the words . . . It's not as tough as it looks.

Thanks,

Karyn

PS – SEND A BUCK IF YOU CAN – THAT'S ONE DOLLAR – UNO – 100 PENNIES – 4 QUARTERS

WEEK 7: THE INTERNATIONAL MEDIA FRENZY

Monday, August 5, 2002

Today I gave myself a manicure. The quick-dry top coat was really old and kind of goopy, but I used it anyway. Now my nails are lumpy.

Tuesday, August 6, 2002

Today I returned a pair of black pants that still had the tag on them to Banana Republic. I mean, how many pairs of black pants

can one have? I have a million. I also had some leftover money on an old Banana Republic gift certificate. So, I used both credits to buy a hot little number to wear to an important meeting today, and didn't spend one dime. Kick butt.

Every single week since I'd started the website, things just got bigger and bigger. Every time something happened, something else happened that 'one-upped' it. This week, a story had run in the Agence France-Presse, which is kind of like the Associated Press in France. And needless to say, the article ended up everywhere, sparking an international media frenzy of sorts. Stories about the website were in newspapers all over the world: the *Mail & Guardian* and the *Cape Times* in South Africa; *Correio Braziliense* in Brazil; the *Nation* in Thailand; *Today* in Singapore; the *India Times*, the *Indian Express* and the *Daily Afternoon* in India; *Korrespondent* in the Ukraine; *Der Standard* in Austria; *Nu* and *de Volkskrant* in the Netherlands, the *Edmonton Journal* and *Winnipeg Free Press* in Canada; *The Gold Coast Bulletin, MX*, and a second story in the *Sunday Herald Sun* in Australia; the *New Zealand Herald* in New Zealand; the *Daily Express, Internet Business News*, Telecomworldwide, the *Metro, Independent on Sunday, Western Daily Press*, and the *Evening Herald of Plymouth* in the UK; *Der Spiegel*, which is like *Time* magazine in Germany; and are you ready for this? The *Oman Daily Observer* and the *Gulf Times* in Qatar – two newspapers in the Middle East – as in Saddam Hussein. Every one of them ran a story about savekaryn.com – the cheesy low-budget website that I created in my apartment in Brooklyn.

I got e-mails from people in India telling me they knew how I felt. I got an e-mail from a girl in Israel telling me that she too was in debt. Some of the stories said that the website had a cult following. They called me ingenious and enterprising. Some other stories talked about Bob and Ben and dontsavekaryn.com. One reporter said that the fact the website was working said a lot about human nature and random acts of kindness. Ain't that the truth?

Aside from the international press that week, stories ran in the *Dallas Morning News*, the *Seattle Times*, the *Salt Lake Tribune*, the *Idaho Statesman*, the *Sunday Gazette Mail* in North Carolina, the *Greenville News* in South Carolina, the *Colorado Springs Business Journal*, the *Press & Dakotan* in South Dakota, the *Morning Journal* in Ohio, the *Mobile Press* in Alabama, the *Wichita Eagle* in Kansas, the *Herald & Review* in Illinois – random papers everywhere started doing stories.

The thing is that I never sought out an interview. I never called anyone and said, 'Will you do a story about my website?' If I did speak to a journalist who wrote an article, then it was because they contacted me. It was so funny! The traffic kept increasing, the donations kept increasing, and the interview requests kept increasing. I started doing like six or seven radio interviews a day. I even did radio shows in Australia, Ireland, the UK, South Africa and Spain. It was so fun!

And every day I woke up feeling nervous because my name and address were floating around on the Internet, and I was just waiting for a journalist to pick up on it, and hunt me down and blow my cover.

And then, in the midst of all the craziness, I got an e-mail from Register.com, saying that they were going to take my website down because I provided false information when I registered it. Meaning my name, address and phone number. But obviously I didn't want to give them the correct information because anyone could look it up. I called the guy who'd given me my money back to see if he could help me, and he said no because it was the legal department that was threatening me, not the accounts payable department. So I had to figure something out.

What made me most angry was that someone turned me in. You know, someone who hated me looked up my information and contacted Register.com to tell them that it was incorrect. It was like every time something cool would happen, something bad would happen to bring me back down.

For the address, I just used my PMB address. But for the phone number, I had no choice but to get a second line. The cheapest way that I found to do it was to get a second cell phone with its own number that shared minutes with my normal cell phone. It was $20 extra a month. For the name, I called up Register.com and asked them if I could register the website to my attorney's name, and they said yes. So I registered it to G. Rosen, which was the name of the partner at my friend Jodi's agency. He was an attorney, just not *my* attorney. I didn't have one. But it worked. And it was funny, because later that week I started to get a ton of calls to that cell phone. And a ton of e-mails that asked who G. Rosen was.

That week, in addition to the letters people sent to my PMB box, I started getting care packages. I got a water filter to put on a bottle of water, anti-stress bath gel, shampoo, conditioner, soap, deodorant, coupons for free Starbucks, a $10 gas card to Shell (which I used to buy some food at the mini-mart), tea, lottery tickets, stamps (to mail my bills), cute necklaces and pins, pens and pencils, Post-it notes, and more mixed tapes and CDs. I got microwave popcorn, a big box of cheese-and-cracker snacks, and jars of Ragu sauce and some macaroni and cheese. I got a hunk of Tillamook cheddar cheese from two college guys who felt sorry for the sad state of the grilled cheese in my apartment. They even sent me a picture of themselves, giving me thumbs-up while holding the brick of cheese. But to top it off, they put a black bar across their eyes like the one on my website covering Elvis's eyes. People also sent me their fashion and beauty magazines that they were done reading, like *Glamour* and *Marie Claire.*

I kept leaving messages for my dad about all the press I was getting, but he still hadn't returned any of my phone calls. But what was weird was that I received an envelope filled with a collector's-edition hat and watch from the 2002 Winter

Olympics in the mail. And it was sent to my home address. Inside the envelope was a typed note that said,

Please accept these items as a donation for your eBay sales. Good luck, Benny (I'm a friend of your dad's).

So my dad couldn't have been too mad at me. I mean, he was telling his friends about my website. So I listed the items.

And in addition to the American money I received, I also started getting foreign money like euros, Canadian dollars, Korean wons, Chilean pesos, and some Chinese yuans. And of course an envelope filled with monopoly money as a joke.

So since people were tuning in, I kept up with my Daily Bucks . . .

Wednesday, August 7, 2002
Tonight I had a friend from out of town come visit. She stayed in a hotel. I went to visit her and took the mini shampoo and bath gel. She'll get more tomorrow. They smell nice.

Thursday, August 8, 2002
Today I canceled my gym membership. I owed them two months of past dues, so I haven't been able to go for the last two months anyway. By canceling my membership, I am saving myself $65 a month. I can run outside instead.

Friday, August 9, 2002
Because I can't afford a facial and I need one, I put tomato slices on my face. I heard they make a good face mask. But they burned, so I took them off and rinsed with cold water. I saved myself $100, but my face stayed really red for a while.

And kept up with my e-mails . . .

DATE: August 9, 2002
FROM: BigFatKoi
TO: Karyn
SUBJECT: Cheaper than membership to a porn site

I'm giving you $1.99 because it's cheaper than membership to a porn site. 'Cause basically all a porn site does is give you a place to fantasize. So I can send you a couple bucks and fantasize about the way you would thank me. Hope it's worth the money to know what I'll be thinking about tonight.
p.s. nice rack

FROM: Karyn
TO: BigFatKoi
SUBJECT: Re: Cheaper than membership to a porn site

Dear BigFatKoi,
Thanks for the buck 99. And I'm glad you like my rack.

And I kept listing tons of stuff on eBay, which had been going really well. In addition to the Big Ticket Items, I started selling books, magazines, anything and everything. I think a lot of people preferred to buy something – even if they didn't want it – rather than just give me money. And listen to this: I sold a Cynthia Rowley green silk dress in a size 8, and got e-mails from people calling me a 'fat ass' because I wore a size 8. How mean is that? Anywho . . .

Saturday, August 10, 2002
Today I went to Starbucks. I know what you are thinking – I fell off the wagon. But I didn't. I had a coupon for a free frappucino courtesy of WKTU-FM in NY. The guy there sent me four of them. Thanks! I even treated my roommate to one for putting up with me during these meek times. Since it was around noon, I counted the frap as breakfast AND lunch, aka brunch. So I paid

nothing AND saved myself an additional $8 for skipping the meals. Thanks! Rock on!

Sunday, August 11, 2002

Today I decided to wear my disposable contacts for another week. I've been wearing the same pair for a month now, because I ran out and have to order new ones. I was going to order some new ones today, but I'm waiting for a check to clear and don't have any money. So another week with dry eyes I go . . . Yesterday I had a close call and dropped one on the bathroom floor. But I found it. They are kind of dry and I blink a lot when I wear them. People think I'm winking at them, but I'm not.

I know it would be cheaper if I just wore my glasses, but I get confused when I wear my glasses. Have you ever tried to grocery shop while wearing your glasses after you've been wearing contacts for a while? WOW! I feel like I'm on drugs! The perception is all funky, I drop things. I reach for the shelf, but just grab air. I usually end up leaving empty-handed and frustrated. Trust me, New York definitely does not want me walking the streets with my glasses on. I'd bump into people, knock them down, and then that could start a riot . . . I NEED MY CONTACTS.

By the end of the week, I had received 146,994 hits and $1,391 in donations. And I'd decided to sell my brown BCBG purse with fringe. It was really difficult to let it go, but I had no choice. It was either that or my Gucci, and I wasn't ready to give that one up yet. It was kind of difficult to part with some stuff because I had memories in things. You know? It wasn't as easy as it looked. That week, I wrote this in my weekly update:

I've been asked this question a lot this week . . .. If you could do it all again, would you? The obvious answer is 'No. If I could turn back time, I would never run up that debt again.' But I don't feel that way. I am a person that has to learn from my mistakes. You can't tell me something is bad, I need to experience it on my own and have it be bad to me. I need to make mistakes to learn. I have always been that way. It's who I am.

I lived a great, fun life being frivolous. I have memories, just like this purse, that I will have forever. So when I part with things like this, I need to remember and distinguish that I'm not parting with the memory, but with the purse. There's a big difference.

So, this week, make mistakes, learn your lesson, and learn how to live life YOUR *way. You'll come out okay in the end. I have faith . . .*

$15,868.25 TOTAL DEBT August 5, 2002
-$132.76 my money
-$1,391.73 your money
-$189.66 eBay sales
$14,154.10 TOTAL DEBT August 11, 2002 – WEEK 7

WEEK 8: HOW MY GRANDPA BLEW MY COVER

Yeah, you read the title right. Not many people saw the Internet posting floating around with my first and last name on it, so to most of the world, I was still anonymous – just Karyn in Brooklyn. Two months had gone by, and my anonymity was about to come to an end. My grandpa blew my cover. By accident, of course, but this is what happened.

On Monday, I got an e-mail from someone at the *Today* show, as in Katie Couric and Matt Lauer. I was absolutely so excited! They asked me if I was interested in coming on the show, but I still wasn't sure because I still didn't want to reveal myself. I kind of wanted to save it for the end. Not like anyone would have cared that much, but so far the momentum had still been building, and the anonymous part was what people seemed to love. My initial gut feeling that told me to hold off when *Good Morning America* contacted me proved to be correct. And my gut said to wait a bit longer this time too.

But I told the girl who e-mailed me that I would think about it and took her number. Meanwhile she was going to pass my name to a producer and check with her bosses to see if they would be willing to do a funny anonymous piece. Kind of like the website – where they would send a camera crew over and do something really silly at my apartment – a very fun segment. When I hung up the phone, I had to take care of something.

Monday, August 12, 2002

Today I killed a roach the size of a small child in my kitchen. I squashed him flat with an Allure magazine after the cat cornered him. That cat's got one good eye. It was really one of the most horrifying things that has ever happened to me. That and the mouse I had this past winter. That little bugger ran right underneath my bed while I was sleeping. The cat cornered him too. He's both a mouser AND a roacher.

I'm not sure if you picked this up from the website or anything . . . but I'm not the type of girl who is used to roaches and mice. But since moving to Brooklyn, I've had both. I figure that's what I have to put up with to compensate for the cheaper rent.

I'm not sure how killing the roach made me save or make a buck today. But I didn't call an exterminator, I got him myself. So I figure I saved a few bucks there.

After that, I got an e-mail from a reporter at the *Milwaukee Sentinel Journal* requesting an interview. So I called her back. After talking to her for a while, she asked me if I had any ties to Wisconsin, because she was looking for a local angle for the story.

'Yes, my grandpa lives there,' I said.

'Really?' she asked. 'Do you think there is any way I could

get a quote from him?' She was a really nice reporter, so I said yes but I needed to talk to him first.

I hung up and called my grandpa, the one who was born in Ireland. He may be a ball of fire, but he's eighty and can only hear out of one ear. And even that good ear has a hearing aid. By now, my mom had told him about my website.

'Grandpa?' I said.

'Karyn!' he said. My grandpa loves me very much and is very proud of me.

'Hi!' I said. 'Grandpa, a reporter from the *Milwaukee Sentinel Journal* wants to talk to you.'

'Why?' he asked.

'Because they are doing a story about my website and are looking for a local angle. And I told her that you live in Wisconsin, and she asked if she could get a quote from you.'

'Okay, just give her my number, anything for my Karyn,' he said.

'Okay, but Grandpa, you have to remember to not tell her my last name,' I said.

'I promise,' he said.

'Okay, I'm going to have her call you right now,' I said before hanging up. 'I love you!'

'I love you too,' he said. I called the reporter back and gave her his number. I trusted her.

Over the next two days, more stories ran in the *Daily Telegraph*, the *Daily Mirror* and the *Guardian* in London. The BBC started e-mailing nonstop, and I did a radio interview where the host surprised me by having Bob and Ben on the line. They weren't mean though. They just said a lot of 'Duh . . .' and 'Uh . . .' and stuff like that. I think they were nervous. Some more stories ran in the *Ottawa Citizen* in Canada, and the *Australian*, the *Canberra Times*, and the *Townsville Bulletin* in Australia.

Tuesday, August 13, 2002

Tonight I went out for drinks with a long-lost friend who came to New York on business. You know what that means? EXPENSE ACCOUNT! Yup! We met at a swanky little place in the meat-packing district . . . and got to catch up and drink up for free! Expense accounts rock.

And by Wednesday the story ran in the *Milwaukee Sentinel Journal.* And it was on the cover of the paper. Page One. Not a lot going on in Milwaukee apparently. Anyway, I found the article and was relieved to see that my last name wasn't printed anywhere. Grandpa had done good and vouched for me, saying that I was legitimate. But then I noticed that the journalist printed *his* first and last name. Damn! I forgot to tell him not to give her his last name. It wasn't the same as mine, so I wasn't too freaked. But anyway . . .

Later that day, my mom called me and told me that some reporter had called my grandpa and started asking questions.

'A reporter from where? What was his name?' I asked.

'Grandpa doesn't remember,' my mom said.

'He has to!' I said.

'All he remembers is that he thinks he worked at Court TV, and he thinks the name began with an A. Andrew or Adam or something.'

This was weird because Court TV had never contacted me for an interview. So for them to call up my grandpa and not me was odd.

'Grandpa didn't give him my last name, right?' I asked.

'He says he didn't, but your Uncle Rob says that he did,' she said. 'I'll have him call you.'

'Okay,' I said. I hung up with my mom and called Jodi, my friend the agent, because she used to work at Court TV. When I asked her if she worked with a producer named Andrew or Adam or something, she said no, but she said it could be someone from The Smoking Gun. The Smoking

Gun is a website that finds court documents and exposes people, so to speak, and it's affiliated with Court TV.

After I hung up with Jodi, I went online to The Smoking Gun website and looked at the staff names. And there, under 'Reporters,' it said Andrew Goldberg.

I called my grandpa.

'Grandpa, did the guy say that his name was Andrew Goldberg?' I asked.

'Yeah, yeah, I think that could have been it,' he said.

'You didn't give him my last name though, right?' I asked.

'No, I didn't,' he said.

'What kind of things did he ask you?' I asked.

'I don't remember,' he said. 'Here, talk to your uncle Rob.' He passed the phone over.

'Karyn,' my uncle said, whispering so my grandpa's one good ear couldn't hear him.

'What did he say?' I asked. It was kind of pathetic that a savvy New York reporter called up my eighty-year-old grandpa to figure out who I was.

'He says he didn't tell him your last name,' my uncle said, 'but listen. He's so proud of you that he talked too much. He told him where you went to high school and college, and told him you were a cheerleader, and that you can sing really well. He told him that your sister lives in Minneapolis with her husband and that they don't have any kids. He told him that your mom and dad are divorced and that your mom owns a frozen custard shop, and that your dad is retired from the phone company. And then I heard him say, "I can't tell you her last name." '

'Well, that's good,' I said.

'No, wait,' he said. 'Then I heard him say, "Oh, her dad's name is Nick Bosnak." So he didn't tell him *your* last name, but he told him *your dad's* last name.'

That fucking reporter tricked my eighty-year-old grandpa! I had to laugh, though, because how could I be mad at grandpa? He is the greatest grandpa in the whole world!

The next day, I looked on The Smoking Gun website and found nothing. I felt like they were going to out me any day. And The Smoking Gun is very popular. So if they outed me, everyone would know. Later that day the phone rang and it was the *Today* show again, asking me to come on the following day and no, they wouldn't do anything anonymous – it was now or never. I said yes.

I quickly called my mom and dad to tell them the good news. My mom was home and was so excited! She said she would call all the relatives and let them know. And my dad, well, he still wouldn't pick up the phone when I called. So I left a message.

'Hi, Dad,' I said. 'It's Karyn. I just want to let you know that I'm going to be on the *Today* show tomorrow. As in Matt Lauer and Katie Couric. I should be on around 8.00 A.M. or so, so tune in. I love you.' I hung up.

Afterward, I made sure my site was completely up-to-date, and then checked on some of my e-Bay auctions. Everything had bids, including the Olympics stuff that my dad's friend had sent me. In fact, they were going for around $30 each. When I looked at the name of the bidder, it said 'Old Crow Jr.' My other grandpa (my dad's dad), used to have the nickname Old Crow Sr. because he was Croatian. So when I saw the name Old Crow Jr. I immediately thought that it must be my dad. I quickly checked the e-mail address of that username, and sure enough it was. My dad was bidding on my e-Bay items! He wouldn't return my phone calls, but he was bidding on my items. I didn't e-mail him, or call him back and tell him that I knew, because I think it was his way of helping me indirectly without giving me money.

Later that afternoon, after logging off, I was a call-in guest on CNN's *TalkBack Live*, and then I got ready for my big day.

Thursday, August 15, 2002

Tonight I applied a really old self-tanner to give myself a bit of color. I really like Clarins, but I can't afford to buy a new bottle, so I am going to try the really old stuff. I do not like to sunbathe because I do not want to get wrinkles. You have to plan early for these types of things. I also do not smoke because I do not want wrinkles OR *lung cancer. The self-tanner smells funny. I hope I don't turn orange.*

Friday morning I woke up and a big black car picked me up at 7.15 A.M. to bring me to the *Today* show's studios at Rockefeller Center. I was so nervous! Scott came with me.

The car dropped us off at a side door, and we checked in with an NBC page. Because it was August and it was a Friday, James Taylor was there to be a guest for the Summer Concert Series.

The night before, the producer had told me that Katie was going to interview me, but when I got there, I found out that it was going to be Matt instead. I was kind of nervous because Matt can be kind of hard-hitting, you know? So I crossed my fingers and prayed that he would be nice.

After checking in, I was directed to a room to get my makeup and hair done. As I sat in the chair and waited, Katie Couric came in for a touch-up. She looked at me.

'Are you the credit card girl?' she asked.

'Yeah,' I said, smiling, 'I am.'

'I think your story is so funny!' she said. 'But Matt's going to interview you.'

'I know, I'm nervous,' I said.

'Oh, you'll be fine!' she said. 'By the way, where'd you get your skirt?'

'Banana Republic,' I said.

'It's cute,' she said.

'Thank you!' I replied. Katie liked my skirt!

'Good luck!' Katie said as she got up to leave. I felt better.

After about five minutes, the makeup and hair girls were done and the producer brought me downstairs. I was so happy. It was a gorgeous day outside and James Taylor was singing. And Matt Lauer is just a babe – let's be honest!

I was directed to my chair in the studio and waited by myself for a few minutes. The studio was dark and cold, and I saw all the people outside, but I couldn't hear them, which helped alleviate some of the nervousness.

A few moments later, Matt Lauer walked up and sat down in the chair opposite me. And wow! Okay, like he's cute on TV and all, but he's a damn dreamboat in person! And that haircut! Despite the criticism, it looked good!

'Hi,' he said to me, smiling. The cameras had not started rolling yet.

'Hi,' I said.

'How are you?' he asked.

'I'm really nervous,' I said.

'Aww, don't worry about it, you'll be fine!' he said. 'Just pretend you are at a cocktail party!'

I wanted to say, 'The thing is, Matt, I don't go to many cocktail parties. I live in Brooklyn with my cat and rodents in the walls.' But I didn't. Before I knew it, the cameras started rolling and we were on the air. Matt started talking.

'What would you do if you were more than $20,000 in debt and had no one to turn to for help? Well, a young woman known to the world just as Karyn set up a website asking people to give her money, and they did, sending her thousands of dollars and expecting nothing in return but good karma. Karyn's true identity has remained a closely guarded secret even to her closest friends. But now Karyn Bosnak is here to reveal herself and tell the world for the first time all about her scheme that apparently is working . . . Karyn, welcome.'

FIVE MINUTES LATER . . . I don't really remember what happened after the introduction! I was too nervous! But after going to Jodi's office, which was right by Rockefeller, and watching the tape, I realized that Matt was nice! I did okay! He asked me how I came up with the idea, he talked about the anti-Karyn sites – all in all it was good! While at Jodi's, I called some radio stations for some more interviews.

Friday, August 16, 2002
Today I made some long-distance calls from my friend's office phone. I was on for about thirty minutes, so I figure I saved about $3.

And then I went home. That day alone, I received over twenty-three hundred e-mails! I felt like Forrest Gump when he caught all those damn shrimp! And I received a gazillion phone calls from people I knew. Let me tell you, everyone watches the *Today* show. Old friends, old boyfriends – they all came out of the woodwork. One of the biggest questions everyone asked was, 'Is Matt Lauer as cute in person as he is on TV?' Well, the females asked that question anyway. No, wait – some guys did too. Anywho, of course I answered 'Yes! You have no idea!'

My mom called me to say she was proud, and she told me that my grandpa cried.

'If only Annamary was here to see her!' she said he said. Annamary was my grandma, who died when I was little. She's the one my mom always prays to. My mom told my grandpa that Grandma probably did see. Moms are good.

After hanging up with her and printing some e-mails so my inbox wouldn't get full, my phone rang again.

'Hello?' I answered.

'Karyn,' a voice said, 'it's your dad.' Finally!

'Hi,' I said. I was so happy he called. 'Did you see me on TV?'

'I did,' he answered. 'And you did a good job. I'm proud of you, honey.'

'Thank you, Dad! See, it's all going to go away,' I said.

'I know,' he said. 'And guess what else?'

'What?' I asked.

'I'm Old Crow Jr and I won some of your eBay auctions,' he answered. I pretended not to know.

'You are? Well, then you owe me $68, Dad,' I said, laughing.

'I noticed on your website that you don't take personal checks,' he said. 'Will you take one from your dad?'

'Yes, I will,' I said. Dads are good.

Sunday, August 18, 2002

Today I may or may not have returned a pair of worn pants to a store in SoHo. It may not be legal to return a pair of worn pants with reattached tags and pass them off as unworn. So I have to be safe and not incriminate myself by admitting that I did it, so I might not have done it. If I did do it, I may have saved myself about $84. But I might not have done it and I might just be making it up.

That week, I received 204,097 hits on the site, and $2,630 in donations. My debt had been cut in half. One guy sent me an e-mail saying this:

Why on earth would people send money to a stranger without getting some sort of payback? Please enlighten me.

And in my weekly update I answered him:

Here's your enlightenment . . . Today I gave two stamps to some random guy at the post office because the line was too long and he didn't want to wait. I was standing there with a whole book of stamps in my hand and he asked me if he could have two and I said sure. He offered me money and I said, 'Don't worry.' It was two stamps, you know? He smiled and said, 'Oh, you made my day.' And I said, 'I'm glad to have made your day.' I gave him something for nothing, and got something in return. It wasn't money, but it was the satisfaction that I helped him out. He left with a smile and so did I.

So to all you people who gave me money, 'You made my day.' I am smiling, just like the guy at the post office. And just by the letters and e-mails that I've received from you, I bet you are smiling too.

I hope it made you feel good like I felt good when I gave that guy two stamps. So, that's what you get, Mr Pessimistic. Hopefully you are enlightened.

You shouldn't do things in life for the sole purpose of getting things back. You should do them because you want to make this world a better place. And what you SHOULD get back is a positive feeling because you've helped someone out. To me, that is satisfaction and payback enough.

I know I've said it once, and I'll say it again. If my website works, and I get my debt paid off, I will SO give back to the community. I will be so indebted to everyone for making my life easier by taking the burden of debt off my shoulders. And I won't do it because it's what I'm supposed to do, but because it's what I WANT to do. When people help you, you feel compelled to help other people. Maybe after I gave that guy two stamps today he went out and gave someone bus fare, or gave someone change at the grocery store. Or maybe he just took that smile of his and smiled at everyone on his way home! I know I did . . . That's what you get back, and that's better than just about anything.

$14,154.10 TOTAL DEBT August 11, 2002
-$432.00 my money
-$2,630.84 your money
-$682.46 eBay sales
$10,408.80 TOTAL DEBT August 18, 2002 – WEEK 8

EIGHTEEN

GRAND DEBT TALLY

-$118.00 my money
-$1,884.80 your money
-$537.82 eBay sales
$7,868.18 TOTAL DEBT August 25, 2002 – WEEK 9

-$75.00 my money
-$1,146.49 your money
-$605.13 eBay sales
$6,041.56 TOTAL DEBT September 1, 2002 – WEEK 10

-$50.00 my money
-$606.07 your money
-$316.79 eBay sales
$5.068.70 TOTAL DEBT September 8, 2002 – WEEK 11

-$100.00 my money
-$426.80 your money
-$254.38 eBay sales
$4,287.52 TOTAL DEBT September 15, 2002 – WEEK 12

-$75.00 my money
-$460.33 your money
-$327.72 eBay sales
$3,424.47 TOTAL DEBT September 22, 2002 – WEEK 13

-$85.00 my money
-$466.68 your money
-$78.50 eBay sales
$2.794.29 TOTAL DEBT September 29, 2002 – WEEK 14

-$75.00 my money
-$447.19 your money
-$0.00 eBay sales
$2,272.10 TOTAL DEBT October 6, 2002 – WEEK 15

-$90.00 my money
-$343.11 your money
-$174.19 eBay sales
$1,664.80 TOTAL DEBT October 13, 2002 – WEEK 16

-$100.00 my money
-$344.48 your money
-$0.00 eBay sales
$1,220.32 TOTAL DEBT October 20, 2002 – WEEK 17

-$100.00 my money
-$103.03 your money
-$287.26 eBay sales
$730.03 TOTAL DEBT October 27, 2002 – WEEK 18

-$100.00 my money
-$220.82 your money
-$19.65 eBay sales
$389.56 TOTAL DEBT November 3, 2002 – WEEK 19

-$114.16 my money
-$136.60 your money
-$138.80 eBay sales
$0.00 TOTAL DEBT November 10, 2002 – WEEK 20

THE AFTERMATH

After the *Today* show appearance, it took me twelve more weeks but my debt was eventually paid off. The money slightly decreased each week, and I did hit a few snags along the way.

I found out that it *was* The Smoking Gun that called my grandpa, and they called him *again* after I was on the *Today* show. So I called the reporter myself and yelled at him. He said that they knew who I was for weeks, but were trying to find 'dirt' on me. They were unsuccessful. A few days later, they ran their story anyway. For the photos they pulled two shots from my *Today* show appearance, one of me looking in the air like a ditz, and the other of me smiling really big like a fool. They couldn't have been more unflattering. The most upsetting part about it though wasn't the photos. It was that the article started out by saying 'Meet Karyn Bosnak. She's the 29-year-old self-described "hottie" behind savekaryn.com . . .' They said my age! Twenty-nine, damn! They *did* find dirt on me!

Anywho, it was a short article, only a paragraph, but at the end it said 'We'd hit it!' After calling around and asking my friends what 'We'd hit it!' meant, I found out that it meant they would have sex with me. Yep, the boys from The Smoking Gun would hit me! Ladies, yes, this may be degrading, but let's be honest: you'd rather have people say they want to 'hit you' than not.

But that wasn't the worst part of it. The worst part of it was that after they published that to the Internet, a popular website called Fark.com linked to The Smoking Gun's article, and a discussion board popped up where dozens of other guys talked about whether or not they'd 'hit me' too. And although I shouldn't have looked, I did.

'I'm not so sure I'd hit it. Who am I kidding, of course I would.'

'I'd hit it . . . then take the $6,000 that idiots sent her and hit the road . . .'

Almost all of the comments said they'd hit me! And once again, ladies, if they're gonna talk about it, wouldn't you rather have them say yes? Anywho, almost at the bottom, things took a turn.

'I wouldn't hit that unless I was blind!'

'Somebody call Jennifer Grey! I think we've located her old nose!'

'Oh I'd hit it all right. Open hand right across the face, and a foot in the ass!'

After getting over the 'she needs a nose job' comments, I came to realize that you can't win them all.

Also right after the *Today* show, the governor's office of the state of Utah sent me a letter saying that it had come to their attention that I was soliciting donations without being registered as a charity in their state. When I refused to register as a charity, because I wasn't one, they threatened to sue me. So after consulting with an attorney friend, she convinced me to put up a disclaimer saying that I wouldn't accept donations from the state of Utah. The thing was, if they did sue me and it went to court, I would probably have won because I clearly didn't fit their state's definition of what a charity was. But since I didn't have the cash to fight the state of Utah, putting a disclaimer up was just safer and cheaper.

After that, someone complained to eBay about me saying that I provided inaccurate contact information, so they canceled all of my auctions and suspended my account until

I gave them the correct information. And, I never got accepted to that PMS study. They said my PMS wasn't 'severe' enough. Right, tell that to my roommate.

By September, more parody sites popped up all over the Web, including 'Save Sheeba' and 'Save Karyn's Complexion.' Like 'Don't Save Karyn,' both were exact replicas of my site. The former was a website set up by a dog asking for a million dollars. It said, 'Help this bitch return to her lap of luxury lifestyle!' and had pages like 'The Daily Bark' and 'Buy Sheeba's Crap,' where you could literally buy Sheeba's crap. There was also an area on the website where you could 'Give Karyn a face lift to make her prettier!' Yes, with the click of a mouse, you could pull my face in all different directions. 'Save Karyn's Complexion' said:

Wanted: Good Skin

Hello!

My name is Darrin, I'm really nice, and I'm asking for you to help save Karyn's Complexion!

You see, Karyn has spent so much time trying to get other people to pay off her credit card debt, that she has completely ignored her complexion. To make matters worse, Karyn is now 29 years old, and her early-morning face looks like a wrinkled sheet that was left in the dryer overnight.

So if you have an extra buck or two, please send Karyn some Retin-A!

All she needs is 1 tube from 200 people, or
2 tubes from 100 people, or
5 tubes from 40 people . . .
You get the picture! . . . AND IT'S NOT A PRETTY ONE, IS IT?

Together, we can banish laugh lines from Karyn's face!

It then provided links to buy Retin-A. I was actually hoping people would buy it and send it to me because Francis told me that was really good for my skin, and well, I couldn't afford it anymore. But no one did. (In other Internet news, I was named 'Dumbass of the Month' on some website called The Blue Site.)

But despite the negative, a lot of good stuff happened along the way too. After the *Today* show, a whole new wave of media happened again because newspapers started doing follow-up stories now that I wasn't anonymous anymore. I also appeared on *CNN* twice and CNBC's *News with Brian Williams*. In addition, fun, big color stories were done in the *Los Angeles Times* and *People* magazine. *People*! A whole page! And guess what else? *Time* magazine. I made *Time* magazine! Me. The biggest screwup ever! But the biggest and the best, the one I was most proud of, was that I made . . . the *National Examiner*! Yes! A tabloid! Right next to an article called 'Anna Nicole's Woes: "I Can't find a Man!"'

In addition to those magazines, British *Glamour* did a two-page article about my website that was very flattering. And it was funny, because the same month, American *Glamour* called me a 'Glamour Don't,' saying that my idea was the worst way to get out of debt. Both *Glamour*'s – the same month – one celebrated my idea, the other knocked it. But the coolest bit of publicity by far was that the *New York Times Magazine* named me and my website one of the best ideas to come out of 2002. And seriously, I'd rather be bashed in *Glamour* and praised in the *New York Times* than the other way around.

HOLLYWOOD ENDING

Oh yeah, did I mention the movies? Well, the guy from Sony kept in touch with me and loved the *Today* show interview, and all the press that the website received. One day, close to paying off my debt, I got a phone call.

'Karyn!' he said. 'We want to bring you to Los Angeles! We want to make you an offer!'

'Really?!' I said, jumping up and down.

'Really!' he said. 'A car is going to pick you up on Monday to bring you to the airport.'

'Pick me up in Brooklyn?' I asked.

'Yes, in Brooklyn,' he said.

'Cool!' I said, thinking I'd have to take the subway.

The next Monday, that car did pick me up and took me to JFK airport. And after taking off and landing, I was in Los Angeles. 'The Sony guy' had a real name, it was Jeff, and he and another producer named Lacy picked me up at the airport. They were so nice!

We walked to their car and they drove me to my hotel, which was the Loews Santa Monica Beach Hotel. It was very fancy and on the ocean. They came in with me to check in.

'Hi,' I said to the woman behind the counter. 'My name is Karyn Bosnak and I'm here to check in.'

'Oh, Miss Bosnak,' she said. 'We have been expecting you. You are a very special guest of Mr Steve Tisch.' I looked at Lacy and Jeff.

'That's our boss,' they said in unison.

'Okay,' I said.

'Now, Miss Bosnak,' she continued. 'You have one of only four rooms in the whole hotel that has a panoramic view of the ocean.'

'Really? Wow, thanks, guys,' I said, turning to Lacy and Jeff. I felt so special!

After the woman finished checking me in, she asked if I needed an escort to my room.

'No, thanks,' I said. 'I'll be fine all by myself.'

Lacy and Jeff walked with me upstairs and I dropped off my bags in my room. The three of us went to dinner and it was so nice to eat a normal meal again. And it was Mexican food! I just love Mexican food! During dinner, they told me that we were going to have a big meeting the following day with their bosses, this Steve Tisch being one of them.

Afterward, we walked back to my hotel, and Jeff gave me $200 spending money while I was there for food and stuff. When they left, I called my friend Tracy, my old sorority sister, who lived in Los Angeles. She came over and we had a slumber party.

I wasn't sure what I was going to wear the next day, so when she showed up, I tried on a few outfits to show her, and she quickly vetoed all of them. So, what was a broke girl to do?

Take her $200 food money and go shopping, that's what! (Before you go and yell at me, you would have done the same thing.) All I had was an ugly pair of pants and an Old Navy skirt with pen marks on it. And I certainly wasn't going to wear *that*!

So after finding a lovely number at the local Banana Republic the next morning, Tracy and I went back to the hotel and she took pictures of me while I got ready. Kind of like how Naomi and I took them at the Plaza. That's what good girlfriends do! And afterward, she drove me to the Sony lot. When she dropped me off, I called Jeff and Lacy from the front gate.

'Hi,' they said. 'Now after you check in, you are going to go left by the *Men in Black* sign, and all the way around to the back to the Astaire Building.'

'Okay,' I said, looking up to find a larger-than-life Will Smith staring back at me.

After gettin' jiggy with it, I took a left where I was instructed to do so. I got a little lost, and after ending up in the Gene Autry Building I asked someone to point me in the right direction. I eventually found it. I walked through the front doors and took the elevator up to the correct floor.

After I checked in at the front desk, both Lacy and Jeff came to greet me and asked me to wait for a bit on a couch in the lobby. While sitting there I looked up at a huge *Forrest*

Gump poster hanging above me. As I looked at it, I did a double take when I saw the first name in the credits. It said 'Produced by Steve Tisch.'

Holy shit! Holy fucking shit! Oh my God! *That's* who their boss was?! The producer of Forrest Fucking Gump?! I tried to calm myself down, but before I knew it Lacy and Jeff were back to get me. (In this case, the 'f-word' is helping me convey the excitement that was going on in my head.)

'Everyone's going to meet in Steve's office,' they said.

'Okay,' I said. I was sweating. I was shaking. I felt like I was on a job interview, only this job interview could change my whole life. I followed them both into a large corner office, and as we walked in a man got up from his desk.

'Hi, Karyn,' he said. 'I'm Steve. It's so nice to meet you.'

'You too,' I said, shaking his hand and sitting down on a big leather couch. I wondered if Forrest sat where I was sitting. Just then, all the other bigwigs came in as well. They were all there just to meet me and see what I had to say. I was so nervous! After they introduced themselves, they started talking.

'So, we think your website is hilarious,' someone said. I don't know who it was, because I was so nervous that I couldn't tell. 'Tell us the story behind it. What happened?'

'Well,' I started, 'I moved to New York about two years ago, and I guess you could say that I went a little hog-wild and charged up a boat-load of stuff.'

I told them about my purses and shoes and lingerie, my dates, my job, and the Buy and Return Credit Payment Management Plan. I told them about losing my job, moving to Brooklyn, the rodents in my walls, and that sign at the grocery store.

'I just didn't want to move home feeling defeated,' I said. 'So I decided to create this silly little website thinking not many people would really go to it.'

'And now she's kind of like the poster child for consumer debt,' Lacy said.

'It's a very funny website,' Jeff said.

I continued telling my story about the anonymity thing, The Smoking Gun and my grandpa. And before I knew it, the meeting was over. I did it! And they loved it!

As I got up to leave Steve's office, I said good-bye to everyone, and Lacy and Jeff walked with me back to Jeff's office.

'That went really well,' they said.

'Really?' I asked.

'Really,' they replied.

'So what do I do now?' I asked.

'Well, we'll get started on the contract, I guess,' Lacy said. 'So nothing really! Go and enjoy yourself! Lay by the pool!'

I thanked them both and said good-bye. On my way downstairs, I was too excited. I couldn't contain myself! I wanted to scream! On my way out, I said good-bye to Will Smith and jumped in a cab by the entrance to go back to my hotel.

'Why were you at the Sony lot?' the cab driver asked me.

'Me? Oh, I . . .' I said shyly, still afraid I would jinx it. 'Someone might make a movie about me.'

'What about you is so interesting?' he asked.

'Oh, I created this website to pay off my debt,' I said, quietly. The driver turned around.

'Are you Karyn?' he asked.

'Yes! Yes, I *am* Karyn!' I answered.

'It's a pleasure to meet you,' he said. 'You are really funny!'

'Really?' I asked.

'Really,' he said.

'Thanks!' I said and leaned back in my seat and smiled.

I finally got that contract the first week in November, and my friend Jodi's agency worked out the deal for me. I think the Sony people planned it that way, waiting to make an offer or give me any money until the debt was paid off so they could see how the story would play itself out. At that time I took down all the PayPal links and stopped collecting money. On November 10, I officially updated my website to say that I was all paid off. Matt Lauer again interviewed me on *Today*, and he was as friendly as he was the first time. And cute!

INTERNET PANHANDLING

The stats are this: approximately 2,718 people gave me cash that amounted to $13,323.08 Of that money, approximately 1,407 people gave me $7,288 by using PayPal, and 1,311 gave me $6,035.08 by using the mail. The largest donation I received was $500 from an anonymous person in New Jersey, and the smallest was one penny. An equal amount of men and women gave me that money.

In addition to money, I received gift baskets, all sorts of beauty products, fresh vegetables from someone's garden, gift certificates, books, coupons, cat food, cat toys, catnip, stamps, calling cards, candles, household products, movie tickets, cans of food, CorningWare, jewelry, hair accessories, clothes – tons of stuff. Also, some guy named Wayne registered the domain names savekaryn.net, savekaryn.org, and savekaryn.us, so mean people wouldn't buy them and start more anti-Karyn sites. I got to pick out two free pairs of shoes from Chinese Laundry's website, but of course when I wrote about which styles I chose, I received e-mails telling me that I again had bad taste in shoes.

I received approximately 2,017,215 hits on my website, and over 37,000 e-mails from people all over the world. I still continue to get about 100,000 hits a month.

On the eBay front, I ended up selling 146 items. I sold purses, sunglasses, shoes, leather belts, jewelry, my $100 shower curtain, part of my new stereo, my feather bed, picture frames, silk flowers, clothing, a couple of watches, books, magazines (people really bought them!), and CDs. I made $4,340.60. I held off on selling my Gucci purse – my most prized possession – until the very end. It wasn't because I was still carrying it, but that it symbolized me at the height of my madness. It was a memory and I didn't want to let it go. But I finally listed it, and a woman in Chicago named Michelle won it. She paid me for it, but didn't want me to send it to her. She said I wasn't allowed to resell it to anyone else, and wanted me to keep it. She said that I shouldn't have to let everything go. I don't carry it anymore. But it's all wrapped up in my closet and it's not going anywhere!

The success of my website started what's called an 'Internet panhandling' phenomenon. I do not like the name Internet panhandling because I choose to think that I provided loads of entertainment to people, and in exchange they gave me some cash to show their gratitude for making them laugh. Anywho, hundreds of sites have started in the wake of my success. Most are very similar to mine, complete with a Grand Debt Tally, weekly update, and a Daily Buck sort of thing. But very few are as successful.

Because of their lack of success, some skeptics have doubted that I collected as much money as I claimed to have collected. However, when mine was 'active,' there were only two other sites out there similar to mine – not hundreds.

Save Karyn wasn't the first Internet panhandling site. Before me, there was 'The Amazing "Send Me A Dollar" Website' at sendmeadollar.com, and 'Odd Todd' at oddtodd.com. The former started in 1998 and has received a total of $4,998. He claims to have received over one million hits. His site is still up. I think the reason that I was more successful than he has been is because his website is really only one page that essentially says 'Give me a dollar.' There's no story and there's no reason. I think savekaryn.com gave people something to invest in – stories, funny bits, and so on. I think a second reason mine was more successful is because he doesn't have a goal. The website is set up to collect as much money as possible. He has a 'count up,' if you will, and I had a 'count down.'

'Odd Todd,' on the other hand, was set up in June 2001 by a guy named Todd Rosenberg, who had just lost his job. He created the website to poke fun at a day in the life of an unemployed person. It's made up of cartoons, and something called the Daily Fact That I Learned From TV, among other things. He didn't create it specifically to collect money, but he 'installed' something called a Tip Jar. Basically if you surfed through his site and liked it, and felt like he deserved a tip for making you laugh, then you could donate to him through PayPal. He never created it with the sole intention of making money. He did it for fun, and the Tip Jar was part of that fun. He never posted anywhere on his site how much money he made either, but he tells me that it's somewhere around $20,000. And like my site, he has also received over two million hits.

So I wasn't the first Internet panhandler out there. I was technically the third. But I offered more than the Amazing Dollar Guy, and I offered something different from Odd Todd. I was 'new' in the Internet panhandling world, and that's why I think it was so successful. I also think people related to it because debt is so universal. No matter where you come from, you can relate to debt.

As for the new sites that popped up after mine, like I said, most are very similar and that's why they aren't as successful. It's been done. The ones whose 'owners' (for lack of a better word) put time into updating and keeping them fresh, obviously collect more money than the sites whose owners don't update at all, but it's still not that much.

It's pretty obvious that I feel indebted to society and to the people who helped me pay my debt back. To pay people back I am going to do a couple of things. First, I've started an area on my website that's sort of a 'Pass the Buck' area. It highlights one Internet Panhandling site a week. And since my website still receives anywhere from 50,000 to 100,000 hits a month, it's a way to get traffic to their sites. I also give them all a small donation to help them get going. Also, as soon as I'm able, I plan to donate to charity the same amount of money that people gave me. I lot of people assume that since I have a book and movie deal, that I am a Rockefeller, but I'm not.

DEBT AND WHAT I LEARNED

I never intended for any of this to happen. Of course, I'm thankful that it did. I needed a wake-up call in my life. A lot of people have said that by not paying off the debt myself, I haven't learned my lesson. But I beg to differ. Through all that's happened I've learned a bigger lesson than if I had continued to make monthly payments all by myself.

First, I've learned that people make mistakes. People screw up in life. It is a fact. But others shouldn't judge them because of it. More importantly, if you've made a mistake, you shouldn't beat yourself up over it, because the bottom line is that you can't go back and change a thing. So, don't have regrets – mistakes make you the person that you are. Even if I had the chance to go back and do things differently, I wouldn't. Learn from your mistakes – don't regret them.

Also, money isn't everything. I think I initially chased a career in daytime television because I saw how much money producers could make down the road. It was never my passion. And to chase a career that wasn't 'me' because I wanted to live a 'fabulous' lifestyle is just wrong.

There's more to life than highlights and high heels. In the long run, it's not going to matter what kind of purse I carried. What's going to matter is how many lives I've touched, how many people I made smile, and how I made this world a better place. And I feel proud that my website made people laugh, and made debt-ridden people all over the world not feel so alone. I still receive e-mails every day from people who say my silly little website motivated them to get serious about paying their debt off. It made them feel like they actually could conquer it. And that makes me feel good – to know that something I've done might have made someone's life a little bit brighter.

Also, sometimes you need to be bold in life. I've always been a go-with-the-flow type of person, and the one time I didn't go with the flow, my life changed. What if I had stayed in Chicago, afraid to make the move? What if I had signed my extension at *Ananda* and stayed there for six more miserable months? I think that I so frequently went with the flow because I was scared of taking chances. And by doing that, I wasn't discovering my true potential or happiness.

So, I moved to New York to get away and go to a place where no one knew my name, to figure out who I was. And what did I find out? Well, sometimes you have to lose yourself to find yourself, and I think that's what happened to me. I'm not a fancy New Yorker – I'm still that greasy little Midwestern girl in the Hot Rollers jacket who just happens to live in Manhattan now. I mean, Brooklyn.

And you know what? I like to make people laugh. And I'm going to keep doing that, whether it's by working in television in another capacity, or writing a book, or just crackin' jokes on the way to the supermarket – I need to make people laugh. It's funny that after working in daytime television for over six years, some silly little website brought me more success.

I moved to New York to figure out who I was. And since I've been here, I've learned more about life, people, humanity, and kindness than I could have ever imagined.

ACKNOWLEDGMENTS

Special thanks goes to my family: Mom, I love you – You are the greatest! Dad, ditto and I swear I have a savings account now. Lisa, you are the best sissy I could ever ask for. I love you and your crazy curly hair. My stepdad, Mick, thanks for always pushing me to be the best that I can. Todd, thanks for loving my big sissy and being a part of my life. A big shout-out also goes to you for always footing the bill when we go to dinner. More thanks to Mrs Rivelli for telling me I was funny all those years ago. Thanks for listening to me when I pray. And last but not least: Grandpa Creaney, I love you so much. Thanks for always having faith in me! You are the best!

Huge thanks also goes to Alison Callahan and everyone at HarperCollins. To every one at RLR: Jodi Turk, you are awesome! Thanks for hooking a girl up. Jennifer Unter, more thanks to you for hooking a girl up with HarperCollins. Bob Rosen, thanks for owning the company that hooked a girl up. Gary Rosen, thanks for being the son of the guy who owned the company who hooked the girl up. And for telling me to 'keep it simple.' And Ezra Fitz, for helping Jennifer hook a girl up. More thanks goes to Jordan Bayer.

I wouldn't be anywhere without my friends. Scott, you are a great roommate. You and Mary Veda will always be close to my heart. Mark, you will always be my gay boyfriend. I love you very much. Tracy & Naomi, you two are the best friends anyone could ask for. I love both of you like family. Naomi's parents, Sharon & Chuck, for the $100! Elvis the Bush Cat – thanks for peeing on my sheets. People really got a big hoot out of your antics. And thanks also to Bev, the new addition to the family.

The BIGGEST thanks goes to the 2,718 people who sent me cash to help me get out of debt, the 147 people who bought my stuff on eBay, and the two million plus people who visited my website.

Miscellaneous thanks goes to: Haribo Gummi Bears and Pepsi-Cola for providing a sugar rush during times of need, and American Express for having loopholes that made the Buy and Return Credit Payment Management Plan possible.

And . . . To whoever hung that sign up at the Brooklyn Met, I hope you got your seven grand!

SHOPAHOLIC & SISTER

Sophie Kinsella

Rebecca Bloomwood thought being married to Luke Brandon would be one big Tiffany box of happiness. But to be honest, it's not quite as dreamy as she hoped. The trouble started on honeymoon, when she told the tiniest little fib to Luke, about the teeniest little purchase. Now she's on a strict budget, she doesn't have a job – and, worst of all, her beloved Suze has a new best friend. She's feeling rather blue – when she receives some incredible news. She has a long-lost sister!

Becky has never been more excited. Finally, a real sister! They'll have so much in common! They can go shopping together . . . choose shoes together . . . have manicures together . . .

Until she meets her – and gets the shock of her life. It can't be true. Surely Becky Bloomwood's long-lost sister can't . . . hate shopping?

A sister. A soulmate. A skinflint?

THE 'SHOPAHOLIC BOOKS'
by Sophie Kinsella

THE SECRET DREAMWORLD OF A SHOPAHOLIC

Meet Rebecca Bloomwood. She's a journalist. She spends her working life telling others how to manage their money. She spends her leisure time . . . shopping. Retail therapy is the answer to all her problems. She knows she should stop, but she can't. She tries Cutting Back, she tries Making More Money. But neither seems to work. The stories she concocts become more and more fantastic as she tries to untangle her increasingly dire financial difficulties. Can Becky ever escape from this dream world, find true love, and regain the use of her Switch card?

'I ALMOST CRIED WITH LAUGHTER'
Daily Mail

0 552 99887 7

SHOPAHOLIC ABROAD

Rebecca Bloomwood's been offered a chance to work in New York. The Museum of Modern Art! The Guggenheim! The Metropolitan Opera House! And Becky does mean to go to them all. Honestly. It's just that it seem silly not to check out a few other famous places first. Like Saks. And Bloomingdales. And Barneys. And one of those fantastic sample sales where you can get a Prada dress for $10. Or was it $100? Anyway, it's full of *amazing* bargains.

'A LAUGH-A-MINUTE READ THAT'S GUARANTEED TO ENTERTAIN YOU'
Glamour

0 552 99940 7

SHOPAHOLIC TIES THE KNOT

Becky Bloomwood's got her dream job as a personal shopper (spending other people's money – and getting paid for it.) She's got a fabulous Manhattan apartment with her boyfriend Luke. Then Luke proposes – and all of a sudden life gets hectic. Mum wants Becky to get married in Oxshott, Elinor wants to host a grand extravaganza at the New York Plaza. Becky knows she has to sit down and decide – but to be honest, it's a lot more fun tasting cake, trying on dresses and registering wedding presents. Time's ticking by, plans are being made both sides of the Atlantic and soon she realizes she's in trouble . . .

'BRILLAINT . . . FUNNY, ROMANTIC AND BELIEVABLE'
Heat

0 552 99957 1

BLACK SWAN

THE FABULOUS GIRL'S GUIDE TO LIFE
by Kim Izzo and Ceri March

The Fabulous Girl is smart, sophisticated and sexy. With her wit and charm, she always seems to know just what to say and do. Yet she understands that despite the best-laid plans life can, and often does, spin out of control.

The Fabulous Girl's Guide to Life shows you how to cope with grace when under pressure. It addresses every aspect of a Fabulous Girl's life in a playful, practical tone including career, socializing, entertaining, family, friendships and sex. There is invaluable advice for those jubilant highs as well as those testing lows, such as how to manage a boy binge, how to be a tactful boss, how to recover from a faux pas, and how to remain poised after discovering your lover in the arms of another. And woven throughout the book is the fictional story of the Fabulous Girl herself.

The Fabulous Girl's Guide to Life is the ultimate survival guide for the extremes of modern life, a must-have for sophisticated and stylish women everywhere.

0 552 15069 X